Cognition
Theory and Applications

Cognition
Theory and Applications

Stephen K. Reed

Florida Atlantic University

Brooks/Cole Publishing Company

Monterey, California

Brooks/Cole Publishing Company
A Division of Wadsworth, Inc.

Printed in the United States of America

10 9 8 7 6 5 4 3 2 1

Library of Congress Cataloging in Publication Data

Reed, Stephen K.
     Cognition : theory and applications.

     Bibliography: p.
     Includes index.
     1. Cognition.   2. Human information processing.
3. Learning, Psychology of.   4. Problem solving.
I. Title.
BF311.R357   153   81-3829
ISBN 0-8185-0462-5   AACR2

Subject Editor: C. Deborah Laughton
Manuscript Editor: Susan Weisberg
Production Editor: Fiorella Ljunggren
Interior and Cover Design: Victoria A. Van Deventer
Illustrations: Cyndie Clark-Huegel and Barbara Hack
Typesetting: Interactive Composition Corporation, Pleasant Hill, California
Cover photo © Stanley Rice

To my parents:

    Anita M. Reed

    Kenneth D. Reed

Preface

The most exciting development in the field of cognitive psychology is not a particular theory or experimental finding but a general trend. Cognitive psychologists have demonstrated an increasing interest in studying complex, real-world tasks and are making significant progress in understanding how people perform on these tasks. I hope that one result of this trend is that undergraduates discover the direct relevance of cognitive psychology to many of their daily activities. A course about cognition should be useful not only to psychology students but to those who have selected other fields of study.

In this book I have attempted to place a greater emphasis on the application of cognitive psychology than is typically found in an undergraduate text. The study of reading, for example, is discussed in the chapters on pattern recognition, attention, language, and text comprehension. Efficient learning strategies are major topics in the chapters on long-term memory and visual imagery. The chapter on classroom problem solving shows how the study of problem solving is currently being extended to include the kinds of problems students encounter in their courses. The chapter on language discusses how the implications of sentences influence legal testimony and advertising, and the chapter on decision making includes a section on medical decision making. In order to help students relate the study of cognition to popular articles they are likely to read, I have included many magazine and newspaper clippings on such contemporary topics as playing blindfolded chess and formulating the odds that someone would be injured by the fall of Skylab.

In presenting this material, I have attempted to avoid overwhelming students with more information than they need. The chapters are each about 25 pages long and include a summary. They cover a wide range of topics, and instructors should be able to expand on whatever topics interest them. The 14 chapters are divided into three parts: Information-Processing Stages, Representation and Organization of Knowledge, and Complex Cognitive Skills. The first part consists of an introductory chapter followed by chapters on pattern recognition, attention, short-term memory, and long-term memory. The chapters describe what occurs during the different information-processing stages and how the stages interact. The second part contains chapters on levels of processing, visual imagery, categorization, and semantic memory. The first two chapters in this part describe qualitatively different memory codes, and the next two chapters discuss the organization of knowledge in long-term memory. The final part consists of chapters on language, text comprehension, problem solving, classroom problem solving, and decision making. The discussion of these complex cognitive skills is often related to ideas presented earlier in the book.

The organization of a book on cognition should perhaps reflect what we actually know about cognition. Research suggests that a hierarchy is a particularly effective way to organize knowledge (see Chapter 9). Recall is facilitated when information is partitioned into categories, which are further partitioned into smaller categories. Hierarchical organization seems to be particularly effective when the number of partitions varies from two to five. I deliberately selected such a structure for this book in the hope that the material will thereby be more accessible to students.

I wrote the first draft of the book while spending a sabbatical year at the University of California at Berkeley. I am grateful to Case Western Reserve University and the Group in Science and Mathematics Education at Berkeley for providing financial support during this year. The Group in Science and Mathematics Education also furnished me with a stimulating environment, and the Institute of Human Learning provided an excellent library.

Shortly after arriving at Berkeley, I had the good fortune to meet C. Deborah Laughton, a psychology editor at Brooks/Cole. She expressed confidence in the book long before it was deserved and, with the assistance of an excellent staff at Brooks/Cole, helped in the development of the book. The development was also facilitated by a number of first-rate reviewers. I would like to thank Ian M. Begg of McMaster University, Bruce K. Britton of the University of Georgia, Dennis Egan of Bell Laboratories, Judith P. Goggin of the University of Texas at El Paso, Richard A. Griggs of the University of Florida, David T. Hakes of the University of Texas at Austin, Kenji Hakuta of Yale University, Robert Haygood of Arizona State University, Stephen M. Kosslyn of Harvard University, Stephen E. Palmer of the University of California, Berkeley, Stan Parkinson of the University of Arizona, John W. Payne of Duke University, John Pittenger of the University of Arkansas at Little Rock,

Peter Polson of the University of Colorado, James R. Pomerantz of the State University of New York at Buffalo, Eleanor Rosch of the University of California, Berkeley, and Robert E. Till of Eastern Illinois University for their insightful comments. The comments of others are always welcome, and I would appreciate receiving suggestions from readers.

Stephen K. Reed

Contents

PART I

Information-Processing Stages

1

Introduction

Cognitive psychology refers to all processes by which the sensory input is transformed, reduced, elaborated, stored, recovered, and used.

ULRIC NEISSER (1967)

Cognition is usually simply defined as the acquisition of knowledge. However, the acquisition and use of knowledge involve many mental skills. If you glanced at the table of contents at the beginning of this book, you saw a list of some of these skills. Psychologists who study cognition are interested in pattern recognition, attention, memory, visual imagery, language, problem solving, and decision making.

The purpose of this book is to provide an overview of the field of cognitive psychology. The book summarizes experimental research in cognitive psychology, discusses the major theories in the field, and attempts to relate the research and theories to cognitive tasks that people encounter in their daily lives—for example, reading, driving, effective learning strategies, advertising, legal testimony, classroom problem solving, and medical decision making.

Neisser's definition of cognitive psychology quoted above reflects how psychologists study cognition. Let me repeat it for emphasis: "Cognitive psychology refers to all processes by which the sensory input is transformed, reduced, elaborated, stored, recovered, and used."

There are several important implications of this definition. The reference to a sensory input implies that cognition begins with our contact with the external world. Transformation of the sensory input means that our representation of the world is not a passive registration of our physical surroundings but an active construction that may involve both reduction and elaboration. We can attend to only a small part of the physical stimulation that surrounds us, and only a small part of what we attend to can be remembered. Reduction occurs when information is lost. Elaboration occurs when we add to the sensory input. For example, when you meet a friend, you may recall many shared experiences.

The storage and the recovery of information are, of course, concerned with memory. The distinction between storage and recovery implies that the storage of information does not guarantee recovery. A good example of this distinction is the "tip of the tongue" phenomenon, where we can almost, but not quite, retrieve a word to express a particular thought or meaning. The later recall of the word proves that the earlier failure was one of retrieval rather than one of storage. The word was stored in memory; it was simply hard to get it back out.

The last part of Neisser's definition is perhaps the most important. After information has been perceived, stored, and recovered, it must be put to good use—for example, to make decisions or to solve problems. We will learn more about problem solving and decision making in Part III, after we review the progress that has been made in understanding perception and memory.

The information-processing approach

The fact that cognitive psychology is often called *human information processing* reflects the predominant approach to the subject used by cognitive psychologists. The acquisition, storage, retrieval, and utilization of information involves a number of separate stages, and the information-processing approach attempts to identify what happens during these stages (Haber, 1969).

Figure 1.1 identifies the stages that researchers most commonly include in information-processing models. They are arranged in temporal order; however, since information flows in both directions, as indicated by the two-headed arrows, an earlier stage can be influenced by information in a later stage. The flow from the input through the sensory store, pattern recognition, and memory stages, is sometimes called *bottom-up processing*. The reverse flow from memory through the pattern-recognition stage is often called *top-down processing*. We will see how information can move in both directions when we look at an interactive model of reading in the next chapter.

A brief consideration of the model in Figure 1.1 will give you a superficial account of the stages, each of which will be elaborated in later chapters. The *sensory store* provides a very brief storage for information in its original sensory form. Presumably, a sensory store exists for each of the senses, although the visual and auditory stores have been the most widely studied. The sensory store extends the amount of time that a person has to recognize a pattern. If a visual pattern is flashed on a screen for 5 msec (5/1000 of a second), the observer has more time than 5 msec to identify it if the visual information can be briefly maintained in a sensory store. Although the sensory store for vision lasts only about one-quarter of a second (250 msec), this is much longer than the 5-msec exposure.

The information in the sensory store is lost at the end of this time unless it can be described during the *pattern recognition* stage. Most of the patterns we encounter are familiar, and recognition consists of classifying a pattern as a cat, the letter *a,* the word *ball,* and so on. When we recognize a familiar pattern, we are using information that we have previously stored in memory. If the description does not match a description of a familiar pattern, the observer may want to store the new description in memory.

The relation between pattern recognition and attention has been a topic of much debate. Some theorists have claimed that we can recognize only one pattern at a time. They argue that attention acts as a filter that determines which patterns will be recognized when many patterns arrive simultaneously. Other theorists have argued that simultaneous patterns can all be recognized but that only some of the recognized patterns will be remembered whereas others are immediately forgotten. The latter view states that attention controls which patterns will be selected into memory. Since the most popular current view is that both theories are correct, depending on the circumstances, attention is represented in Figure 1.1 by both the *filter* and the *selection* stages. The filter limits the amount of information that can be recognized at one time, and the selection limits the amount of material that can be entered into memory.

Memory is represented in Figure 1.1 by *short-term* and *long-term* memory. We use short-term memory (STM), for example, to remember a telephone number as we are dialing it. STM is limited in both the amount of information it can hold (capacity) and the length of time it can⋅ hold the information (duration). Most adults can remember a seven-digit number, but they find it very difficult to remember a ten-digit number, such as an unfamiliar area code in addition to the telephone number. The

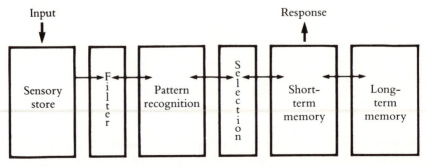

Figure 1.1. Stages of an information-processing model.

limited duration of STM is illustrated by the fact that we can quickly forget the number if we don't repeat it to ourselves by using verbal rehearsal. Long-term memory (LTM) has neither of the two limitations of STM. It has no limitations on the amount of information it can hold, and forgetting occurs relatively slowly.

The "higher" cognitive skills such as decision making and problem solving do not have a stage in our information-processing model. However, they depend greatly on the other stages. For example, pattern-recognition skills are important in playing chess, a very demanding intellectual task. The limited capacity of STM is a major determinant of performance on tasks that require complex decision making or problem solving. The role of problem solving in learning new information is receiving increasing emphasis as cognitive psychologists discover more about the active nature of learning. Specifying the interactions among perception, memory, and thought is one of the challenges that confront cognitive psychologists.

The beginning of cognitive psychology

It is difficult to pinpoint the exact beginning of any field of study, and cognitive psychologists would likely offer a wide variety of dates if asked when cognitive psychology began. William James's *Principles of Psychology,* published in 1890, included chapters on attention, memory, imagery, and reasoning. F. C. Bartlett's book *Remembering: A Study in Experimental and Social Psychology,* published in 1932, contained a theory of memory for stories that is very consistent with current views. We could find other important articles or books that would seem modern but did not cause a major shift toward the way cognitive psychology is currently studied.

One book that did have a major impact was *Behaviorism,* written in 1924 by John B. Watson. The book's central theme was that psychologists should study only what they could directly observe in a person's behavior. Watson's argument lent support to a stimulus-response (S-R) approach, in which experimenters measure how people respond to stimuli. The stimulus-response approach is consistent with Watson's view because the stimulus and response are both observable. The problem with this approach is that it does not reveal exactly what the person does with the information presented in the stimulus. By contrast, the information-processing approach attempts to identify how a person transforms the information between the stimulus and the response. Psychologists who follow the latter approach seek to understand what occurs during each of the stages shown in Figure 1.1. The discovery of what occurs during each of these stages is particularly important when a person has difficulty performing a task—the psychologist can then attempt to identify which stage is the primary source of the difficulty.

Information Processing Gathers Momentum

The change from the S-R to the information-processing approach began to gather momentum in the middle to late 1950s, stimulated by the growing popularity of computers and computer programs that illustrated the different operations in the processing of information. Psychologists became interested in using the computer as an analogy of how people process information and attempted to identify how different stages of processing influence performance. One stage that can have a dramatic influence on how people perform mental tasks is STM. George Miller argued in a classic paper published in 1956 that STM capacity limited performance on many cognitive tasks. Miller's paper was important in demonstrating how a single stage—STM—can influence performance on a wide variety of tasks.

Two years later Donald Broadbent (1958) proposed one of the first models based on an information-processing analysis—a filter model to account for performance on selective listening tasks. When subjects were asked to listen to different messages played in each ear, they found it difficult to listen to both messages simultaneously. Broadbent's filter model (Figure 1.2) shows that many sensory inputs can simultaneously enter a short-term store, but only a single input can enter a limited-capacity channel (perceptual system). The purpose of the filter is to determine which message gains access to the perceptual system. The filter model proposes that the listener can attend to only one message at a time; attention is controlled by the filter. Two simultaneous messages can both be recognized only if the unattended message passes through the filter before it decays from the short-term store. Although the identity of the short-term store was not firmly established when Broadbent wrote his book, it now seems reasonable to equate the short-term store in Figure 1.2 with the sensory store shown in Figure 1.1. Broadbent's limited-capacity channel corresponds to the pattern-recognition stage in Figure 1.1. The filter model implied that a perceptual limitation prevented people from comprehending two messages spoken at the same time.

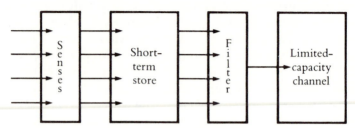

Figure 1.2. The major components of Broadbent's filter model. *(From Perception and Communication, by D. E. Broadbent. Copyright 1958 by Pergamon Press, Ltd. Reprinted by permission.)*

The year after Broadbent published *Perception and Communication,* George Sperling completed his doctoral dissertation at Harvard. In one of Sperling's (1960) tasks, observers viewed a very brief exposure of an array of letters and were required to report all the letters in one of the rows of the display. The pitch of a tone signaled which row was to be reported. Sperling designed the procedure to determine whether perception or memory limited the number of letters people could report from the brief exposure. His analysis of this task resulted in an information-processing model that proposed how the sensory store, pattern recognition, and short-term memory combined to influence performance on the task (Sperling, 1963).

Both Broadbent's and Sperling's models had an important influence on subsequent information-processing theory, the former on models of auditory attention and the latter on visual recognition.

Higher Cognitive Processes

The information-processing analysis of perceptual tasks was accompanied in the late 1950s by a new approach to more complex tasks. The excitement of this new approach is described by Newell and Simon (1972). The development of digital computers after World War II led to active work in artificial intelligence, a field that attempts to program computers to perform intelligent tasks such as playing chess and constructing derivations in logic. A seminar was held at the RAND Corporation in the summer of 1958 with the aim of showing social scientists how computer-simulation techniques could be applied to create models of human behavior. The RAND seminar had a major impact on integrating the work on computer simulation with other work on human information processing.

One consequence of the RAND seminar was its influence on three psychologists who spent the 1958–1959 academic year at the Center for Advanced Study in the Behavioral Sciences at Stanford University. The three—George Miller, Eugene Galanter, and Karl Pribram—shared a common dissatisfaction with the then-predominant theoretical approach to psychology, which viewed the human being as a bundle of stimulus-response reflexes. Miller brought with him a large amount of material from the RAND seminar, and this material, along with other recent work in artificial intelligence, psychology, and linguistics, helped shape the view that is expressed in their book *Plans and the Structure of Behavior* (Miller, Galanter, & Pribram, 1960).

The authors argued that much of human behavior is planned. A plan, according to their formulation, consists of a list of instructions that can control the order in which a sequence of operations is to be performed. A plan is essentially the same as a program for a computer. Since the authors found it difficult to construct plans from stimulus-response units, they proposed a new unit called TOTE, an abbreviation for Test-Operate-Test-Exit. A plan consists of a hierarchy of TOTE units.

Consider a very simple plan for hammering a nail into a board (see Figure 1.3). The goal is to make the head of the nail flush with the board. At the top of the hierarchy is a test to determine whether the goal has been accomplished. If the nail is flush, one can exit. If the nail sticks up, it is necessary to test the hammer. The position of the hammer determines which one of two operations, lifting or striking, should be performed.

The ideas expressed by Miller, Galanter, and Pribram were influenced by earlier work in two areas outside of psychology. The work of Newell, Shaw, and Simon (1958a) in the area of artificial intelligence identified strategies that people use to perform complex tasks such as playing chess. A second major influence came from the linguist Noam Chomsky, who argued that a stimulus-response theory of language learning could not account for how people learn to comprehend and generate sentences (Chomsky, 1957). His alternative proposal—that people learn a system of rules (a grammar)—was consistent with Miller, Galanter, and Pribram's emphasis on planning. We will return to both contributions, as well as the contributions of Miller, Broadbent, and Sperling, in the following chapters.

The ideas expressed by these theorists have continued to be developed and refined over the past 25 years. Neisser's *Cognitive Psychology* (1967) brought many of these ideas together into a single source; other books on cognition have followed. Although some of the early ideas

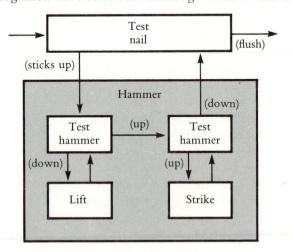

Figure 1.3. A hierarchical plan for hammering nails. *(From* Plans and the Structure of Behavior, *by G. A. Miller, E. Galanter, and K. Pribram. Copyright 1960 by Holt, Rinehart and Winston. Reprinted by permission of E. Galanter.)*

about the stages shown in Figure 1.1 have proven oversimplified, the model still provides a good explanation of how people perform on many cognitive tasks.

Our understanding of cognition has greatly increased over the past 25 years, even though cognitive psychology is still a young science. Elliot Aronson, in the introduction to his popular book *The Social Animal* (1972) explained the major reason he wrote the book: he once told one of his classes that social psychology was a young science, and it made him feel like a coward. He went on to write that labeling social psychology as a young science was a gigantic cop-out—a way of pleading with people not to expect too much, a way of avoiding the responsibility for applying findings to the problems of the world we live in. Aronson wrote his book to demonstrate that social psychology does have a lot to contribute. I hope you feel the same way about cognitive psychology after reading this book.

Organization of the book

This book is divided into three major parts. The first part discusses information-processing stages; the second part discusses the representation and organization of knowledge; and the third part discusses complex cognitive skills.

In this chapter I have attempted to present a brief overview of the information-processing approach to the study of cognition. One of the primary objectives of that approach, as was illustrated in Figure 1.1, is to identify the major information-processing stages. The first part of the book summarizes our knowledge of what occurs during each of these stages. Chapters 2 and 3, on pattern recognition and attention, are both concerned with perception. Theories of pattern recognition attempt to specify how people recognize and store descriptions of patterns in memory. These theories also attempt to identify why performance limitations occur when a person cannot report all the letters in an array of letters and why it is easier to perceive letters when they form a word. Theories of attention are needed to explain performance when too much perceptual information arrives at the same time. Usually a person can respond to only some of the information. Experiments designed to measure how much is processed have resulted in theories about whether a particular stage causes the limitation or whether the tasks simply require too much mental effort to be performed at the same time.

Chapters 4 and 5 are both concerned with memory and discuss the distinction between STM and LTM, respectively. STM is a "working memory" that enables us to combine information that is retrieved from LTM with information that arrives from the environment. STM's limited capacity and fast decay rate make it necessary for us to enter into

LTM new information we want to remember over a long time period. The chapter on LTM discusses various strategies that can be used in learning and focuses on verbal rehearsal. Both chapters distinguish between recall and recognition tests and show how theories of recognition memory differ depending on whether the information is retained in STM or LTM.

The second part of the book is concerned with the representation and organization of knowledge in memory. Chapters 6 and 7 illustrate different kinds of memory codes; our ability to remember depends on the kind of memory code that is constructed. The most influential theory of memory over the past decade has been the levels-of-processing theory proposed by Craik and Lockhart (1972). Their theory was stimulated by research showing that a person's ability to remember a word depended on what characteristics of the word were emphasized in a judgment task. Memory codes can also be distinguished by whether they emphasize verbal information or visual information. The study of visual and verbal codes has resulted in many findings that have implications for how efficiently people can perform on different tasks.

Chapters 8 and 9 emphasize the organization of LTM. Chapter 8 is primarily theoretical; it examines how knowledge is organized into categories and how categories are organized into hierarchies. The ability to categorize is a skill that is frequently used in pattern recognition. Identification usually occurs when an item is classified as a member of a particular category. The organization of knowledge in LTM can also be studied by measuring how quickly people can make classification decisions. Chapter 9 examines how psychologists have used this and other techniques to study the relations among concepts in semantic memory, the part of LTM that represents the meaning of words.

The last part of the book contains five chapters on cognitive skills. The section begins with a discussion of language in Chapter 10. Language involves not only the meaning of individual words but the combination of words to form sentences that are grammatically correct and convey the intended meaning. Chapter 11, on text comprehension, focuses on our ability to comprehend paragraphs rather than individual sentences. Over the past several years psychologists have made significant progress in identifying factors that influence the comprehension of text. They have even developed some rather detailed models of how the organization of ideas in a text interacts with STM and LTM to determine what is remembered.

Chapter 12, the first of two chapters on problem solving, shows how cognitive psychologists have studied this area. The chapter describes attempts to identify the skills that are needed to solve different kinds of problems, identify general strategies, and examine the role of memory in problem solving. Chapter 13, on classroom problem solving, discusses performance on material that is typically encountered in a classroom, such as mathematics. Topics include the initial analysis of a problem, the use of planning, and the role of instruction in teaching solution strategies and identifying mistakes.

Chapter 14 discusses decision making. The study of decision making has shown that people often find it difficult to combine information in an optimal way when evaluating alternatives. The term *risky decision making* is used to describe situations in which there is uncertainty regarding possible outcomes. People's estimates of probabilities are often biased. The study of how people make probability estimates, how they revise their estimates when they receive new information, and how they use their estimates to make decisions constitutes most of the research on risky decision making.

Recommended reading

An early statement of the assumptions of the information-processing approach is given by Haber (1969). Estes (1978a) provides a more recent overview of this approach. Lachman, Lachman, and Butterfield's (1979) book on cognitive psychology contains an excellent discussion of how other disciplines—behaviorism, verbal learning, human engineering, information theory, and linguistics—contributed to the information-processing paradigm. An interesting paper by Roediger (1980) discusses how people have used familiar analogies to help them understand memory. He begins with Aristotle's and Plato's comparison of memory to a wax tablet and ends with the computer analogy that is currently emphasized. Readers interested in how other major theoretical approaches influenced the history of psychology should read Heidbreder's *Seven Psychologies* (1961). The book contains chapters on prescientific psychology, the beginning of scientific psychology, the psychology of William James, functionalism, behaviorism, dynamic psychology, Gestalt psychology, and psychoanalysis.

2

Pattern Recognition

*About patterns, philosophers and psychologists have been strangely silent;
yet most interesting phenomena are almost certainly patterned. Of course,
this silence is really not at all strange, for patterns are amazingly complicated
things to come to grips with. Even a consensus of what we mean by the word
"pattern" is lacking, but a growing number of people are beginning to feel
that many of the central problems of behavior, intelligence, and information
processing are problems that involve patterns.*

LEONARD UHR (1966)

We begin our study of cognitive psychology by starting with a skill that
people use very well—pattern recognition. The study of pattern recognition is primarily the study of how people identify the objects in their
environment. Our ability to recognize patterns should seem impressive
if we stop to consider how much variation there is in different examples
of the same pattern. Each letter of the alphabet, for example, is one kind
of pattern. Figure 2.1 shows various styles of handwriting. It is obvious
that all people do not have the same style of writing and that some
handwriting is much less legible than others. However, unless it is very
illegible, we usually are successful in reading it—that is, in recognizing
the words.

The ease and accuracy with which we can recognize patterns make
it difficult to study this ability. It is not very interesting or revealing if
someone easily identifies all of a variety of patterns. In order to make the
task more difficult, psychologists often resort to using a tachistoscope—a
device for presenting patterns very rapidly under controlled conditions.
If the patterns are presented for only a few milliseconds, people start to

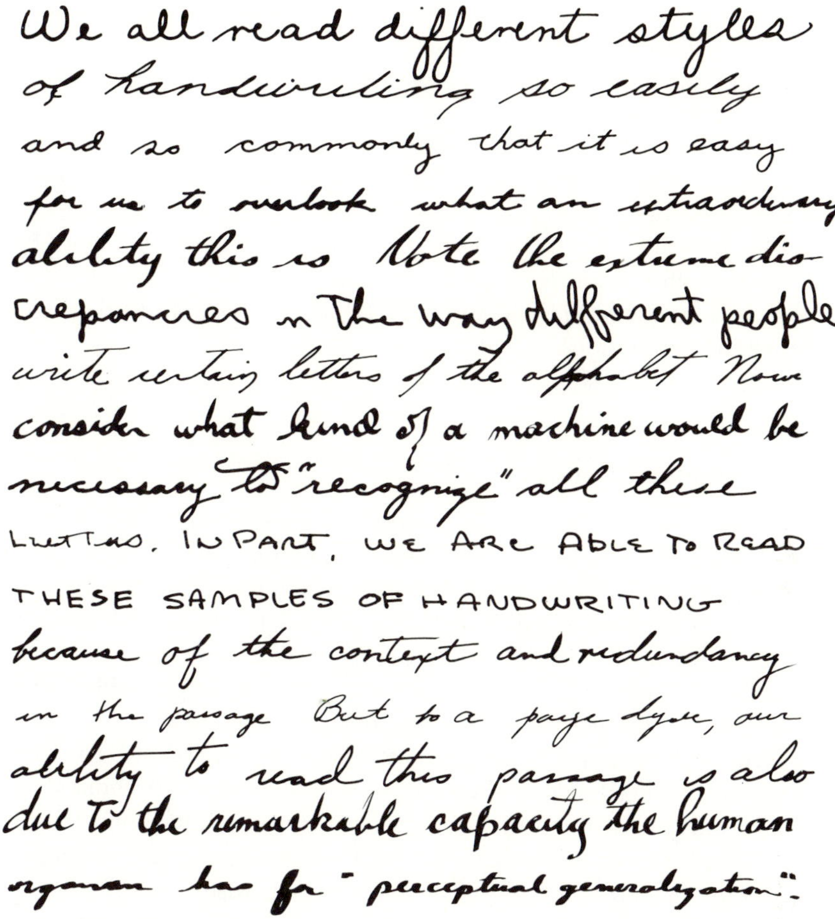

We all read different styles of handwriting so easily and so commonly that it is easy for us to overlook what an extraordinary ability this is. Note the extreme discrepancies in the way different people write certain letters of the alphabet. Now consider what kind of a machine would be necessary to "recognize" all these letters. IN PART, WE ARE ABLE TO READ THESE SAMPLES OF HANDWRITING because of the context and redundancy in the passage. But to a page typer, our ability to read this passage is also due to the remarkable capacity the human organism has for "perceptual generalization".

Figure 2.1. Variations in handwriting. (*From* Man-Machine Engineering, *by A. Chapanis. Copyright © 1965 by Wadsworth, Inc. Reprinted by permission of the publisher, Brooks/Cole Publishing Company, Monterey, California.*)

make mistakes and psychologists start to take notes about the kinds of mistakes that result.

A large part of the literature on pattern recognition is concerned with alternative ways of describing patterns. The first section of this chapter discusses three kinds of descriptions that represent different theories of pattern recognition. The second section is about information-processing models of visual pattern recognition. We will take a more detailed look at Sperling's research and how his results influenced later theories. The third section deals with word recognition and will give us the opportunity to consider some of the factors that influence reading.

Describing patterns

Consider the following explanation of how we recognize patterns. Our LTM contains descriptions of many different kinds of patterns. When we see or hear a pattern, we form a description of it and compare the description to the descriptions stored in our LTM. We are able to recognize the pattern if its description closely matches one of the descriptions stored in LTM. Although this is a plausible explanation, it is rather vague. For example, what form do these descriptions take? Let us consider three explanations that have been suggested: (1) templates, (2) features, and (3) structural descriptions.

Template Theories

Template theories propose that patterns are really not "described" at all. Rather, they are holistic, or unanalyzed, entities that are compared to other patterns by measuring how much two patterns overlap. Imagine that you made a set of letters out of cardboard. If you made a cutout to represent each letter of the alphabet, and I gave you a cutout of a letter that I made, you could measure how my letter overlapped with each of your letters—the templates. The identity of my letter would be determined by the template with the greatest amount of overlap. The same principle would apply if you replaced your cardboard letters with a visual image of each letter and used the images to make mental comparisons.

There are a number of problems with using the degree of overlap as a measure of pattern recognition. First, the comparison requires that the template be in the same position and the same orientation, and be the same size, as the pattern you are trying to identify. Thus the position, orientation, and size of the templates would have to be continuously adjusted to correspond to the position, orientation, and size of each pattern you wanted to recognize. A second problem is the great variability of patterns, as was illustrated in Figure 2.1. It would be difficult to construct a template for each letter that would produce a good match with all the different varieties of that letter. Third, a template theory doesn't reveal how two patterns differ. We could know from a template theory that the capital letters P and R are similar because one overlaps substantially with the other. But in order to know how the two letters differ, we have to be able to analyze or describe the letters. By contrast, the feature theory, considered in the next section, allows us to analyze patterns into their parts. A fourth problem is that a template theory does not allow for alternative descriptions of a pattern. The pattern in Figure 2.5, for example, can be perceived as either a stingray or a full-blown sail. The two interpretations depend on which lines are grouped together. The structural theory, considered later, will allow us to specify the relations of parts of the pattern.

These weaknesses of a template theory make it very unpromising as a general theory of pattern recognition, and it is usually quickly dismissed. There are, however, some situations in which a template theory might provide a useful model. The description of the sensory store in Chapter 1 indicated that it briefly preserved sensory information to give the observer more time to recognize patterns. But how are the patterns preserved in the sensory store if they are unrecognized? One possibility is that the patterns can be represented as unanalyzed templates, which are analyzed into their features during the pattern recognition stage.

This interpretation of the sensory store is most clearly presented by Phillips (1974). Subjects in Phillips's experiment viewed patterns made by randomly filled cells in a square matrix. The size of the matrix was either 5 cells × 5 cells or 8 cells × 8 cells. The first pattern was presented for one second and was followed after a variable interval by either an identical or a similar pattern. The subject's task was to decide, as quickly as possible, whether the two patterns were the same or different. On half of the trials the second pattern occurred in the exact location as the first. Since the second pattern was exactly superimposed over the sensory image of the first pattern, it might be possible to use the sensory store to make a template match. On the other half of the trials, the second pattern was moved horizontally by the width of one cell. The slight shift in position should prohibit a template match because the two patterns are not correctly aligned.

Figure 2.2 shows the results of Phillips's experiment. The interstimulus interval—the time separating the two patterns—was 20, 60, 100, 300, or 600 msec. When the two patterns were presented in identical locations (labeled *still* on Figure 2.2), accuracy declined as a function of the interstimulus interval. This finding suggests that the subjects were making use of a sensory store that was rapidly decaying. When the second pattern was moved, subjects could not use the sensory store to make a template match, so accuracy was not influenced by the interval separating the patterns. It should be noted that the use of the sensory store resulted in more accurate performance when the interstimulus interval was less than 300 msec. This result suggests that the sensory store lasts only about a quarter of a second. When the separation was only 20 msec (the data points to the extreme left on the graph) and the patterns were presented in the same location, the performance was almost perfect, even for the most complex pattern.

When the second pattern was moved, subjects had to rely on a description of the first pattern rather than a sensory image. The description might be in the form of a visual image, but unlike a sensory image, in which the pattern still appears to be physically present, a visual image

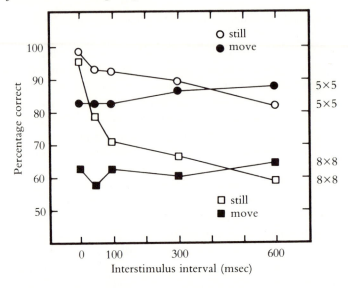

Figure 2.2. Percentage of correct responses as a function of the inter-stimulus interval, matrix size, and movement. *(From "On the Distinction between Sensory Storage and Short-Term Visual Memory," by W. A. Phillips. In* Perception & Psychophysics, *1974, 16, 283–290. Copyright 1974 by the Psychonomic Society, Inc. Reprinted by permission.)*

has to be retrieved from memory. Thus the description was less accurate than the sensory image and was greatly influenced by complexity even at very short separations. Since comparing the descriptions of two patterns takes longer than making a template match, the speed of response was highly correlated with accuracy. The reaction time results would look very much like the accuracy results in Figure 2.2 if we were to replace "% Correct" with "Speed of response." Reaction times were very fast for the "still" condition but became slower as the interstimulus interval increased. Reaction times were slower for the "move" condition and were uninfluenced by the interstimulus interval. Both the accuracy and reaction time results suggest that the sensory store can be used for a rapid template match if the two patterns are separated by less than 300 msec and are presented in the same location.

Feature Theories

The success of the template theory in accounting for Phillips's results depends on matching the second pattern to a sensory image of the first pattern. The sensory image can be thought of as a kind of afterimage in which the pattern still appears to be physically present until the sensory store decays away. But it is questionable whether the sensory store plays an important role outside the laboratory, and, even if it did, the information would be quickly lost. Since we usually cannot rely on the sensory store to match patterns, we must compare decriptions of patterns. Feature theories allow us to describe patterns by listing the parts of a pattern. For example, we might describe a friend as having long, blond hair, a short nose, and bushy eyebrows.

Feature theories are convenient for describing perceptual learning, and one of the best discussions of feature theories is contained in Eleanor Gibson's *Principles of Perceptual Learning and Development* (1969). The theory proposed in Gibson's book is that perceptual learning occurs through the discovery of features that distinguish one pattern from another. Children learn to identify an object by being able to identify differences between it and other objects. For example, when first confronted with the letters *E* and *F,* the child might not be aware of how the two differ. Learning to make this discrimination depends on discovering that the lowest horizontal line is present in the letter *E* but not in the letter *F.* The lowest horizontal line is a *distinctive feature* for distinguishing between an *E* and an *F*; that is, it enables us to distinguish one pattern from the other.

Perceptual learning can be facilitated by a learning procedure that highlights the distinctive feature. An effective method for emphasizing a distinctive feature is initially to make it a different color from the rest of the pattern and gradually change it back to the original color. Egeland (1975) used this procedure to teach prekindergarten children how to distinguish between the confusable letter pairs *R–P, Y–V, G–C, Q–O, M–N,* and *K–X.* One letter of each pair was presented at the top of a card with six letters below it, three of which matched the sample letter and three of which were the comparison letter. The children were asked to select those letters that exactly matched the sample letter.

One group of children received a training procedure in which the distinctive feature of the letter was initially highlighted in red; for example, the stem of the *R* in the *R–P* discrimination initially appeared red. During the training session the distinctive feature was gradually changed to black to match the rest of the letter. Another group of children received feedback regarding which of their choices were correct, but they were not informed about the distinctive features of the letters. Both groups were given two tests—an immediate test at the end of the training session and a delayed test one week later. The distinctive features group made significantly fewer errors on both tests, even though the features were not highlighted during the tests. They also made fewer errors during the training sessions.

Emphasizing the distinctive features produced two benefits. First, it enabled the children to learn the distinctive features so they could continue to differentiate letters after the distinctive features were no longer highlighted. Second, it enabled the children to learn the features without making many errors during the training session. The failure and frustration that many children experience in the early stages of reading (letter discrimination) can result in increased lack of interest in later classroom learning.

Evaluating Feature Theories

Although most pattern recognition theorists make use of the feature concept, it is often a challenging task to find a good set of features. Gibson (1969) proposed the following criteria as a basis for selecting a set of features for uppercase letters.

1. The features should be critical ones, present in some members of the set but not in others, so as to provide a contrast.
2. The identity of the features should remain unchanged under changes in brightness, size, and perspective.
3. The features should yield a unique pattern for each letter.
4. The number of proposed features should be reasonably small.

Gibson used these criteria, empirical data, and intuition to derive the set of features for uppercase letters shown in Figure 2.3.

A set of features is usually evaluated by determining how well it can predict perceptual confusions since confusable items should share many common features. For example, Figure 2.3 reveals that the only difference in features for the letters *P* and *R* is the presence of a diagonal line for the letter *R*; therefore, the two should be highly confusable. The letters *R* and *O* differ in five features, and so they should seldom be confused.

There are several experimental procedures for generating perceptual confusions. The feature set shown in Figure 2.3 was initially tested by examining confusion errors made by 4-year-old children (Gibson, Osser, Schiff, & Smith, 1963). Since these children made errors on a perceptual matching task, it was possible to determine which pairs of letters were likely to be confused. One problem with this procedure was that even 4-year-old children made few errors, and many letters were never confused at all.

A second procedure projected a pair of letters on a small screen and required that subjects respond whether the two letters were the "same" or "different" by pushing one of two buttons as soon as they could make their decision (Gibson, Schapiro, & Yonas, 1968). The subjects were college students and 7-year-old children. Since all the possible combinations of "different" pairs and an equal number (to prevent a response bias toward saying "different") of "same" pairs required too many judgments, two sets of nine letters were used. The assumption of this

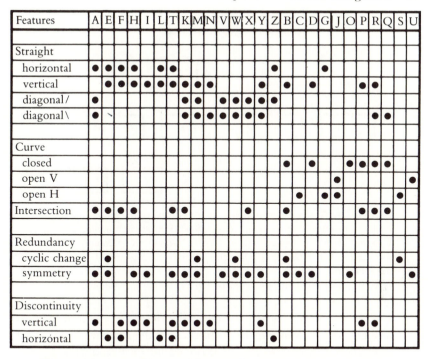

Figure 2.3. A possible set of features for capital letters. *(From* Principles of Perceptual Learning and Development, *by E. Gibson, p. 88. © 1969 by Prentice-Hall, Inc., Englewood Cliffs, New Jersey. Reprinted by permission.)*

procedure is that it should take longer to decide that two similar letters are different than to decide about two dissimilar letters. The results supported this assumption. The average time for adults to decide that *G* and *W* are different was 458 msec, compared to 571 msec to decide that *P* and *R* are different.

The reaction times were analyzed by hierarchical cluster analysis (Johnson, 1967). The analysis partitions letters into finer and finer categories on the basis of their perceived similarity. The letters in each category are difficult to distinguish from each other, as revealed by the longer reaction times to discriminate between any pair of letters in a category. An analysis of the children's reaction times revealed that the letters *C*, *G*, *P*, and *R* belonged to one category and the letters *E*, *F*, *M*, *N*, and *W* to another (see Figure 2.4). By looking at the letters in each category, it is possible to infer the features of the letters that were important in determining perceived similarities: all the letters with curves were grouped into one category and the letters composed of straight lines into another. This grouping reveals that people are slower in responding that two letters are different when both letters contain curves or when both letters contain only straight lines.

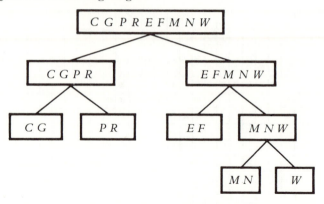

Figure 2.4. A hierarchical cluster analysis illustrating perceived simi-
larities among letters. *(From "Confusion Matrices for Graphic Patterns
Obtained with a Latency Measure," by E. Gibson, R. Schapiro, and A.
Yonas. In* The Analysis of Reading Skill: A Program of Basic and
Applied Research. *Final report, project no. 5–1213, Cornell University and
USOE, 1968. Reprinted by permission of Dr. Eleanor J. Gibson.)*

The cluster analysis next partitioned the curved letters into the two
confusable pairs *C G* and *P R,* distinguished by the presence of a vertical
line. The other branch was then partitioned into *E F* and *M N W,* distinguished by the presence of either a horizontal line or a diagonal line.
Finally, the pair *M N* was established as a confusable pair. The analysis
of the adult reaction times yielded very similar results. The cluster analysis of both groups showed that the straight/curved contrast was the
major determinant of perceived similarity. The presence of a particular
line orientation (vertical, diagonal) also influenced reaction times.

A third method for measuring perceived similarity is to ask an observer to identify letters that are presented very rapidly in a tachistoscope
(Townsend, 1971). It is often difficult to discriminate physically similar
letters under these conditions, and the errors provide a measure of perceived similarity. Holbrook (1975) compared two feature models to determine how successfully each could predict the pattern of errors found
by Townsend. One was the Gibson model shown in Figure 2.3, and the
other was a modification of the Gibson model proposed by Geyer and De
Wald (1973). The major change in the modification was the specification
of the number of features in a letter (such as "two" vertical lines for the
letter *H*) rather than simply a listing of whether that feature was present.
A comparison of the two models revealed that the feature set proposed
by Geyer and De Wald was superior in predicting both the confusion
errors made by adults (Townsend, 1971) and the confusion errors made
by 4-year-old children (Gibson et al., 1963). The prediction of both
models improved when the features were optimally weighted to allow
for the fact that some features are more important than others in account-

ing for confusions. Since the straight/curved distinction is particularly important, it should be emphasized more than the others.

A potential source of embarrassment for proponents of feature models is that even the best predicting model did not predict Townsend's data as well as a template model that measured the physical overlap of each pair of letters. The correlation between predicted errors and obtained errors was .70 for the template model and .50 for the Geyer model using optimally weighted features. The higher correlation for the template model indicates that it was more successful than the feature model in predicting correct responses. Why did the template model do better if it is not a very good theory of how people recognize patterns? Perhaps one reason it predicted well in these circumstances is that all the letters came from the same type font and there were no variations of each letter. A more important reason is that a template preserves the relations among the features. The letters *E* and *F* would produce considerable overlap because the vertical line and two horizontal lines in the letter *F* are connected in the same way as the vertical line and the upper two horizontal lines in the letter *E*. However, the similarity of two letters is determined not only by what features each contains but by the way the features are joined together. In order for the prediction of feature theories to be more accurate, the relation among features would have to be made more explicit. This is the main objective of structural theories.

Structural Theories

The importance of the relations among the features of a pattern was a guiding principle of Gestalt psychology. To the Gestalt psychologists a pattern was more than the sum of its parts. The relations among pattern features were later formalized by people working in the field of artificial intelligence who discovered that the interpretation of patterns usually depended on making explicit how the lines of a pattern were joined to other lines. I pointed out previously that a template theory would be unable to distinguish between the two interpretations of Figure 2.5. A feature theory would also have problems because, although it could identify the four sides as features, the features are identical for both interpretations. Structural theories, however, emphasize the relationships among the features, and Clowes (1969) used Figure 2.5 as an example of why structural theories are often necessary to produce adequate descriptions of patterns. Perceiving the pattern as a stingray requires grouping adjacent lines: line *a* with line *d* and line *b* with line *c*. Perceiving the pattern as a sail requires grouping opposite lines: line *a* with line *c* and line *b* with line *d*.

Structural theories build upon feature theories. Before we can specify the relation among features, we have to specify the features. A structural

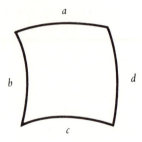

Figure 2.5. An ambiguous pattern, showing a stingray or a sail. *(From "Transformational Grammars and the Organization of Pictures," by M. Clowes. In A. Graselli (Ed.), Automatic Interpretation and the Organization of Pictures. Copyright 1969 by Academic Press, Inc. Reprinted by permission.)*

theory allows for the specification of how the features fit together. For example, the letter *H* consists of two vertical lines and a horizontal line. But we could make many different patterns from two vertical lines and a horizontal line. What is required is a precise specification of how the lines should be joined together: the letter *H* consists of two vertical lines connected at their midpoints by a horizontal line.

Structural models describe how lines are joined together and therefore give a more precise description of line patterns than feature models do. Sutherland (1968) was one of the first to argue that, if we want to be able to account for our very impressive pattern recognition capabilities, we will need the more powerful kind of descriptive language contained in a structural model. Psychologists have been slow to follow his advice, however, and pattern recognition theories are still based primarily on feature models.

One exception is Palmer's (1977) research, which established the importance of structural variables in the analysis and synthesis of patterns. *Analysis* refers to breaking down a pattern into its parts, and *synthesis* refers to combining the parts to make a pattern. The synthesis task is illustrated in Figure 2.6. Subjects were shown two three-segment parts in adjacent 3 × 3 dot matrices. They were required to mentally combine the two parts to form a six-segment pattern. When they completed the synthesis of the two parts, they pushed a button and were shown a six-segment pattern that was either similar or identical to the correct synthesis. Subjects then responded whether the pattern matched their synthesized pattern, and the correctness of their response was used to verify that their synthesis was correct.

The objective of this experiment was to test the hypothesis that the structure of the parts determines how quickly they can be combined. If structural variables are important, "good" parts should be easier to combine than unnatural parts. Each of the two patterns in Figure 2.6 is

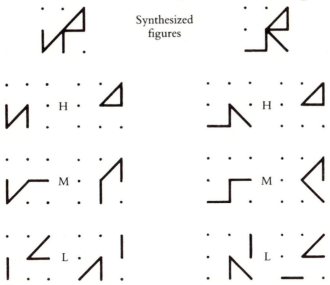

Figure 2.6. Patterns used in a mental synthesis task. The patterns are divided into high- (H), medium- (M), or low- (L) goodness parts. *(From "Hierarchical Structure in Perceptual Representation," by S. E. Palmer. In* Cognitive Psychology, *1977, 9, 441–474. Copyright 1977 by Academic Press, Inc. Reprinted by permission.)*

divided into high-, medium-, and low-goodness parts, defined on the basis of both theoretical and rated measures of goodness. As hypothesized, the high-goodness parts were much easier to synthesize. Subjects took about 1.5 seconds to mentally construct a pattern from high-goodness parts and about 4.5 seconds to construct a pattern from medium- or low-goodness parts.

The analysis task was similar to the embedded figures task invented by the Gestalt psychologists. A six-segment figure and a three-segment part appeared side by side. The subject was required to respond as quickly as possible whether the part was contained in the figure. The reaction times demonstrated that responses to high-goodness parts were significantly faster than responses to medium- or low-goodness parts. The findings from both the analysis and the synthesis tasks supported the hypothesis that there is a predominant way of organizing the features of a pattern. When the analysis or synthesis of a pattern makes use of parts that correspond to this organization, the task is relatively easy compared to the use of parts that violate the organization.

By specifying how features are joined together into patterns and parts, structural models allow us to describe the structure of patterns. They are particularly useful for describing line patterns such as letters of the alphabet or the more artificial patterns used by Palmer. When there are not important structural relations among the features, feature models are very adequate, and a pattern can be described by simply listing its features. The moral is that the kind of descriptive language we need depends on the kinds of patterns we want to describe.

Information-processing stages

The Partial-Report Technique

In order to understand how people perform on a pattern recognition task, we have to identify what occurs during each of the information-processing stages discussed in Chapter 1. Sperling (1960) is responsible for the initial construction of an information-processing model of performance on a visual recognition task. Subjects in Sperling's task saw an array of letters presented for a brief period of time (usually 50 msec) in a tachistoscope and were asked to report all the letters they could remember from the display. Responses were highly accurate if the display contained fewer than five letters. But when the number of letters was increased, subjects never reported more than an average of 4.5 letters correct, regardless of how many letters were in the display.

A general problem in constructing an information-processing model is to identify the cause of a performance limitation. Sperling was interested in measuring the number of letters that could be recognized during a brief exposure, but he was aware that the upper limit of 4.5 might be caused by an inability to remember more than that. In other words, subjects might have recognized most of the letters in the display but have forgotten some before they could report what they had seen. Sperling therefore changed his procedure from a whole-report procedure (report all the letters) to a partial-report procedure (report only some of the letters).

In the most typical case the display consisted of three rows, each containing four letters. Subjects would be unable to remember all twelve letters in a display, but they should be able to remember four letters. The partial-report procedure required that subjects report only one row. The pitch of a tone signaled which one of the three rows should be reported: the top row for a high pitch, the middle row for a medium pitch, and the bottom row for a low pitch. The tone occurred immediately after the physical termination of the display, so subjects would have to view the entire display and could not look simply at a single row.

The use of the partial-report technique is based on the assumption that the number of letters reported from the cued row equals the average number of letters perceived in each of the rows since subjects did not know in advance which row to look at. This turned out to be a faulty assumption, but it seemed reasonable at the time, so let's accept it for a while for the purposes of discussion. The results of the partial-report procedure indicated that subjects could correctly report three of the four letters in a row, implying that they had recognized nine letters in the entire display.

Sperling's Model

It often happens that what is best remembered about a scientist's work is not what that person originally set out to investigate. Although Sperling designed the partial-report technique to reduce the memory requirements of his task and obtain a "pure" measure of perception, his work is best remembered for discovery of the importance of a visual sensory store. How did this come about? The estimate that subjects had perceived 9 letters was obtained when the tone occured immediately after the termination of the 50-msec exposure. In this case, subjects could correctly report about three-quarters of the letters, and three-quarters of 12 is 9. But when the tone was delayed until 1 second after the display, subjects' performance declined to the point that the estimated number of letters perceived was only 4.5. The estimates showed a gradual decline from 9 letters to 4.5 as the delay of the tone increased from 0 to 1 second (Figure 2.7).

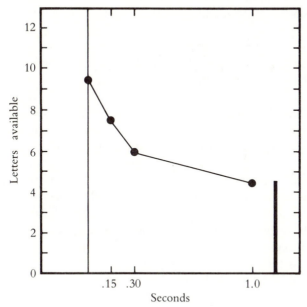

Figure 2.7. Number of "letters available" as a function of delay of the tone. *(From "The Information Available in Brief Visual Presentations," by G. Sperling. In* Psychological Monographs, *1960, 74(11, Whole No. 498). Copyright 1960 by the American Psychological Association. Reprinted by permission.)*

The most interesting thing about the number 4.5 is that it is exactly equal to the upper limit of performance on the whole-report task. The partial-report procedure has an advantage over the whole-report procedure only if the tone is delayed by less than 1 second. In order to explain the gradual decline in performance illustrated in Figure 2.7, Sperling proposed that subjects were using a visual sensory store to recognize letters in the cued row. When they heard the tone, they selectively attended to the cued row in the store and attempted to identify the letters in the row. Their success in making use of the tone depended on the clarity of information in the sensory store. When the tone occurred immediately after the termination of the stimulus, the clarity was sufficient for recognizing additional letters in the cued row. But as the clarity of the sensory image faded, it became increasingly difficult to recognize additional letters. When the tone was delayed by 1 second, subjects could not use the sensory store at all to focus on the cued row, so their performance was determined by the number of letters they had recognized from the entire display that happened to be in that row. Their performance was therefore equivalent to the whole-report procedure, in which they attended to the entire display.

In 1963 Sperling proposed an information-processing model of performance on his visual report task. The model consisted of a visual information store, scanning, rehearsal, and an auditory information store.

The *visual information store,* VIS, is a sensory store that preserves information for a brief period lasting from a fraction of a second to a second, the decay rate depending upon such factors as the intensity, contrast, and duration of the stimulus. It also depends on whether exposure of the stimulus is followed by a second exposure. Visual masking occurs when a second exposure, consisting of a brightly lighted field or a different set of patterns, reduces the effectiveness of the visual information store.

In order for pattern recognition to occur, the information in the sensory store must be scanned. Sperling initially considered *scanning* to occur one item at a time, as if one had a sheet of cardboard with a hole in it just large enough for only a single letter to appear.

The next two components of the model consisted of *rehearsal* (saying the letters to oneself) and an *auditory information store,* AIS (remembering the names of the letters). In order to remember the items until recall, subjects usually reported rehearsing the items. Additional evidence for verbal rehearsal was found when recall errors often appeared in the form of auditory confusions—in other words, producing a letter that sounded like the correct letter. The advantage of the auditory store is that items can be continuously recycled by means of rehearsal. Sperling's auditory store is part of short-term memory, a topic we will consider later in the book.

Sperling revised his initial model in 1967. By this time evidence had begun to accumulate suggesting that patterns were not scanned one at a time but were analyzed simultaneously. Sperling therefore modified his idea of the scan component to allow for pattern recognition to occur simultaneously over the entire display, although the rate of recognition in a given location depended on where the subject was focusing attention. Another change in the 1967 model was the inclusion of a *recognition (R) buffer* for converting the visual image of a letter into a program of motor instructions for pronouncing the names. Sperling added the recognition buffer to the model because a person would not have time to actually rehearse the letters during the brief exposure of the stimulus. Recognition of a letter would therefore activate the program for rehearsal, which would be carried out after the visual information store had decayed. Figure 2.8 shows a diagram of the revised model.

Rumelhart's Model

In 1970 Rumelhart proposed a detailed mathematical model of performance on a wide range of information-processing tasks, including the whole-report and partial-report procedures studied by Sperling. Rumelhart's model assumes that recognition occurs by identification of the features of a pattern. Feature recognition occurs simultaneously over the entire display, but it takes time to recognize features, and the more time the observer has, the more features can be recognized. Imagine that you are looking at the screen of a tachistoscope and the experimenter presents a brief exposure of the letters *F, R,* and *Z.* If the exposure were very short, you might see only the vertical line of the letter *F,* the curve of the letter *R,* and the diagonal line of the letter *Z.* If forced to guess at this

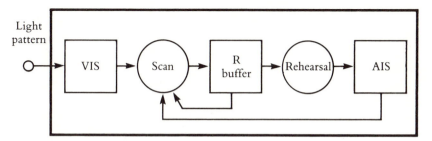

Figure 2.8. Model of processing stages in the Sperling paradigm. *(From "Successive Approximations to a Model for Short-Term Memory," by G. Sperling. In Acta Psychologica, 1967, 27, 285–292. Copyright 1967 by North-Holland Publishing Company. Reprinted by permission.)*

point, you would most likely use this information. You might guess that the *R* was an *R, P,* or *B* because these letters have curved segments at the top. If the exposure were a little longer, you would be able to see more features, and it would be easier to guess or even recognize the entire letter.

Your success in identifying the letters would be determined not only by the length of the exposure but also by how quickly you could recognize the features. The rate of feature recognition in Rumelhart's model is influenced by both the clarity of the information and the number of items in the display. When the exposure terminates, the clarity declines as the visual information store decays. The number of items in the display affects the rate of feature recognition because the model assumes that people have a limited amount of attention, which is divided across all the items in the display. As the number of items in the display increases, the amount of attention that can be focused on each item declines, and this slows down the rate of recognizing that particular item.

The assumption that the rate of feature recognition depends on both the number of items in the display and the clarity of the information is used by Rumelhart to account for performance on Sperling's task. Rumelhart's model proposed that people could only report an average of 4.5 letters in the whole-report procedure because of a perceptual limitation rather than a memory limitation. As the number of letters is increased up to 12, people continue to try to recognize all the letters simultaneously. But the rate of recognizing each letter slows down as more letters are added to the display. Although there are more letters that could be recognized, the increase is compensated for by the lower probability of recognizing each letter.

Rumelhart's model assumes that in the partial-report procedure the observer attempts to recognize letters over the entire display before hearing the tone. Then, on hearing the tone, the observer attends only to the cued row in the visual information store and attempts to recognize additional letters in that particular row. The rate of recognition is increased by the fact that the observer now has to attend to only 4 letters rather than 12. But as the visual information store decays, not only is there less time to use it, but it becomes more difficult to use because of decreasing clarity. Success in focusing on the cued row therefore depends very critically on the delay of the tone, as is illustrated in Figure 2.7. Rumelhart's assumptions were adequate not only for making quantitative predictions about performance on Sperling's tasks but for making quantitative predictions in a number of other tasks.

One difference between Rumelhart's interpretation and that suggested by Sperling is that Sperling claimed that performance in the whole-report task was limited by memory and Rumelhart claimed that performance was limited by perception. The relative roles of perception and memory as limiting factors in this task should depend on the number of letters in the display and the exposure time. We will see in the next chapter that STM could limit performance if the number of letters in the display exceeded the limited capacity of STM. However, if people could recognize only 4.5 letters because of the very brief exposure, the limiting factor would be perception rather than memory.

Because memory is a limiting factor when people have time to recognize more letters than they can remember, the whole-report procedure is no longer used to measure perception. A better procedure, called the *detection paradigm,* was designed by Estes and Taylor (1966). This procedure requires that the observer report which one of two target letters is in a display of letters. For instance, the subject might be told that a display will contain either the letter *B* or the letter *F,* and the task is to report which letter is present. The memory requirements are minimal because the subject must report only a single letter. By using the percentage of trials on which the observer was correct, and correcting for guessing, Estes and Taylor were able to calculate the average number of letters perceived on each trial. The detection procedure has also been analyzed by Rumelhart (1970) as a part of his general model—a model that provided an impressive account of performance on the visual information-processing tasks studied during the 1960s.

Word recognition

The Word Superiority Effect

Much of the research on pattern recognition during the 1970s shifted away from how people recognize isolated letters to how people recognize letters in words. This research was stimulated by a finding that has been labeled the *word superiority effect.* Gerald Reicher (1969), in his dissertation at the University of Michigan, investigated a possible implication of the scan component in Sperling's 1967 model. If the observer attempts to recognize all the letters in an array simultaneously, is it possible to recognize a four-letter unit in the same amount of time as it takes to recognize a single letter? In an attempt to answer this question, Reicher designed an experiment in which observers were shown a single letter, a four-letter word, or a four-letter nonword. The task was always to identify a single letter by selecting one of two alternatives. The exposure of the stimulus was immediately followed by a visual masking field with the two response alternatives directly above or below the critical letter. For example, one set of stimuli consisted of the letter *D,* the word *WORD,* or the nonword *OWRD.* The two alternatives in this case were the letters *D* and *K,* which were displayed above the critical letter *D* (see Figure 2.9).

Observers indicated whether they thought the letter in that position had been a *D* or a *K*.

This example illustrates several characteristics of Reicher's design. First, the four-letter word has the same four letters as the four-letter nonword. Second, the position of the critical letter is the same for both the word and the nonword. Third, both of the response alternatives make a word (*WORD* or *WORK*) for the word condition and a nonword for the nonword condition. And fourth, the memory requirements are minimized by requiring that subjects identify only a single letter, even when four letters are presented.

The results showed that subjects were significantly more accurate in identifying the critical letter when it was part of a word than when it was part of a nonword or when it was presented alone. Eight of the nine subjects did better on single words than on single letters. The one subject who reversed this trend was the only subject who said that she saw the words as four separate letters, which she made into words; all other subjects said that they experienced a word as a single word and not as four letters making up a word.

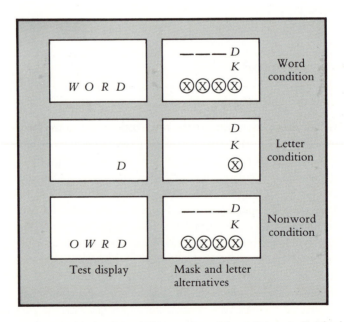

Figure 2.9. Example of the three experimental conditions in Reicher's (1969) experiment. The mask and response alternatives followed the test display. The task was to decide which of the two alternatives occurred in the tested position. *(From* Cognitive Psychology, *by Robert L. Solso, copyright © 1979 by Harcourt, Brace Jovanovich, Inc. Reprinted by permission of the publisher.)*

This word superiority effect can possibly tell us something useful about reading. Over the past ten years it has been the subject of numerous investigations, which have been reviewed by Baron (1978b). Baron points out that it is still unresolved which of several possible explanations of the effect is the best. The explanation that Baron seems to favor is simply that more features of letters are identified when the letters are parts of words than when they are parts of nonwords.

An alternative explanation—the inference view—is that the perceptual information is easier to interpret for words than for nonwords (Krueger & Shapiro, 1979; Massaro, 1979). This view implies that the same number of features is perceived for words as nonwords. Imagine that you saw a four-letter word and identified the first three letters as *WOR*. You didn't have time to identify the fourth letter but noticed that it contained a curved segment. The curved segment suggests that the fourth letter must either be a *D, O,* or *Q.* Since only the letter *D* completes a word, you can eliminate the *O* or *Q.* If you identified *ORW* and a curved segment in a nonword, you wouldn't know whether the last letter was a *D, O,* or *Q.* The correct inference in the first case depends on using knowledge of what letters occur in words.

Reicher's procedure attempted to limit the use of inferences by requiring that people choose between only two alternatives, such as the letters *D* and *K* in the above example. It is not obvious how well the inference view can explain his results when there are only two alternatives, both of which form a word. The detection of a curved segment, for example, should result in selecting a *D* rather than a *K* regardless of whether the letter occurred in a word or a nonword.

Some of the studies on the word superiority effect have used variations of Reicher's procedure, and the inference view may provide a better explanation of their results (see Krueger & Shapiro, 1979; Massaro, 1979). We also know that inferences are important during normal reading, since we can use our knowledge of language to infer information that we do not perceive. I mentioned in the previous chapter that reading is a good example of how we use both bottom-up and top-down analysis. The bottom-up analysis begins with the perceptual information that we are reading. The top-down analysis begins with our knowledge of language. Let us look at how an interactive model of reading combines both sources of information.

An Interactive Model of Reading

The recognition of words during reading is determined by both the information in the text and the observer's knowledge of the world. A major problem is how the skilled reader puts all this information together to make reading an easy task. Although we do not yet have a detailed answer to this question, we do know the general form a model should take.

It is clear from the many studies related to reading that a model of how people recognize words will have to be an interactive model in which different sources of information are combined. Figure 2.10 shows an interactive model proposed by Rumelhart (1977). As the reader scans the text, letters are registered in the visual information store (VIS), where the reader attempts to identify the features of the letters. This perceptual information is then combined with the reader's knowledge to recognize words. The knowledge includes information about the orthographic structure of the language, lexical items in the language, syntactic possibilities, and semantic context.

Orthographic knowledge is knowledge about the probability of various strings of letters—for example, knowing that a *u* typically follows a *q* and a *z* is unlikely to follow the letter *t*. *Lexical* knowledge is knowledge of which letter combinations form a word in a language. As was previously shown, the constraint that the letters must form a word places restrictions on which letters can occur.

Syntactic knowledge concerns the grammar of a language. It uses the previous words in a sentence to determine whether the next word is likely to be a noun, verb, adjective, or some other grammatical unit. Children make use of grammatical information quite early in learning to read (Weber, 1970). Observers who classified oral reading errors made during the first-grade reading class found that about 90% of the errors were grammatically acceptable with the preceding context. An error was judged grammatically acceptable if the child's response could be completed to form a grammatical sentence. If the child reads *Spot and* for the

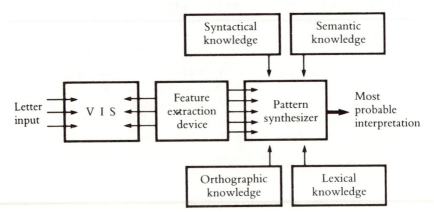

Figure 2.10. An interactive model of reading. *(From "Toward an Interactive Model of Reading," by D. E. Rumelhart. In S. Dornic (Ed.),* Attention and Performance *(Vol. 6). Copyright 1977 by Lawrence Erlbaum Associates, Inc., Publishers. Reprinted by permission.)*

words *Spot can,* the error is grammatically acceptable because *Spot and* can be completed to form a grammatical sentence. The substitution of *she cold* for *she could* would be classified as ungrammatical.

Semantic knowledge refers to the meaning of what we are reading. Consider the experience of trying to read handwriting that is almost illegible. If we isolate single words from their context, we may not be able to recognize them at all even if we have very good orthographic and lexical knowledge. If a word appears in a sentence, we can make use of grammatical knowledge to determine whether the word is likely to be a noun, verb, or adjective. This would provide some help, but each of these grammatical classes is very large, so we would most likely resort to semantic knowledge for further help. The meaning of the sentence and surrounding sentences should help us identify the illegible word.

A specific example might help us to understand how all this information can be combined (Rumelhart, 1977). Consider the following procedure. You view the picture shown in Figure 2.11 for a few seconds and are then given a tachistoscopic presentation of a noun phrase, which you know will refer to one of the objects in the picture. The picture provides a semantic context for the noun phrase. The noun phrase is

Figure 2.11. A scene illustrating a context. *(From "Toward an Interactive Model of Reading," by D. E. Rumelhart. In S. Dornic (Ed.),* Attention and Performance *(Vol. 6). Copyright 1977 by Lawrence Erlbaum Associates, Inc., Publishers. Reprinted by permission.)*

THE CAR, but because of the fast exposure, you identify only some of its features—shown in Figure 2.12.

Since the perceptual information is rather meager, you must use other sources of knowledge to interpret the stimulus. The syntactic

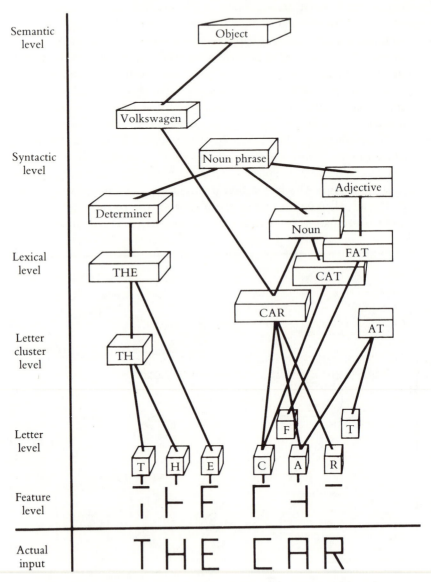

Figure 2.12. Sources of information for reading. *(From "Toward an Interactive Model of Reading," by D. E. Rumelhart. In S. Dornic (Ed.), Attention and Performance (Vol. 6). Copyright 1977 by Lawrence Erlbaum Associates, Inc., Publishers. Reprinted by permission.)*

knowledge that a noun phrase usually starts with a determiner (*a, an, the*) makes it relatively easy to identify the first word as *THE.* This decision is also facilitated by the orthographic knowledge that *TH* is a frequent letter pair. Orthographic knowledge is represented at the letter cluster level in Figure 12.12. The syntactic knowledge that the second word of a noun phrase is a noun or an adjective is much less restrictive, and the words *FAT, CAT,* and *CAR* are considered at the lexical level as being consistent with the perceptual information. The fact that *AT* is a frequent letter pair is counterproductive because it suggests an incorrect answer. If you gave the correct answer in this case, it would likely be because of the influence of the semantic context. Identifying the second word as *CAR* is consistent with the fact that there is a car (a Volkswagen) in the picture.

We might want to question whether this example overemphasized the importance of nonperceptual knowledge by providing so little perceptual information. Don't we usually have time to recognize all the features of a letter when we read? I have two answers to this question.

First, the features can often be very difficult to recognize when we are reading handwriting, making it necessary to use nonperceptual information. In fact, we may not even realize that a letter or word is ambiguous, because the context makes it clear which word is intended. The two sentences in Figure 2.13 contain a physically identical word, yet we have little difficulty in identifying the word as *went* in the upper sentence and as *event* in the lower sentence.

Second, even when we read typewriting and therefore have very legible letters before us, the use of nonperceptual knowledge can reduce the amount of perceptual analysis we have to perform. The difficulty of doing a very careful perceptual analysis is illustrated by proofreading errors. I was often surprised to find about three or four errors in each of the chapters of this book even after I had carefully read the manuscript on two previous occasions in an attempt to identify errors. And proofreading is done much more carefully and slowly than normal reading.

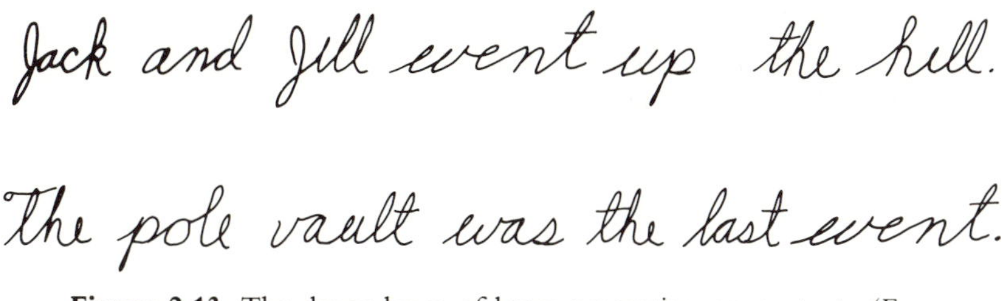

Jack and Jill event up the hill.

The pole vault was the last event.

Figure 2.13. The dependence of letter perception on context. *(From "Toward an Interactive Model of Reading," by D. E. Rumelhart. In S. Dornic (Ed.),* Attention and Performance *(Vol. 6). Copyright 1977 by Lawrence Erlbaum Associates, Inc., Publishers. Reprinted by permission.)*

The purpose of normal reading, of course, is to extract meaning from text. This section illustrates that the extraction of meaning not only depends on pattern recognition but helps to guide pattern recognition. The way in which people attempt to comprehend text is one of the most challenging problems in cognitive psychology. We will return to this issue in a later chapter. Our immediate task is to continue examining the perceptual aspects of cognition by studying the role of attention in limiting the amount of information we perceive and enter into memory. You will notice as you read the next chapter that the experiments in this area use primarily auditory messages. Our ability to process many visual patterns simultaneously and control what we are looking at by moving our eyes makes it easier to study attention by using auditory messages. The findings reported in the next chapter will generalize some of the ideas expressed in this chapter. The role of context, for example, is as important in understanding speech as it is in reading written material. As you read further, look for related ideas and concepts. I will try to make your task easier by pointing out some of the similarities between visual and auditory perception.

Summary

Pattern recognition is a skill that people perform very well. The three most popular explanations of pattern recognition are template, feature, and structural theories. A template theory proposes that two patterns are compared by measurement of their degree of overlap. A template theory has difficulty accounting for many aspects of pattern recognition, but it is a useful way of representing information in the sensory store before it is analyzed during the pattern recognition stage. The most common theories of pattern recognition assume that patterns are analyzed into features. Feature theories are often tested by determining how well they can account for perceptual confusions. Structural theories state explicitly how the features of a pattern are joined together. They provide a more complete description of a pattern and are particularly useful for describing patterns consisting of intersecting lines.

Sperling's interest in the question of how many letters can be perceived during a brief tachistoscopic exposure resulted in the construction of information-processing models for visual tasks. Sperling proposed that the information is preserved very briefly in a visual information store, where all the letters can be simultaneously analyzed. When a letter is recognized, its name can be verbally rehearsed and preserved in an auditory store (short-term memory). Rumelhart's model proposed that patterns are recognized by identification of their features. The rate of feature identification is a function of both the clarity and the number of letters in a display. The model accounts for performance on Sperling's partial-report task by assuming that the observer focuses attention on the cued row as soon as the tone is heard. The probability of recognizing additional letters in the row depends on the clarity of the visual information store.

Recognition of letters while reading is influenced by perceptual information and the context of the letter. The finding that a letter could be recognized more easily when it was part of a word than when it was part of a nonword or was presented by itself has been called the word superiority effect. A perceptual explanation of this finding assumes that the recognition of some letters can facilitate the recognition of other letters that frequently occur together or form a word. An alternative explanation assumes that it is easier for people to infer what letter occurred when the letter is part of a word. An interactive model of reading proposes that perceptual information interacts with orthographic, lexical, syntactic, and semantic knowledge to influence word recognition and thus facilitate reading.

Recommended reading

My book *Psychological Processes in Pattern Recognition* (Reed, 1973) provides a summary of research on pattern recognition, emphasizing the information-processing approach. Garner's (1974) book *The Processing of Information and Structure* reviews research on the structural characteristics of patterns. The relation between his work and Eleanor Gibson's is discussed in his chapter on letter identification in Garner (1979). Lockhead and Crist (1980) demonstrate that letters can be made more distinctive by emphasizing how features are related to other features. Bower and Glass (1976) demonstrate how structural descriptions of visual patterns determine the effectiveness of memory cues. A chapter by Estes (1978b) contains a thorough discussion of the perceptual requirements of reading. Articles by Baron (1978b) and Adams (1979) discuss the theoretical attempts to explain the word superiority effect. Rumelhart and Siple (1974) propose a quantitative model of how people recognize tachistoscopically presented words. Marslen-Wilson and Welsh (1978) demonstrate how bottom-up and top-down analyses interact to influence word recognition during speech. Other areas of research on pattern recognition include scene recognition (Biederman, 1981) and recognition of the facial transformation that occurs in aging (Pittenger & Shaw, 1975). The characteristics of the visual information store are discussed in a recent review paper (Long, 1980).

3

Attention

Everyone knows what attention is. It is the taking possession by the mind, in clear and vivid form, of one out of what seem several simultaneously possible objects or trains of thought. Focalization, concentration, of consciousness are of its essence.

WILLIAM JAMES (1890)

The above words from William James's famous *Principles of Psychology*, published in 1890, refer to two characteristics of attention that continue to be studied today—focalization and concentration. *Focalization* implies selectivity. We are usually bombarded by all kinds of perceptual stimuli and must decide which of these are of interest to us. The selective nature of attention is illustrated by the behavior of subjects in Sperling's partial-report task: when a cue signaled which row to report, subjects were able to attend selectively to the cued row and ignore the information in the other two rows.

The selective nature of perception is necessary to keep us from becoming overloaded with information. This is particularly true in large cities. According to Stanley Milgram (1970), a well-known social psychologist, it has been calculated that in midtown Manhattan it is possible to encounter 220,000 people within a 10-minute radius of one's office. This kind of overload, Milgram argues, can affect our life on several levels, influencing role performance, the evolution of social norms, and cognitive functioning. Adaptive responses to information overload include spending less time on each input, disregarding low-priority inputs, or completely blocking off sensory inputs. The first part of this chapter is concerned with theories that attempt to locate the stage at which this selection occurs. Do we block off the sensory input before it reaches the pattern recognition stage, or do we make the selection after recognition?

Theories that attempt to answer this question are called *bottleneck theories* because they assume that selection is necessary whenever too much information reaches a bottleneck—a stage that cannot process all of it.

The second aspect of attention is *concentration*. Imagine that you are the first to arrive at a cocktail party, and you carry on a conversation with the hostess. As long as there are no other conversations in the room, it would require little concentration or mental effort to follow what the hostess was saying. If she were not speaking in your native language, however, comprehension would be less automatic and would require more mental effort. You would also have to concentrate more to follow what she was saying if you were surrounded by many other conversations. If you wanted to eavesdrop on one of the other conversations while you were listening to the hostess, still more concentration or mental effort would be required.

The second section of this chapter discusses *capacity theories* of attention, which attempt to identify how capacity or mental effort is allocated to different activities. Such theories propose that attention is limited in capacity, and when we attempt to attend to more than one event—studying while watching television, for instance—we pay the price of doing each less efficiently. Rumelhart's model, discussed in Chapter 2, is a theory that assumes a limited capacity. According to his model, feature recognition slows down as the number of items increases because a limited amount of attention must be distributed over more patterns.

An important area of research related to capacity theories is the study of automatic processing. *Automatic processing* occurs when the capacity required for carrying out a task is very minimal. If a task requires very little capacity to perform, it should not interfere with other tasks. The third section of this chapter examines the characteristics of automatic processing and illustrates how the concept can be applied to memory and the acquisition of reading skills.

The final section presents some research on using selective listening tests to predict success in a pilot training program or the accident rate of commercial drivers. There are other potential applications of research on selective attention. One example is the diagnosis of heart murmurs. Rushmer (1970) pointed out that it is a difficult task for medical students to learn how to classify heart murmurs. Part of the difficulty results from the demands of selective attention—to be able to hear the murmur embedded in the sound of a heart beat. Perhaps we will see still more applications of selective attention research in the future.

Before I talk about attention in my own course on cognitive psychology, I have the students try to listen to two verbal messages at once. Two volunteers come to the front of the class and read different passages from one of their books. The rest of the class usually finds it very difficult to comprehend both of the messages simultaneously. It is easier to try to comprehend only one of the messages, but the difficulty of the task depends on physical characteristics such as pitch and separation. The level of difficulty increases as the pitch of the two speakers becomes more similar or the two speakers stand closer together. If you have the opportunity, try to participate in such a demonstration and observe some of these effects for yourself. It will give you a better understanding of the listener's task.

Bottleneck theories

Broadbent's Filter Model

As you will recall, the discussion of information-processing models in Chapter 1 included a summary of Broadbent's (1958) filter model. The model could account for much of the data on attention that had been collected at that time. One example is an experiment in which enlisted men in England's Royal Navy listened to three pairs of digits (Broadbent, 1954). One member of each pair arrived at one ear at the same time that the other member of the pair arrived at the other ear. For example, if the sequence were 73–42–15, the subject would simultaneously hear 7 and 3, followed by 4 and 2, followed by 1 and 5.

Left ear	Right ear
7	3
4	2
1	5

The pairs were separated by a ½-second interval, and the subjects were asked to report the digits in whatever order they chose. They were able to report 65% of the lists correctly, and almost all of the correct reports involved recalling all the digits presented to one ear, followed by all the digits presented to the other ear. In other words, if 741 had been presented to the left ear and 325 to the right ear, the subject would recall either in the order 741–325 or 325–741.

Another group of men was instructed to recall the digits in the actual order of their arrival: the first pair of digits, followed by the second pair of digits, followed by the third pair of digits. The time between successive pairs of digits varied from ½ second to 2 seconds. Figure 3.1 shows the percentage of lists correctly recalled as a function of the interval between pairs. The results indicated that performance was better at the longer intervals; nevertheless, it was much worse than when subjects could recall the digits on one ear followed by the other ear.

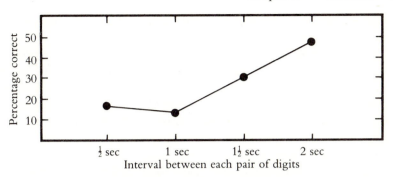

Figure 3.1. Recall of digit sequences as a function of the interval between pairs. *(From "The Role of Auditory Localization in Attention and Memory Span," by D. E. Broadbent. In* Journal of Experimental Psychology, *1954, 47, 191–196. Copyright 1954 by the American Psychological Association. Reprinted by permission.)*

To account for these findings, Broadbent used the filter model, which can be represented by the mechanical model shown in Figure 3.2 (Broadbent, 1957). The mechanical model consists of a Y-shaped tube and a set of identifiable balls. The tube has a narrow stem that can accept only a single ball at a time (the limited–capacity perceptual channel) but upper branches (the sensory store) that are wider and can accept more than one ball at a time. At the junction of the stem and branches is a hinged flap

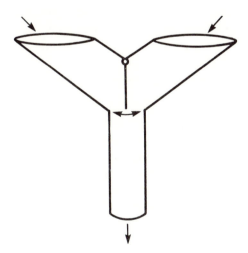

Figure 3.2. A mechanical model of attention. *(From "A Mechanical Model for Human Attention and Immediate Memory," by D. E. Broadbent. In* Psychological Review, *1957, 64, 205–215. Copyright 1957 by the American Psychological Association. Reprinted by permission.)*

(the filter), which can swing back and forth to allow balls from either branch of the **Y** to enter the stem.

In this case the balls represent digits, and the two branches represent the two ears. Two balls are simultaneously dropped, one into each branch. The flap door would be set to one side to allow one of the balls to enter the stem, while the other ball would be held in a sensory store. If the observer wanted to report all the digits entering one ear, the flap would stay to one side until all three balls from one branch entered the stem. The flap would then be shifted to the other side, allowing the three balls from the other branch to enter the stem. If the observer were forced to report the digits as they arrived, the flap would have to be shifted back and forth to allow balls to enter the stem in the order they arrived.

The model accounts for performance on Broadbent's (1954) task by assuming that it takes time to switch attention (represented by the flap, or filter) from ear to ear. If the interval separating pairs of balls is too short, the flap will not have time to switch back and forth, and performance will deteriorate as it did when the interval was 1 second or less (Figure 3.1). The easiest case should be when the listener can report all the digits entering one ear before reporting all the digits entering the other ear. In this case, the listener can recognize all the digits entering one ear before recognizing the digits entering the other ear, and only a single shift of attention is required. But the shift has to occur before the information entering the unattended ear decays from the auditory sensory store. A limitation of the filter model is that the sensory store would have to last fairly long in order for the model to operate as proposed; otherwise, the information would decay before it could be recognized.

Treisman's Attenuation Model

A common experimental paradigm for testing Broadbent's assumption that the listener can recognize information on only one channel at a time is to present a different, but continuous, message to each ear and ask the listener to "shadow," or repeat aloud, one of the messages. Shadowing a message provides proof that the listener is following instructions and attending to the correct ear. The initial findings from shadowing experiments supported the filter model. As predicted, subjects were almost completely unaware of the content of the message played on the unattended ear (Cherry, 1953).

However, later research indicated that listeners occasionally could report information on the unattended channel. Moray (1959) discovered that subjects sometimes heard their own names on this channel. Treisman (1960) found that the contextual effects of language would sometimes cause subjects to report words on the unattended channel and therefore shadow inappropriately. A few examples of the intrusions that occurred were the following:

1. . . . I SAW THE GIRL / song was WISHING . . .
   . . . . me that bird / JUMPING in the street . . .
2. . . . SITTING AT A MAHOGANY / three POSSIBILITIES . . .
   . . . . let us look at these / TABLE with her head . . .

The first line in each example is the message that the listener was asked to shadow. The second line is the unattended message. The words in capital letters are the words actually spoken by the subjects. The intrusions from the unattended channel fit the semantic context better than the words on the attended channel. The contextual cues were not sufficient to cause subjects to change permanently to the unattended message in order to follow the meaning of the passage, but the results did raise some questions for the filter theory. If the filter completely blocks out the unattended message, how could subjects report hearing their names or shadow words on the unattended channel?

To answer this question, Treisman (1960) proposed a model consisting of two parts—a selective filter and a "dictionary" (Figure 3.3). The filter distinguishes between two messages on the basis of their physical characteristics, such as location, intensity, or pitch. However, the filter in Treisman's model does not completely block out the unattended message but merely attenuates it, making it less likely to be heard. The recognition of a word occurs in the dictionary if the intensity or subjective loudness of the word exceeds its threshold (the minimum intensity needed for recognition). The thresholds have two important characteristics. First, they vary across words. Some words have permanently lower thresholds than others and thus are more easily recognized—for example, important words such as a person's own name or perhaps danger signals such as *fire*. Second, the thresholds can be momentarily lowered by the listener's expectations. For instance, if the words *I sang a* were heard, the threshold for the word *song* would be momentarily lowered, making it more likely that the word *song* would be recognized.

The model proposed by Treisman was able to explain why usually very little is heard on the unattended channel, but occasionally some words are recognized. The attenuation of words on the unattended channel implies that they will be subjectively less loud than words on the attended channel. They will usually not be loud enough to exceed their threshold unless they have a very low threshold or their threshold is momentarily lowered. Figure 3.3 shows a schematic representation of this effect. The height of the arrows represents the subjective loudness of the two messages, and the height of the thresholds represents the loudness that is necessary for recognition of the word. Since important words have permanently low thresholds, they can occasionally be heard on the

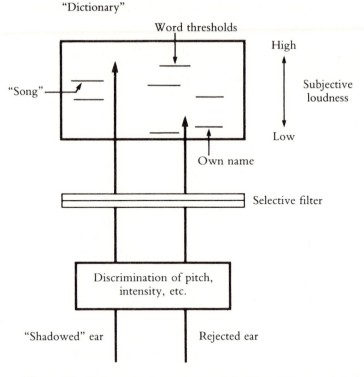

"Dictionary"

Figure 3.3. Treisman's attenuation model. *(From "Contextual Cues in Selective Listening," by A. M. Treisman. In Quarterly Journal of Experimental Psychology, 1970, 12, 242–248. Copyright 1970 by the Experimental Psychology Society. Reprinted by permission.)*

unattended channel, as was found by Moray (1959). A word like *song* normally has a high threshold, but its threshold can be momentarily lowered by expectations. This aspect of the model could account for Treisman's (1960) finding that words on the unattended channel were sometimes incorrectly shadowed if they better fit the context of the message on the attended channel.

The Deutsch-Norman Memory Selection Model

The models proposed by Broadbent and Treisman placed the bottleneck at the pattern recognition stage. Attention was represented by a selective filter that completely blocked out the unattended message in Broadbent's model and attenuated it in Treisman's model, with the implication that very few words should be recognized on the unattended channel. An unattended message could be recognized in Broadbent's model only if attention switched to that message before it decayed from the sensory store. In Treisman's model words in the unattended message could be recognized only if their thresholds were low enough to be exceeded by the attenuated message.

We have previously seen that a frequent problem in constructing information-processing models is the identification of the stage at which a performance limitation occurs. Constructing models of attention is no exception. According to the models proposed by Deutsch and Deutsch (1963) and Norman (1968), the bottleneck occurs after pattern recognition. The problem is not one of perception but one of selection after perception occurs. In their models attention is equivalent to the selection stage in Figure 1.1 (Chapter 1).

The model proposed by Deutsch and Deutsch involves two different conversations (messages). The model assumes that words in both conversations are recognized but are quickly forgotten unless they are important. Words on the attended channel are important because people have to shadow them. Words on the unattended channel are usually unimportant because the listener is asked to attend to another channel. Although recognized, they are quickly forgotten unless they are important—a person's own name, for instance. The probability that information will enter memory depends on the general level of arousal in addition to the importance of the material. Much more will enter memory when a person is alert than when the person is drowsy.

Norman expanded the Deutsch and Deutsch model in a 1968 paper. Figure 3.4 shows a schematic diagram of Norman's model. Three sensory inputs—*i, j,* and *k*—are recognized by being matched to their representations in memory. They will be quickly forgotten, however, unless they can be selected for more permanent storage. Selection is determined not only by the strength of the sensory input but also by the pertinence or the importance of each input. Certain words have a permanently high level of importance, whereas others have low levels but can fluctuate as a result of expectations formed from contextual, grammatical, or semantic cues. The input that is acted on or stored more permanently in memory is determined by a combination of sensory activation and importance (labeled σ and π in Figure 3.4). Stimulus *i* has the highest combination in the example, so it is the one selected for further processing.

Capacity theories

The models proposed by Broadbent, Treisman, Deutsch and Deutsch, and Norman stimulated many experiments and arguments regarding the location of the bottleneck. Some data seemed to support the assertion that the bottleneck was caused by the limitations of perception, whereas other data supported the assertion that the bottleneck occurred after perception. The failure to agree on the location of the bottleneck has had two con-

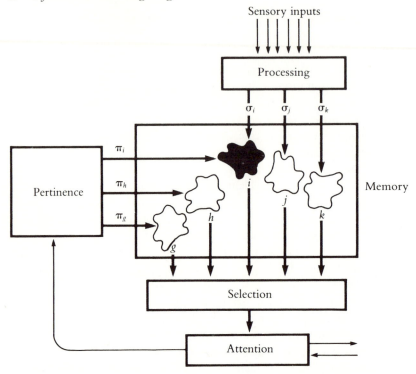

Figure 3.4. Norman's memory selection model. The example shows five words, represented by the subscripts g, h, i, j, and k. Words g, h, and i are important, and words i, j, and k are consistent with the sensory input. The word selected for further processing is the one with the greatest combination of pertinence (importance) and sensory activation. *(From "Toward a Theory of Memory and Attention," by D. A. Norman. In* Psychological Review, *1968, 75, 522–536. Copyright 1968 by the American Psychological Association. Reprinted by permission.)*

sequences. First, psychologists have become more interested in studying the capacity demands of different tasks rather than in locating the bottleneck (Kahneman, 1973). Second, it now seems reasonable to assume that the observer has some control over where the bottleneck occurs depending on what is required in a particular task (Johnston & Heinz, 1978).

We will look first at a capacity model of attention proposed by Kahneman to see how a capacity model differs from a bottleneck model. Then we will review the theory proposed by Johnston and Heinz (1978), which suggests that attention is flexible and the observer has control over where the bottleneck occurs. The Johnston and Heinz theory is particularly interesting because it shows how a bottleneck theory can be related to a capacity theory, since the location of the bottleneck determines how much capacity is required to perform a task.

Example of a Capacity Model

Capacity theories are concerned with the amount of mental effort required to perform a task. Daniel Kahneman's *Attention and Effort* (1973) helped to shift the emphasis from bottleneck theories to capacity theories. Kahneman argued that capacity theory assumes there is a general limit on a person's capacity to perform mental work. It also assumes that a person has considerable control over how this limited capacity can be allocated to different activities. For example, we can usually drive a car and carry on a conversation at the same time if both activities do not exceed our capacity for attending to two different tasks. But when heavy traffic begins to challenge our skills as a driver, it is better to concentrate only on driving and not try to divide our attention between two activities.

A model of the allocation of capacity to mental activities is shown in Figure 3.5. Any kind of activity that requires attention would be represented in the model because all such activities compete for the limited capacity. Different mental activities require different amounts of atten-

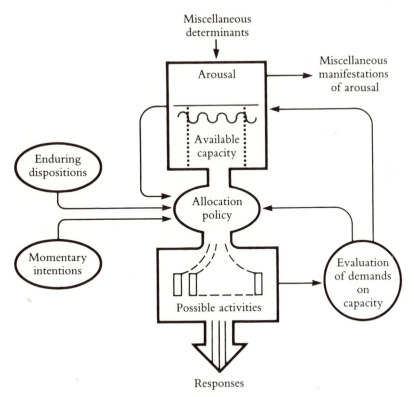

Figure 3.5. A capacity model for attention. *(From Daniel Kahneman, Attention and Effort, © 1973, p. 10. Reprinted by permission of Prentice-Hall, Inc., Englewood Cliffs, New Jersey.)*

tion; some tasks require little mental effort and others require much effort. When the supply of attention does not meet the demands, the level of performance declines. An activity can fail entirely if there is not enough capacity to meet its demands or if attention is allocated to other activities.

Kahneman's model assumes that the amount of capacity available varies with the level of arousal; more capacity is available when arousal is moderately high than when it is low. However, very high levels of arousal can interfere with performance. This assumption is consistent with the Yerkes-Dodson (1908) law that performance is best at intermediate levels of arousal.

The level of arousal can be controlled by feedback from the attempt to meet the demands of ongoing activities, provided that the total demands do not exceed the capacity limit. The choice of which activities to support is influenced by both *enduring dispositions* and *momentary intentions*. Enduring dispositions reflect the rules of involuntary attention. A novel event, an object in sudden motion, or the mention of our own name may automatically attract our attention. Momentary intentions reflect our specific goals or objectives at a particular time. We may want to listen to a lecturer or scan a crowd at an airport in order to recognize a friend.

The capacity model proposed by Kahneman was designed to supplement rather than to replace the bottleneck models. Both types of theories predict that simultaneous activities are likely to interfere with each other, but they attribute the interference to different causes. A bottleneck theory proposes that interference occurs because the same mechanism is required to carry out two incompatible operations at the same time, whereas a capacity model proposes that interference occurs when the demands of two activities exceed the available capacity. Thus a bottleneck model implies that the interference between tasks is specific and depends on the degree to which the tasks use the same mechanisms. A capacity model, on the other hand, implies that the interference is nonspecific and depends on the total demands of the task. Both kinds of interference occur, and both kinds of theories are therefore necessary.

Capacity and Stage of Selection

The flexibility of attention and the interaction between a bottleneck and a capacity theory have been demonstrated by Johnston and Heinz (1978). They used selective listening tasks to develop their theory, so a bottleneck would be likely to occur. However, unlike the early bottleneck theories, their theory proposed that the listener has control over the location of the bottleneck. The location can vary along a continuum ranging from an early mode of selection—in other words, before recognition (as represented by Broadbent's theory)—to a late mode of selection—in other words, following a semantic analysis (as represented by the Deutsch and Deutsch theory). Johnston and Heinz call their theory a multimode theory because of its flexibility: the observer can adopt any mode of attention demanded by, or best suited to, a particular task.

Although a listener can attempt to understand the meaning of two simultaneous messages by adapting a late mode of selection, the use of a late mode is achieved at a cost. As the perceptual processing system shifts from an early to a late mode of selection, it collects more information about the secondary message but requires more capacity to comprehend the primary message. The predicted result is that comprehension of the primary message will decline as the listener attempts to more fully process a secondary message.

Johnston and Heinz tested these predictions in a series of five experiments. A common procedure for measuring the amount of capacity required to perform a task is to determine how quickly a person can respond to a subsidiary task. The main task in their research was a selective listening task. A light signal occurred randomly throughout the listening task, and as the subsidiary task, subjects were instructed to respond to it as quickly as possible by pushing a button. The experimenters assumed that the greater the portion of capacity allocated to selective listening, the less should be available for monitoring the signal light, causing longer reaction times.

One of the experiments used a paradigm in which subjects heard pairs of words presented simultaneously to both ears. Undergraduates at the University of Utah were asked to shadow words defined either by the pitch of a voice or by a semantic category. One set of stimuli used a male and a female voice, and the undergraduates were asked to shadow the words spoken by either the male or the female. These subjects could use an early, sensory mode of selection because the two messages were physically different. Another group of undergraduates heard two messages spoken by the same voice. One message consisted of words from a category such as names of cities, and the other message of words from a different category, such as names of occupations. Subjects were asked to report the words from one of the categories and ignore the words from the other category. These subjects had to use a late, semantic mode of selection because it was necessary to know the meaning of the words in order to categorize them.

The multimode theory predicts that more capacity is required to perform at a late mode of selection. The use of the semantic mode should therefore cause slower reaction times to the light signal and more errors on the selective listening task. The theory also predicts that listening to two lists should require more capacity than listening to and shadowing one list, which should require more capacity than listening to no lists.

Reaction times to the subsidiary task supported the predictions. The average time to respond to the light signal was 310 msec for no lists, 370 msec for one list, 433 msec for two lists that could be distinguished by using sensory cues (pitch), and 482 msec for two lists that could be distinguished by using only semantic cues (categories). These results were accompanied by different levels of performance on the shadowing task. The percentage of errors was 1.4 for a single list, 5.3 for the two lists that could be separated using sensory cues, and 20.5 for the two lists that could be separated using only semantic cues.

The authors interpreted the results as supporting their view that selective attention requires capacity, and the amount of capacity required increases from early to late modes of selection. The first assumption received support from the consistent finding across experiments that reaction times were slower when the listener had to listen to two lists rather than only one. The second assumption received support from the consistent finding that reaction times were slower when the listener had to attend on the basis of semantic cues rather than sensory cues. This latter finding, when combined with the performance results on the selective listening task, suggests that a person can increase the breadth of attention, but only at a cost in capacity expenditure and selection accuracy. But there are two silver linings to this otherwise dark cloud. First, if attention is as flexible as suggested by the multimode theory, a person at least has the choice of how best to use it. And second, psychologists have demonstrated that, with sufficient practice, some tasks can become so automatic that they do not appear to require any of the precious capacity postulated by a capacity theory.

Automatic processing

Of particular interest to psychologists are skills that require very minimal capacity to perform. Psychologists have used the term *automatic processing* to refer to such skills. The first part of this section describes the characteristics of automatic processing and shows how the concept can be applied to memory.

There are two ways in which automatic processing can be achieved—heredity and learning (Hasher & Zacks, 1979). *Heredity* implies that we are born with the ability to carry out some activities at an automatic level. The discussion of automatic processing in memory focuses on such activities. *Learning* implies that a skill becomes automatic through practice. Riding a bicycle is an example. Most of us have learned how to ride a bicycle, and perhaps we can still remember the early experience of wobbling back and forth for a few feet before stopping and having to start over again. When we were just beginning to learn how to ride, the task required a lot of attention. Once we learned how to ride, however, it was difficult to imagine why we had so much trouble initially. Furthermore, we were able to attend to the scenery or our thoughts while bicycling because we no longer had to concentrate on riding. The same could be said about other well-learned motor skills, such as dribbling a basketball or juggling five balls while riding a unicycle.

The second part of this section shows how automatic processing can be acquired in a task like learning to read. LaBerge and Samuels (1974) suggest that, in order to learn new component skills of a complex task, it is important to judge not only whether a skill has been learned but how much capacity is required to perform it. Beginning readers who have mastered some component skills of the main task still may not be ready to learn new component skills if the learned skills require most of their available capacity. The implication is that acquiring automatic processes through practice may be a necessary requirement for learning complex skills.

Automatic Processing and Memory

Let us begin the discussion of automatic processing by considering a general framework for combining research on capacity and memory. Hasher and Zacks (1979) distinguished between two kinds of memory activities—those that require very little or no capacity and those that require considerable capacity. The former, or *automatic processes,* include the recording of frequency, spatial, and temporal information. The latter, or *effortful processes,* include various strategies to improve memory, such as visual imagery, elaboration, organization, and verbal rehearsal.

Frequency information is information about how frequently different stimuli occur. An experimenter might vary the number of times people see different pictures during an experiment and then ask them to estimate how many times each picture appeared. Spatial information is information about where objects occur in the environment. The experimenter could present pictures in different locations and then ask people to recall the locations. Temporal information is information about when or for how long objects occur. The experimenter might ask people about the relative recency or the relative duration of events that occurred during the experiment.

The claim that all three kinds of information can be automatically recorded in memory cannot be tested unless we specify the implications of automatic processing. Hasher and Zacks proposed five criteria that distinguish between automatic and effortful processing. Table 3.1 summarizes the criteria and their predicted effects. The predictions are:

1. *Intentional versus incidental learning.* Intentional learning occurs when we are deliberately attempting to learn and incidental learning

TABLE 3.1. Predicted Effects for Automatic and Effortful Processing.

	Automatic processing	Effortful processing
Intentional versus incidental learning	No difference	Intentional better
Effect of instructions and practice	No effects	Both improve performance
Task interference	No interference	Interference
Depression or high arousal	No effects	Decreased performance
Developmental trends	None	Decreased performance in young children or elderly

From "Automatic and Effortful Processes in Memory," by L. Hasher and R. T. Zacks. In *Journal of Experimental Psychology: General*, 1979, *108*, 356–388. Copyright 1979 by the American Psychological Association. Reprinted by permission.

occurs when we are not consciously attempting to learn. Incidental learning is as effective as intentional learning for automatic processes, but is less effective for effortful processing. People should therefore have knowledge of frequency, spatial, and temporal information even when they are not trying to learn this information.

2. *Effects of instructions and practice.* Instructions on how to perform a task and practice on the task should not affect automatic processes because they can already be carried out very efficiently. Both instructions and practice should improve performance on effortful processes.

3. *Task interference.* Automatic processes should not interfere with each other because they require little or no capacity. Effortful processes require considerable capacity and should interfere with each other when they exceed the amount of available capacity.

4. *Depression or high arousal.* Emotional states such as depression or high arousal can reduce the effectiveness of effortful processes. Automatic processes should not be affected by emotional states.

5. *Developmental trends.* Automatic processes show little change with age. They are acquired early and do not decline with old age. Effortful processes show developmental changes; they are not performed as well by young children or the elderly.

The predictions state that memory for frequency, temporal, and spatial information should not be affected by intentional versus incidental learning, instructions or practice, task interference, depression or high arousal, and developmental trends. There has not yet been enough research to evaluate all these predictions, but the existing data are quite supportive for three criteria that have been extensively evaluated. Evidence indicates that people can effectively record frequency, spatial, and temporal information when they are not trying to learn this information. Research also indicates that these processes do not interfere with each other and show little developmental change. There is not yet enough evidence to evaluate the other two predictions—that practice and emotional states should not influence this kind of information.

In contrast to automatic processes, the use of various memory strategies requires considerable capacity. Review of the relevant research literature provides substantial support for the predicted effects summarized in the right column of Table 3.1. First, these are strategies that people often use during intentional learning to help them learn but usually do not use during incidental learning. Second, people generally learn more when they are specifically instructed to use these strategies. Third, emotional states such as depression can reduce their effective use. Fourth, there is evidence that young children and the elderly do not use these strategies as often as young adults. The prediction that these strategies can interfere with each other has limited support, but there is less available data to evaluate this prediction.

The theoretical framework proposed by Hasher and Zacks cannot be completely evaluated at this time because there is not enough data, although the existing data are generally supportive and are likely to stimulate further research. The advantage of Hasher and Zack's proposal is that it has sufficient breadth to interrelate different areas of psychology. Their synthesis not only ties together attention and memory—two central areas of cognitive psychology—but relates both of these areas to developmental differences and changes associated with emotional states. Theoretical formulations of this magnitude should help build the bridges that link different areas of research.

Automatic Processing and Reading

Presumably, the automatic recording of spatial, temporal, and frequency information is achieved through heredity. Other cognitive skills require extensive practice to achieve automatic processing. One of the most demanding cognitive skills that faces the young child is learning how to read. Learning to read requires many component skills, some of which we considered in the previous chapter. The child must analyze the features of letters, combine the features to identify the letters, convert the letters into sounds for pronouncing words, understand the meaning of individual words, and combine the meaning of the words to comprehend the text. According to a theory proposed by LaBerge and Samuels (1974), the ability to successfully acquire complex, multicomponent skills such as reading depends on the capability of automatic processing. Their criterion for deciding when a skill or subskill is automatic is that it can be completed while attention is directed elsewhere. The rationale behind this argument is that unless at least some of the component skills can be completed without requiring capacity, the total demands of all the component skills will be simply too great for the individual to perform the task.

As we saw in the previous chapter, an initial component skill for successful reading is the ability to identify the features of a letter. The features must then be organized or combined to form a letter, a process which initially requires attention, according to LaBerge and Samuels. However, after sufficient practice in recognizing letters, the features can be combined automatically to form a letter, freeing some capacity for the other necessary component skills. Learning to read depends not only on learning the component skills but on learning them so well that they make very little demand on the limited capacity of attention.

LaBerge and Samuels used a letter-matching task to illustrate the acquisition of the automatic processing of letters. They studied how quickly people could decide whether two letters were the same or different. The pairs were either familiar letters (*b d, p q*) or artificial letters (ı ɹ ʔ ʕ). When subjects were presented letters from one of these sets, they could match the artificial letters as quickly as they could match the familiar letters; familiarity didn't make any difference as long as the subjects were attending to the correct set of letters. However, when subjects matched a different set of letters (*a n u v*) and were occasionally presented one of the above pairs, they could match a familiar pair faster than an artificial pair. The time to match the artificial pairs declined with practice, however, and after five days of practice, the subjects could match the artificial pairs as quickly as they could match the familiar pairs (see Figure 3.6).

LaBerge and Samuels interpreted these results as demonstrating the acquisition of automatic processing. When subjects were expecting a different group of letters, they had to switch their attention to the appropriate set when artificial letters were presented. This would require additional time and delay their response. But a switch of attention was not required for the familiar letters because these letters could be identified automatically without attention. The finding that artificial letters eventually were compared as quickly as familiar letters suggested that something was being learned about the unfamiliar letters over the five days of practice. Since there was no difference in matching pairs when subjects were expecting the correct set of letters, LaBerge and Samuels proposed that subjects were learning to automatically process the artificial pairs when their attention was directed elsewhere. They suggested that acquiring the ability to carry out a component skill automatically is an im-

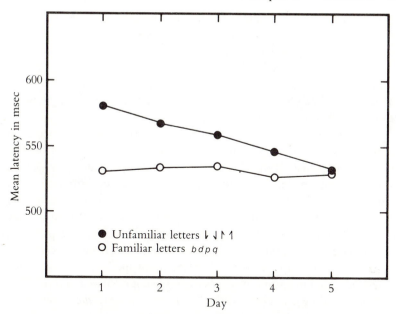

Figure 3.6. Average response times for matching familiar and un-familiar letters when subjects were expecting a different letter set. *(From "Toward a Theory of Automatic Information Processing in Reading," by D. LaBerge and S. J. Samuels. In* Cognitive Psychology, *1974, 6, 293–323. Copyright 1974 by Academic Press, Inc. Reprinted by permission.)*

portant part of learning that should be tested in addition to accuracy. The accurate performance of a component skill (such as recognizing letters) could nonetheless hinder the acquisition of a new component skill (such as pronouncing words) if the performance required so much capacity that little was left for learning the new component.

LaBerge and Samuels argued that the automatic processing of letters became possible when people could recognize a letter as a unit rather than attend to the individual features. To extend their argument, words should require less capacity to recognize if we can recognize the word as a unit rather than as a string of individual letters. You may recall that almost all the people who participated in Reicher's (1969) experiment reported that they perceived a four-letter word as a unit rather than as four separate letters.

One consequence of perceiving a word as a unit is that it should cause us to attend less to the individual letters in the word. You can test your own ability to perceive individual letters in words by reading the follow-ing sentence. Read it once and then read it again, counting the number of *f*'s.

> Finished files are the
> result of years of scientific
> study combined with the
> experience of many years.

There is a total of six *f*'s in the sentence. If you counted fewer than six, please try again.

Most people find this a difficult task because they fail to detect the *f* in one of the words (*of*) even though it occurs three times in the sentence. One explanation of why we overlook this particular *f* is that it is pronounced like the letter *v*. Although this may be a contributing factor, results obtained by Healy (1980) indicate that we often recognize frequently occurring words as units and therefore find it difficult to focus on the individual letters. Healy asked people to read a prose passage at normal reading speed but to encircle the letter *t* whenever it occurred in the passage. She found that people were more likely to miss the letter when it occurred in common words than when it occurred in rare words. In particular, they often missed the letter *t* in the word *the,* which is the most common word in the English language.

Healy's results are consistent with the theory advocated by LaBerge and Samuels. Since people encounter frequent words more often than rare words, they should be better able to recognize a frequent word as a unit. This explanation is analogous to the explanation that familiar letters are more likely than unfamiliar letters to be recognized as units. Less capacity should be required to recognize a frequent word because the reader does not have to pay as much attention to the individual letters. If less capacity is required to recognize a familiar word, the reader should have more capacity available for comprehending the meaning of the sentence.

Individual differences and applications

The preceding section demonstrated how a capacity theory could help us understand complex skills such as reading. Research on the selective nature of attention also has potential applications. The effective design of emergency instructions, for example, depends on making certain that people attend to the instructions. When the emergency could create a panic, this requirement is not trivial (see Box 3.1). Another application is the evaluation of individual differences in order to select people who will perform well in occupations that require selective attention. We will now look at studies in which the selective listening task has been successfully applied to predict flight performance and road accidents.

Box 3.1. Emergency Instructions

Our May colloquium speaker, Dr. Elizabeth Loftus, spoke at the Document Design Center about her pioneering work on the design and testing of emergency instructions for public places. Dr. Loftus, a cognitive psychologist at the University of Washington, began working in the field of public messages in 1973, when she and a colleague, Dr. Jack Keating, were asked by the Government Services Administration to develop emergency evacuation messages for a 37-story Federal building. They extracted what they could from the published psychological literature on perception, attention, memory, and crowd behavior and began to answer questions about the design of messages: Should there be a warning tone? Should a male or a female voice speak the message? How should the message be logically constructed? What types of sentences should be used? What words should be included or avoided?

Their initial success with applying psychological principles to the design of emergency messages led the National Bureau of Standards to request Loftus to extend her findings to hospital situations, where the words of emergency messages must be carefully chosen to avoid panic among patients. Loftus found still another way to develop and apply cognitive principles when San Francisco's subway system, BART, asked her to redesign their evacuation instructions following a disastrous fire. Three recommendations that emerged from that project were: parts of the message must be repeated, since there is no assurance that people are attending to the message the first time it is uttered; the message should be pre-recorded, since a conductor's accent or emotional state can interfere with intelligibility; the structure and timing of the message need to be coordinated with the movement of people as they are obeying the instructions—too much information given too soon can prevent people from carrying out the instructions. In most of these emergency situations, designers must also carefully coordinate vocal and written instructions to make them most effective.

Predicting Flight Performance

The ability to selectively attend is important in many activities outside the laboratory. For example, Gopher and Kahneman (1971) found that flight instructors frequently emphasized the importance of selective attention in learning to fly high-performance aircraft. Flight cadets often failed because they could not appropriately divide their attention among simultaneous activities or were slow to recognize crucial signals that arrived on unattended channels. Although the selective listening paradigm was a popular laboratory task, psychologists had not developed it to study individual differences or predict performances outside the laboratory. Gopher and Kahneman attempted to remedy this situation by determining whether a test of selective listening would help them predict progress in a flight-training program.

The subjects were 100 cadets in the Israeli Air Force. The test consisted of a series of messages that simultaneously presented different information to the two ears. Each message contained two parts: an 8-second period that contained 16 pairs of words (a mixture of verbs and digits), followed by 3 pairs of digits. Each part was preceded by a tone that signaled which ear was relevant. The task was to report every digit on the relevant ear as soon as it was heard. There were either two or four relevant digits during the first part of the message and three relevant digits during the second part.

The 100 cadets were divided into three groups according to how far they had progressed during flight school: (1) 17 cadets had been rejected during initial training on light aircraft; (2) 41 cadets had been rejected early in training on jet aircraft; and (3) 42 cadets had reached advanced training on jet aircraft. The cadets' performance on the second part of the selective listening task was the best predictor of their progress in flight school. Cadets who made three or more errors on this part of the test included 76% of those rejected during training on light aircraft, 56% of those rejected early in jet training, and 24% of those who had progressed to advanced training. The findings indicate that selective listening tasks have promise as a test, particularly since these results were obtained from a select group of people who probably all possessed good attentive skills relative to the general population.

Predicting Road Accidents

Kahneman, Ben-Ishai, and Lotan (1973) evaluated the generality of these findings by testing the validity of the task as a predictor of the accident rate of bus drivers. The study involved three groups of drivers. The accident-prone drivers had at least two moderately severe accidents during a single year; the accident-free drivers did not have any accidents during the same time period; and the intermediate group fell between these two extremes. The drivers from the three groups took the selective listening test, and their performance was correlated with their driving records. Performance on the second part of the test again produced the highest correlation with the accident rate. Kahneman and his co-investigators concluded that the test should enable a company to reject from 15% to 25% of the accident-prone drivers with a relatively negligible cost in rejecting potentially safe drivers.

The potential usefulness of the test was confirmed by Mihal and

Barett (1976), who included a slightly modified version in a battery of seven tests. The test that best predicted the accident involvement of 75 commercial drivers was the selective listening test. Mihal and Barett's findings are interesting because we might have thought that some other tests, such as a visual test of selective attention, would have produced the highest correlation as driving would seem to emphasize visual skills over auditory skills. However, an embedded figures test was not as good a predictor, nor was a simple reaction time test.

The results suggest that the selective listening test has merit as a predictor of driving records, particularly since accidents depend not only on driving skill but on various chance factors in the environment. However, exactly what is being measured by the test is not entirely clear. Kahneman and his associates argue that the test measures how quickly a person can switch attention. They base their argument on the finding that the second part of the test—during which the subject has to decide whether to switch attention to the other ear—produced the highest correlations. But the second part of the test also differed from the first part in what stimuli occurred on the irrelevant channel. A relevant digit was never paired with another digit on the first part but was always paired with another digit during the second part. This may make a difference if some subjects use a late mode of selection, as defined by Johnston and Heinz (1978). Also, Mihal and Barett's results were obtained by using only the first part of the test. The attempt to discover what selective attention tests measure is a good example of the kind of interaction that should occur between theoretical and applied areas of psychology.

We are now ready to consider the two memory stages in the information-processing model. Let us assume at this point that information has been successfully identified during the perceptual analysis stages: it has been attended to, recognized, and entered into a temporary store called short-term memory (STM). What will happen next? To answer this question, let us turn to the investigation of the characteristics of STM in Chapter 4.

Summary

Two characteristics of attention are selectivity and mental effort. Selectivity is necessary to keep us from becoming overloaded with too much information. The initial theories developed within the information-processing approach proposed that selectivity occurred at a bottleneck—a stage that could process only one message at a time. Broadbent's filter theory specified that the bottleneck occurred at the perception or pattern recognition stage, and attention was represented by a filter that preceded this stage. Treisman modified the filter theory to allow for the occasional recognition of words on the unattended channel. She proposed that the filter attenuated the unattended message and did not completely block it out. Important words or expected words could be recognized on the unattended channel if their thresholds were low enough to be exceeded by the attenuated message. Unlike Broadbent and Treisman, Deutsch and Deutsch suggested that the bottleneck occurs after perception and determines what is selected into memory. Norman further developed the latter theory and argued that the quality of the sensory information is combined with importance to determine what enters memory.

The results of many experiments on selective listening failed to agree on the location of the bottleneck. The effect was to shift the emphasis to capacity theories of attention and to encourage a more flexible view of the stage at which selection occurs. Capacity theories emphasize the amount of mental effort that is required to perform tasks and are concerned with how effort is allocated to different activities. A capacity theory supplements a bottleneck theory by proposing that the ability to perform simultaneous activities is limited when the activities require more mental effort than is available. The interaction between a capacity theory and a bottleneck theory is illustrated by results obtained by Johnston and Heinz. They effectively argue that a person has control over the stage at which selection occurs, but late modes of selection (following recognition) require more capacity than early modes of selection. The attempt to comprehend two messages therefore results in a decline in accuracy on the primary message and slower responses to a subsidiary task designed to measure capacity.

Automatic processing occurs when a task requires very little capacity to perform. Automatic processes occur under incidental learning, do not benefit from instruction or practice, do not interfere with other processes, are not influenced by emotional states, and show little change with development. Recording temporal, spatial, and frequency information are examples of automatic processes.

The work on selective attention has a number of implications for performance outside the laboratory. LaBerge and Samuels suggested that the acquisition of complex, multicomponent skills such as reading depends on the ability to automatically carry out some of the skills without attention. The ability to perform some components correctly does not necessarily mean that a person is ready to acquire new components if all the available capacity must be used to perform the already learned components. The performance of flight cadets and commercial drivers on selective listening tasks is one of the best predictors of success in flight school and of accident rates. It is not entirely clear, however, what the tests measure; hopefully, further research linking theory and applications will prove beneficial to both areas.

Recommended reading

Kahneman's *Attention and Effort* (1973) provides a comprehensive discussion of attention in addition to presenting a capacity theory. Chapters by Egeth and Bevan (1973) and Keele and Neill (1978) also summarize much of the work on attention. Neisser and Becklen (1975) studied selective attention by using a visual task that was somewhat analogous to the selective listening tasks we have looked at. Schneider and Shiffrin (1977; Shiffrin & Schneider, 1977) describe their research on the acquisition of automatic processing through extensive practice. Their work is similar to the work of Hasher and Zacks (1979) in presenting a general theoretical framework for integrating a large number of experimental findings. Posner and Snyder (1975) discuss an interesting question: to what extent are our conscious intentions and strategies in control of the way information is processed in our minds? Their analysis emphasizes the distinction between automatic processing and the conscious selection of strategies. Hirst, Spelke, Reaves, Caharack, and Neisser (1980) evaluate different theoretical explanations of how people can perform two complex tasks (dictation and reading) at the same time. Navon and Gopher (1979) propose a general theory of how people allocate their attention when the demands of a task exceed their capacity.

4

Short-Term Memory

My problem is that I have been persecuted by an integer. For seven years this number has followed me around, has intruded in my most private data, and has assaulted me from the pages of our most public journals. This number assumes a variety of disguises, being sometimes a little larger and sometimes a little smaller than usual, but never changing so much as to be unrecognizable. The persistence with which this number plagues me is far more than a random accident. There is, to quote a famous senator, a design behind it, some pattern governing its appearances. Either there really is something unusual about the number or else I am suffering from delusions of persecution.

GEORGE A. MILLER (1956)

The above quotation is the first paragraph of George Miller's famous paper "The Magical Number Seven, Plus or Minus Two: Some Limits on Our Capacity for Processing Information." Miller found that people were limited in the number of items they could keep active in memory and that this limited capacity influenced their performance on a variety of tasks. The previous chapter on attention also dealt with a capacity limitation, but our concern there was with simultaneously arriving information. The capacity model of attention proposed that our ability to carry on several activities at the same time was restricted by the total amount of mental effort that was available for distributing to these activities.

The tasks in this chapter do not require that people recognize simultaneously arriving information. There is no perceptual overload, and there is enough time to recognize each item and enter it into short-term memory (STM). The problem is that STM can hold only a limited number of items, causing a profound effect on the many tasks that require use of STM. The implications of this limitation are evident throughout the book—not only in this chapter but in later chapters on text comprehension, problem solving, and decision making.

The fact that STM will be referred to throughout the book reflects its important role as a working memory. Figure 4.1 shows that STM can combine information from both the environment and LTM whenever a person attempts to learn new information, make decisions, or solve problems. When you add the numbers in your checking account, you are receiving some information from the environment (the numbers in your account) and other information from LTM (the rules of addition). Obtaining a correct answer depends on using both sources of information appropriately.

The goal of this chapter is to summarize the major characteristics of STM. We begin by examining both the rate and the cause of forgetting. The emphasis will be on interference as the primary cause. The second section discusses the capacity of STM. After looking at Miller's (1956) insights about capacity, we will learn how the formation of groups of items in LTM can partially compensate for limited capacity. The third section deals with acoustic codes and rehearsal since acoustic codes are often used to maintain information in STM. We will examine whether they are necessary for reading. The final section presents a model of how we recognize whether an item is in STM. In particular, we will consider how quickly people can examine the contents of their STM.

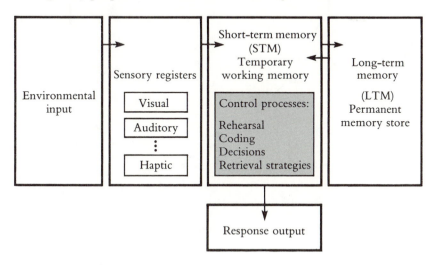

Figure 4.1. Flow of information through the memory system. *(From "The Control of Short-Term Memory," by R. C. Atkinson and R. M. Shiffrin. In* Scientific American, *1971,* 225, *82–90. Copyright © by Scientific American, Inc. All rights reserved. Reprinted by permission.)*

Forgetting

Rate of Forgetting

The label *short-term memory* indicates that information in STM is lost rapidly unless it is preserved through rehearsal. The rapid rate of forgetting from STM was established by Peterson and Peterson (1959) at Indiana University. They tested undergraduates on the ability to remember three consonants over a short retention interval. In order to prevent them from rehearsing the letters, subjects were required to count backward by threes, starting with a number that occurred after the consonants. For example, a subject might hear the letters *C H J* followed by the number 506. She would then count backward until she saw a light, which was a signal for recalling the three consonants. The light occurred 3, 6, 9, 12, 15, or 18 seconds after the subject began counting.

The results of the experiment are shown in Figure 4.2. The data show that the probability of a correct recall declined rapidly over the 18-second retention interval. The rapid forgetting rate implies that we must rehearse verbal information to keep it available in STM. It also shows why it is very likely that, if we are momentarily distracted after

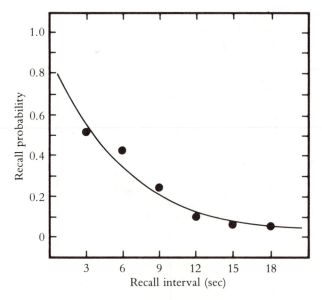

Figure 4.2. Correct recall as a function of the recall interval. *(From "Short-Term Retention of Individual Verbal Items," by L. R. Peterson and M. J. Peterson. In* Journal of Experimental Psychology, *1959, 58, 193–198. Copyright 1959 by the American Psychological Association. Reprinted by permission.)*

looking up a telephone number, we will have to look it up again before dialing.

This rapid rate of forgetting can be very frustrating when we are trying to learn new information, but it can also be beneficial. There are many occasions when we only need to remember something over a short period of time. Think of all the phone numbers you have dialed. Most of these you dialed only once or twice and will never need again. If all of these numbers were permanently stored in LTM, it could be very difficult to retrieve the few numbers that you constantly use.

Decay versus Interference

One question raised by Peterson and Peterson's findings is whether the loss of information from STM is caused by decay or by interference. Try to remember the consonants *R Q W* over a short interval without thinking about them. Since it's difficult not to think about them if you have nothing else to do, subjects in memory experiments are asked to perform some other task. An interference theory proposes that memory for other material or the performance of another task interferes with memory and causes forgetting. A decay theory proposes that forgetting should still occur even if the subject had to do nothing over the retention interval, as long as the subject did not rehearse the material.

A decay theory and an interference theory make different predictions about whether the passage of time or the number of interfering items is the primary cause of forgetting. If memory simply decays over time, then the amount of recall should be determined by the length of the retention interval. If memory is disrupted by interference, then recall should be determined by the number of interfering items.

Waugh and Norman (1965) tested whether the loss of information from STM is caused primarily by decay or by interference. Their procedure consisted of presenting lists of 16 single digits. The last digit in every list (a probe digit) occurred exactly once earlier in the list. The task was to report the digit that followed the probe digit. For example, if the list was 5 1 9 6 3 5 1 4 2 8 6 2 7 3 9 4, the probe digit would be 4 and the correct answer (the test item) would be 2. For this particular example, there are 7 digits that occur after the test item. The number of interfering items is therefore equal to 7. Waugh and Norman varied the number of interfering items by varying the location of the test digit in the list. There were many interfering items if the test item occurred early in the list and only a few if the test item occurred late in the list.

The experimenters also varied the rate of presentation in order to determine whether the probability of recalling the test digit would be influenced by the length of the retention interval. They presented the 16 digits in a list at a rate of either 1 digit or 4 digits a second. A decay theory would predict that performance should be better for the fast rate of presentation because there would be less time for the information to decay from memory. Figure 4.3 shows the results. The rate of presentation had very little effect on the probability of recalling the test digit. Consider the case in which there are 12 interfering items. The retention interval would be 12 seconds for the 1-per-second rate and 3 seconds for the 4-per-second rate. Memory is only slightly (and insignificantly) better for the shorter retention interval. In contrast, the number of interfering items has a dramatic effect on retention. The probability of recall declines rapidly as the number of interfering items increases.

Waugh and Norman's findings support the contention that inter-ference, rather than decay, is the primary cause of forgetting. Although some decay may occur (see Reitman, 1974), the amount of forgetting caused by decay is substantially less than the amount caused by inter-

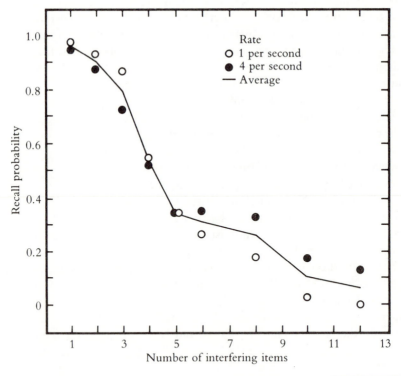

Figure 4.3. Effect of rate of presentation and number of interfering items on recall probability. *(From "Primary Memory," by N. C. Waugh and D. A. Norman. In* Psychological Review, *1965, 72, 89–104. Copyright 1965 by the American Psychological Association. Reprinted by permission.)*

ference. As has been demonstrated by Reitman and many others, the extent of forgetting is determined not only by the number of interfering items but by the degree of similarity between the interfering and test items. Increasing the similarity makes it more difficult to recall the test items.

The finding that interference is the primary cause of forgetting is good news. If information spontaneously decayed from memory, we would be unable to prevent its loss. If information is lost through interference, we can attempt to improve retention by structuring learning so as to minimize interference. A phenomenon known as release from proactive interference illustrates how interference can be reduced by decreasing the similarity among items.

Release from Proactive Interference

Psychologists have distinguished between two kinds of interference—proactive interference and retroactive interference. *Retroactive interference* is caused by information that occurs after an event. The Waugh and Norman (1965) study demonstrated the effect of retroactive interference: the number of digits that followed the probe digit influenced how well it could be recalled. *Proactive interference,* on the other hand, is caused by events that occurred before the event that someone attempts to recall.

Keppel and Underwood (1962) had previously demonstrated the effect of proactive interference in the Peterson STM task. They found that people initially performed very well in recalling three consonants after a short retention interval, but their performance deteriorated over subsequent trials. The reason is that the consonants they had tried to remember during the initial trials began to interfere with their memory for consonants during the later trials. People found it increasingly difficult to distinguish between consonants that were presented on the current trial and consonants that were presented on earlier trials.

The reduction of this interference is referred to as the *release from proactive interference* (Wickens, Born, & Allen, 1963). The study by Wickens and his colleagues was the first of many studies to demonstrate that the recall of later items can be improved by making them distinctive from early items. Figure 4.4 shows a clear illustration of release from proactive interference. Students in this particular experiment were required to remember either three numbers or three common words over a 20-second interval, during which time they performed another task to keep from rehearsing. The control group received items from the same class (either numbers or words) on each of four trials. The interference effect is evident from the decline in performance over trials. The experimental

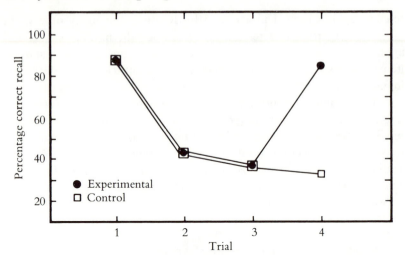

Figure 4.4. Release from proactive interference is demonstrated on Trial 4 for the experimental group. *(From "Characteristics of Word Encoding," by D. D. Wickens. In A. W. Melton and E. Martin (Eds.),* Coding Processes in Human Memory. *Copyright 1972 by V. H. Winston & Sons. Reproduced with permission from Hemisphere Publishing Corporation, Washington, D.C.)*

group received items from the same class over the first three trials but on the fourth trial received items from the other class. If they had been remembering words, they now remembered three numbers; if they had been remembering numbers, they now remembered three words. The shift in categories caused a dramatic improvement in performance, as is illustrated in Figure 4.4. The interference effect was specific to the class of material being presented and was greatly reduced when three distinctive items occurred.

Release from proactive interference also occurs when people are asked to remember more complex events (Gunter, Clifford, & Berry, 1980). The events consisted of television news items that people heard while they viewed a videotape of the same events. People heard three items during each trial and attempted to recall them after a 1-minute delay. The control group received items from the same class (either politics or sports) over a series of four trials. The experimental group received items from the same class over the first three trials, but on the fourth trial they received items from the other class. If they had been recalling sports events, they now recalled political events; if they had been recalling political events, they now recalled sports events. The results were very similar to the results shown in Figure 4.4. The proportion of correct responses declined for the control group over the four trials—87% on the first trial, 67% on the second, 55% on the third, and 43% on the fourth trial. The recall of the experimental group showed a similar decline over the first three trials but improved dramatically on the fourth trial, when they heard items from a different category. The experimental group recalled 82% of the items on the first trial, 67% on the second, 55% on the third, and 74% on the fourth trial.

The practical implications of these results are simply that, whenever possible, we should attempt to reduce interference by ordering material in an appropriate sequence. Items that are likely to interfere with each other should be studied at different times rather than during a single session. The reduction of interference through appropriate sequencing can partially compensate for the rapid forgetting from STM. Let us now look at how we can partially compensate for the limited capacity of this store.

Capacity

The Magic Number Seven

A second limitation of STM is that it can hold only about seven items. The limited capacity of STM is demonstrated by a task that is often used as a measure of its capacity. It is called a *digit span* or, more generally, a *memory span* task. The task requires that a person recall a sequence of items in their correct order. Memory span is the longest sequence that a person can typically recall. An example of a memory span task is shown below. Read each row of letters once, then shut your eyes, and try to recall these letters in the correct order.

T M F J R L B
H Q C N W Y P K V
S B M G X R D L T
J Z N Q K Y C

If you are like most other adults, you could probably easily recall a string of seven digits (Rows 1 and 4) but not a string of nine digits (Rows 2 and 3). It was this number seven that plagued George Miller. The "magic number seven" kept appearing in two different kinds of studies: experiments on absolute judgment and on memory span. The absolute judgment task consists of presenting stimuli that vary along a sensory continuum such as loudness. The experimenter selects different levels of loudness that are easy to discriminate and assigns each a label. The labels are usually numbers that increase as the values on the continuum increase: if there were seven stimuli, the least-loud stimulus would be labeled 1, and the loudest would be labeled 7. The subject's task is to learn to identify each stimulus by assigning the correct label. The experimenter presents the stimuli in a random order and corrects mistakes by providing the correct answer.

The experimenter is primarily interested in how many stimuli the subject can label correctly before the task becomes too difficult. The results vary depending on the sensory continuum, but Miller was impressed with the finding that the upper limit for a single dimension was usually around seven, plus or minus two. The upper limit was about five for loudness, six for pitch, five for the size of squares, and five for brightness. The average across a wide variety of sensory tasks was 6.5, and most of the upper limits were between five and nine.

It is important to point out that these results are not caused by an inability to discriminate adjacent values of the stimuli. All the stimuli would be easy to discriminate if the subject had to judge which one of two adjacent stimuli was louder, larger, brighter, or higher in pitch. The limitation was caused by the inability to keep more than about seven sensory values available in STM because of its limited capacity. The results represent performance during the early stages of learning before the different sensory stimuli are stored in LTM. With sufficient experience, the upper limits can be increased, as is illustrated by a musically sophisticated person who can accurately identify any one of 50 or 60 different pitches. However, that person is using LTM, which is not limited in capacity.

The upper limit found in the absolute judgment experiments corresponds very well with the upper limit found in memory span tasks. Miller cited the results found by Hayes (1952), which indicated that the memory span ranged from five items for English words (*lake, jump, pen, road, sing*) to nine items for binary digits (001011101). The memory span for numbers or letters fell in about the middle of this range.

Miller's paper was important for drawing attention to how little the upper limit varied in performance on absolute judgment and memory span tasks. His paper was also important for suggesting that recoding the information to form chunks can help one overcome the limited capacity of STM. Chunks consist of individual items that have been learned and stored as a group in LTM. You can demonstrate for yourself how chunking can increase the number of letters that can be recalled from STM. Tell a person that you will read 12 letters to him and you would like him to repeat them back in the correct order. Then read the 12 letters grouped in the following way: *FB–ITW–AC–IAIB–M*. Next read the same 12 letters to another person grouped in a different way: *FBI–TWA–CIA–IBM*. You will likely find that the second person could recall more letters. The first person had to recall 12 separate letters, but the second person could recall four chunks, each containing three letters. Miller argued that the capacity of STM should be measured in chunks rather than in individual items. The 12 letters should be easy for the second person to recall because they take up only four "slots" in STM rather than 12.

Individual Differences in Chunking

There is increasing evidence that a major determinant of individual differences in memory is how effectively people can group material into familiar chunks. The initial evidence for this conclusion came from the study of how chess players reproduce the pieces on a chess board. The classic study of this task was begun by de Groot, a Dutch psychologist, during the 1940s and was later published in his book *Thought and Choice in Chess* (1965). The main conclusion of the study was that the difference between the skills of the chess master and lesser players is the result more of differences in perception and memory than of differences in the quality of their operational thinking.

Empirical support for de Groot's conclusion came from a series of clever experiments that required players of different abilities to reproduce a chess board as it might appear 20 moves into a game (de Groot, 1966). Figure 4.5 shows two of the board configurations that were used in the study. The subjects were given 5 seconds to view the board, the pieces were then removed, and the subjects were asked to place the pieces back on the board in order to reproduce what they had just seen. When the subject was finished, the experimenter removed the pieces that were incorrectly placed and asked the subject to try again. The subjects con-

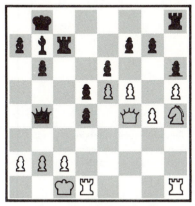
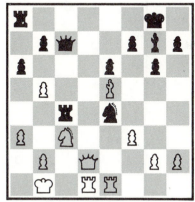

From: Janosevic-Krisnik;   From: Bannik-Geller;
Zenica 1964   Moskou 1961

Figure 4.5. Examples of experimental positions used in the guessing and reproduction experiments. *(From "Perception and Memory versus Thought: Some Old Ideas and Recent Findings," by A. D. de Groot. In B. Kleinmuntz (Ed.), Problem Solving: Research, Method and Theory. Copyright 1966 by John Wiley & Sons, Inc. Reprinted by permission.)*

tinued to try to replace the incorrect pieces until they correctly reproduced the board or until 12 trials were completed.

The average performance of five master players and five weaker players is shown in Figure 4.6. The master players correctly reproduced about 90% of the pieces on their first attempt, compared to only 40% for the weaker players. In order to determine whether the results were caused by the masters' ability simply to guess where the pieces should be located, de Groot chose other board configurations and asked the players to guess where the pieces were located, without ever seeing the board or receiving any clues. Figure 4.6 shows that the master players were only slightly better at guessing where the pieces were located. The weaker players, in fact, did about as well guessing as when they actually saw the board. De Groot argued that the master players depended on their ability to code the pieces into familiar groups. When the players viewed pieces that were placed randomly on the board, the master players no longer had an advantage over the weaker players, and both groups performed about the same.

Chase and Simon (1973) extended de Groot's paradigm in order to

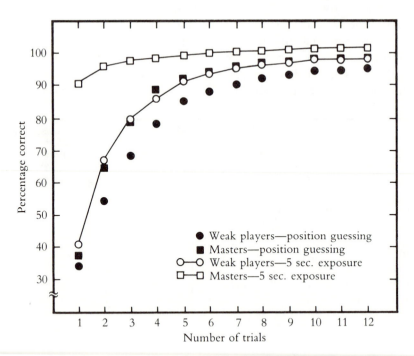

Figure 4.6. Percentage of correctly located chess pieces. *(From "Perception and Memory versus Thought: Some Old Ideas and Recent Findings," by A. D. de Groot. In B. Kleinmuntz (Ed.),* Problem Solving: Research, Method and Theory. *Copyright 1966 by John Wiley & Sons, Inc. Reprinted by permission.)*

identify the groups of pieces (chunks) that presumably produced the superior coding ability of master chess players. A master chess player, a Class A player, and a beginner were tested on de Groot's reproduction task. Chase and Simon assumed that pieces belonging to the same chunk would be placed on the board as a group. They measured the time between successive pieces and classified pauses greater than 2 seconds as indicating chunk boundaries. The latencies suggested that, for middle-game positions, the average number of chunks per trial was 7.7 for the master player, 5.7 for the Class A player, and 5.3 for the beginner, with the number of pieces per chunk averaging 2.5, 2.1, and 1.9, respectively. There was some tendency for more skilled players to use more chunks, particularly for end-game positions in which the average number of chunks per trial was 7.6, 6.4, and 4.2, respectively.

A simulation program (Memory-Aided Pattern Perceiver, or MAPP) of the chess reproduction task was developed by Simon and Gilmartin (1973) to gain further insight into the kinds of chunks stored in LTM. The memory of the program contained 572 chunks, with two to seven chess pieces in each. The simulation program was somewhat more effective than the Class A player in coding the configurations, but less effective than the master player. There was, however, a substantial correlation between which pieces were remembered by MAPP and those remembered by the master player, even though the patterns stored by MAPP were selected independent of a detailed knowledge of the master's performance. Extrapolating from the performance of the simulation model, Simon and Gilmartin estimated that master players have between 10,000 and 100,000 chunks stored in LTM. Their estimate implies that there is no shortcut to becoming a chess master.

Recall of Circuit Diagrams

Skill in reading nonverbal symbolic drawings is important for a wide range of occupations, including electronics, engineering, chemistry, and architecture. A skilled electronics technician, for example, must be able to understand circuit diagrams and relate the symbols to hardware in need of repair or to circuit design problems. The purpose of a study conducted by Egan and Schwartz (1979) was to determine what differences distinguish the novice and the skilled technician in their ability to reproduce a circuit diagram. Discovering what the skilled technician actually knows should be useful for assessing skill levels, developing job aids for skilled performance, or improving training in such skills.

The earlier work of de Groot, Chase, Simon, and Gilmartin on chess influenced the design of the experiments. Chunks were determined by asking an expert (a skilled electronics technician at Bell Laboratories who had over 25 years of experience working with electronic circuits) to indicate meaningful groups of symbols in circuit drawings by circling symbols that served a common function. Figure 4.7 shows an example of a circuit drawing. The enclosed groups and verbal labels indicate how the technician organized the diagram.

The subjects in one of Egan and Schwartz's experiments were six skilled electronics technicians and six novices. The technicians had been employed at Bell Laboratories for at least six years. The novice subjects were college students who had little knowledge of electronics. Each subject participated in 12 meaningful recall tasks, 12 random recall tasks, and 12 construction tasks, all involving different circuit diagrams. The meaningful recall tasks used actual circuit diagrams that were copied from texts. The random recall tasks used drawings that had the same wiring pattern and circuit symbols as the meaningful diagrams but with the symbols positioned randomly in the spaces. After viewing the diagrams for either 5 or 10 seconds, subjects attempted to reconstruct the drawings from memory by placing magnetized circuit symbols on the blank spaces of the answer sheet. The construction task required that subjects guess the location of the symbols on the answer sheet without having seen the diagrams.

The performance of the two groups of subjects on each of the three tasks is shown in Figure 4.8. The technicians did significantly better than the novices in reproducing a meaningful configuration but did no better in reproducing a random configuration. Both of these findings replicate

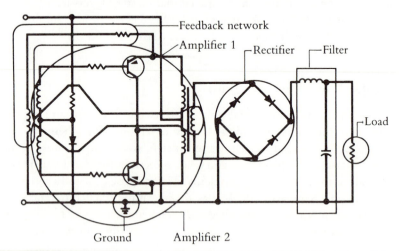

Figure 4.7. An example of a circuit drawing. Enclosed groups and verbal labels indicate the organizational description provided by a skilled technician. *(From "Chunking in Recall of Symbolic Drawings," by D. E. Egan and B. J. Schwartz. In* Memory & Cognition, *1979, 7, 149–158. Copyright 1979 by the Psychonomic Society, Inc. Reprinted by permission.)*

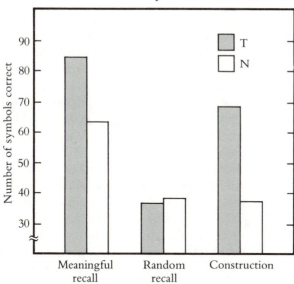

Figure 4.8. Performance by technicians (T) and novices (N) on meaningful recall, random recall, and construction tasks. *(From "Chunking in Recall of Symbolic Drawings," by D. E. Egan and B. J. Schwartz. In Memory & Cognition, 1979, 7, 149–158. Copyright 1979 by the Psychonomic Society, Inc. Reprinted by permission.)*

the results obtained for chess (de Groot, 1965; Chase & Simon, 1973). Although an expert's opinion, rather than latencies, was used to determine chunk boundaries, the time between replacing successive symbols was significantly faster for pieces belonging to the same chunk. This finding is consistent with the research on chess, as is the finding that the recall of circuit diagrams by skilled technicians (whether measured by number correct, chunk size, or number of chunks) was very similar to the recall of chess positions by chess players in the Class A to master range (Chase & Simon, 1973). One difference between the results obtained by de Groot (1966) and those obtained by Egan and Schwartz (1979) is that the skilled technicians, but not the master chess players, did significantly better on the construction task. This finding raises the question of whether the superior performance of the skilled technicians was caused by more sophisticated guessing rather than by encoding more information into memory. Egan and Schwartz present several arguments against the guessing interpretation; more research might prove beneficial in answering this question.

Rehearsal and acoustic codes

Rapid forgetting rate and limited capacity are the two most important characteristics that distinguish STM from LTM. Psychologists once emphasized a third distinction based on differences in memory codes. They argued that acoustic codes are the predominant memory codes in STM, and semantic codes are the predominant codes in LTM. The emphasis on acoustic codes occurred because of the nature of the material used to study STM and because of the usefulness of verbal rehearsal for retaining information. The material usually consisted of sequences of letters, numbers, or nonsense syllables, all of which could be labeled but were not very meaningful. It is therefore not surprising that a person would use acoustic codes rather than visual or semantic codes to maintain information in STM.

The emphasis on acoustic codes declined when psychologists used material that would activate other kinds of codes. Release from proactive interference, for example, is often cited as evidence that semantic codes influence STM, as recall improves greatly when the material changes to a different semantic category. There is also evidence that people can use visual images to maintain information in STM, particularly when they attempt to remember the details of visual patterns. We will examine this evidence in Chapter 7.

Although the acoustic code is no longer considered the only code that influences STM, it continues to be studied extensively. The acoustic code is important because verbal rehearsal provides an effective means for retaining information in STM. However, one limitation of rehearsal is that it can result in acoustic confusions. Let us now look at the evidence for acoustic confusions and then at a model that demonstrates how they can occur.

Acoustic Confusions

We saw in Chapter 2 that one of the early information-processing models provided for the translation of visual information into acoustic information (Sperling, 1963). Evidence for this translation included Sperling's finding that subjects made acoustic confusions—errors that sounded like the correct response. The subsequent work of Conrad (1964) also established that acoustic confusions occur in STM. Conrad selected two groups of letters that had high within-group confusability but low between-group confusability. One group consisted of the letters *B C P T V,* and the other group of the letters *F M N S X.* Conrad used a film projector to present visually six-letter sequences consisting of letters from both sets. After each sequence subjects had to write the six letters in their correct order.

If acoustic confusions occur, an error would be more likely to involve substitution of a letter from the same group than substitution of a letter from a different group. Conrad's data indicated that 75% of the errors involved one of the other four letters belonging to the same acoustic group, and 25% of the errors involved one of the five letters in the other acoustic group. It is particularly easy for acoustic confusions to occur when all the letters in a sequence sound alike. Try to recall the letters in each of the two following rows. You should find that the letters in the second row are easier to recall than the letters in the first row.

G Z D B P V C T

M J Y F H R K Q

The finding that acoustic confusions occur in an STM task demonstrates that acoustic codes are important, but it does not reveal how the errors occur. One way of accounting for the errors is to use auditory components to represent the names of items. Laughery (1969) developed a computer program to simulate the standard memory span procedure, in which subjects are presented with a sequence of digits or letters and asked to reproduce as many items as they can remember. The names of the items are represented in memory by specifying their auditory components. The components—called *phonemes*—are the basic sounds of the English language.

Table 4.1 lists the phonemes used in English. Notice that some letters are represented by several phonemes because they can be pronounced in different ways. The letter *a* is pronounced differently in the words *father, had, call,* and *take;* each pronunciation is represented by a different phoneme. The letter *e* has two pronunciations: the long-*e* sound in *heat* and the short-*e* sound in *head*. It is also possible for two letters to combine to form a phoneme—for example, *ch* and *th*.

TABLE 4.1. Phonemes of General American English.

Vowels	*Consonants*	
ee as in h*ea*t	*t* as in *t*ee	*s* as in *s*ee
I as in h*i*t	*p* as in *p*ea	*sh* as in *sh*ell
e as in h*ea*d	*k* as in *k*ey	*h* as in *h*e
ae as in h*a*d	*b* as in *b*ee	*v* as in *v*iew
ah as in f*a*ther	*d* as in *d*awn	*th* as in *th*en
aw as in c*a*ll	*g* as in *g*o	*z* as in *z*oo
u as in p*u*t	*m* as in *m*e	*zh* as in ga*rage*
oo as in c*oo*l	*n* as in *n*o	*l* as in *l*aw
Λ as in t*o*n	*ng* as in si*ng*	*r* as in *r*ed
uh as in th*e*	*f* as in *f*ee	*y* as in *y*ou
er as in b*ir*d	*θ* as in *th*in	*w* as in *w*e
oi as in t*oi*l		
au as in sh*ou*t		
ei as in t*a*ke		
ou as in t*o*ne		
ai as in m*i*ght		

It is convenient to use phonemes to account for acoustic confusions because words that sound alike usually have some phonemes in common. Let's look again at the two sets of letters in Conrad's experiment. The names of the letters in the set $F M N S X$ (*ĕf, ĕm, ĕn, ĕs, ĕks*) have the same initial phoneme—the short e ($ĕ$) sound—but their second phoneme differs. The letters in the set $B C P T V$ (*bē, sē, pē, tē, vē*) all share a common phoneme—the long e ($ē$) sound—but all have different first phonemes.

The major assumption of Laughery's model is that each of the auditory components representing an item can be independently forgotten. In other words, if a name consists of two phonemes, a person could remember one phoneme but not the other. The model also assumes that the auditory components can be forgotten at different rates; the decay rates were determined from experimental results (Wickelgren, 1965). Laughery makes the reasonable assumption that a person who cannot recall all the auditory components of a letter uses whatever is recalled to limit the number of possible responses. It is therefore easy for the model to account for acoustic confusions. Whenever only the $ē$ phoneme is recalled, the subject will guess one of the letters in the $B C P T V$ set. If only the $ĕ$ phoneme is recalled, the subject will guess one of the letters in the $F M N S X$ set. An incorrect guess in either case will result in an acoustic confusion. Although acoustic confusions occasionally occur, it is usually advantageous to use verbal rehearsal when we want to maintain information in STM. The translation of visual material into an acoustic code is not limited to remembering strings of letters or digits. The most common example of converting visual material into acoustic codes occurs when we read.

Acoustic Codes in Reading

Most of us read by subvocalizing (saying to ourselves) the words in the text. Although subvocalizing can help us remember what we read, it limits how fast we can read. Since covert speech is not much faster than overt speech, subvocalization limits reading speed to the rate of speaking; we could read faster if we didn't translate printed words into a speech-based code (see Box 4.1).

When I was a graduate student, I attempted to improve my reading rate by enrolling in a speed-reading course. A prerequisite for increasing my speed was that I learn to eliminate subvocalization. The trick is to go directly from the printed word to its meaning without covertly pronouncing the word. I was successful at increasing my reading rate while maintaining comprehension when the material was fairly simple. However, I found it quite difficult to read more complex or technical material without using subvocalization. I soon returned to my slower rate. I don't know either how representative my experience was or what percentage

Box 4.1. Does Speed Reading Really Exist?

ALEXANDRA D. KORRY

Begin reading now.
Use your hand to guide your eyes.
Don't regress.
Stop subvocalizing.
Faster.

This is the message of Evelyn Wood Reading Dynamics, the California company that has made millions teaching Americans how to glide through that pile of bestsellers sitting on the shelf.

Evelyn Wood claims it will have you reading at up to 5,000 words a minute at the conclusion of a seven-session course. They'll triple your reading, they say, or your money back.

More than one million speed-reading aspirants, including President Carter, John F. Kennedy's military advisers, actor Charlton Heston, and a host of members of Congress have enrolled in the courses since they were first offered in 1959.

But now a growing number of reading specialists are raising serious questions about speed reading. They dispute the value of the $395 Evelyn Wood course and others like it, saying simply that no one—regardless of their training—can read that fast.

"They have the illusion of improving their reading when in fact they are skimming," charged John Guthrie, director of research for the 70,000-member International Reading Association. To Evelyn Wood officials, those are fighting words.

"Skimming is a nasty word in our business," said M. Donald Wood, husband of the woman who founded the system and helped organize a national franchise system that teaches speed reading in 26 cities around the country. "It works. We know that."

"I think it's the greatest invention since the printing press," said Evelyn Wood, now 72, and recovering from a stroke in her native Salt Lake City. She was a graduate student at the University of Utah when she discovered the technique after years of observing naturally fast readers.

Many reading experts challenge the system. Although they differ as to what is the proper upper limit for reading speed, most agree that anyone who claims to be reading more than 900 words a minute is, in fact, skimming.

"I can't imagine that someone reading 4,000 words a minute is reading," said Keith Rayner, a professor of psychology at the University of Massachusetts in Amherst. "Given the anatomy of the eye . . . I have a hard time believing that people can read beyond 900 words per minute."

Ronald Carver, an education professor at the University of Missouri, says tests he gave students there tend to support that notion. When the students were tested at 600 words a minute, they were "simply getting an idea of what they were reading," in effect, skimming.

Evelyn Wood officials, who regularly claim to have students reading at 2,000 words a minute, said such studies ignore a basic premise of their ap-

(Box 4.1 continues)

Box 4.1 (*continued*)

proach. At Evelyn Wood, people learn a new way to read—one that teaches readers to take in whole ideas rather than single words, they said.

"It's a visual form of reading," said Verla Nielson, director of the program's Salt Lake City operations. "It's seeing words in chunks—reading as the author thought it. It's like learning to read music—you can see many notes at the same time."

To prove that the method works, the company cites the results of comprehension tests given to their students at the beginning and end of the course. Some reading specialists take issue with those multiple-choice quizzes.

Carver, a reading specialist for 13 years, told a group of college students to imagine they were reading material from the Wood course and then gave them the Wood tests. The students averaged a 60% comprehension level without ever reading the material, a reflection of what Carver says is the tests' shortcomings.

"They claim you can increase your perception of the number of words taken at once. That's absurd," said the Reading Association's Guthrie. "There's a lot of scientific evidence that shows you can only take in 20 characters at a time."

Carlos Garcia Tunon, a Washington marketing consultant and an Evelyn Wood alumnus who reportedly went from 362.5 to 5,024 words per minute with a 20% increase in comprehension, said he didn't feel he was seeing every word he was supposed to be reading at the faster speeds. What you get from the speed reading, he said, is the basic theme, the characters, and the plot of a book.

Tunon was one of thousands of people who have been drawn to the reading system's free mini-lessons by advertising that features students flipping through texts as if they were looking at picture books.

Once at the mini-session, an instructor tells the student that anyone can learn the necessary skills, that all it takes is practice, that if you break the bad habits you learned as a child, you'll be reading six times faster. It's a 15-minute buildup that ends with a passing reference to the $395 price tag ($295 if another member of your family enrolls).

The students are told if they stop subvocalizing—reading the individual word to yourself—and regressing—rereading a line—they'll save 40% of reading time.

They also show a 15-minute film on the reading method. The highlight is a 1975 "Tonight Show" segment of an interview with Elizabeth Jaffee, then a 13-year-old wunderkind of speed reading, who reads 30 pages of a highly technical book in one minute.

What they don't tell you is that Jaffee, now a college freshman, isn't really a speed reader anymore. That the Evelyn Wood alumna sued and received a $25,000 out-of-court settlement because she claimed that the technique works only for certain kinds of reading.

© 1980 *The Washington Post*. Reprinted by permission.

---

of graduates from speed-reading courses successfully eliminate subvocalization. However, the experimental analysis of speech processing during reading has produced results that seem consistent with my own experience. The results suggest that, although we can comprehend the meaning of words without subvocalization, subvocalization is useful in facilitating the detailed recall of a text (Levy, 1978).

Levy attempted in her own experiments to suppress subvocalization by requiring that subjects repeatedly count from one to ten as they read a short paragraph. They were told to count quickly and continuously in a soft voice while reading the sentences and to try to remember all the sentences in the paragraph. You may want to try this as you read the two paragraphs in Table 4.2. When they finished reading the paragraph, people were shown one of the sentences in the paragraph or a slight variation and were asked to judge whether the test sentence was identical to the one presented earlier.

TABLE 4.2. Examples of Lexical, Semantic, and Paraphrase Tests.

1. An emergency

The hospital staff paged the busy doctor.
The solemn physician distressed the anxious mother.
The sobbing woman held her unconscious son.
A speeding truck had crossed the mid-line.
Her oncoming car was hit and damaged.
Her child had plunged through the windshield.
The medical team strove to save him.

The solemn physician distressed the anxious *woman*. (lexical)

The solemn *mother* distressed the anxious *physician*. (semantic)

The solemn *doctor upset* the anxious mother. (paraphrase - yes)

The solemn *officer helped* the anxious mother. (paraphrase - no)

2. A lost boy

The lost boy searched the crowded street.
His careless mother had forgotten about him.
The concerned policeman approached the worried child.
The kindly man dried the boy's tears.
The yound lad gave his home address.
And the police cruiser escorted him home.
In future his mother was more careful.

The concerned policeman approached the worried *youngster*. (lexical)

The concerned *child* approached the worried *policeman*. (semantic)

The concerned *officer* approached the *upset* child. (paraphrase - yes)

The concerned *woman* approached the *carefree* child. (paraphrase - no)

From "Speech Processing during Reading," by B. A. Levy. In A. M. Lesgold, J. W. Pellegrino, S. D. Fokkema, and R. Glaser (Eds.), *Cognitive Psychology and Instruction.* Copyright 1978 by Plenum Publishing Corporation. Reprinted by permission.

Since the altered sentences were only slightly changed, people had to remember the details to do well on this task. The first two sentences following each paragraph in Table 4.2 are examples of altered sentences. The lexical alteration changes a single word but preserves the meaning of the sentence—the word *mother* is changed to *woman* for the first paragraph and the word *child* to *youngster* for the second paragraph. The semantic alteration changed the meaning of the sentence by switching the order of the two nouns in the test sentence and the original sentence—for the first paragraph, the order of *mother* and *physician*. The results of this study revealed that people performed more poorly when they had to count while reading. They were not as accurate in identifying when changes occurred, regardless of whether there were lexical changes or semantic changes.

Suppressing subvocalization did not interfere with performance when people listened to the sentence, however. The fact that counting while listening did not affect performance demonstrates that suppression interfered specifically with reading and not with language comprehension in general. The difference between listening and reading is that the listener receives an acoustic code rather than a visual code. The fact that counting interfered only with recall following reading suggests that translating visual material into an acoustic code helps preserve detailed information in the text.

Although the acoustic code improved recall of detailed information, it was not necessary to preserve the gist of the paragraph (Levy, 1978). Support for this claim comes from a second experiment, in which subjects made paraphrase judgments. These subjects were not encouraged to maintain the exact wording of sentences because word changes occurred in all the test sentences. However, positive examples preserved the general meaning of an original sentence and negative examples altered the meaning. Unlike the semantic changes, the meaning was altered by replacing two words in the sentences rather than changing the order of words (see Table 4.2) Therefore, less information was required to distinguish between positive and negative examples in the paraphrase task than to judge correctly in the lexical or semantic tasks. People could do well on the paraphrase task if they remembered the general ideas expressed in the paragraph. Since the counting task did not interfere with performance, acoustic coding was not required to remember the more important ideas.

Levy's findings are consistent with my own experiences in preventing subvocalization. When the material is relatively simple and detailed recall is not required, people can recall the major ideas without subvocalization. However, subvocalization did facilitate the detection of more subtle changes, such as changing the order of two words or replacing a word with a semantically similar word. Additional evidence also supports this conclusion. Hardyck and Petrinovich (1970) measured subvocalization by recording the muscle activity of the larynx. Subjects in the experimental group were trained to keep their muscle activity at nonreading relaxation levels. Any increases in activity during reading activated an audio signal to remind them to suppress subvocalization. A control group read the same material but was allowed to subvocalize as they read. A comprehension test revealed that the two groups did not differ in recall of easy material, but the subvocalization group recalled more of the difficult material than the suppression group.

The studies on speech processing during reading suggest that, although subvocalization is not necessary for comprehension, it does facilitate retention of detailed or complex information. A popular explanation of these findings is that subvocalization makes it easier to retain words in STM until they can be integrated with other words in the sentence or paragraph (Conrad, 1972; Kleiman, 1975). We would be able to evaluate this suggestion more accurately if we had a better understanding of the role of STM in reading. Fortunately, considerable progress has been made over the past several years in understanding the psychological processes involved in text comprehension. Chapter 11 summarizes this progress and indicates how STM is used in reading.

Recognition of items in STM

Searching STM

Our discussion of STM up to this point has emphasized the *recall* of material, as shown in the experiments asking for recall of three consonants, a string of letters or digits, a chess board, or a circuit diagram after a short delay. Psychologists have also been interested in how people attempt to "recognize" whether a given item is contained in STM. First, they present a sequence of items, which the subject stores in STM. The sequence is usually six items or fewer so all the items can be easily maintained. Then a test item occurs, and the subject must decide whether that item is one of the items in the sequence.

This procedure was invented by Saul Sternberg at Bell Laboratories in order to study how people encode a pattern and compare it to other patterns stored in STM. Sternberg first showed a sequence of digits (the memory set), which the subject stored in STM. Then he presented a test digit, and the subject made a rapid decision as to whether the test digit was or was not a member of the memory set. When Sternberg (1966) varied the size of the memory set from one to six digits, he discovered that the time required to make the decision increased as a linear function of the number of digits in STM. Whenever the size of the memory set was increased by one additional digit, the response time was lengthened by 38 msec. Sternberg proposed that the test digit was sequentially compared to each item stored in STM and that it required about 38 msec to make each comparison.

In one of the early applications of the paradigm, Sternberg (1967) varied the quality of the test digit in addition to the size of the memory set. The memory set consisted of one, two, or four digits, and the test digit was either intact or degraded to make it difficult to recognize. Sternberg suggested that two operations were needed to perform the task. First, the observer had to encode the test digit in order to compare it to other digits stored in STM. The subject then had to scan the memory set to determine whether any of the digits matched the test digit.

Sternberg showed how it would be possible to determine whether a degraded pattern would influence the encoding time or the memory scan time. The slope of the function relating reaction time (RT) to memory-set size indicated the amount of time needed to compare the test digit with a digit stored in STM: it is the amount of additional time needed whenever another digit is added to the memory set. If a degraded digit slows down the rate of comparison, the slope should increase. Figure 4.9(a) shows this prediction. Notice that the more items in the memory set, the greater the difference in RT. The encoding of the test digit occurs only once, however, and should be independent of the number of items in the memory set. If the degraded digit lengthens the encoding time, the reaction time should increase by a constant amount (the additional time needed for encoding), which is independent of the number of items in the memory set. Figure 4.9(b) shows this prediction.

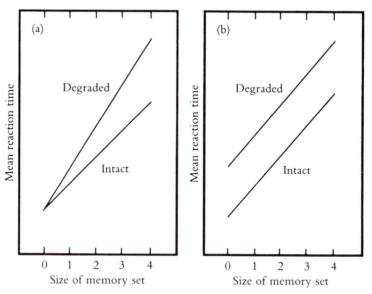

Figure 4.9. Predicted reaction time functions if degrading affects the memory comparison time (a) or the encoding time (b). *(From "Two Operations in Character Recognition: Some Evidence from Reaction Time Measurements," by S. Sternberg. In* Perception & Psychophysics, 1967, *2, 45–53. Copyright 1967 by the Psychonomic Society, Inc. Reprinted by permission.)*

Figure 4.10 shows the results actually obtained by Sternberg over two sessions. Degradation greatly affected the encoding time in both sessions. The data for degraded and intact digits form nearly parallel lines, similar to those shown in Figure 4.9(b). The effect on the memory comparison time (as measured by differences in slopes) was very minimal. Degrading the test digit primarily affected the time needed to encode the pattern and had little effect on the time required to compare the test digit with other digits stored in STM. This finding implies that a visually degraded digit was not directly compared with the other digits since this would have slowed down the comparison. The longer encoding time suggests that the effect of degradation was compensated for during the encoding stage. The subject may have changed the degraded image into a normal image and matched the normal image against the visual images stored in STM. Or the subject may have named the test digit and compared it to the names of digits stored in STM. The latter explanation is particularly attractive because acoustic codes are usually used to maintain information in STM. It should take longer to name a degraded digit, and hence the encoding time would be slowed down. However, once named, the degraded image would no longer be used, so the rate of comparison would be relatively unaffected.

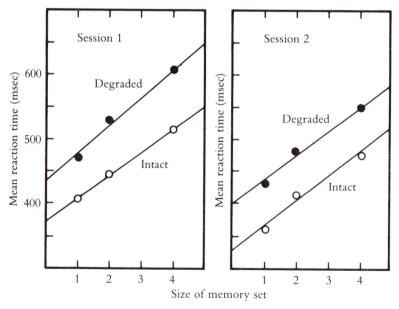

Figure 4.10. Mean reaction time for intact and degraded test stimuli. *(From "Two Operations in Character Recognition: Some Evidence from Reaction Time Measurements," by S. Sternberg. In* Perception & Psychophysics, *1967, 2, 45–53. Copyright 1967 by the Psychonomic Society, Inc. Reprinted by permission.)*

Some Determinants of the Memory Comparison Rate

Although the degradation of the test digit had very little effect on the comparison rate, the use of qualitatively different kinds of stimuli does influence the comparison rate. Furthermore, there is a very orderly relation between the memory span and the rate of searching STM. Cavanagh (1972) found seven classes of stimuli in which measures were available for both the number of stimuli that could be recalled in a memory span test and the comparison rate of stimuli in a Sternberg task. Both measures were available for the digits 0 through 9; colors; the letters of the alphabet; familiar words; geometrical shapes such as squares, circles, and triangles; random forms; and nonsense syllables composed of a vowel between two consonants.

The average comparison rate ranged from 33 msec for digits to 73 msec for nonsense syllables. The average memory span ranged from 3.4 items for nonsense syllables to 7.7 items for digits. Figure 4.11 shows the almost perfect inverse relation between the two measures: the greater the memory span, the faster the processing rate. An interesting implication of the results shown in Figure 4.11 is that the same amount of time is always required to search STM when it is filled to its capacity. The average capacity of STM is 3.4 nonsense syllables, 3.8 random forms, 5.3

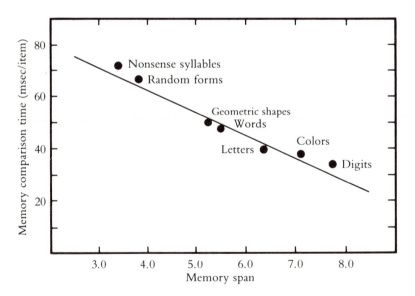

Figure 4.11. Relation between the memory comparison rate and the memory span. *(From "Relation between the Immediate Memory Span and the Memory Search Rate," by J. P. Cavanagh. In* Psychological Review, *1972, 79, 525–530. Copyright 1972 by the American Psychological Association. Reprinted by permission.)*

geometrical shapes, 5.5 words, 6.4 letters, 7.1 colors, and 7.7 digits. It takes about one-quarter of a second to search STM in each of these cases. When there are more items to search, the rate of search is faster, so the total search time remains constant.

We still don't know the cause of this inverse relation, but Cavanagh suggests several possible explanations. One of the simplest is that the items are represented in memory by a list of features. Short-term memory has a constant, limited amount of "space," which can hold only a fixed number of features. Since nonsense syllables, random forms, and geometric shapes are more complex than letters, colors, and digits, they would have more features and each item would take up more space in STM. The feature explanation of the comparison rate would assume that the time it takes to compare a test item with an item in the memory set is determined by how many features have to be compared. The complexity of the stimulus, as defined by number of features, would therefore affect both how many items could be stored in STM and the time required to compare two items. The feature explanation is consistent with many of the ideas regarding pattern recognition discussed in Chapter 2; however, further research is necessary in order to determine whether it is the best explanation.

Although the stimuli studied by Cavanagh differed in their rate of comparison, they all caused the typical increase in response time as the size of the memory set increased. Is it possible to find cases in which the size of the memory set does not influence response time? There are a few such interesting cases, one of which was revealed by DeRosa and Tkacz (1976). The subjects in their experiment were shown a series of three, four, or five pictures. The pictures were part of an ordered sequence of pictures shown in Figure 4.12. If the pictures were randomly selected from the sequence, the response time increased as a linear function of the number of items in the memory set. If people were shown the five birds numbered 3, 7, 6, 9, and 1 in Figure 4.12, it would take them longer to search STM than if they were shown only birds 3, 7, and 9. However, the size of the memory set did not make any difference when they were shown sequences of adjacent items. They could search memory as fast for the sequence 3, 4, 5, 6, and 7 as they could for the sequence 3, 4, and 5. Furthermore, the sequence did not have to be presented in an ascending order to obtain this result. People who were shown items 3 to 7 in a 5, 3, 7, 4, 6 order could also search a five-item sequence as fast as they could search a three-item sequence.

The results indicate that people can represent a sequence of adjacent items as a single unified whole rather than as separate items. The finding that the order of presentation within the sequence did not make a difference suggests that we are able to rapidly reorganize items to make a unified whole. Perhaps we quickly establish the two boundaries of the sequence and examine whether the test item falls within the boundaries. This interpretation is supported by the fact that the speed of negative responses is determined by how far the test item is from the nearest boundary of the sequence. If the memory set consisted of items 2, 3, 4, and 5, it would take much longer to reject the sixth item than the ninth item in the sequence. The finding that organization facilitates the search of information in STM is but one example of how organization can improve performance.

I have attempted in this chapter to discuss some of the major characteristics of STM. We use STM in so many different cognitive tasks that it would be impossible to confine this discussion to a single chapter. The next chapter focuses on LTM but also emphasizes the interaction between STM and LTM. If we are interested in learning information, rather than simply maintaining it over a short period of time, we must attempt to enter that information into a more permanent store. We will begin our study of learning by looking at a model that represents learning as the transfer of information from STM into LTM.

Stimulus type   Ordinal position

Figure 4.12. Five organized sequences of visual stimuli. *(From "Memory Scanning of Organized Visual Material," by D. V. DeRosa and D. Tkacz. In* Journal of Experimental Psychology: Human Learning and Memory, *1976, 2, 688–694. Copyright 1976 by the American Psychological Association. Reprinted by permission.)*

Summary

Short-term memory has several limitations that distinguish it from long-term memory. First of all, STM results in rapid forgetting. Items that are not actively rehearsed can be lost in 20 to 30 seconds. Evidence suggests that interference, rather than decay, is the primary cause of forgetting. Interference can result from items presented either before (proactive interference) or after (retroactive interference) the tested item. Release from proactive interference illustrates how the reduction of interference improves memory.

Another limitation of STM is its capacity. After reviewing a large number of findings on absolute judgment and memory span, George Miller identified the capacity limitation as consisting of about seven chunks. A chunk is a group of items that is stored as a unit in LTM. For instance, the sequence *FBITWACIAIBM* is easy to recall when grouped as *FBI–TWA–CIA–IBM* because the 12 letters have been grouped as four chunks. De Groot argued that the superior ability of a master player to reproduce a chess board is a result of the ability to group the pieces into familiar configurations. Using pauses as a measure of chunk boundaries, Chase and Simon concluded that master chess players have both more chunks and larger chunks stored in LTM than less experienced players. Success in reproducing other configurations, such as circuit diagrams, also depends on the availability of chunks.

The use of verbal rehearsal to maintain information in STM is confirmed by acoustic confusions—errors that sound like the correct response. Laughery's simulation model accounts for acoustic confusions by assuming that acoustic codes consist of phonemes, and phonemes can be independently forgotten. Although we usually rely on an acoustic code when we read, we can remember the general ideas from our reading without subvocalizing. However, subvocalization improves our ability to recall details and complex material.

A recognition task consists of showing an item and asking the subject to verify whether the item is contained in a set of items stored in STM. The finding that the time required to make this decision increases as a linear function of the number of items stored in STM suggests that people search the items one at a time. Degrading the test item has relatively little effect on the rate of search, but it does lengthen the time needed to encode the test item before comparing it to the other items in STM. However, the comparison rate is influenced by whether the items are relatively simple—such as letters or digits—or more complex—such as random forms or nonsense syllables. There is an inverse relation between search rate and memory span: the faster the search rate, the greater the number of items that can be stored in STM. A possible explanation is that both findings are influenced by the number of features composing each item. There are a few cases in which search time is uninfluenced by the number of items in STM, one example being items that can be sequentially organized.

Recommended reading

The relation between absolute judgment and paired-associate learning is discussed in Siegel and Siegel (1972). Baddeley and Hitch (1974; Hitch & Baddeley, 1976) have been actively involved in exploring the properties of STM as a working memory. Slowiaczek and Clifton (1980) investigated the role of subvocalization in reading and found that subvocalization is useful when people have to combine ideas expressed in different sentences. There are several good books on memory, including Baddeley (1976); Crowder (1976); and Klatzky (1980). A book edited by Gruneberg, Morris, and Sykes (1978) contains articles on practical aspects of memory. Reviews of memory research frequently occur in the *Annual Review of Psychology* (for example, Craik, 1979a; Peterson, 1977) and provide a summary of research over the past several years.

5

Long-Term Memory

Memory is that part of the brain that reminds us on Friday what we should have done the previous Monday.

POPULAR SAYING

Most of us at one time or another have envied someone who has a very good memory and wished that we could improve our own memory. It's questionable whether we would all be more successful if we had better memories, but at least some people attribute their success to their ability to remember a lot of details. One such person is Isaac Asimov, the author of more than 200 books, 1300 articles, and 250 short stories. In an article titled " 'Computer' Memory Helps Him Write a Book a Month," Asimov claimed that he is able to write on such a wide variety of topics because of his talent for retention: "I read, and I have read a lot. I've heard a lot. And I remember it all and have it on tap. I can recall instantly from the files in my head so I never take notes. My memory is my staunch and unfailing support" (*The Oakland Tribune,* March 11, 1979).

The storage of all this information obviously does not occur in STM, so psychologists have proposed a more permanent store, called long-term memory (LTM). The first section of this chapter describes some ways in which information can be transferred from a temporary to a more permanent store. We start by considering the basic characteristics of LTM, including learning strategies. Much of what was known about this topic was summarized in an important paper by Atkinson and Shiffrin published in 1968. The authors discussed several strategies that could facilitate learning, but they studied primarily verbal rehearsal. They assumed that each time an item was rehearsed, information about that item was entered in LTM. Direct support for their position came from research that required people to rehearse aloud so the experimenter could determine whether the probability of recalling information was related to the number of times it was rehearsed.

The attempt to learn new information by using rehearsal or some other strategy raises the question: When is the new information entered in LTM? Imagine that you are attempting to learn some important historical dates in order to pass a history exam. You may be able to recall the dates after a short study session, but the information could be stored in either STM or LTM. The second section of this chapter discusses research on how effectively people can identify when learning has occurred. We will look at how young children and college students decide which items they need to study. We will then examine a learning model that is successful in identifying whether information is recalled from STM or LTM. This is an important distinction because an item is learned and doesn't have to be studied only if it is retrieved from LTM.

The final section follows the discussion of short-term memory by considering recognition memory. However, the theory of recognition in LTM attempts primarily to account for errors rather than response times, and the procedure used to study LTM recognition is different from that for STM.

The Atkinson-Shiffrin model

Structural Components and Control Processes

The interaction between STM and LTM was emphasized in the theory proposed by Atkinson and Shiffrin (1968, 1971). In their theory the structural components consist of a sensory store, a short-term memory, and a long-term memory. The sensory store preserves information for a few hundred milliseconds; its characteristics were identified by George Sperling (1960) for the storage of visual information. STM, the second basic component of Atkinson and Shiffrin's system, is regarded as a person's working memory. Information is lost from STM within 15 to 30 seconds if it is not rehearsed.

The third component, LTM, differs from the other two components because it contains information that is relatively permanent. Some psychologists have suggested that information is never lost from LTM, though we lose the ability to retrieve it. Whether information is lost or impossible to recover may not be of much practical significance, but if we knew that it was still in memory, we might hope to recover it eventually.

The rate of forgetting from LTM varies from a few minutes to many years. Ideally, we would like to have a single forgetting rate for STM and a single forgetting rate for LTM. The fact that there is a wide range of forgetting rates is one of the criticisms that has been directed at theories about the distinction between STM and LTM. In order to be more specific about the rate of forgetting, we have to know how information is coded, a topic we will study in Chapter 6.

Another difference between STM and LTM is that LTM is unlimited in its capacity. We never reach the point where we cannot learn new information because LTM is filled. Nevertheless, it is not always easy to enter new information into LTM. Atkinson and Shiffrin proposed several control processes that could be used in an attempt to learn new information. The control processes are strategies that a person uses to facilitate learning; they include rehearsal, coding, and imaging.

Rehearsal is the repetition—either aloud or silently of information—over and over until it is learned.

Coding attempts to place the information to be remembered in the context of additional, easily retrievable information, such as a mnemonic phrase or sentence. For example, many of us learned that the lines of a treble clef are E, G, B, D, F by remembering the sentence "Every good boy does fine."

Imaging is creating visual images to remember verbal information. This is an old memory trick—it was even recommended by Cicero for learning long lists or speeches.

The list of control processes could be further expanded, but rehearsal, coding, and imaging are three of the primary ways of learning. Because there are so many control processes to study, Atkinson and Shiffrin (1968) decided to focus their research on only one—verbal rehearsal. More recent work by psychologists has emphasized coding, organizational strategies, and imagery; these strategies are discussed in the second part of this book.

Verbal Rehearsal and Learning

Verbal rehearsal is usually considered to be a form of "rote learning" because it involves simply repeating information over and over until we think we have learned it. It can be useful when the material seems rather abstract, making it difficult to use strategies such as coding or imaging. The task designed by Atkinson and Shiffrin (1968) required the learning of abstract, meaningless material and therefore encouraged the use of rehearsal.

The undergraduates in their experiment tried to learn associations between a two-digit number (the stimulus) and a letter (the response). The paired associates included items such as 31–*Q*, 42–*B*, and 53–*A*. Each pair was shown for three seconds, followed by three seconds before the next trial. Interspersed throughout these study trials were test trials, in which only the two-digit number was presented and the subject was asked to supply the letter that had accompanied it earlier. One of the variables in the experiment was the number of trials that occurred between the study and test trials. Some associates were tested on the very next trial and others after a delay that could last as long as 17 trials.

Atkinson and Shiffrin interpreted the data from this experiment by proposing a model in which verbal rehearsal was used to learn the associates. They assumed that the students maintained a fixed number of items in STM and that these items were rehearsed whenever the student was not viewing a new item or responding during a test trial. The effect of rehearsal was to transfer information about that item into LTM. The extent of learning depended on how long a particular pair was maintained in the rehearsal set. Atkinson and Shiffrin proposed that learning increased as a linear function of the number of trials over which the item was rehearsed. Once the item was no longer rehearsed, information about that particular item decreased as each succeeding item was presented for study. The predicted probability of a correct response therefore depended on both the number of trials in which the item was rehearsed and the number of intervening trials that occurred between the time the item left the rehearsal set and the test trial. Figure 5.1 shows how both factors influenced the predictions.

The prediction shown in Figure 5.1 is the probability of retrieving the correct response from LTM. If an item has been kept active in STM through rehearsal, it will be responded to correctly if it is still in STM at the time of the test. If the subject has been rehearsing 31–Q right up until the time of the test on 31, it is easy to respond Q. If the item had been rehearsed but is no longer in STM, the answer has to be retrieved from LTM. A third possibility exists when an item is not rehearsed at all. Since

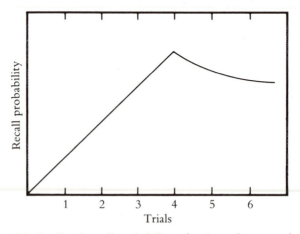

Figure 5.1. Predicted recall probability of an item that was rehearsed for four trials and tested two trials after it left the rehearsal set.

the model assumes that only a limited number of items can be maintained in the rehearsal set, rehearsing a new item will be done at the expense of eliminating one of the items already in the set. Atkinson and Shiffrin proposed that an item that is not rehearsed can be responded to correctly only if it is tested on the trial immediately following its presentation.

The assumptions made by Atkinson and Shiffrin were formulated in a mathematical model, which they used to make a number of successful quantitative predictions over a wide array of experiments. They used their model to estimate four parameters:

1. The number of items maintained in the rehearsal set
2. The probability of including a new item in the rehearsal set
3. The amount of information transferred to LTM each time an item was rehearsed
4. The rate of decay from LTM after an item left the rehearsal set

Although their model allowed Atkinson and Shiffrin to obtain estimates of these parameters and make a number of successful predictions, it lacked direct support for the proposal that rehearsal results in learning. Dewey Rundus, working in Atkinson's laboratory at Stanford University, designed an experiment that provided this support by asking students to rehearse aloud.

Rehearsal and the Serial Position Effect

An easy way to test the proposal that verbal rehearsal results in learning is to ask someone to rehearse out loud. The experimenter can then count the number of times each item was rehearsed and determine whether the probability of recalling an item is related to the number of rehearsals. The task designed by Rundus (1971) was exactly of this type. He presented lists of 20 nouns to undergraduates at Stanford. The words were presented one at a time for a period of 5 seconds each. Rundus instructed the students to study by repeating aloud words on the list during each 5-second interval. They were free to rehearse any word on the list as long as their rehearsal filled the intervals. Following the presentation of the list, the students attempted to recall the words in any order.

Figure 5.2 shows the results of the experiment. The probability of recalling a word depended on its position in the list. Words at the beginning and words at the end of the list were easier to recall than words in the middle of the list. The U-shape of the recall curve, which is called a *serial position effect,* is often obtained in recall experiments. The better recall of words at the beginning of the list is called a *primacy effect,* and the better recall of words at the end of the list is called a *recency effect.*

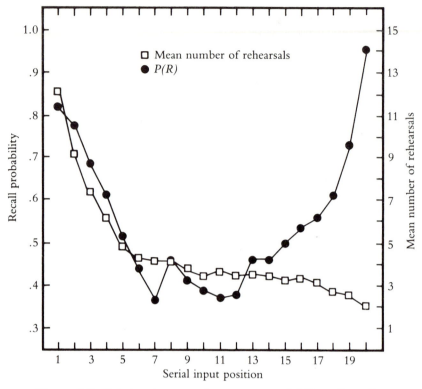

Figure 5.2. Relation between the average probability of recall—
P(R)—and the average number of rehearsals as a function of serial
position. *(From "Analysis of Rehearsal Processes in Free Recall," by D.
Rundus. In* Journal of Experimental Psychology, *1971, 89, 63–77.
Copyright 1971 by the American Psychological Association. Reprinted by
permission.)*

The curve showing the number of times each word was rehearsed illustrates that words at the beginning of the list were rehearsed more often
than the other words. Because a person does not have much choice in
what to rehearse at the beginning of the list, these words are rehearsed
more often, as is illustrated by the example shown in Table 5.1. The
relation between the rehearsal and recall curves reveals that the primacy
effect can be explained by Atkinson and Shiffrin's theory. Since early
words were rehearsed more often than the other words, they should have
a higher probability of being retrieved from LTM. This explanation implies that the primacy effect should be eliminated if all the words on the
list are rehearsed equally often. In fact, when subjects were instructed to
rehearse each word equally often by rehearsing only the displayed word,
the primacy effect disappeared (Fischler, Rundus, & Atkinson, 1970).

Although the number of rehearsals can predict the primacy effect, it

TABLE 5.1. A Partial Listing of Items Rehearsed by One of the Subjects.

Item presented	Items rehearsed (rehearsal set)
1. Reaction	Reaction, reaction, reaction, reaction
2. Hoof	Hoof, reaction, hoof, reaction
3. Blessing	Blessing, hoof, reaction
4. Research	Research, reaction, hoof, research
5. Candy	Candy, hoof, research, reaction
6. Hardship	Hardship, hoof, hardship, hoof
7. Kindness	Kindness, candy, hardship, hoof
8. Nonsense	Nonsense, kindness, candy, hardship
.	.
.	.
.	.
20. Cellar	Cellar, alcohol, misery, cellar

From "The Control of Short-Term Memory," by R. C. Atkinson and R. M. Shiffrin. In *Scientific American,* 1971, *225,* 82–90. Copyright © 1971 by Scientific American, Inc. All rights reserved. Reprinted by permission.

does not predict the recency effect. People were very good at recalling the words at the end of the list even though they did not rehearse them any more than the words in the middle of the list. The recency effect is usually explained by the proposal that the words at the end of the list are still in STM when a person begins the recall. The students in Rundus's experiment recalled the words immediately after the last item was presented; therefore, it is reasonable to assume that the words they had just seen were still available in STM.

We learned from the Peterson and Peterson experiment discussed in Chapter 4 that information is rapidly lost from STM if people have to perform another task. If the recency effect is caused by retrieving the most recent items from STM, it should be eliminated if a person has to perform another task before recalling the items. Subjects in an experiment designed by Postman and Phillips (1965) had to perform an arithmetic task for 30 seconds before they attempted to recall a list of words. The arithmetic task was successful in eliminating the recency effect, implying that the words at the end of the list had decayed from STM.

One of the successes of an information-processing model that distinguishes between STM and LTM is that it can account for the serial position effect. Words at the beginning of the list are rehearsed more often than the other words, making it easier to retrieve these items from LTM, and words at the end of the list can be retrieved from STM. Thus items at the beginning and the end of a list are more likely to be recalled than items in the middle, but for different reasons.

Appropriation of study time

Rehearsal is a rather obvious learning strategy, and we have all used it at one time or another. What to rehearse is a little less obvious, but we could probably agree that we should rehearse material we haven't already learned. For instance, imagine that you are trying to learn a list of vocabulary words in a foreign language. Some are easy to learn and you learn them very quickly, but others are more difficult. You would not want to spend an equal amount of time on each word but would spend more time studying the difficult words.

Although this strategy seems very obvious to us, it would not be to a young child. A variety of evidence suggests that, as they get older, children become increasingly able to discover efficient learning strategies and to benefit from training on what to do in a learning task (Brown, 1978). Examples of strategies acquired by children include the ability to use rehearsal spontaneously, to estimate the number of items they can recall (memory span), to determine when they have learned items well enough to repeat them all back to the experimenter, and to divide their study time so as to spend more time on the unlearned items.

I will focus on one of these strategies—the division of study time—so we can examine it from several different perspectives. The first part of this section shows that the efficient use of study time is acquired relatively early in elementary school, though it is not found in the first grade. The second part reviews a study that attempted to train mentally retarded children to use their study time more efficiently. The third part shows that even college students can benefit from a good learning model that selects for them the items they need to study.

Developmental Changes in the Effective Use of Study Time

Masur, McIntyre, and Flavell (1973) designed an experiment to measure how efficiently students could divide their study among a list of items. Groups of first-grade, third-grade, and college students were asked to learn a set of items 50% longer than their own previously assessed memory spans. For example, if a student's memory span was 8 items, there would be 12 items on the list. The student would initially make some errors when attempting to recall all 12 items. After the first recall period, the student would see all the items again and could select half of them for additional study. This procedure was repeated for several trials. The experimenters were primarily interested in whether the student included in the study set those items that were not recalled. Since these items were not yet learned, including them in the study set should be an efficient strategy—at least for adults.

The first-grade children included unrecalled items in the study set

62% of the time, third-graders included them 80% of the time, and college students included them 85% of the time. Since students were allowed to study half of the items, the probability is .5 that an item would be included by chance. The first-grade children did better than chance on only one of the three trials. The results imply that, although first-grade children are deficient in their use of this particular study skill, third-grade children use the skill about as well as college students. First-grade children fail to study unrecalled items even though they can easily identify which items they didn't recall.

Can we therefore design a procedure to train these children to study unrecalled items? We could try, but we would be assuming from our adult perspective that studying unrecalled items is an efficient strategy. It is—for adults. This conclusion is based on the fact that college students could study unrecalled items without affecting their performance on recalled items. If they recalled an item on one trial, the probability that they would recall it on the next trial was uninfluenced by whether they studied it between the two trials. This was not true for the first-grade children, who did better in recalling any item if they could study it some more. In fact, the advantage gained from studying an item was almost as high for recalled items as it was for unrecalled items. It didn't really make much difference for first-graders which items they decided to study because recalling an item on one trial was no guarantee that they could recall it on the next trial unless they studied it some more. Therefore, training first-grade students to study unrecalled items would show little gain in performance. A gain would only occur when the children could retain recalled items in memory while they studied other items.

Training Memory Strategies

The importance of adapting training strategies to cognitive abilities is emphasized in a study by Brown and Campione (1977). Their study was influenced by the results of the experiment just described. The children in their experiment were mentally retarded, although they were in the upper range of children so classified. The younger group had a mental age of 6 years 10 months, and an older group had a mental age of 7 years 11 months. Children of both ages were assigned to one of three experimental groups, designed to compare two training conditions with a control (nontraining) condition. Each child was seen individually for six consecutive days. The first two days were devoted to pretesting, the third and fourth days to training, and the last two days to posttesting. The pretesting was a modification of the procedure used by Masur, McIntyre, and Flavell (1973). The children attempted to recall the names of 12 pictures. They were allowed to study half of the pictures before each recall attempt.

Although the children selected the items for further study during pretesting, the experimenter selected the items during the two days of training. Children in the "standard" group received items they had failed to recall. This should be an optimal strategy for older children and adults who could maintain the recalled items in memory while they attempted to learn new items. The second training procedure was designed to help younger children who could not maintain recalled items in memory. Children in this "creeping" group were allowed to study the items they had just recalled plus one additional missed item. Brown and Campione hoped that these children would gradually "creep" up to a better level of performance by learning one new item on each trial. A third condition, the "random" group, served as a control for the two training procedures. Approximately half the items given to this group had been recalled and half had been missed.

The final two days of the study consisted of a posttest that was very similar to the pretest in that children were allowed to select their own items for study. If the training procedures were effective, children in the two training groups should use a more sophisticated strategy on the post-test and perform better than on the pretest.

The results of the study are shown in Figure 5.3. The standard training procedure, as predicted, was successful in improving performance for the older children (left panel) but not for the younger children (right panel). Unfortunately, the younger children also did not benefit from the creeping procedure as had been hoped. They did improve their performance during the training session if they followed the creeping procedure, but they did not continue to use the creeping strategy when asked to select items on the posttest. The children's failure to continue using a strategy has been the major stumbling block in trying to teach effective memory strategies to mentally retarded children. The children often learn to use the strategy to improve their performance during a training session but then discontinue using it when they are no longer prompted (Brown, 1978).

Brown and Campione (1977) suggested that one reason the younger children may not have used the creeping strategy on the posttest was that they were never explicitly told the reason for the experimenter's selection of items during the study session. They were not informed that the experimenter was adding a single unrecalled item to the study set after each trial so they could gradually learn all the items. The children may have failed to notice exactly what the experimenter was doing or failed to understand why such a choice might be helpful. Very explicit feedback and instruction might change the outcome, and future studies will explore this possibility.

An important implication of the two studies just described is that a researcher cannot simply improve performance by teaching children a

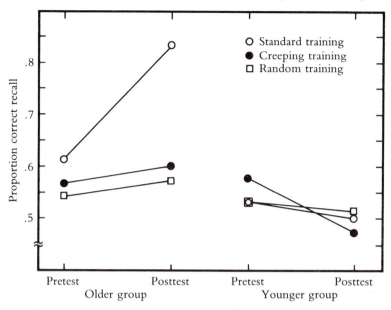

Figure 5.3. Mean proportion of correct recall on pre- and posttests as a function of age and training condition. *(From "Training Strategic Study Time Apportionment in Educable Retarded Children," by A. L. Brown and J. C. Campione. In* Intelligence, *1977, 1, 94–104. Copyright 1977 by Ablex Publishing Corp. Reprinted by permission.)*

common adult strategy without considering the cognitive capabilities of the children. We seen that third-grade children spontaneously used a strategy quite similar to the adult strategy of studying unrecalled items. Older mentally retarded children can be taught to use this strategy: only 36% of the older children in the standard group initially used this strategy on the pretest, but 82% did so on the posttest, with the resultant improvement of performance shown in Figure 5.3.

The first-grade children did not use this strategy. Furthermore, it is questionable whether they would benefit by adding all unrecalled items to their study set because they needed to study both recalled and unrecalled items. This is why the creeping procedure was designed to gradually introduce unrecalled items into the study set. The creeping approach would seem to have the most promise for improving the performance of younger children, as was suggested by the improvement of the younger retarded children during the training session.

Using Study Time More Efficiently

The preceding discussion suggested that adults—and even older children—know how to utilize study time efficiently. They know that an unrecalled item needs further study, and therefore they tend to study unrecalled, rather than recalled, items. One reason this strategy was successful was that the retention interval was not very long in the previous two experiments. Since the experiments alternated between study and recall sessions, some of the correct responses could have been retrieved from STM. When people need to learn material more permanently, it is important to distinguish whether a correct response was retrieved from STM or LTM. Even recalled items need further study if the information was retrieved from STM.

Imagine that you have to learn some foreign vocabulary words. You will want to be able to recall the translations not only during the time you study the words, but also on subsequent days. To succeed, you must be able to tell when you have really learned the translation and are not simply retrieving it from STM. My own experience has been that I sometimes find it difficult to judge when I have really learned what I was studying. Although the information appeared easy to recall shortly after I read or heard about it, it was gone the next day.

There are many tasks that a computer can do much better than people can, so why not let the computer decide when we have really learned an item? Since a computer can only follow the instructions of a programmer, it must be given instructions derived from a good model of learning. The advantage of using a formal model of learning and a computer to improve recall was demonstrated in a study by Atkinson (1972a, 1972b). The task required that undergraduates learn the English translation of 84 German words. The words were divided into seven lists, each containing 12 words. One of the lists was displayed on each trial of an instructional session, and either the student or the computer selected one of the items for test and study. After the student attempted to provide the English translation, the correct translation was presented. The computer then displayed the next list, and the procedure repeated for a total of 336 trials. Figure 5.4 shows a typical list and the design of the instructional session.

Atkinson designed the experiment to compare the learning of three different groups of students. Students in one group were allowed to pick which words they wanted to study. They were told that they should try to learn all the vocabulary words, and the best way to proceed was to test and study words that they did not already know. Students in a second group received items to study that were selected according to a learning model. Atkinson formulated the model in an attempt to optimize learning by presenting those words that the students most needed to study. The words were selected on the basis of a response-sensitive strategy that carefully kept track of a student's previous responses. Students in a third group received words that were randomly selected. Random selection, of course, is not a very good procedure, because it would include words that a student had already learned. The performance of this third group is of

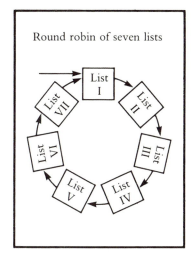

Round robin of seven lists

Typical list

1. das   Rad
2. die   Seite
3. das   Kino
4. die   Gans
5. der   Fluss
6. die   Gegend
7. die   Kamera
8. der   Anzug
9. das   Geld
10. der Gipfel
11. das Bein
12. die Ecke

Figure 5.4. Illustration of the language-learning task designed by Atkinson. *(From "Ingredients for a Theory of Instruction," by R. C. Atkinson. In* American Psychologist, *1972, 27, 921–931. Copyright 1972 by the American Psychological Association. Reprinted by permission.)*

interest because it provides a standard against which to compare the other two groups.

The learning model assumes that an item can be in one of three states:

1. An *unlearned* state. Items in this state have not yet been learned, so the learner will respond incorrectly.
2. A *temporary* state. Items in this state have been temporarily learned. The student will initially give the correct answer but will forget the translation as she attempts to learn other items. We might think of these items as being stored in STM.
3. A *permanent* state. The translations of items in this state are relatively permanent in the sense that the learning of other vocabulary items will not interfere with them. We might think of these items as being stored in LTM.

The goal of the learning model is to select for study those items that are not yet in LTM in order to maximize the number of items in LTM at the end of the session. Items in the unlearned state are easy to identify because the student will be unable to provide the correct translation. Clearly, these items need further study, and, on the basis of the research discussed previously, we might expect that students would study them. Items in the temporary state are more difficult to identify because the student will be able to provide the correct answer on some of the trials. Let's consider the case in which a student receives two tests on the same item and responds correctly on both occasions. Is that item in a permanent state, implying that it wouldn't have to be presented again? We don't know for certain, but our decision should be influenced by the number of trials that occurred between the two tests. The greater the number of intervening trials, the greater the probability that the item is in the permanent state because studying other items should cause the student to forget the translation if it had been only temporarily learned.

The advantage of a computer is that it can record and remember exactly how a student responded on each of the items. When this information is used in a model that attempts to optimize learning, it is possible that the model could better select items for study than the student could. The results of Atkinson's experiment demonstrated that this possibility can be realized. Figure 5.5 shows the performance of each of the three groups during a delayed test given one week later. It is apparent that the worse the students did during instruction, the better they did on the test. The reason is that successful instruction requires identifying and presenting the unlearned words, resulting in many errors during the instruction. The response-sensitive strategy based on the learning model was the most

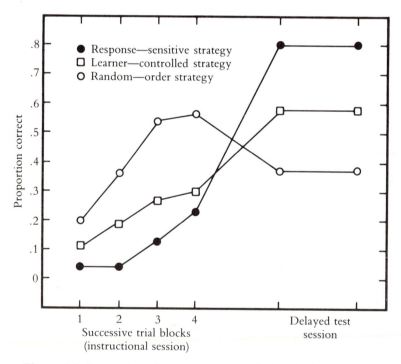

Figure 5.5. Proportion of correct responses during the instructional session and during the delayed test administered one week later. *(From "Ingredients for a Theory of Instruction," by R. C. Atkinson. In* American Psychologist, *1972, 27, 921–931. Copyright 1972 by the American Psychological Association. Reprinted by permission.)*

successful in identifying unlearned items. Those students who could select their own items for study (the learner-controlled strategy) did much
better on the test than when the items were randomly selected, but they
did much worse than the model. Performance on the test indicated that
the learner-controlled strategy yielded a gain of 53% compared to the
random procedure, but the computer-controlled strategy yielded a gain
of 108%.

The results provide a clear demonstration of the usefulness of a good
learning model that can be carried out by a computer. Although learner-
controlled instruction was better than random selection, it was worse
than selection of items by the learning model. It seems clear that serious
consideration should be given to using the model on a wide scale. The de-
clining cost of computers should make instructional programs like the
one developed by Atkinson a possibility in more situations.

Recognition memory

Recognition is studied by showing people a sequence of items and then
showing them test items, asking them to decide whether each test item
was a member of the original sequence. Recognition differs from recall
because in a recall experiment people see the items only during the initial
presentation, whereas in a recognition experiment they see at least some
of the items again during the test. We saw in Chapter 4 that recognition
of items in STM has been studied by using the Sternberg paradigm. The
sequence is short enough to fit within the limited capacity of STM, and
people are shown a test item immediately after seeing the sequence. Since
people make very few errors on this test, interest has focused on the variables that influence decision time.

Recognition of items in LTM is studied by using a much longer list,
one that greatly exceeds the limited capacity of STM. The test items may
also be presented after a considerable delay, preventing the use of STM.
If we wanted to test recognition for items stored in LTM, we might do
the following experiment: First we could show people a list of 100 items,
such as words or pictures. The next day we would show them a sequence
of 200 items, half of which they saw previously, and ask them to identify
each item they recognized from the experiment the previous day.

After we had collected our data, we would be faced with the problem
of how to measure performance. What would we do if one of the participants couldn't say "no" and responded positively to each of the 200 items?
This person would have "recognized" every item that was on the original
list, but would also have "recognized" 100 items that were not on the list.
Although this is an extreme case, it does point out the need for a measure
of performance on a recognition task. The measure most often used,
called d', is derived from signal-detection theory.

A Signal Detection Theory of Recognition

The theory we're about to consider was originally developed to describe performance in signal-detection experiments. The signal-detection task requires that an observer report whether a signal occurred—for instance, whether a tone occurred in a background of noise. The listener can make two different kinds of errors. First, he can respond negatively when a signal did occur. This kind of error is called a *miss* because the subject failed to detect the signal. Second, the listener can respond positively when a signal did not occur. This kind of error is called a *false alarm*.

James Egan (1958) showed that the theory developed to describe performance in a signal-detection task could also be used to describe performance on a recognition memory test. There are two kinds of items on the memory test—old items that occurred before in the experiment and new items that did not occur. Although the task requires distinguishing between old and new items rather than between signals and noise, the same kinds of errors can occur when people attempt to identify old items. A person can respond negatively to an old item by failing to remember that it occurred before. This error is called a *miss,* as when a person misses a signal. Or a person can respond positively to a new item that hadn't occurred before. The error is called a *false alarm,* as when a person incorrectly states that a signal occurred.

The signal-detection theory assumes that items vary along a continuous dimension, which is labeled *memory strength* or *familiarity*. The effect of presenting an item during the experiment is to increase its familiarity in the experiment. Since old items were previously presented in the experiment, they will generally have higher familiarity values than new items. This situation is represented in Figure 5.6 by the placement of the two distributions (representing new items and old items) along the continuum. The height of the distribution on the left shows how many new items have that particular familiarity value. The average value for new items is represented by the vertical line labeled *Ave(N)*. The height of the distribution on the right shows how many old items have that particular familiarity value. The average value for old items is represented by the vertical line labeled *Ave(O)*.

Notice that the two distributions overlap and that some new items actually have higher familiarity values than old items. Why should this be? First, we must remember that the term *familiarity* is being used to define how familiar an item seems to be within the context of the experiment. You are very familiar with your name, but if it didn't occur in the experiment, it would have a low familiarity value. Since the familiarity values reflect how confident you are that an item occurred in the experiment, your name should have a very low familiarity value because you should be very confident that it was not one of the old items. Other new

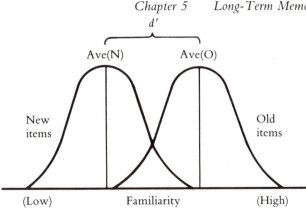

Figure 5.6. A signal-detection representation of old and new items along a familiarity continuum. Ave(N) is the average familiarity value for new items, and Ave(O) is the average familiarity value for old items.

items, however, would be more difficult to judge. For example, if the word *boat* was presented and you were later tested on the word *ship,* you might respond positively because the two words have similar meanings. The word *ship* would seem familiar even though it did not occur.

A measure called d' is used to represent how much the two distributions overlap or how well a person performs on a recognition test. It is a measure of the difference in the means of the two distributions (Ave(O)–Ave(N)) relative to the variance of the new item distribution. A high value of d' implies that there is a considerable overlap of the two distributions because a person makes many mistakes. The extreme case is $d' = 0$, which indicates that the average familiarity value is the same for old and new items. A d' of 0 would occur if a person couldn't remember any of the items in the experiment and simply guessed when given the memory test.

Since d' is a measure of how well a person performs on a recognition memory test, it reflects the probability of making an error on the test. It does not, however, tell us the kinds of errors that occur. In order to know the kinds of errors, we have to know how a person distinguishes new items from old items. Since old items generally have higher values on the continuum than new items, a person should respond that familiar items were previously presented and unfamiliar items were not previously presented. This sounds simple enough, but exactly where should the cutoff be placed separating familiar from unfamiliar items if familiarity varies along a continuum? The placement of the dividing line differs across people and tasks, so it is necessary to calculate the location of the boundary. The vertical line labeled β in Figure 5.7 shows two possible locations. Signal-detection theory assumes that people respond that an item was not previously presented if its familiarity value is less than

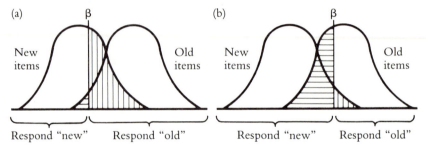

Figure 5.7. Influence of the response criterion (β) on the probability of a miss (horizontal lines) and false alarm (vertical lines).

β and that it was previously presented if its familiarity value is greater than β.

The location of β determines how a person's errors are divided into misses and false alarms. Notice in Figure 5.7 that part of each distribution is on the wrong side of the dividing line. The familiarity values of most new items are less than β, so they will be correctly labeled as new items. But a few new items have a familiarity value greater than β, so they will be incorrectly identified as having previously occurred, resulting in a false alarm. The probability of a false alarm is represented by the proportion of new items that have familiarity values greater than β, the areas of vertical lines in Figure 5.7. The probability of a miss is represented by the proportion of old items that have familiarity values less than β, the areas shaded with horizontal lines. Since the latter do not seem very familiar, they will be classified as new items.

Notice in Figure 5.7 that there is a trade-off between misses and false alarms as the criterion is moved either to the left or to the right. Moving the criterion to the left (Figure 5.7a) implies that a person responds positively more often. This causes a decline in the number of misses but an increase in the number of false alarms. Moving the criterion to the right (Figure 5.7b) implies that a person responds positively less often. This causes an increase in the number of misses but a decline in the number of false alarms. The exact placement of the criterion can be calculated by making use of this trade-off between the proportion of false alarms and misses.

The application of signal-detection theory to recognition memory therefore provides two measures of performance. The first measure—d'—is a measure of accuracy. It indicates how well a person can distinguish between old items and new items. Accuracy is determined by such factors as individual differences in memory, length of the retention interval, and degree of similarity between old and new items. The second measure—β—indicates the response criterion selected by an individual. It is a value on the familiarity continuum that is used by the individual for deciding whether an item was previously presented. Items with familiarity values greater than the criterion are classified as old, and items with familiarity values less than the criterion are classified as new. The location of the criterion determines whether the errors are primarily misses or false alarms.

Eyewitness Identification

The discussion of recognition memory has been rather abstract so far, so let's see how it is used in a particular task. Recognition memory is studied in the laboratory by showing people a sequence of items and then asking them whether a test item was a member of the sequence. The subjects have to remember not only that they saw that item before but that they saw it during the experiment. In other words, they have to remember the context in which they saw the item. Recalling the correct context is often useful in everyday situations. For instance, you may recognize someone as a person you met before but may not be able to remember where the meeting took place. Remembering the appropriate context might help you recall additional information about that person.

Eyewitness identification is a situation in which recalling the context of information is important. Accurate identification depends not only on being able to recognize a face as someone familiar but on recalling that the person was seen performing a crime rather than seen in a newspaper, on television, or in police mugshots. The possibility that the witness might be able to recognize a face without being able to recall the correct context was addressed by the U.S. Supreme Court in *Simmons* v. *United States* 390 U.S. 377 (1968) (cited in Brown, Deffenbacher, & Sturgill, 1977). The court noted the potential biasing effect caused by showing a witness a single mugshot or showing mugshots that emphasized a particular suspect. They held that the biasing effects would be particularly misleading if the witness originally had only a brief glimpse of the suspect or saw him under poor conditions (Buckhout, 1974).

The possible biasing effects that can occur during eyewitness identification were investigated in two experiments conducted by Brown, Deffenbacher, and Sturgill (1977). In one experiment students in a large introductory psychology class were asked to view ten ".criminals" (graduate and upperclass undergraduate white males) for 25 seconds each. The experimenter told the class to observe them carefully because they would have to pick them out from mugshots later that evening and from a lineup the following week. One and one-half hours later, the students looked at 15 mugshots consisting of color slides showing a front and side view. They were asked to indicate for each mugshot whether that person had appeared earlier in front of the class. Five of the 15 mugshots were of people who had actually appeared. The five criminals were correctly identified as criminals 72% of the time; however, the ten noncriminals were also identified as criminals 45% of the time. The value of d' calculated from these percentages is significantly above 0, but it is not very large. This finding implies that, although the accuracy of identification was significantly above chance, it was not very good. Furthermore, the high false alarm rate (45%) indicates that many people in the mugshots were falsely accused.

A major goal of this experiment was to determine whether presenting a mugshot would cause a bias toward identifying the person in the photograph as a criminal. Notice that the students saw the mugshots of only five of the ten criminals. Would they be more likely to later identify these five as criminals than the five criminals whose mugshots were not presented? One week later students saw a lineup and were asked to indicate whether each person in the lineup was one of the original criminals who appeared in the front of the class. The criminals whose mugshots were shown were identified on 65% of the occasions, compared to 51% for criminals whose mugshots were not shown. Showing a mugshot made it significantly more likely that a person would be identified as a criminal, perhaps because the "witnesses" could not recall whether they previously saw the person or the photograph.

At this point we might say, "So what, they were all guilty anyway." But what about innocent people? Would showing their mugshots make it more likely that they would be identified as criminals during the lineup? This was the issue that concerned the Supreme Court in the *Simmons* v. *United States* decision. In the Brown, Deffenbacher, and Sturgill experiment, nine of the people included in the lineup had not initially appeared in front of the class, but pictures of four of the nine were included among the mugshots. If showing a mugshot of an innocent person biases the witnesses to label that person as a criminal, these four should be identified as criminals more often than the other five. The results support this hypothesis. The four people whose pictures had been included in the mugshot session were incorrectly identified as criminals on 20% of the occasions, compared to 8% for people whose pictures had not appeared. The greater tendency to identify a person as a criminal after seeing a mugshot affected the "innocent" people as well as the "guilty."

One objection to this experiment is that students were initially asked to remember what ten people looked like rather than only one or two, a more typical situation in a real crime. Brown and his colleagues eliminated this objection in a second experiment, in which a different class of students was asked to identify only two people. The two people handed out the first midterm exam in the class; members of the class were not told that they would later be asked to identify the two people. The design of the experiment was similar to the one described above except that the mugshots were shown two or three days after the exam and the lineup occurred four or five days after the students viewed the mugshots. The same pattern of results occurred as in the previous experiment: presenting a mugshot of a person made it more likely that the person would be identified in the lineup.

Although these experiments do not pretend to duplicate what an actual witness is confronted with during a crime, they do raise serious questions regarding a person's ability to identify the context in which a person is perceived. The findings suggest that great care should be taken in what material is shown to a witness who must make the final identification of a suspected criminal.

Familiarity versus Searching

As we saw in Chapter 4, people judge whether an item is in STM by sequentially comparing it to the items stored there. When the number of stored items is very small, this procedure provides a fast and reliable way of arriving at an answer. When a person has stored a long list of items in LTM, searching the entire list would take more time, particularly if there was uncertainty about what items were on the list. The possibility that a person makes a judgment on the basis of familiarity, as suggested by the signal–detection model, therefore provides an attractive alternative to the Sternberg (1967) model.

There are circumstances when it might be beneficial to search LTM —for instance, when the list of stored items is not very long or when the items are well learned so searching would guarantee a correct response. Both of these conditions were created in an experiment conducted at Stanford University (Juola, Fischler, Wood, & Atkinson, 1971). Undergraduates were given a list that contained 10, 18, or 26 words. They were asked to memorize the words on the list and were tested the following day on their ability to recall the items. After it was clear that each person had learned the words, the experiment began. The subjects pushed a button, which caused a word to appear on the screen of a tachistoscope. They then responded positively or negatively whether the word was contained in the memorized list. The experiment was like the Sternberg (1966) experiment except, instead of seeing a new list of items on each trial, the subjects had learned a single, longer list of items, which was stored in LTM. Since the list was learned, it did not have to be shown before each trial.

Some of the results of this experiment could be easily explained by Sternberg's model. One such finding was the linear relation between reaction time and list length. Those subjects who learned the shortest list responded the fastest, and those who learned the longest list responded the slowest. This result is consistent with the idea that people searched the items in the list: the longer the list, the greater the search time.

Other findings could be more easily explained by the signal-detection model. Words that were semantically similar to words on the list took longer to reject than neutral words. If the word *ship* was on the list and a subject was tested on *boat,* the response time would be greater than for a neutral word like *tree.* We saw previously that this effect is consistent with the idea that the familiarity of a word varies along a continuum, making some words more difficult to reject than others.

Since Juola and his colleagues hoped to explain both sets of findings, they proposed a model that combined the major characteristics of the Sternberg and the signal-detection models (Figure 5.8). The model borrows from signal-detection theory the assumption that the familiarity of words varies along a continuum. Old words (those on the list) are generally more familiar than new words (those not on the list), but the two distributions overlap. It is very easy to classify words that have extreme values on the continuum. Very familiar words are obviously on the list, so a person can respond "yes" immediately. Very unfamiliar words are obviously not on the list, so a person can respond "no" immediately. It is not obvious, however, how to classify a word that is only somewhat familiar. The model proposes that in this case people search the list before responding.

The model differs from the signal-detection model by assuming that there are two response criteria instead of only one. Familiarity values less

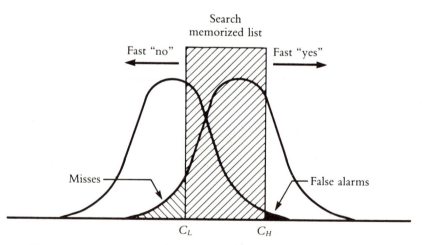

Figure 5.8. Distribution of old items and new items along a familiarity continuum. The two criteria—C_L and C_H—determine whether the subject will respond immediately or search the memorized list. *(From "Recognition Time for Information Stored in Long-Term Memory," by J. F. Juola, I. Fischler, C. T. Wood, and R. C. Atkinson. In* Perception & Psychophysics, *1971, 10, 8–14. Copyright 1971 by the Psychonomic Society, Inc. Reprinted by permission.)*

then the lower criterion (C_L) result in an immediate "no" response, and familiarity values greater than the higher criterion (C_H) result in an immediate "yes" response. The intermediate values between the two criteria result in a search of the list. Figure 5.8 shows that both misses and false alarms can occur, but they are relatively rare because a person has the option of searching the list to assure a correct response. In fact, the error rate in this study was quite low.

The strength of this model is that it can account for results that are consistent with both the Sternberg and the signal-detection models since it combines them into a single model. The finding that the average response time was longer when the list was longer is explained by the assumption that people search the list before classifying some of the words —the response time is longer because it takes more time to search a longer list. The finding that semantically similar words are more difficult to reject than neutral words is explained by the assumption that a neutral word has a low familiarity value. A neutral word is therefore rejected immediately, but a semantically similar word is rejected only after a search of the list.

The model proposed by Juola and his colleagues should provide a useful account of results obtained from people who use more than one strategy to classify items. When the list is short and can be maintained in STM, the search strategy should be predominant. When the list is long and it is not obvious what items are on the list, decisions based on familiarity should be predominant. When the demands of the task are between these two extremes, the Juola model provides an attractive explanation of how the two strategies can be combined.

Earlier in this chapter I mentioned that a person can use different kinds of memory codes in an attempt to remember information. The next two chapters examine how memory codes differ and how different codes influence retention. To use Atkinson and Shiffrin's terminology, the emphasis will shift from a consideration of the structural components of memory to a consideration of the ways control processes or strategies can influence the construction of qualitatively different memory codes.

Summary

Learning can be represented as the transfer of information from STM to LTM. The decay rate for information in LTM is relatively slow compared to the rapid decay rate from STM. Furthermore, LTM does not suffer from a capacity limitation; that is, it is not limited in the amount of information it can store. The distinction between STM and LTM, as well as the role of rehearsal in transferring information into LTM, was emphasized in a model proposed by Atkinson and Shiffrin. One of the findings that can be accounted for by their model is the serial position effect. Atkinson and Shiffrin suggested that the primacy effect—the bet-ter recall of words at the beginning of the list—could be explained by the finding that these words were rehearsed more often, resulting in their storage in LTM. The recency effect—the better recall of words at the end of the list—could be explained by the finding that these words were still available in STM.

A good strategy for learning a list of items is to study those items that haven't already been learned. Although first-graders are deficient in us-ing this strategy, third-graders follow the strategy about as often as col-lege students. The attempt to train children to study unrecalled items must take into account their capability for performing memory tasks. Al-though older children benefited from training, younger children did not because they needed to study both recalled and unrecalled items. A dif-ficult decision, even for adults, is to decide whether successfully retrieved new information came from STM or LTM. The ability to make this dis-tinction is useful because the student should concentrate on items that are not yet stored in LTM. A learning model used this distinction to deter-mine which items should be presented during an instructional session in order for students to recall them during a test given one week later.

A recognition task differs from a recall task because it tests judgment of whether an item was previously presented, usually within a specified context. A model of recognition memory derived from signal-detection theory assumes that items vary in familiarity along a continuum. Items that were presented before (old items) generally have higher familiarity values than items that were not presented before (new items), but the two distributions overlap. A person must select a criterion value along this continuum in order to decide whether an item is old or new. The lo-cation of the criterion determines whether the errors are primarily misses or false alarms. False alarms in eyewitness identification are increased by showing mugshots to a witness. The witness may falsely identify a per-son because of a failure to recall the context in which that person was seen. The signal-detection model can be combined with the Sternberg scanning model by assuming that a person responds immediately to items having extreme values on the familiarity continuum but searches mem-ory for items having intermediate familiarity. The combined model can explain more findings than either model by itself, but it best accounts for the recognition of items on lists of intermediate length.

Recommended reading

The general references on memory cited at the end of Chapter 4 discuss LTM as well as STM. Bahrick (1979) studied very long-term memory by asking alumni to recall various kinds of information (such as street and building names) about their college town. Herrmann and Neisser (1978) designed an *Inventory of Everyday Memory Experiences* that contained 48 questions about everyday forgetting and 24 questions about memory for events from early childhood. Readers interested in children's learning strategies should consult Baron (1978a) and Campione and Brown (1978). Readers interested in eyewitness testimony should consult Goldstein (1977) and Yarmey (1979)—both authors emphasize the limitations of evidence based on eyewitness testimony.

PART **II**

Representation and Organization of Knowledge

6

Levels of Processing

It is abundantly clear that what determines the level of recall or recognition of a word event is not intention to learn, the amount of effort involved, the difficulty of the orienting task, the amount of time spent making judgments about the items, or even the amount of rehearsal the items receive; rather it is the qualitative nature of the task, the kind of operations carried out on the items, that determines retention.

F. I. M. CRAIK AND ENDEL TULVING (1975)

The preceding two chapters developed a theory of memory as consisting of a short-term store and a long-term store. This theory provides a beginning, but it leaves us with many questions. Why are there many different decay rates in LTM? Does verbal rehearsal always cause learning? What other control processes can we use to enter information into LTM? How is memory organized? And what about visual knowledge?

In the next four chapters I will attempt to provide some answers to these questions about the representation and organization of knowledge. Our immediate objective is to learn the ways memory codes differ and the consequent implications for learning and retrieval. When people try to learn, they most likely form several different kinds of memory codes and psychologists have little control over what people do. So instead of asking people to learn, we often ask them to make judgments about words without telling them they will have to recall the words after the judgment task. The purpose of the judgment task (often called an *orienting task*) is to try to control the kind of memory code formed by requesting that a person make decisions about a specific characteristic of the word, such as its pronunciation or its meaning. We can then examine how well that person can recall the word as a function of the emphasized characteristics.

The first section of this chapter examines a theory of memory called *levels of processing,* proposed by Craik and Lockhart (1972), which proposes that success in recalling a word depends on the kinds of operations carried out while encoding the word. That is, retention is determined by the characteristics that are emphasized during initial perception or rehearsal. Evidence supporting the theory is reviewed in the second section. The third section attempts to explain why semantic codes are better than structural codes. The argument that memory for an event is improved by making the code more elaborate and distinctive is used to explain how coding influences retention. The final section considers the encoding specificity principle, which states that the effectiveness of a retrieval cue depends on how well its characteristics correspond to the characteristics of the stored event.

The levels-of-processing theory

Emphasis on Coding Strategies

The paper written by Craik and Lockhart (1972) had three objectives: (a) to examine the reasons for proposing multistore models; (b) to question the adequacy of such models; and (c) to propose an alternative framework in terms of levels of processing. We have already considered some of the major characteristics of the three memory stores (sensory store, STM, and LTM) in the previous chapter. The commonly accepted differences among these stores were summarized by Craik and Lockhart (see Table 6.1).

The sensory store is preattentive in the sense that it occurs before perceptual recognition. Attention influences what observers recognize, as when they attend to a particular row of letters after hearing a tone. The sensory store provides a literal copy of the stimulus input but rapidly decays away. It isn't possible to use a control process or strategy to maintain the store, so information must be read out using pattern recognition in order to preserve it in a more permanent store.

In order to enter STM, the information must be attended to and described. It can be maintained in STM by continued attendance to it or by use of verbal rehearsal. Since verbal rehearsal is often used, the format is primarily phonemic, but it can also be visual or semantic. STM is limited by its small capacity and fast decay rate, but retrieval is easy because so few items have to be searched.

Information is entered into LTM primarily through verbal rehearsal. Long-term memory is largely semantic; that is, it is organized according to meaning. It has no known limits in capacity, and its contents, if lost at all, are lost through interference. The ability to retrieve information

TABLE 6.1. Commonly Accepted Differences among the Three Stages of Verbal Memory.

Feature	Sensory registers	Short-term store	Long-term store
Entry of information	Preattentive	Requires attention	Rehearsal
Maintenance of information	Not possible	Continued attention Rehearsal	Repetition Organization
Format of information	Literal copy of input	Phonemic Probably visual Probably semantic	Largely semantic Some auditory and visual
Capacity	Large	Small	No known limit
Information loss	Decay	Displacement Possibly decay	Possibly no loss Loss of accessibility or discriminability by interference
Trace duration	¼–2 seconds	Up to 30 seconds	Minutes to years
Retrieval	Readout	Probably automatic Items in consciousness Temporal/phonemic cues	Retrieval cues Possibly search process

From "Levels of Processing: A Framework for Memory Research," by F. I. M. Craik and R. S. Lockhart. In *Journal of Verbal Learning and Verbal Behavior*, 1972, *11*, 671–684. Copyright 1972 by Academic Press, Inc. Reprinted by permission.

from LTM can last from minutes to years. Cues are very useful in retrieving information from LTM, as we will see later in this chapter, but retrieval may require a lengthy search and a considerable amount of time.

Although most psychologists had accepted the characterization of memory represented in Table 6.1, Craik and Lockhart felt that the evidence for a distinction between STM and LTM was not as clear as it should be. They argued first that the capacity of STM was really more variable than Miller's estimate of from five to nine chunks. For example, people can reproduce strings of up to 20 words if the words form a sentence. One might reasonably argue that the words in a sentence form chunks and that it should be easy to recall 20 words from STM if there are about three words in each chunk. But this argument requires objective evidence that such chunks exist. Second, although the format is primarily phonemic in STM and semantic in LTM, there is evidence for visual and semantic codes in STM (see Shulman, 1971) and visual and phonemic codes in LTM. An example of an attempt to eliminate acoustic confusions in LTM is the ad campaign directed against Goodyear Tire and Rubber Company by B. F. Goodrich, which was motivated largely by the similarity of the two companies' names (see Box 6.1). Third, as we have already seen, decay rates vary considerably depending on the material being learned. Ideally, we would like to see a single, fast rate of decay for STM and a single, slow rate of decay for LTM.

The distinction between the three memory stores summarized in Table 6.1 is therefore an idealized view of how the stores differ. Although I believe there is much experimental support for this view, we must remember that most theories, including the theory that proposes three separate memory stores, are oversimplified. The part of the theory that seems the weakest to me is the variety of decay rates. Where do all these decay rates come from? The strength of the levels-of-processing theory is its attempt to answer this question.

The levels-of-processing theory proposes that there are different ways to code material and that memory codes are qualitatively different. Preliminary processing is concerned with the analysis of physical features such as lines, angles, brightness, pitch, and loudness. Later stages of analysis are concerned with pattern recognition and identification of meaning. After the stimulus is recognized, it may be further elaborated— a word, sight, or smell may trigger associations, images, or stories on the basis of the individual's past experience with that particular stimulus. The levels-of-processing theory claims that analysis proceeds through a series of sensory states to levels associated with pattern recognition to semantic-associative stages.

Each level of analysis results in a different memory trace—but a

---

Box 6.1. It Flies

Four years ago when B. F. Goodrich Co. launched its ad campaign directed against Goodyear Tire and Rubber Co., many ad people said it wouldn't fly.

The point of the exercise was to inform the public about the sometimes overlooked company and its products by employing a whimsical touch.

Not only did the campaign fly, said Patrick C. Ross, president of Goodrich's tire division, it set records in consumer recall, brand awareness and brand preference.

The Goodrich campaign was met with a mixed and sometimes hostile reaction from the business and advertising community. Malcomb Forbes, publisher of Forbes magazine, called it "dumb advertising," while New York adman Al Ries, prominent supporter of the positioning doctrine, said Goodrich would have been better off changing its name.

Even the blimp, long the symbol of Goodyear, was dragged into the fray. Goodrich ads and posters pictured a clear blue sky, saying that it was the tire company WITHOUT the blimp.

But Ross said last week that the straight talk and humor of the ad effort was credible to the public and got through the psychological barriers in the audience.

Since the campaign began, consumer awareness of Goodrich is up 122% and preference for the company's radial tires is up 85%, he said. Large gains also were made in the perception of Goodrich as the most innovative tire company and recognition that the firm was the first U.S. maker of radials, he added.

From the *Plain Dealer,* Cleveland, May 8, 1977. © 1977 by the *Plain Dealer,* Cleveland, Ohio. Reprinted by permission.

---

memory trace that varies in its decay rate. The memory code and its persistence are therefore both by-products of perceptual processing. When only the physical features of a stimulus have been analyzed, the memory trace is fragile and quickly decays. When the stimulus has been identified and named, the memory trace is stronger and can be represented by an intermediate decay rate. Memory is best when a person elaborates the meaning of the stimulus.

The levels-of-processing theory is a theory of control processes or strategies—of the way we analyze the stimulus and of the memory codes that result from different levels of analysis. Unlike the Atkinson-Shiffrin (1968) theory, it is not concerned with the structural components or stages of memory; the two theories, therefore, can coexist. Craik (1979b) has recently stated that the point of most levels-of-processing studies has been to gain a fuller understanding of memory codes operating in LTM, not to deny the distinction between STM and LTM. When viewed from this perspective, the work on levels of processing extends rather than replaces a stage analysis by showing how control processes can influence the retention of material.

Implications for Verbal Rehearsal

We saw in the previous chapter that the Atkinson-Shiffrin model emphasized verbal rehearsal as a means of transferring information from STM to LTM. Since most of us have used this method to learn material, the role of rehearsal in learning seems intuitively attractive. But rehearsal does not automatically result in learning, according to Craik and Lockhart. The effectiveness of rehearsal, like other methods of study, depends on the level at which material is processed. The reason rehearsal often results in learning is that people usually attend to the meaning of the material during rehearsal.

Nor is rehearsal always used for learning. Sometimes it is used to maintain information in STM, as when we dial a telephone number. Would rehearsal result in learning if people used it simply to maintain items in STM? Does rehearsal automatically result in learning, or are there different kinds of rehearsal, only some of which promote learning? To answer these questions, Craik and Watkins (1973) asked people to perform a fairly simple task. Students were instructed to listen to a series of word lists and, at the end of each list, to report the last word beginning with a particular letter. The experimenter told them the critical letter before each list and assumed that they would maintain a word starting with that letter in STM until they heard another word beginning with that letter or the list ended. The task was quite easy, and students almost always gave the correct answer at the end of the list.

The purpose of the experiment was to vary the length of time a word would have to be maintained in STM. For example, if *g* were the critical letter and the list contained, in order, the words *daughter, oil, rifle, garden, grain, table, football, anchor,* and *giraffe,* the word *garden* would be immediately replaced by *grain,* which would eventually be replaced by *giraffe.* Since there are no intervening words between *garden* and *grain,* but three intervening words between *grain* and *giraffe, grain* would have to be maintained in STM for a longer time than *garden.* The word *grain* should therefore be rehearsed more often than *garden.* Craik and Watkins controlled the amount of time a word would have to be maintained in STM by varying the number of intervening (noncritical) words from 0 to 12. If maintenance rehearsal results in learning, the probability of recalling a word at the end of the experiment should be a function of the length of time it was maintained in STM.

After hearing 27 lists of words, the students were asked to recall as many words as they could from all the lists. Craik and Watkins found that the probability of recalling a word was independent of the length of time it was maintained in STM. To consider the two extreme cases, students recalled 12% of the words that were immediately replaced in STM by the next word on the list and 15% of the words that were maintained over 12 intervening words.

The small difference between 12% and 15% shows that rehearsal does not automatically cause learning. According to the levels-of-processing view of memory, the students did not attempt to form a lasting memory code because they thought they would only have to remember the word over a very short period of time. In particular, they did not emphasize the meaning of the words. A good analogy might be reading the words in a book without thinking about what you are reading. You would be rehearsing the words in the sense that you would be covertly pronouncing them, but your thoughts might be on yesterday's football game or tonight's party. Suddenly you realize that you can't remember what you just read because you weren't thinking about what it meant. Let's look now at the evidence that the way material is processed determines what kind of memory code is formed, which in turn determines how well the material is remembered.

Supporting evidence

The Hyde-Jenkins Experiment

The influence of levels of processing on retention was nicely demonstrated in a study by Hyde and Jenkins (1969) at the University of Minnesota. Their results were published several years before Craik and Lockhart's theory and most likely influenced its development. Like most of the studies used later to test the levels-of-processing theory, Hyde and Jenkins's used an incidental learning paradigm. In an incidental learning task people are given some material but are not told that they have to learn it. The experimenter then later gives them a recall or recognition test on the items presented during the experiment. In an intentional learning task, by contrast, the subjects are explicitly told to learn the material.

The first experiment in Hyde and Jenkins's study compared seven groups of subjects, but we will consider only four to simplify the discussion. One of the four groups was given an intentional learning task in which the subjects were asked to try to remember 24 words. The words consisted of 12 pairs of primary associates—words that are highly associated. For example, the word *red* is highly associated with the word *green,* and *table* is highly associated with *chair.* The 24 words were presented in a random order, with the restriction that primary associates could not occur together in the list. After the subjects in the "intentional" group had listened to a tape recording of the 24 words, they attempted to recall as many as they could, in any order.

The other three groups were incidental learning groups who were not informed that they should try to remember the words. They heard the same recording of 24 words but were asked to make a judgment about each item on the list. One group simply rated the words as pleasant or unpleasant, another group judged whether each word contained the letter *e,* and a third group estimated the number of letters in each word. The purpose of using three judgment groups was to try to create different levels of processing. The first group would have to consider the meaning of the words. The latter two groups would have to consider the spelling of the words; the meaning of the words would be irrelevant to them. Since, according to the levels-of-processing theory, semantic processing should result in better recall than nonsemantic processing, the undergraduates who rated the pleasantness of the words should show better recall than those who considered the spelling of the words.

The results supported the prediction. The average number of words recalled was 16.3 for those students who rated pleasantness, 9.9 for the students who estimated the number of letters, and 9.4 for the students who judged the presence of the letter *e.* The most striking aspect of the results is that students in the pleasant-unpleasant group recalled virtually as many words as those students who were instructed to try to learn the words (16.3 versus 16.1). In other words, incidental learning was as efficient as intentional learning when the students considered the meaning of the words.

We have been assuming, along with Hyde and Jenkins, that differences in recall among the three incidental groups were caused by the possibility that the students in the pleasant-unpleasant group were more likely to attend to the meaning of the words than students in the other two groups. Do we have any direct evidence for this assumption? The fact that the list consisted of pairs of words that are semantically related provides a clue. Recognizing that words are related in meaning can make it easier to recall them. For example, the recall of *green* may remind a person that *red* was also on the list. One indication that people were attending to the meaning of words would be if they recalled the primary associates together—*red* followed by *green* or vice versa.

Hyde and Jenkins defined the percentage of clustering as the number of associated pairs recalled together, divided by the total number of words recalled. The amount of clustering was 26% for the group that made judgments about the letter *e,* 31% for the group that estimated the number of letters, 64% for the group that was told to study words, and 68% for the group that judged the pleasantness of the words. These results support the assumption that groups differed in how much they used meaning to aid recall. Those groups that were the most sensitive to the meaning recalled the most words.

Structural, Phonemic, and Semantic Processing

Tests of the levels-of-processing theory have generally focused on three levels—the structural, phonemic and semantic. Table 6.2 shows

TABLE 6.2. Typical Questions Used in Levels-of-Processing Studies.

Level of processing	Question	Answer Yes	No
Structural	Is the word in capital letters?	TABLE	table
Phonemic	Does the word rhyme with WEIGHT?	crate	MARKET
Category	Is the word a type of fish?	SHARK	heaven
Sentence	Would the word fit the sentence "He met a _____ in the street"?	FRIEND	cloud

From "Depth of Processing and the Retention of Words in Episodic Memory," by F. I. M. Craik and E. Tulving. In *Journal of Experimental Psychology: General*, 1975, *104*, 268–294. Copyright 1975 by the American Psychological Association. Reprinted by permission.

examples of questions that have been asked in order to emphasize different levels of coding. The structural question asks whether the word is in capital letters. Coding at the phonemic level is encouraged by asking whether a word rhymes with another word—the question emphasizes pronunciation. Questions about whether a word is a member of a certain category or whether it fits into a sentence encourage coding at the semantic level—a person must evaluate the meaning in order to answer correctly.

In a series of experiments conducted by Craik and Tulving (1975) one of the questions preceded each brief exposure of a word. The participants were informed that the experiment concerned perception and speed of reaction. After a series of question and answer trials, the subject was unexpectedly given a retention test for the exposed words. Craik and Tulving anticipated that memory would vary systematically with depth of processing.

Figure 6.1 shows the results from one of Craik and Tulving's experiments that used a recognition test. When students were asked which words were presented during the initial judgment task, they recognized the most words when they had initially judged whether the word fit into a sentence and the fewest words when they had initially judged whether the letters were upper- or lowercase. Recognition accuracy was at an intermediate level when the students were asked whether one word rhymed with another. The findings supported the prediction that retention would increase as processing proceeded from the structural to the phonemic to the semantic level. The same pattern of results occurred when Craik and Tulving used a recall, rather than a recognition, test. Questions about a word's meaning resulted in better memory than those about either a word's sound or the physical characteristics of its letters.

The left half of Figure 6.1 shows the average response time required to answer the three different kinds of questions. The "case" questions

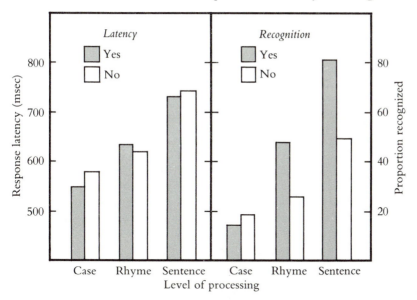

Figure 6.1. Initial decision latency and recognition performance for words as a function of the initial task. *(From "Depth of Processing and the Retention of Words in Episodic Memory," by F. I. M. Craik and E. Tulving. In* Journal of Experimental Psychology: General, *1975, 104, 268–294. Copyright 1975 by the American Psychological Association. Reprinted by permission.)*

could be answered most quickly, followed by the "rhyme" questions, followed by the "sentence" questions. Although the recognition results on the right can be predicted from the response times on the left, it is not always true that slower responses lead to better memory. It is possible to design a structural decision task that results in slow responses and poor retention.

Imagine that an experimenter shows you a card with a five-letter word such as *stoop* or *black*. Your task is to respond positively if the word consists of two consonants followed by two vowels followed by a consonant, and negatively for any other sequence of consonants and vowels. As you might guess, your response times would be relatively slow. In fact, it takes about twice as long to make this kind of structural decision as to make a semantic decision about whether a word fits into a sentence. If good retention is caused by long response times, the structural processing should now result in better retention than the semantic processing. However, recognition is still much better after semantic processing, proving that the level of processing, and not the time spent processing, is the best determinant of retention.

Criticisms and modifications

Criticisms

The levels-of-processing theory has had a major impact on memory research: many investigators designed studies to explicitly test its implications; others found it a convenient framework in which to discuss their results. As much of this research was quite supportive of the theory, it wasn't until about five years after the Craik and Lockhart paper that psychologists began to seriously question the usefulness of the theory (Baddeley, 1978; Eysenck, 1978; Nelson, 1977). One of the main criticisms was that it was too easy to account for differential rates of forgetting by appealing to the theory. An investigator could always claim that differences in rates of forgetting were caused by differences in level of processing, which was an example of circular reasoning.

In order to avoid circular reasoning, it is necessary to be able to measure depth of processing independently of retention. The argument that depth increases from structural to phonemic to semantic processing appealed to most psychologists because it is consistent with the ordering of the information-processing stages shown in Figure 1.1 (Chapter 1). Analyzing the physical structure of a pattern leads to retrieving its name, which in turn leads to considering its meaning by retrieving stored associations from LTM. One problem with this assumption is that, although this sequence provides a reasonable account of how information is analyzed, it is not a *necessary* sequence (Baddeley, 1978; Craik, 1979b). Although Craik and Lockhart originally hoped that encoding time would provide an independent measure of depth of processing, we have seen that this measure has its limitations (Craik & Tulving, 1975).

Another difficulty with the concept of depth of processing is that, even if we had an objective ordering of the "depth" of different memory codes, it still would not tell us why some codes are more effective than others. Why are semantic codes better than phonemic codes and phonemic codes better than structural codes? Psychologists have suggested two possible answers. One is that memory codes differ in how elaborate they are, and more elaborate codes result in better memory. The other is that memory codes differ in distinctiveness, and more distinctive codes result in better memory.

Elaboration

One explanation of how memory codes differ proposes that they differ in the number and types of elaborations stored in memory (Anderson & Reder, 1979). This view assumes that people store much more than simply the items presented to them by forming additional associations to help them remember the items. Anderson and Reder have proposed that, although it is very easy to elaborate material at the semantic level, it is difficult to construct elaborations at the structural or phonemic level. Most of the associations we have are concerned with meaning rather than with the physical structure of letters, spelling, or pronunciation. They suggest that the reason for this difference is that people usually try to remember the meaning of what they read rather than such details as what the letters looked like. As a consequence, people have learned to elaborate on the semantic content because it is generally more useful than elaborating on nonsemantic content.

One virtue of the elaboration hypothesis is that it provides a possible explanation of how differences can occur within a particular level of processing (Craik, 1979b). Although the original levels-of-processing proposal predicted that semantic processing should be superior to nonsemantic processing, it could not account for differences in retention for two different semantic tasks. The elaboration hypothesis predicts that such differences should occur if the two tasks differ in the extent of semantic elaboration.

This prediction was tested in a study at Wayne State University (Klein & Saltz, 1976). Undergraduates were given a semantic orienting task similar to the one used by Hyde and Jenkins (1969), but some of the students rated words along two semantic dimensions rather than only one. If the task required judging the word on two different dimensions—such as pleasant-unpleasant and big-little—students chose the appropriate adjective from each dimension and wrote the two adjectives after each word. After completing the judgment task, they were unexpectedly asked to recall all the words. Words that were rated on two dimensions were recalled significantly more often than words that were rated on only a single dimension, suggesting that the improved recall was caused by a greater amount of semantic elaboration. When people rated a word along two dimensions, they considered it from two different perspectives.

Another method for increasing semantic elaboration is to provide a richer, more elaborate context. This approach is illustrated by one of the experiments in the Craik and Tulving (1975) study. The experiment tested for the recall of words following a semantic judgment task in which people determined whether a word would fit into a sentence frame. There were three levels of sentence complexity—simple, medium, and complex. For example:

Simple. She cooked the _____.
Medium. The ripe _____ tasted delicious.
Complex. The small lady angrily picked up the red _____.

After completing 60 judgments, subjects were asked to recall as many words as they could from the initial phase of the experiment. They were then shown the original sentence frames and asked to recall the word associated with each sentence. The first part of the recall task is called *noncued recall* and the second part is called *cued recall* because students could use the sentence frames as retrieval cues. Figure 6.2 shows the proportion of words recalled as a function of sentence complexity. Sentence complexity had a significant effect on recalling words that did fit the sentence. This was true for both cued recall (CR-yes) and noncued recall (NCR-yes), although the effect was greater for cued recall. The effect of sentence complexity supported Craik and Tulving's hypothesis that more complex sentence frames would produce a more elaborate memory code and improve recall.

The more elaborate code was ineffective, however, if the word did not fit the sentence. This finding suggests that the elaboration must be consistent with the meaning of the word in order to be effective. Even when elaboration is generally consistent with the meaning of a word, it can vary in effectiveness depending on how precisely it relates to the word's meaning. Imagine that you read the sentence *The fat man read the sign*. Sometime later someone shows you the same sentence with the word *fat* replaced by a blank and asks you to recall the missing word. If elaboration is effective, you might do better if you read an elaborated sentence such as

1. The fat man read the sign that was 2 feet high.
   or
2. The fat man read the sign warning about thin ice.

Although both sentences provide additional information, there is an important distinction between the two elaborations. The first is an *imprecise elaboration* because there is no apparent relation between the adjective *fat* and the height of the sign. The second is a *precise elaboration* because the relative danger of thin ice should depend on a person's weight.

Stein and Bransford (1979) tested the effectiveness of precise and imprecise elaboration by comparing four groups of students in an incidental learning task. Students in the control group read ten short sentences and were told that the purpose of the experiment was to measure sentence comprehensibility. The second and third groups of students also were told that the experiment was to measure comprehensibility. They read the same ten sentences elaborated by an additional phrase that was either precisely or imprecisely related to a target word in the sentence. A fourth group of students was told to generate their own elaborations so the experimenters could measure the probability of certain phrases being generated. At the end of the experiment everyone was shown the unelaborated sentences and asked to recall a missing target word.

Students in the control group recalled an average of 4.2 words, compared to 2.2 words for the imprecise elaboration group, 7.4 words

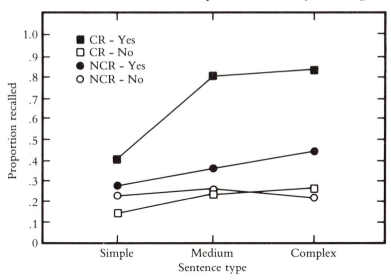

Figure 6.2. Proportion of words recalled as a function of sentence complexity. CR = cued recall; NCR = noncued recall. *(From "Depth of Processing and the Retention of Words in Episodic Memory," by F. I. M. Craik and E. Tulving. In* Journal of Experimental Psychology: General, *1975, 104, 268–294. Copyright 1975 by the American Psychological Association. Reprinted by permission.)*

for the precise elaboration group, and 5.8 words for the self-generation group. The results demonstrate that elaboration is not always effective in recall since imprecise elaboration actually caused a decline in performance relative to the control group. In order to be effective, the elaboration should clarify the significance or relevance of a concept (such as fat man) relative to the context (thin ice) in which it occurs.

The fact that recall following self-generation was intermediate between that for precise and imprecise elaboration suggests that the students' elaborations contained a mixture of each type. Two judges therefore divided the subject-generated elaborations into two groups (precise and imprecise), depending on whether the information clarified the relevance of the target words in the sentence. Students were able to recall 91% of the target words when they generated precise elaborations and 49% when they generated imprecise elaborations. A second experiment revealed that instructions were effective in encouraging subjects to generate precise elaborations. Subjects in the imprecise elaboration group were asked to elaborate with the question "What else might happen in this context?" Subjects in the precise elaboration group were prompted to elaborate with the question "Why might this man be engaged in this particular type of activity?" Students in the latter group recalled significantly more target words, indicating that elaboration is particularly effective when it is directed toward understanding the potential relevance of the presented information.

Distinctiveness

Memory codes can differ in distinctiveness as well as in the extent of elaboration. The term *distinctive* refers to how easy it is to distinguish one item from another. In order to remember something, we would like to make it really stand out from other items that could interfere with our memory. Elaboration is one possible strategy to make an item more distinctive, but the elaboration should emphasize characteristics that differentiate that item from other items (Eysenck, 1979).

You can probably think of events that are easy to recall because they were particularly distinctive. I once played a game of "cootie" with my two sons, who were then 3 and 4 years old. One threw the die and it landed in the toilet, an event that both thought was very funny. I was surprised when, a week later, they could both recall the number that they were trying to get at that time and the number they actually got. That particular event was different enough from all the other rolls of the die that the numbers before and after it did not interfere with their memory.

Release from proactive interference, discussed in Chapter 4, illustrates another means of improving recall in a memory task—shifting to a new semantic category. People recalled more items when the material changed from words to numbers or from numbers to words than when the material stayed the same. Recall also improved when the items changed from sports events to political events or from political events to sports events. All the changes made the material more distinct from preceding items.

The recall of nonsemantic material is also facilitated when it is made more distinct. The nonsemantic tasks studied by Hyde and Jenkins (1969) required that people make judgments about the spelling of a word, such as estimating its length or indicating whether it contains the letter *e*. Another characteristic of a word's spelling is called *orthographic distinctiveness*. A word is orthographically distinctive when it has an unusual shape —that is, sequencing of short and tall letters. Orthographically distinctive words include *lymph, khaki,* and *afghan.* Examples of orthographically common words are *leaky, kennel,* and *airway.* The first three words have unusual shapes, and the last three have more typical shapes.

When people are asked to recall a list of words, half of which are orthographically distinctive and half of which are orthographically common, they recall significantly more of the distinctive words (Hunt & Elliott, 1980). It is clear that the shape of the words, rather than some other factor, causes the results. When the same list is presented auditorily, rather than visually, there is no difference in recall. There is also no difference in recall when the words are typed in capital letters—people do not recall *LYMPH, KHAKI,* and *AFGHAN* any better than *LEAKY, KENNEL,* and *AIRWAY.* Apparently the different heights of lowercase letters contribute to the effect since all letters are the same height when they are capitalized.

Release from proactive interference and the effect of orthographic distinctiveness demonstrate that distinctiveness can account for different amounts of recall at a specific level of processing. Can distinctiveness account for different levels of recall between levels of processing? In order to demonstrate that distinctiveness can account for the levels-of-processing effect, it would be necessary to show that semantic codes are more distinct than phonemic codes and phonemic codes are more distinct than physical codes. Some research has already been directed toward the first comparison.

Several psychologists (Eysenck, 1979; Moscovitch & Craik, 1976) have argued that semantic codes result in better retention than phonemic codes because semantic codes are much more distinctive than phonemic codes. They base their argument on the assumption that there is a relatively small number of phonemes so phonemic codes necessarily overlap with each other, whereas the domain of possible meanings is essentially limitless.

In Chapter 4 we saw that a phonemic model of STM could account for acoustic confusions by assuming that phonemes can be forgotten independently (Laughery, 1969). Since many letters share a phoneme with other letters, the loss of a single phoneme can make it impossible to identify a letter uniquely. This overlap of phonemes is consistent with the view that phonemic codes are not very distinctive. The remainder of the argument—that there are many different semantic codes—has an intuitive appeal, but it would be strengthened if we could agree on what constitutes the set of semantic codes. Unfortunately, though the set of phonemic features is well defined, the set of semantic features is not.

One way of making memory codes less distinct at both the phonemic and the semantic level is to ask the same question repeatedly during an orienting task instead of asking a unique question for each word (Moscovitch & Craik, 1976). For example, one might preface each semantic judgment with the sentence form *The girl dropped the _____ on the floor.* Many words fit the context of the sentence, and they would all be evaluated in the same way—by considering if they could be dropped. The phonemic judgments might ask whether each word rhymed with *ring.* When the same questions were asked repeatedly, substantially fewer words were recalled after the semantic task than when each sentence was unique. However, the recall of words following the rhyming task was unaffected by whether or not the questions were unique. Moscovitch and Craik interpreted these results as supporting their hypothesis that semantic codes are more distinctive than phonemic codes and therefore are more affected by conditions that make them less distinctive. Since phonemic codes are less distinctive to begin with, they have less to lose—presumably because there is a considerable overlap of phonemes even when unique questions are asked.

The experimental study of elaboration and distinctiveness has modified the original conception of levels of processing (Craik, 1979b). Some of the original ideas have survived, however. The central idea that there are qualitative differences in memory codes, that different orienting tasks can determine which codes are emphasized, and that memory codes differ in their decay rate remains a useful conception of memory. The major shift in emphasis has been the attempt to provide a theoretical basis for these findings by determining how structural, phonemic, and semantic codes can differ in distinctiveness and elaboration.

Encoding specificity and retrieval

The Encoding Specificity Principle

The change in emphasis from "levels" to "elaboration" and "distinctiveness" was accompanied by another refinement in the theory. The original theory (Craik and Lockhart, 1972) had much to say about how words were coded but little about how they were retrieved. The usefulness of providing an appropriate context for facilitating retrieval is illustrated by the difference between positive and negative responses in Figure 6.1. Words that resulted in positive responses, because they either formed a rhyme or fit the context of a sentence, were recalled more often than words that resulted in negative responses. We have also seen that the use of more complex, elaborate sentence frames facilitated recall for positive responses but not for negative responses (Figure 6.2). This effect was particularly evident when the context was provided as a retrieval cue. Craik and Tulving (1975) interpreted this finding as support for their view that a more elaborate context is beneficial only when the test word is compatible with the context and forms an integrated unit. A complex sentence like *The small lady angrily picked up the red* _____ makes it easier to retrieve a positive response *(tomato)* but does not make it easier to retrieve a negative response *(walking)*.

These results show that, under certain conditions, some retrieval cues are more effective than others. A general answer to the question of what makes a retrieval cue effective is provided by the *encoding specificity principle,* which can be stated as follows: "Specific encoding operations performed on what is perceived determine what is stored, and what is stored determines what retrieval cues are effective in providing access to what is stored" (Tulving & Thomson, 1973, p. 369).

Let's dissect this definition into two parts. The first part states that memory traces differ not only in their durability but in the kind of information they contain. The second part states that the information memory traces contain determines what kind of retrieval information should facilitate their recovery. The first part is essentially equivalent to the levels-of-processing framework; the second part forces us to take a closer look at retrieval. The second part implies that it is possible to hold constant the encoding conditions of an item and still observe large differences in its recall, depending upon the retrieval conditions. The encoding and retrieval conditions can interact in the sense that a cue effective in one situation may or may not be effective in another.

Interaction between Encoding and Retrieval Operations

A study by Thomson and Tulving (1970) provided some initial support for the encoding specificity principle. It seems intuitively obvious that the effectiveness of a retrieval cue should depend on how closely the cue is associated with a test item. The following are good retrieval cues: *white* for *BLACK, meat* for *STEAK, dumb* for *STUPID, woman* for *MAN, ice* for *COLD,* and *dark* for *LIGHT.* People who are asked to remember *BLACK, STEAK, STUPID, MAN, COLD,* and *LIGHT* can recall more of these words if they are given the retrieval cues during the recall test. It is also intuitively obvious that weakly associated words do not make good retrieval cues—for example, *train* for *BLACK, knife* for *STEAK, lamb* for *STUPID, hand* for *MAN, blow* for *COLD,* and *head* for *LIGHT.* When people were given the weakly associated cues during the recall test, they recalled fewer words than subjects who were given no retrieval cues.

Tulving and Thomson demonstrated, however, that even ineffective retrieval cues can become effective if they are presented with the test words during the study session. When a weak associate was paired with a test word, it became a more effective retrieval cue than a strong associate. If people studied *train* and *BLACK* together, then the presentation of *train* during the recall test would more likely lead to the recall of *BLACK* than would the presentation of *white.* The effectiveness of a retrieval cue therefore depends on what occurs during the initial encoding of a word, as the encoding specificity hypothesis predicts.

A somewhat similar finding was reported by Light and Carter-Sobell (1970) using a recognition test. Subjects in their experiment were shown sentences that contained an adjective and a noun printed in capital letters. For example, they might see the sentence *The CHIP DIP tasted delicious*. They were informed that there would be a memory test on the adjective–noun phrases after they had read all the sentences. The recognition test required that they decide whether a noun appeared in the previous sentences. Some nouns on the recognition test were preceded by the same adjective *(CHIP DIP)*, some were preceded by a different adjective *(SKINNY DIP)*, and some were preceded by no adjective *(DIP)*. Presenting the same adjective resulted in better recognition of the noun than presenting no adjective, but presenting a different adjective resulted in worse recognition.

Perhaps one reason a different adjective produced a decline in performance is that the different adjective was consistent with an alternative meaning of the noun—*skinny dip* as opposed to *chip dip*. The experimenters argued that the adjective determines which semantic features of a noun are stored in memory. If their hypothesis is correct, then a different adjective that is consistent with the encoded meaning should be a more effective retrieval cue than a different adjective that is inconsistent with the encoded meaning. *Raspberry jam* should be a more effective retrieval cue than *traffic jam* if the original phrase were *strawberry jam*. The results supported the hypothesis, although the most accurate performance was still the condition in which the same adjective occurred during both the study and the test sessions.

The studies by Thomson and Tulving (1970) and Light and Carter-Sobell (1970) both investigated encoding specificity within the semantic domain. The first study demonstrated that an ineffective retrieval cue—a weak semantic associate—can become an effective retrieval cue if it is associated with a test item during the study session. The second study demonstrated that an adjective that preserves the semantic encoding of a word is more effective than an adjective that changes the semantic encoding.

Let us now consider how the encoding specificity principle applies when there are two different processing levels—semantic and phonemic. Imagine that you are in an experiment and have to respond positively or negatively to the question *associated with sleet?* You then see the word *hail* and respond positively. After making a series of judgments about rhymes and associations, you are given one of the following retrieval cues:

1. Associated with *sleet*
2. Associated with *snow*
3. Rhymes with *bail*

Which of the three retrieval cues do you think would be most helpful for retrieving the word *hail*?

We would probably agree that the first cue would be most effective because it is identical to the question asked during the encoding trials. But what about cues (2) and (3)? The second cue is similar to the original context since, like the initial question, it emphasizes semantic associations. The third cue, by contrast, emphasizes the phonemic code and is therefore different from the original context. The encoding specificity principle predicts that the original context is the best retrieval cue, a similar context is the next best cue, and a different context is the least effective cue. The results shown in Table 6.3 support this prediction (Fisher & Craik, 1977).

Now consider what might have happened if the word *hail* was preceded by the question *Rhymes with pail?* The same principle applies. Reproducing the exact context is the best cue, and providing a different context—a semantic association in this case—is the worst cue (see Table 6.3). The interaction between encoding and retrieval is illustrated by the fact that the effectiveness of a retrieval cue depends on how a word was coded. When its semantic characteristics were emphasized, a semantic cue was more effective than a phonemic cue. When its phonemic characteristics were emphasized, a phonemic cue was more effective than a semantic cue. In other words, the specific encoding of an item determines which retrieval cues are most effective for gaining access to what is stored—the encoding specificity principle.

Transfer-Appropriate Processing

A general implication of the encoding specificity principle is the use of *transfer-appropriate processing,* a term used by Morris, Bransford, and Franks (1977). The latter concept emphasizes that the value of a particular learning strategy is relative to a particular goal. Transfer-appropriate pro-

TABLE 6.3. Proportions of Words Recalled as a Function of the Similarity between the Encoding Context and Retrieval Cue.

	Rhyme	*Associate*
Encoding context		
Example: *hail*	Rhymes with *pail*	Associated with *sleet*
Retrieval context		
Identical	Rhymes with *pail* .24	Associated with *sleet* .54
Similar	Rhymes with *bail* .18	Associated with *snow* .36
Different	Associated with *sleet* .16	Rhymes with *bail* .22

From "Interaction between Encoding and Retrieval Operations in Cued Recall," by R. P. Fisher and F. I. M. Craik. In *Journal of Experimental Psychology: Human Learning and Memory,* 1977, *3,* 701–711. Copyright 1977 by the American Psychological Association. Reprinted by permission.

cessing implies that the quality and durability of a memory trace can only be determined relative to the testing situation. For example, if the test emphasized phonemic information and you had been concentrating on semantic information, you could be in trouble.

A situation from my own undergraduate education provides a good example of transfer-appropriate processing. I had taken three semesters of German in which there was very little emphasis on pronunciation, although we were occasionally asked to read aloud. I therefore did not attend very closely to the phonemic code but concentrated on the meaning of the passage so I could provide a correct translation. After three semesters I enrolled in a conversation course in which the emphasis was on correct pronunciation. I quickly learned how poorly I pronounced German words.

It's relatively rare, however, that we must emphasize the phonemic code since we are generally required to recall or recognize semantic information. Transfer-appropriate processing, therefore, usually means semantic processing. There are different ways to process material semantically, and knowledge of the test format should help you decide how to study. If the test is a multiple-choice test, it is likely that knowledge of details will be more useful than knowledge about the general organization of the material. If the test is an essay test, it is likely that a careful organization of the material will be more useful than knowledge of many details.

There is evidence to support the claim that students' performance on a test is influenced by the kind of test they expect. Half of the subjects in an experiment by d'Ydewalle and Rosselle (1978) expected a multiple-choice test, and half expected a series of open questions. Only some of the subjects in each group received the expected test, and those subjects did better than the subjects who received an unexpected test. Apparently each group used different learning strategies that were appropriate for the expected test.

Our discussion of different kinds of memory codes continues in the next chapter. So far the emphasis has been on verbal material, and I have said very little about visual knowledge. The next chapter examines the important role of visual imagery in performing many cognitive tasks.

Summary

The levels-of-processing theory proposes that how an item is encoded determines how long it can be remembered. Qualitatively different memory codes are established by asking people in an incidental learning task to make decisions about a word's physical structure, pronunciation, or meaning. When people are unexpectedly asked to recall the words, they recall the most words following semantic processing and the fewest words following structural processing. Further support for the theory is the finding that rehearsal does not necessarily result in learning, presumably because subjects do not attend to the meaning of words they only want to keep active in STM.

Although the theory originally proposed that retention is determined by the depth of processing (with physical, phonemic, and semantic processing, respectively, representing increasing depth), the failure to find an independent measure of depth resulted in an increasing emphasis on the elaborateness and distinctiveness of memory codes. The elaboration hypothesis claims that it is easier to retrieve more elaborate codes and easier to provide associations at the semantic level. The distinctiveness hypothesis claims that it is easier to retrieve distinctive codes and that semantic codes are more distinctive than phonemic codes. Studies of elaborateness and distinctiveness using semantic material have demonstrated that increasing either one results in improved recall. Making the semantic context more elaborate (by using complex sentences) or making words more distinctive (by shifting to a new semantic category) increases the number of words recalled.

The encoding specificity principle states that the effectiveness of a retrieval cue is determined by how well it corresponds to the characteristics of the memory trace. When the memory trace emphasizes semantic characteristics, a semantic cue is the most effective; when the memory trace emphasizes phonemic information, a phonemic cue is most effective. The best retrieval cue is one that exactly duplicates the original context, and for the cue to be at all effective, the item should fit the context.

Transfer-appropriate processing emphasizes the need to form memory codes that will be useful relative to the context in which they will be retrieved. Although transfer-appropriate processing is usually semantic processing, some situations may require an emphasis on nonsemantic codes.

Recommended reading

The book edited by Cermak and Craik (1979) contains many excellent chapters on how the levels-of-processing concept evolved during the 1970s. Bransford's (1979) book *Human Cognition* includes a discussion of research on the levels-of-processing approach to memory. Another factor influencing memory—the amount of cognitive effort used during an orienting task—is discussed by Tyler, Hertel, McCallum, and Ellis (1979). Paivio's dual coding theory, which is discussed in the next chapter, has also been used to explain the levels-of-processing effect (D'Agostino, O'Neill, & Paivio, 1977).

7

Visual Images

Mental imagery has long played a central role in psychologists' and philoso-phers' accounts of cognitive processes and the representation of knowledge in the mind. The construct of the image, however, has never been oper-ationalized well enough to satisfy most psychologists, and so it is not sur-prising that imagery has disappeared periodically from the mainstream of Western psychology. Nevertheless, the concept has such magnetism that it has never stayed away for long, and it is currently enjoying remarkable pop-ularity.

STEPHEN KOSSLYN AND JAMES POMERANTZ (1977)

The discussion in the preceding chapters emphasized verbal knowledge. The stimuli studied usually consisted of items that could be easily as-signed a verbal label, such as words, letters, digits, or even nonsense syllables. We may question, however, whether we assign verbal labels to everything we perceive. Some events may be hard to describe verbally and others simply may be easier to remember as an image. Although images can exist for each of the sensory modalities, psychologists have been primarily interested in visual images. This chapter considers how visual images contribute to knowledge.

A distinction between verbal knowledge and visual or spatial knowl-edge is often made on intelligence tests. Verbal knowledge is usually measured by vocabulary questions or questions that test comprehension of written material. Spatial knowledge is usually measured by per-formance of such operations as mentally folding connected squares into a cube or mentally rotating an object to determine whether it matches another object. Although most tests place a much greater emphasis on verbal knowledge than spatial knowledge, some specialized tests contain rather difficult questions on spatial transformations. One example is the Dental Admissions Test, used to help select applicants to dental schools. Since spatial skills are very useful in dentistry, the test includes some challenging problems on spatial relations. People would presumably answer the question illustrated in Figure 7.1 by forming a visual image of the object and rotating the image to align it with the openings.

The study of visual imagery has been one of the main contributions of cognitive psychology. However, psychologists ignored imagery for many years because of the influence of John B. Watson's *Behaviorism* (1924), which was dedicated to wiping out the study of mental events. Watson argued that only behavior could be objectively studied, an argument that certainly had some merit but almost completely eliminated the study of mental processes such as visual imagery. It wasn't until the 1960s that psychologists once again began to try to understand the role of visual images in the acquisition of knowledge. Visual imagery is still difficult to study because it cannot be directly observed, but research over the past two decades has provided strong evidence that visual images are used in performing many tasks.

The first section of this chapter presents some evidence for visual images. The results of the experiments would be difficult to explain if we believed that all knowledge was verbal. The second section argues that forming visual images is an effective method for remembering information. However, the formation of a visual image is much easier for concrete material than for abstract material, and we will examine the implications of this finding. For many centuries people have recognized the potential usefulness of imagery in aiding memory, and many mnemonic strategies are based on visual imagery. The third section describes several memory strategies and shows how they can be used to learn names of people, foreign languages, and lists of items. The final section shows that even visual images have limitations. Fortunately, their lack of detail usually doesn't restrict their usefulness.

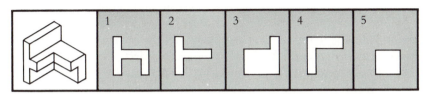

Figure 7.1. A sample question from the Dental Admissions Test. Students must select the opening through which the object at the far left could pass. *(Reproduced with permission from the American Dental Association.)*

Evidence for images

Although psychologists have seldom questioned that images exist, some have questioned the usefulness of images as explanatory constructs. The most influential paper challenging the usefulness of images in psychological theories was written by Pylyshyn (1973). Pylyshyn argued that it was misleading to think of images as uninterpreted photographs, analogous to pictures in the head. He supported the alternative view that an image is much closer to being a description of a scene than a picture of it. The emphasis on the descriptive characteristics of images, rather than their sensory characteristics, is the central theme of a *propositional theory*.

Kosslyn and Pomerantz (1977) agreed with Pylyshyn that images are interpreted and organized, but they argued that we often process images in the same way that we process perceptual information. In response to Pylyshyn's paper, they summarized five experimental findings that they thought could be better explained on the basis of imagery than non-sensory information. Two of the five findings were concerned with scanning visual images, a task studied by Kosslyn and his associates. We will look first at one variable influencing scanning time—the effect of distance between objects. We will then examine the other three findings on visual matching, mental rotation, and selective interference.

Scanning Visual Images

Many explanations of performance based on visual imagery assume that an image is a spatial representation analogous to the experience of seeing an object during visual perception. Furthermore, many of the operators that are used in analyzing visual patterns are also used to analyze visual images (Kosslyn & Pomerantz, 1977). One such operator is visual scanning. The analogy between pictures and images suggests that the time it takes to scan between two objects in an image should be a function of their distance from each other. Evidence obtained by Kosslyn, Ball, and Reiser (1978) supports this prediction.

One of their experiments required that undergraduates at Johns Hopkins University learn the exact locations of the objects shown in Figure 7.2. The map was then removed, and the students were given a series of trials that began with the name of an object. The task required they form a mental image of the entire map and focus on the named object. Subjects then heard the name of a second object and scanned the map in the way they had been instructed—by imagining a black speck moving in a straight line from the first object to the second. When they reached the second object, they pushed a button that stopped a clock. There are 21 possible distances among the seven objects, and the longest distance is nine times greater than the shortest distance. If distance deter-

Figure 7.2. A fictional map used to study the effect of distances on mental scanning time. *(From "Visual Images Preserve Metric Spatial Information: Evidence from Studies of Image Scanning," by S. M. Kosslyn, T. M. Ball, and B. J. Reiser. In* Journal of Experimental Psychology: Human Perception and Performance, *1978, 4, 47–60. Copyright 1978 by the American Psychological Association. Reprinted by permission.)*

mines the scanning time, as predicted, reaction time should be a linear function of the distance between two locations. Figure 7.3 shows how closely the prediction was supported.

The results demonstrate that images, like pictures, preserve the spatial relations among objects. However, there is also evidence that the spatial relations can be ignored if subjects are not explicitly asked to scan their image at a constant rate. Lea (1975) presented a map that was somewhat similar to Kosslyn's, except that the objects were arranged in a circle. The locations were not evenly spaced around the circle—some were close together and some were far apart. Subjects in Lea's experiment were given the name of an object and had to indicate the name of another object that was *n* locations away (in either a clockwise or a counter-clockwise direction). The time required to answer the question was a linear function of the number of locations that had to be considered (*n*), but it was not influenced by the distance between locations. Although subjects had learned the distances separating the objects, the distances were not needed to carry out the task. Since the subjects were not explicitly instructed to base their answers on a visual image, it is quite likely that

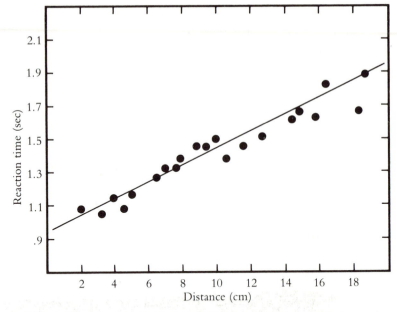

Figure 7.3. Scanning time between all pairs of locations on the imaged map. *(From "Visual Images Preserve Metric Spatial Information: Evidence from Studies of Image Scanning," by S. M. Kosslyn, T. M. Ball, and B. J. Reiser. In* Journal of Experimental Psychology: Human Perception and Performance, *1978, 4, 47–60. Copyright 1978 by the American Psychological Association. Reprinted by permission.)*

they ordered the objects in a verbal list and answered the questions by scanning the list.

The contrasting results of the two experiments demonstrate the flexibility that people have in being able to use either a visual code or a verbal code. The results shown in Figure 7.3 suggest that, when a task emphasizes spatial information, people can scan an image in a way that preserves spatial information. When the task requires the retrieval of verbal information, scanning a list that ignores spatial information is more efficient.

Sequential versus Parallel Processing

One difference between information maintained in a visual image and information maintained as a verbal code is that a visual image makes it possible to match information in parallel. When you look at the schematic faces in Figure 7.4, you can perceive many features of the faces simultaneously. However, when you describe these same features verbally, you do not have access to all the features at the same time because language is sequential. You have to decide the order in which you describe each feature.

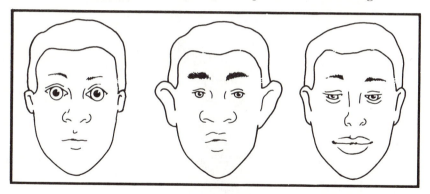

Figure 7.4. Three sample faces illustrating size differences of feature values. *(From "Representation and Retrieval Processes in Short-Term Memory: Recognition and Recall of Faces," by E. E. Smith and G. D. Nielsen. In* Journal of Experimental Psychology, *1970, 85, 397–405. Copyright 1970 by the American Psychological Association. Reprinted by permission.)*

The parallel representation of spatial information and the sequential representation of verbal information influences how quickly a person can determine whether a perceived pattern matches a memorized pattern. If the memorized pattern is stored as a visual image, the match should occur quickly and be relatively uninfluenced by the number of features that have to be matched. If a pattern is stored as a verbal description, the match should occur more slowly and be influenced by the number of features that have to be compared.

Nielsen and Smith (1973) tested these predictions by showing students either a picture of a schematic face or its verbal description. There were five features of the face—ears, eyebrows, eyes, nose, and mouth—that varied in size. Each of the features could assume one of three values—large, medium, or small (see Figure 7.4 for an example). After students studied either the description or the picture for 4 seconds, the stimulus was removed. Following a retention interval that lasted either 4 or 10 seconds, the experimenters presented a test face and the students decided whether it matched the face or description presented earlier.

In order to test the prediction that the number of features would influence reaction time only when people compared the test face to a verbal description, Nielsen and Smith varied the number of relevant features from three to five. The students knew that they could ignore the ears and eyebrows when there were three relevant features because these features never changed, and they could ignore the ears when there were four relevant features. But they had to compare all five features when all five were relevant. Figure 7.5 shows the amount of time needed to respond that either the initial face (Task FF) or description (Task DF) matched the test face. The response times indicate that matching was

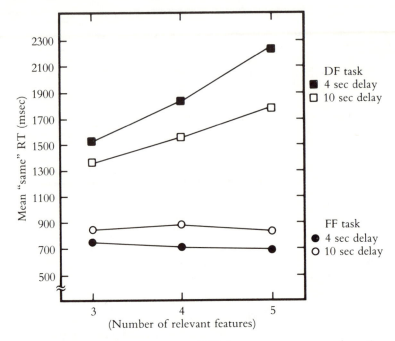

Figure 7.5. Mean reaction time (RT) for correct responses when stimuli were the same, as a function of the task, delay, and number of relevant features. *(From "Imaginal and Verbal Representations in Short-Term Recognition of Visual Forms," by G. D. Nielsen and E. E. Smith. In* Journal of Experimental Psychology, *1973, 101, 375–378. Copyright 1973 by the American Psychological Association. Reprinted by permission.)*

relatively fast and independent of the number of relevant features only when the initial item was a visual pattern.

The results imply that, when a person can maintain a visual image of a pattern in STM, a second visual pattern can be compared to it very quickly. It's almost as if the person is superimposing the two patterns and comparing all the features simultaneously. When the features are verbally described, a match requires sequentially retrieving information from the description, such as large ears, small eyebrows, small eyes, medium nose, and large mouth. Each feature on the list is individually compared to the corresponding feature on the test face. The response time therefore increases as a function of the number of relevant features on the list. The reaction time functions for the DF task in Figure 7.5 may remind you of the reaction time functions found in the Sternberg memory scanning task (Figure 4.10, Chapter 4). The similarity is not surprising since both tasks require that people sequentially scan a list of items in STM. The maintenance of an image in the FF task avoids a list of separate items by combining the individual features on the list into a single integrated pattern. The efficiency with which this integrated pattern can be compared to other visual patterns is an important difference between a visual image and a verbal description.

Mental Rotation

Deciding if two patterns match is considerably more difficult if they differ in orientation. The task shown in Figure 7.6 requires judging whether the two patterns in each pair are the same object (Shepard & Metzler, 1971). The two patterns of pairs A and B are different orientations of the same pattern, but pair C consists of two different patterns. One method for determining whether two patterns are identical is to rotate one pattern mentally until it has the same orientation as the other pattern. When both patterns have the same orientation, it is easier to determine whether they match.

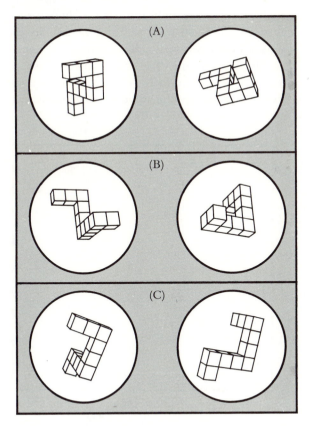

Figure 7.6. Examples of pairs of patterns differing in orientation. *(From "Mental Rotation of Three Dimensional Objects," by R. N. Shepard and J. Metzler. In* Science, *1971, 171, 701–703. Copyright 1971 by the American Association for the Advancement of Science. Reprinted by permission.)*

The pairs used by Shepard and Metzler differed in orientation from 0 degrees to 180 degrees in 20-degree steps. Half of the pairs could be rotated to match each other, and half of the pairs were mirror images that did not match. Figure 7.7 shows that the time required to decide that two patterns were identical increased linearly with an increase in the number of degrees they differed in orientation, suggesting the subjects were rotating a visual image of one of the forms until it had the same orientation as the other form. Self-reports were consistent with this interpretation: subjects reported that they imagined one object rotating until it had the same orientation as the other and that they could rotate an image only up to a certain speed without losing its structure.

Similar results occur when people have to make judgments about familiar patterns. Cooper and Shepard (1973) showed subjects letters of the alphabet and asked them to indicate whether the pattern was a normal letter *(R)* or its mirror image *(Я)*. Response times depended on how much the pattern was rotated from its normal upright position. Response times were shortest when the pattern was upright and longest when the pattern was upside down or rotated 180 degrees. However, response times were not a linear function of the angle of rotation, as was found for the block patterns. A 60-degree increase in rotation increased response time more between 120 degrees and 180 degrees than between 0 degrees and 60 degrees.

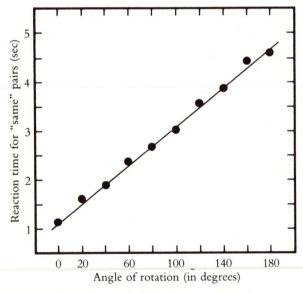

Figure 7.7. Reaction time to judge that two patterns have the same three-dimensional shape. *(From "Mental Rotation of Three Dimensional Objects," by R. N. Shepard and J. Metzler. In* Science, *1971, 171, 701–703. Copyright 1971 by the American Association for the Advancement of Science. Reprinted by permission.)*

A plausible explanation of why letters are less affected by small degrees of rotation than block patterns are is that letters may appear to be upright even when they are slightly rotated (Hock & Tromley, 1978). Some letters (such as *F*) can be rotated more than others (such as *G*) and still appear upright. Hock and Tromley used the physical characteristics of letters to classify them into sets that should appear either tilted or upright when slightly rotated. The "tilted" letters produced results that were similar to block patterns. Since these letters are very sensitive to orientation, response time to decide whether the letter was normal or reversed increased as a linear function of rotation. The "upright" letters produced results similar to those obtained by Cooper and Shepard. Since these letters were less affected by small changes in orientation, decision time changed very little for small angles of rotation.

Interference

We have seen in earlier discussions that a major cause of forgetting is interference. The research on release from proactive interference (Wickens, 1972) demonstrated that interference could be reduced by shifting semantic categories. Interference can also be reduced by shifting between visual and verbal material, as was demonstrated in a study by Lee Brooks (1968).

In the visual task in this study, subjects were shown a block diagram of a letter (see Figure 7.8). The letter was then removed and the subjects had to use their memory of the letter to respond *yes* to each corner that was on the extreme top or bottom and *no* to each corner that was in between. The correct answer for the example, starting at the asterisk at the lower left and proceeding in the direction of the arrow, is *yes, yes, yes, no, no, no, no, no, no, yes.*

The verbal task in Brooks's experiment required that people respond

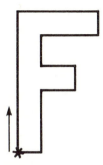

Figure 7.8. A block diagram of a letter. *(From "Spatial and Verbal Components of the Act of Recall," by L. R. Brooks. In* Canadian Journal of Psychology, *1968, 22, 349–368. Copyright 1968 by the Canadian Psychological Association. Reprinted by permission.)*

positively to each word in a sentence that was a noun. For example, people listened to the sentence *A bird in the hand is not in the bush* and then classified each word as a noun or a nonnoun. The correct answer for the example is *no, yes, no, no, yes, no, no, no, no, yes*.

Brooks assumed that his subjects would rely on a verbal code to maintain the sentence in memory and a visual image to maintain the block diagram in memory. If his assumption is correct, it should be possible to interfere selectively with performance by using two different methods of responding. One method required that the answers be given verbally, by overtly responding *yes* or *no*. A verbal response should cause a greater conflict when classifying the words of a sentence than when classifying the corners of a block diagram. Another method required that a subject point to a *Y* for each positive response and an *N* for each negative response, using a diagram like the one shown in Figure 7.9. The diagram shows the correct answers for classifying the words in the sample sentence. Pointing to the correct letter requires close visual monitoring and should interfere more with the block task than with the sentence task.

The selective nature of interference is revealed by the average response time required to complete each task. Classifying the words in a sentence required more time when people gave a verbal response; classifying the corners of a letter required more time when people pointed to the correct response. In other words, giving a verbal response interfered more with memory for verbal material (a sentence) than with memory for visual material (a block diagram), and vice versa.

The selective nature of interference within a modality has implications for the number of items that can be maintained in STM. When we reviewed the evidence on STM capacity in Chapter 4, we looked at research that presented items from the same modality, such as a string of letters in a memory span task or different levels of brightness in an absolute judgment task. What would happen if we designed a memory span task in which some items could be retained by using a verbal code and other items could be retained by using a visual code? If there is a reduction in interference because of the variety, people should be able to recall more items.

An experiment by two Dutch psychologists (Sanders & Schroots, 1969) revealed that a person's memory span can, in fact, be increased by using material from two different modalities. One modality was the typical verbal modality, created by showing a string of consonants. The other modality was a visual or spatial modality, created by showing students a random sequence of lights on a two-dimensional light board. In the second condition students responded by pointing to the lights on the board in the correct order of their appearance.

The lack of interference between modalities suggests that people should be able to increase their memory span by storing the consonants

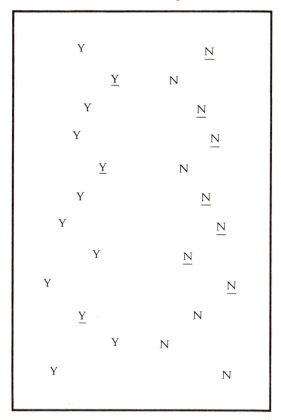

Figure 7.9. A sample answer sheet for responding *yes* or *no* in classifying words in the sample sentence. Correct responses are underscored.
*(From "Spatial and Verbal Components of the Act of Recall," by L. R.
Brooks. In* Canadian Journal of Psychology, *1968, 22, 349–368. Copyright 1968 by the Canadian Psychological Association. Reprinted by permission.)*

as a verbal code and the light sequence as a visual code. Recall was, in fact,
better when a sequence consisted of both visual and verbal items. For
example, when people were asked to recall a string of 11 consonants, they
correctly recalled an average of 5.4 items. When they were asked to recall
a string of 6 consonants followed by a string of 5 spatial positions, they
correctly recalled an average of 8.3 items. The improvement in recall was
not due to the possibility that spatial positions were easier to recall than
consonants as previous research had shown that recalling spatial positions
was actually more difficult. Rather, the findings were caused by the
relative lack of interference between the visual and verbal codes. The
results, along with those obtained by Brooks and many other psychologists, show that using two different modalities can reduce interference
and improve performance.

This research illustrates how visual images can be used to improve performance on many cognitive tasks, including preserving the spatial relations among different parts of a picture, lowering reaction time for processing spatial information, and reducing interference between visual and verbal codes. We will now look more closely at additional evidence that visual codes can be used effectively to improve recognition and recall.

Visual imagery and learning

You may be able to recall instances in which you relied on visual imagery to learn material. When I moved to Cleveland to begin an academic appointment at Case Western Reserve University, my home telephone number was 283-9157. I decided to learn the number by verbal rehearsal. I wrote it on a sheet of paper and rehearsed it several times before I was confident that I had learned it. After two days of unsuccessful practice, I decided to look for a different learning strategy.

My choice was influenced by the old "sing along with Mitch" routine, in which a bouncing ball appears over the words of a song. Where would the ball go if I pictured it bouncing over a sequence of numbers— 1 2 3 4 5 6 7 8 9? If you try it for the sequence 283-9157, you will see that it has a rather nice pendulum motion, swinging back and forth and ending up in the middle. Once I discovered this relationship, I immediately learned the number, and I have been able to reconstruct it even though it ceased being my number quite a few years ago.

This may be an unusual example of how the creation of an image can facilitate learning. But there are many other ways in which imagery is used in learning, as we will see in the next two sections. The most obvious example is when we attempt to remember pictures without having to translate the entire picture into words.

Memory for Pictures

One indication that visual imagery might provide an effective memory code is that people usually find it easier to recognize pictures than to recognize words. Roger Shepard (1967) was one of the first to demonstrate that recognition accuracy for visual material is very high. Subjects in his experiment viewed 612 pictures at a self-paced rate and were later given a recognition memory test on pairs of pictures. Each pair consisted of a picture they had previously seen and a novel picture. When they were tested two hours later, the participants were virtually perfect in identifying which member of the pair they had seen. Another group of participants, tested one week later, was still able to identify the correct picture in 87% of the pairs.

The high level of performance is partially a function of the easy test. We could remember very little about a picture itself and still be able to indicate which one of two possibilities had been presented. But when the same test was repeated using words instead of pictures, recognition accuracy wasn't as high. Subjects tested immediately after seeing the words could identify which one of two words had been presented in only 88% of the pairs (Shepard, 1967). Their level of performance on the immediate verbal test was about the same as when pictures were tested after a week's delay.

An experiment by Standing (1973) provided further evidence that it is easier to remember pictures than words. One group of dedicated subjects viewed 10,000 pictures over a five-day period. Immediately following the learning session on the fifth day, the participants were given a recognition memory test similar to the one designed by Shepard. Standing estimated the number of items they must have retained in memory in order to reach the level of performance they obtained on the test (taking into account the probability of guessing correctly). His estimate was that the participants must have remembered 6600 pictures. This estimate does not imply that the participants remembered all the details of a picture—but they did remember enough details to distinguish that picture from a novel picture.

Subjects in Standing's experiment were not shown 10,000 words for comparison, but other groups were shown 1000 words, 1000 ordinary pictures (such as a dog), or 1000 vivid pictures (such as a dog holding a pipe in its mouth). Two days later subjects attempted to identify which one of two possibilities occurred in the experiment. Standing estimated that the participants had retained enough information about 880 vivid pictures, 770 ordinary pictures, and 615 words to make the correct choice without guessing. The finding that recognition memory is better for pictures than for words replicates Shepard's results.

Images and Advertising

The finding that people are better at recognizing pictures than words should have important implications for a number of applied fields. Let's consider advertising as an example. Advertisers often spend a lot of money trying to convince people that they should purchase a product. Part of their task, particularly for a new or relatively unknown product, is to help people remember the name of the product. An ad may seem very interesting and even enjoyable, but it would not be effective if the potential buyer couldn't remember the name of the product that was advertised.

When I was a graduate student in Los Angeles, I participated in a marketing study that tested an audience's response to two new television shows scheduled to appear the following September. We were asked to rate the shows and a series of commercials that occurred between them. When the second show finished, the staff asked us to recall the names of the products that were advertised 30 minutes earlier. This was a surprisingly difficult task.

The possible role that imagery can play in advertising was studied by Lutz and Lutz (1977). Learning the names of products is an example of paired-associate learning, in which the advertiser wants us to associate the brand name with the product being advertised. Research on memory for pictures suggests that combining the product and brand name into a single interactive picture should facilitate recall of the brand. When people shop for that particular product, they may remember the picture of the product and the associated brand name.

Lutz and Lutz searched the Yellow Pages of a telephone directory to collect samples of two kinds of pictures: (1) an *interactive* illustration, which integrates the brand and product into a single illustration, and (2) a *noninteractive* illustration, which shows either the brand or the product by itself. The second type of illustration is the most common and usually includes a picture of the product with the brand name written next to it. Figure 7.10 shows two examples of interactive illustrations and two examples of noninteractive illustrations. The interactive illustrations combine the brand and product into a single picture, either by including an illustration of each (picture interaction) or by combining the illustration of a product and a letter of the brand name (letter accentuation). The noninteractive pictures contained either an illustration of the brand name or an illustration of the product.

The students' task was to learn to associate the company's brand name with its product or service. Each student was assigned to one of four groups consisting of two imagery groups (interactive and noninteractive) and their corresponding control groups. Students in each of the four groups studied 24 brand–product pairs for 10 seconds each. The interactive imagery group was shown pictures like the ones at the top of Figure 7.10. The control group had to learn the same pairs (such as Rocket Messenger Service or Dixon Crane Company) but saw only the words without the pictures. The noninteractive group saw a picture of either the product or the brand name, but the pictures were not shown to its control group.

In the recall test participants were given a list of the 24 products and asked to supply the appropriate brand name for each. The results of the test indicated that only the interactive pictures facilitated recall of the brand names. People in the interactive group recalled significantly more names than people who attempted to learn the same pairs without the pictures. However, this finding was based almost entirely on the picture

Interactive Imagery

Picture Interaction

Rocket Messenger Service

Letter Accentuation

Dixon Crane Co.

Non-interactive Imagery

Name

OBear Abrasive Saws

Product or Service

Figure 7.10. Interactive and noninteractive advertisements. *(From "Effects of Interactive Imagery on Learning: Applications to Advertising," by K. A. Lutz and R. J. Lutz.* In Journal of Applied Psychology, *1977, 62, 493–498. Copyright 1977 by the American Psychological Association. Reprinted by permission.)*

interaction condition; the letter accentuation condition was much less effective. People in the noninteractive group did not learn more pairs than the people in their control group.

The experimenters interpreted the results as supporting the use of pictures in ads—if the pictures form interactive images. Picture interaction is the most effective type of imagery, but it requires that both the product and the brand name be portrayable as pictures. This constraint is usually easy to satisfy for products but is more difficult for brand names unless the company has a name like Lincoln National Life or Bell Telephone. The fact that words vary in how easy they are to translate into images implies that the successful use of imagery depends on the nature of the material that has to be learned.

Effect of Material on Image Formation

The work of Alan Paivio at the University of Western Ontario established how the effectiveness of visual and verbal codes is influenced by the abstractness of material. Following an extensive series of studies, Paivio (1969) argued that there were two major ways a person could elaborate on material in a learning experiment. One form of elaboration emphasizes verbal associations. A word like *poetry* may result in many associations that could help you distinguish it from other words. You might think of different styles of poetry, specific poems, or experiences in an English class. We saw in the previous chapter that verbal associations helped people recall words in the Hyde and Jenkins (1969) experiment. People who considered the meaning of the words recalled primary associates together because recalling one word reminded them of its associate.

The other form of elaboration is creation of a visual image to represent a word. If I asked you to remember the word *juggler,* you might form an image of a person juggling three balls. If I asked you to remember the word *truth,* however, you would probably have difficulty forming an image. The difference between the two words is that the first refers to a concrete object and the second to an abstract concept. It is easy to form an image to represent a concrete object but difficult to form an image for an abstract concept. Paivio (1969) argued that the concrete–abstract dimension is the most important determinant of ease in forming an image. At the concrete end of the continuum are pictures because the picture itself can be remembered as a visual image and the person doesn't have to create an image. Pictures often result in better memory than concrete words, which usually result in better memory than abstract words.

If visual images and verbal associations represent the two major forms of elaboration, is one more effective than the other? In order to answer this question, we have to know how easy it is to form either an image or a verbal association to a word. The imagery potential of words is usually measured by asking people to rate on a scale how easy it is to form an image for a given word. As we might expect, concrete words are rated high on imagery and abstract words rated low. The association value of a word is usually measured by asking people to give as many associations as they can over a 1-minute interval. Paivio and his colleagues have found that the imagery potential of words is a more reliable predictor of learning than the association potential of words. High-imagery words are easier to learn than low-imagery words, but high-association words are not necessarily easier to learn than low-association words (Paivio, 1969).

The beneficial effect of imagery on learning is revealed in a study by Paivio, Smythe, and Yuille (1968). Students at the University of Western Ontario were asked to learn a list of paired associates consisting of 16 pairs of words. The words were equally divided between high-imagery (H) words—such as *juggler, dress, letter, hotel*—and low-imagery (L) words—such as *effort, duty, quality,* and *necessity*. The list contained four pairs each that were high–high, high–low, low–high, and low–low, where the first term refers to the imagery value of the stimulus and the second term refers to the imagery value of the response. Examples include *juggler–dress* (H–H), *letter–effort* (H–L), *duty–hotel* (L–H), and *quality–necessity* (L–L).

Figure 7.11 shows how well the students could recall the response when given the stimulus. The powerful effect of imagery is quite evident. The H–H pairs resulted in the best recall and the L–L pairs the worst. When only one member of the pair had a high-imagery value, recall was better when that word was used as the stimulus (H–L). The fact that H–H pairs were easiest to learn is consistent with the previously mentioned finding that interactive pictures improve the recall of brand names. When images can be created for both members of a word pair, the images can be combined to form an interactive image. For example, one can associate

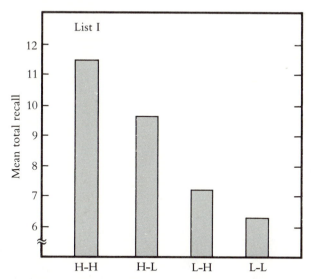

Figure 7.11. Mean total recall over four trials as a function of high (H) and low (L) imagery values. *(From "Imagery versus Meaningfulness of Nouns in Paired-Associate Learning," by A. Paivio, P. C. Smythe, and J. C. Yuille. In* Canadian Journal of Psychology, *1968, 22, 427–441. Copyright 1968 by the Canadian Psychological Association. Reprinted by permission.)*

the word *dress* with *juggler* by forming an image of a juggler wearing a dress.

It is interesting to note that high-imagery words were easier to recall than low-imagery words even though the learners were not told to use visual imagery. Perhaps the participants spontaneously generated images whenever they could. Support for this hypothesis was obtained in a questionnaire completed after the learning task. The students indicated, for each of the 16 pairs on the list, which one of five strategies they used in an attempt to learn that particular pair. Their options were *none, repetition* (rehearsal), *verbal* (a phrase or rhyme connecting two words), *imagery* (mental pictures that include the items), and *other*. The *none* and *other* options were reported relatively infrequently. The distribution of the other three responses depended on whether the pairs consisted of high- or low-imagery words (see Figure 7.12). The reported use of imagery was the highest for the H–H pairs and lowest for the L–L pairs. The striking resemblence between learning (Figure 7.11) and the reported use of imagery (Figure 7.12) suggests that imagery is an effective learning strategy.

The reason images are effective, according to Paivio (1975), is that an image provides a second kind of memory code that is independent of the verbal code. Paivio's theory is called a *dual-coding* theory because it proposes two independent memory codes, either of which can result in

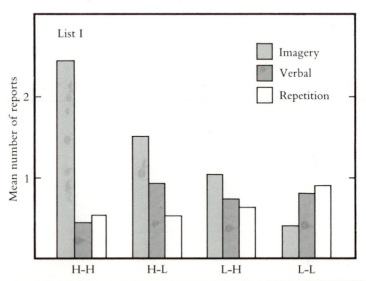

Figure 7.12. Mean number of pairs for which imagery, verbal, and repetition strategies were reported as a function of high (H) and low (L) imagery values. *(From "Imagery versus Meaningfulness of Nouns in Paired-Associate Learning," by A. Paivio, P. C. Smythe, and J. C. Yuille. In* Canadian Journal of Psychology, *1968, 22, 427–441. Copyright 1968 by the Canadian Psychological Association. Reprinted by permission.)*

recall. A person who has stored both the word *cat* and an image of a cat can remember the item if she retrieves either the image or the word. Evidence suggests that the two memory codes are independent in the sense that a person can forget one code without forgetting the other code (Paivio, 1975). Having two memory codes to represent an item therefore provides a better chance of remembering that item than having only a single code. Since images facilitate recall, it is only natural that they should play a key role in suggestions for improving memory.

Mnemonic strategies

Every so often a book appears on how to improve memory. Such a book is usually written by a person who not only has practiced memory (mnemonic) techniques but can successfully apply them to demonstrate rather remarkable acts of recall. One example, *The Memory Book* by Lorayne and Lucas (1974), was on the best-seller list for a number of weeks.

Although memory books always discuss several different techniques for improving memory, there is usually an emphasis on visual imagery. The author presents a mnemonic strategy, in which imagery usually plays a key role, and claims that the use of the strategy will improve recall. The claim, however, is seldom supported by experimental data. Is there proof that the proposed strategy works? Fortunately, supportive data exist in the psychology journals. We will now consider some of those data.

Comparison of Association Learning Strategies

The results obtained by Paivio, Smythe, and Yuille (1968) suggested that visual imagery is a particularly good strategy to use when images can be generated to represent words. Their study, however, was not designed to teach people to use a particular strategy, unlike an experiment conducted by Bower and Winzenz (1970). Subjects in the latter experiment were asked to learn paired associates consisting of concrete nouns. Each participant was assigned to one of four groups given different instructions on how to learn the associations. Students in the "repetition" condition were asked to rehearse each pair silently. Students in the "sentence-reading" condition read aloud a sentence in which the two words of a pair were capitalized as the subject and object of the sentence. The experimenters told the members of this group to use the sentence to associate the two critical nouns. Students in the "sentence-generation" condition made up their own sentence to relate the two words in a sensible way. Students in an "imagery" condition formed a mental image that combined the two words in a vivid interaction. They were encouraged to make their image as elaborate or bizarre as they wished.

Following a single study trial on each of 30 word-pairs, the students were given a recall test on 15 pairs and a recognition test on the other 15 pairs. Recognition of the correct response was easy, and all four study strategies resulted in a high level of performance. Recall of the correct response was more difficult, however, and here the differential effectiveness of the strategies was apparent. The average number of correct recalls was 5.6 for the repetition group, 8.2 for the sentence-reading group, 11.5 for the sentence-generation group, and 13.1 for the imagery group. The data dramatically illustrate that, although verbal rehearsal does result in some learning, it is a relatively ineffective method compared to the elaboration strategies. A comparison of the imagery and sentence-generation conditions illustrates that visual elaboration was more effective than semantic elaboration. Although the use of concrete nouns made visual elaboration possible, the fact that sentence generation was also an effective strategy suggests that this technique could be used when it is necessary to learn abstract words.

A specific application of the imagery strategy in paired-associate learning is learning to associate a name to a face. I would guess that just about everyone has had difficulty learning names at one time or another. Authors of memory books can often perform a very impressive demonstration in which they repeat back the names of everyone in an audience after hearing them only once. The method used by Lorayne involves first converting the name into a visual image and then linking the image to a prominent feature of the person's face. For example, if Mr. Gordon has a large nose, the image might be a garden growing out of his nose. Although the method may seem rather bizarre, it has experimental support.

A group of British psychologists found that people who were taught this strategy learned significantly more names than a control group that was not taught the strategy (Morris, Jones, & Hampson, 1978). The learning task required associating a different name (randomly selected from a telephone directory) to each of 13 photographs of male adults. After a short study period of 10 seconds for each item the imagery group could correctly name ten of the photographs, compared to five for the control group. The authors admit that the use of mnemonic strategies requires some effort, and not everyone will be willing to make that effort to learn names. However, their results should provide encouragement to those who wonder whether the effort will be worthwhile.

The Mnemonic Keyword Method and Vocabulary Learning

The use of imagery to remember names obviously depends on how easy it is to form an image from a name. Some names should be fairly easy, such as Smith (form an image of a blacksmith) or Green (form an image of the color). Other names, such as Gordon or Detterman, may require associating a concrete word to the name and then forming an image of the associated word. The associated word, called a *keyword,* should sound like the name that is being learned. The association of *garden* with *Gordon* is an example of the keyword method. *Garden* provides a keyword that can be used to form an image. The words *debtor-man* might be a good keyword for Detterman if one formed an image of Mr. Detterman dressed in ragged clothes.

You may have some reservations at this point about the keyword method. It's certainly more complicated than simply forming an image because you have to remember not only the image but also the association between the keyword and the name in order to remember the original name correctly. Mr. Gordon might not appreciate being called Mr. Garden, and Mr. Detterman would certainly not like being called Mr. Debtorman.

Even though the keyword method requires two stages—learning the association between the name and the keyword and forming an image of the keyword—the method is still very effective. A striking demonstration of its effectiveness is illustrated in a study by Atkinson and Raugh (1975) on the acquisition of a Russian vocabulary. The keyword method divides the study of a vocabulary word into two stages. The first stage requires associating the foreign word with an English word, the keyword, that sounds approximately like some part of the foreign word. The second stage requires forming a mental image of the keyword interacting with the English translation. For example, the Russian word for *building* (*zdanie*) is pronounced somewhat like *zdawn-yeh,* with the emphasis on the first syllable. Using *dawn* as the keyword, one could imagine the pink light of dawn being reflected in the windows of a building.

The appropriate selection of keywords is an important aspect of the method. A good keyword should satisfy the following criteria: It should (1) sound as much as possible like a part of the foreign word, (2) be different from the other keywords, and (3) easily form an interactive image with the English translation. Table 7.1 shows a sample of 20 Russian words and their associated keywords. As an exercise in using the method, you can try to create an image linking the first pair of words.

Students in the Atkinson and Raugh study attempted to learn the English translation of 120 Russian words over a three-day period. The students were divided into two groups—the "keyword" group and a control group. Subjects in the keyword group were instructed on the use of the keyword method. After the pronunciation of each foreign word they were shown both a keyword and the English translation. The instructions indicated that the students should try to picture an interactive image linking the keyword and the English translation or should generate a sentence incorporating both words if they could not form an image.

The keywords were not shown to students in the control group, who were told to learn the translations in whatever manner they wished. The control group did not receive instructions on the use of keywords or mental imagery.

On the day following the three study sessions students in both groups were tested on the entire 120-word vocabulary. Students in the keyword group provided the correct translation for 72% of the Russian words, whereas students in the control group provided the correct translation for 46% of the words. This difference is particularly impressive considering that Russian was selected as a special challenge to the keyword method because the pronunciation of most Russian words is quite different from English pronunciation. Since many people find that the Russian vocabulary is more difficult to learn than the vocabulary of other foreign languages, it is valuable to have a method that can facilitate learning. Atkinson and Raugh planned to use the keyword method in a computerized vocabulary-learning program designed to supplement a college course on Russian. Students would be free to study the words in any way they wished but would have the option of requesting a keyword by pressing an appropriate button on the terminal.

TABLE 7.1. A Sample of 20 Items from the Russian Vocabulary with Related Keywords.

Russian	Keyword	Translation
VNIMÁNIE	[pneumonia]	ATTENTION
DÉLO	[jello]	AFFAIR
ZÁPAD	[zap it]	WEST
STRANÁ	[strawman]	COUNTRY
TOLPÁ	[tell pa]	CROWD
LINKÓR	[Lincoln]	BATTLESHIP
ROT	[rut]	MOUTH
GORÁ	[garage]	MOUNTAIN
DURÁK	[two rocks]	FOOL
ÓSEN'	[ocean]	AUTUMN
SÉVER	[saviour]	NORTH
DYM	[dim]	SMOKE
SELÓ	[seal law]	VILLAGE
GOLOVÁ	[Gulliver]	HEAD
USLÓVIE	[Yugoslavia]	CONDITION
DÉVUSHKA	[dear vooshka]	GIRL
TJÓTJA	[Churchill]	AUNT
PÓEZD	[poised]	TRAIN
KROVÁT	[cravat]	BED
CHELOVÉK	[chilly back]	PERSON

From "An Application of the Mnemonic Keyword Method to the Acquisition of a Russian Vocabulary," by R. C. Atkinson and M. R. Raugh. In *Journal of Experimental Psychology: Human Learning and Memory,* 1975, *104,* 126–133. Copyright 1975 by the American Psychological Association. Reprinted by permission.

The Method of Loci

The mnemonic methods we have reviewed so far have been applied to paired-associate learning such as associating a name with a face or an English word with a Russian word. Another method is *serial learning,* which requires memorizing a sequence of items in their correct order. For example, if you are going shopping, you may want to remember a list of items in the order you plan to purchase them.

A long list of items can be memorized by using the method of *loci,* a technique that was invented many centuries ago. The need for a good memory was particularly important in the ancient world, which lacked printing and even paper for notes. The classical art of memory was primarily taught as a technique for delivering long speeches (Yates, 1966). An unknown teacher of rhetoric recorded the principles in *Ad Herennium,* a book written about 86–82 B.C. The first step was to commit to memory a series of loci, or places—usually parts of a building such as the forecourt, living room, bedrooms, and parlors—including statues and other ornaments in the rooms. The topics of the speech were then translated into images that were placed at the various locations in the order they would be discussed. The orator imagined walking through the building in a specified order, retrieving each image as he came to the next location. The method assures that the topics are remembered in their correct order since the order is determined by the sequence of locations in the building.

The memory section of *Ad Herennium* did more than simply describe the method of loci; it gave a detailed set of rules for how the method should be used. For instance, there were rules for selecting locations:

> Memory loci should not be too much like one another, for instance too many intercolumnar spaces are not good, for their resemblance will be confusing. They should be of moderate size, not too large, for that renders the images placed on them vague, and not too small for then an arrangement of images will be overcrowded. They must not be too brightly lighted for then the images placed on them will glitter and dazzle; nor must they be too dark or the shadows will obscure the images [Yates, 1966, p. 23].*

And rules for creating images:

> We ought, then, to set up images of a kind that can adhere longest in memory. And we shall do so if we establish similitudes as striking as possible; if we set up images that are not many or vague but active; if we assign to them exceptional beauty or singular ugliness; if we ornament some

---

*From *The Art of Memory,* by Dame Frances Yates. Copyright 1966 by Routledge and Kegan Paul Ltd. and the University of Chicago Press. This and all other quotations from this source are reprinted by permission.

of them, as with crowns or purple cloaks, so that the similitude may be more distinct to us; or if we somehow disfigure them, as by introducing one stained with blood or soiled with mud or smeared with red paint, so that its form is more striking, or by assigning certain comic effects to our images, for that, too, will ensure our remembering them more readily [Yates, 1966, p. 25].

Two aspects of these rules are rather striking. The first is the concern with the visual precision of images. The recommendation that images be of a certain size to be most effective is consistent with current research on imagery (Kosslyn, 1975; Kosslyn, Ball, & Reiser, 1978). However, the recommendation that the loci not be too bright or too dark seems unusual to me. Do our images so closely reflect reality that we have to be concerned about lighting? Perhaps people who relied extensively on imagery had images that were so detailed and accurate that lighting was a concern. My own belief is that the images of most people are highly schematic and not very detailed, a belief I will try to support in the next section.

The second significant aspect of the rules is their attempt to reduce interference by creating loci and images that are highly distinctive. The importance of distinctiveness is still emphasized in current theories of memory, as we saw in the previous chapter. The author of *Ad Herennium* recommended that the loci should be different enough from one another that they would not be confused. One implication of this rule is that storing more than one image in a single location interferes with retrieval.

Crovitz (1971) tested this implication by asking undergraduates at Duke University to learn a set of 32 English words. Another set of 32 items (such as pet store, zoo, fire station, hospital) were selected as memory loci. The locations were typed individually on cards, which were placed on the experimenter's table. The number of cards or locations varied across groups. The control group was given no memory instructions and no cards. Six other groups received 1, 2, 4, 8, 16, or 32 locations, along with instructions to picture each word on the list vividly at the successive locations. The instructions indicated that subjects would hear 32 words and would have to store more than one word at a location if there were fewer than 32 cards.

Figure 7.13 shows the percentage of words that were recalled in their correct order as a function of the number of locations. The group that was asked to associate all the words to a single location did not do significantly better than the control group (0 locations), which attempted to learn the words without using the method of loci. However, the level of performance improved rapidly as the number of locations increased to 16, suggesting that two images could be stored at each location without producing interference. Storing more than two images at a location made it difficult to remember the words, particularly in their correct order. It is important to note, however, that even a few locations led to better

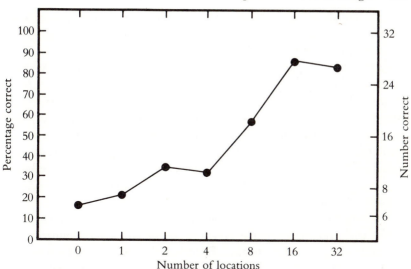

Figure 7.13. Recall of items in their correct order as a function of number of locations. *(From "The Capacity of Memory Loci in Artificial Memory," by H. F. Crovitz. In* Psychonomic Science, *1971, 24, 187–188. Copyright 1971 by the Psychonomic Society, Inc. Reprinted by permission.)*

recall than the control group produced, and many locations produced a substantial improvement in recall.

Limitations of images

The usefulness of visual images as memory codes may seem surprising. If you are like me, you may feel that you cannot create very vivid images and perhaps even question whether you use any images at all. Let me give you a chance to form an image by asking: Does the Star of David contain a parallelogram (a four-sided figure whose opposite sides are parallel)? Try to form an image of the Star of David and examine it to answer the question. Many people have difficulty identifying the parts of patterns, even after they have just seen the pattern (Reed & Johnsen, 1975). Since we have seen many results that show the usefulness of images, it is only fair to discuss a few of their limitations before leaving the topic.

Memory for Details

Our discussion so far has focused on the successful use of visual images to improve memory. We learned that memory for pictures is better than memory for words and memory for concrete words better than memory for abstract words. Both of these findings are related to the ease with which an image can be created to represent a concrete word or picture. We also saw how instructions to form interactive images facilitated the learning of people's names, vocabulary words, and lists of items. If images can do all this, how are they limited?

One answer is that the tests that showed good memory for visual material were not very challenging. For example, the experiments by Shepard (1967) and Standing (1973) used a recognition memory test in which a person selected which one of two pictures had occurred in the experiment. Although the results of these studies suggest that visual memory contains an abundance of information, in reality the results do not allow us to conclude how much information is stored. All we know is that people retained enough information to distinguish the "old" picture from the new one.

Nickerson and Adams (1979) investigated how completely and accurately people remember visual details by asking them to recognize a very common object, a U.S. penny. Figure 7.14 shows 15 drawings of a penny, only one of which is correct. If you can identify the correct choice, you did better than the majority of the subjects in the experiment, who selected incorrectly. Although we have seen a penny on many occasions, most of us have never learned its details, probably because they are not very useful in everyday life. Attributes such as color and size allow us to distinguish quickly between a penny and other coins, making the learning

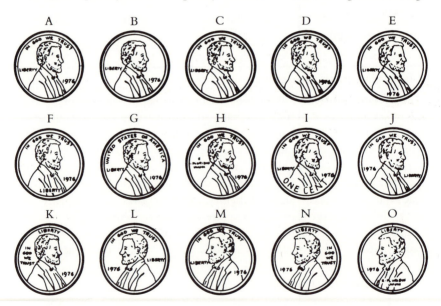

Figure 7.14. Fifteen drawings of a penny that were used in a recognition memory test. *(From "Long-Term Memory for a Common Object," by R. S. Nickerson and M. J. Adams. In Cognitive Psychology, 1979, 11, 287–307. Copyright 1979 by Academic Press, Inc. Reprinted by permission.)*

of additional details unnecessary. When a new coin is introduced (such as the Susan B. Anthony dollar) that requires more attention to details to distinguish it from another coin, there is considerable resistance to its acceptance.

The retention of details is usually unnecessary when we use images to remember words. Your image of a penny would not have to be detailed or accurate to help you remember the word *penny;* it would only have to be detailed enough to allow you to recall the correct word when you retrieved your image. Experimental results have shown that people who were good at recalling the names of pictures they had seen two weeks earlier did not have more detailed images than people who could not recall as many names (Bahrick & Boucher, 1968). For example, people who could recall that they had seen a cup did not necessarily remember many details of the cup when they were given a recognition test similar to the one illustrated by Figure 7.14. The evidence suggested that people were using visual images to aid their recall, but it was necessary to remember only enough details about an object to recall its name. Visual images can therefore be incomplete if the task does not require memory for details.

Structural Descriptions

At the beginning of this chapter I argued that the existence of both visual codes and verbal codes allows us considerable flexibility in performing many tasks. This is beneficial to us but detrimental to psychologists who would like to know what we are doing. Are we using visual information, verbal information, or a combination of both when we recall information? One method for reducing the influence of verbal information is to ask people to make judgments about parts of patterns that they did not notice when they looked at the pattern. Pattern 1 in Figure 7.15 is a particularly good candidate because it can be perceived in many different ways. To use the terminology introduced in Chapter 2, people can choose from a variety of structural descriptions to remember the pattern. Examples include two adjacent hourglasses, two overlapping triangles, a diamond inside a large hourglass, or two overlapping parallelograms. Any one of these descriptions could be stored in memory by using a combination of verbal and visual codes. Words like *triangle, overlap,* and *inverted* could help us remember the pattern, as could a visual image. But words should be of relatively little use in helping people identify parts of the pattern they did not perceive. For example, if a person perceived the pattern as two adjacent hourglasses, a verbal description involving only hourglasses would not be very useful in helping him decide that a triangle or a parallelogram is also part of pattern 1.

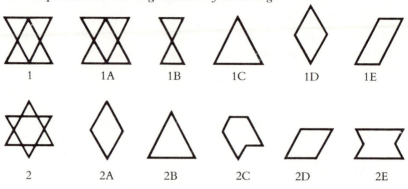

Figure 7.15. Two patterns used to test for recognition of parts. *(From "Detection of Parts in Patterns and Images," by S. K. Reed and J. A. Johnsen. In* Memory & Cognition, *1975, 3, 569–575. Copyright 1975 by the Psychonomic Society, Inc. Reprinted by permission.)*

The alternative is to examine a visual image of the pattern to see whether it contains a triangle or a parallelogram. This alternative should not be particularly difficult if people have images that are fairly vivid and detailed. Performance would then be comparable to examining a picture of the pattern. But if images are not very vivid and detailed, locating a part in an image would be much more difficult than locating a part in a perceived pattern. Jeff Johnsen and I compared these two conditions by assigning undergraduates at Case Western Reserve University to one of two groups (Reed & Johnsen, 1975). Students in the "perception" group saw a possible part of a pattern followed by the complete pattern, such as part 1C followed by pattern 1. They then had 10 seconds to examine the pattern to see whether it contained the part. Students in the "image" group saw the part and pattern in the reverse order—the pattern before the part—and had 10 seconds to examine their image of the pattern to see whether it contained the part. Both groups had to make the same decisions, but the perception group could examine a perceived pattern, whereas the image group had to examine an image of the pattern. Figure 7.15 shows some examples of the tasks: students had to decide whether parts 1B, 1C, 1D, and 1E were contained in pattern 1 and whether parts 2A, 2C, 2D, and 2E were contained in pattern 2 (parts 1A and 2B were not tested in this particular experiment).

The results were that the undergraduates in the perception group failed to detect the part on 14% of the trials, whereas those in the image group failed on 48% of the trials. Some of the correct responses in the image condition occurred because people saw the part when the pattern was presented rather than successfully examining their image to locate the part. When these responses were dropped from the analysis, undergraduates in the image group were unable to detect the part on 72% of the trials.

The subjects frequently failed to detect a part in an image even though they could remember what the complete pattern looked like—they could draw pattern 1 or pattern 2 when asked. The difficulty of the imagery task seems to be caused by the lack of clarity of visual images relative to perceived patterns. The subjects formed a structural description of a pattern that was sufficient for reproducing the pattern or recognizing parts that matched the description but usually inadequate for recognizing parts not contained in the description. These results suggest that most people's images are highly structured, somewhat vague, and difficult to reorganize.

Studies showing the limitations of visual images provide both good news and bad news. The bad news is that our attempt to use visual images is not a universal solution for improving memory performance. The good news is that, even if people believe they have poor images, their images may still be sufficient for performing the many tasks that do not require great detail. In either case, the study of visual images has greatly increased our understanding of how people perform on many intellectual or memory tasks.

Summary

There is a variety of evidence suggesting that visual images play an important role in our ability to perform many cognitive tasks. Visual images preserve the spatial relations among the objects of a scene or the features of a pattern. The time it takes to mentally scan between two objects in an image is therefore a function of the distance between them. Visual images also make it possible to compare all the features of a pattern simultaneously when we attempt to match a visual pattern with an image of another pattern. In contrast, features described verbally must be compared one at a time because of the sequential nature of language. When we are comparing two patterns that are in different orientations, a visual image makes it possible to rotate one pattern mentally until both have the same orientation. The distinction between visual and verbal codes is also suggested by selective interference between the two codes. Experiments revealed, for instance, that circling responses on an answer sheet interfered more with classifying the corners of a block diagram, whereas responding verbally interfered more with classifying the words in a sentence.

The usefulness of visual images in memory is supported by research showing that people usually remember pictures better than concrete words and concrete words better than abstract words. These results correspond to the fact that images are easiest to form from pictures and most difficult to form from abstract words. Learning pairs of items is facilitated by forming an interactive image that combines both members of the pair. For example, the recall of advertisements was best when people saw an illustration that combined a picture of the brand name with a picture of the product. The dual-coding theory explains the usefulness of visual imagery in recall by proposing that a visual image provides an extra memory code that is independent from the verbal code. A person therefore has two chances to recall the item rather than only a single chance.

The knowledge that visual imagery improves memory has existed for centuries and has resulted in the use of imagery in many mnemonic strategies. A study that compared four strategies—verbal rehearsal, sentence reading, sentence generation, and imagery—found that people who used the imagery strategy recalled the most words. However, the two sentence elaboration strategies produced much better recall than simple rehearsal, suggesting that the former strategies could facilitate learning abstract words. Visual images can also be used to learn people's names and a foreign vocabulary, although it is often necessary to translate a name or foreign word into a similar-sounding concrete keyword first. An interactive image is then formed to link the keyword with a face or the English translation of the foreign word. The method of loci is a mnemonic strategy that can be used to learn a sequence of items, such as the major topics in a speech. A person selects a familiar physical structure, such as a building, and produces an interactive image linking a word or topic with each location in the building. The order of the topics is preserved by locating the topics in the order they would be encountered as one walked through the building. Experiments evaluating the effectiveness of mnemonic strategies have usually found a dramatic improvement in performance.

Although the use of visual images often produces a dramatic improvement in recognition or recall, the images of most people seem to be limited in clarity and detail. An experiment that asked people to select the correct drawing of a penny from a set of similar alternatives found that most people made the wrong choice. A likely explanation is that we do not need to remember the details of a penny. This is also true for the images used to represent words in a memory task: it is only necessary to remember enough about the image to recall the word. People store visual patterns in memory as structural descriptions and find it very difficult to recognize a novel part that does not match their structural description—for example, locating a parallelogram in the Star of David.

Recommended reading

Paivio's *Imagery and Verbal Processes* (1971) discusses the experimental work during the 1960s that helped restore imagery as a major topic in experimental psychology. *The Function and Nature of Imagery,* edited by

Sheehan (1972), contains chapters on a wide variety of topics including clinical implications of imagery. One of the chapters is on individual differences in the use of imagery (Marks, 1972), a topic that was also studied by MacLeod, Hunt, and Mathews (1978). Articles by Anderson (1978), Finke (1980), Kosslyn (1981), Pylyshyn (1981), and Shepard and Podgorny (1978) discuss the representation of information in images and the relation between imagery and perception. Research by Posner, Boies, Eichelman, and Taylor (1969) provided evidence regarding the maintenance of visual codes in STM. However, their conclusion that visual codes are quickly replaced by verbal codes has been challenged by Kroll and Parks (1978). Psychologists continue to study the practical implications of imagery, including its use as a mnemonic (McCarty, 1980; Pressley, Levin, Hall, Miller, & Berry, 1980) and its role in the acquisition of spatial knowledge (Thorndyke & Stasz, 1980).

8

Categorization

We begin with what seems to be a paradox. The world of experience of any normal man is composed of a tremendous array of discriminably different objects, events, people, impressions. But were we to utilize fully our capacity for registering the differences in things and to respond to each event encountered as unique, we would soon be overwhelmed by the complexity of our environment. The resolution of this seeming paradox—the existence of discrimination capacities which, if fully used, would make us slaves to the particular—is achieved by man's capacity to categorize. To categorize is to render discriminably different things equivalent, to group the objects and events around us into classes, and to respond to them in terms of their class membership rather than their uniqueness.

J. S. BRUNER, J. J. GOODNOW, AND G. A. AUSTIN (1956)

This chapter and the following one discuss ways in which people organize knowledge. One way to organize knowledge is to form categories. Categories consist of objects or events that we have grouped together because we feel that they are somehow related to one another. The ability to categorize enables us to interact with our environment without becoming overwhelmed by its complexity. Bruner, Goodnow, and Austin, in their influential book *A Study of Thinking* (1956), listed five benefits of forming categories.

1. Categorizing objects "reduces the complexity of the environment." Scientists have estimated that there are more than 7 million discriminable colors. If we responded to all of these as unique, we could spend our entire lifetime just trying to learn the names of colors. When we classify discriminably different objects as being equivalent, we respond to them in terms of their class membership rather than as unique items.

2. Categorizing is "the means by which objects of the world are identified." We usually feel that we have recognized a pattern when we can classify it into a familiar category such as *dog, chair,* or the letter *A.*

3. This achievement is a consequence of the first two: the establishment of categories "reduces the need for constant learning." We do not have to be taught about novel objects if we can classify them; we can use our knowledge of items in the category to respond to the novel object.

4. Categorizing allows us to "decide what constitutes an appropriate action." A person who eats wild mushrooms must be able to distinguish between poisonous and nonpoisonous varieties. Eating a poisonous variety is clearly not an appropriate action.

5. Categorizing "enables us to order and relate classes of objects and events." Although classification is by itself a useful way to organize knowledge, classes can be further organized into subordinate and superordinate relations. The category *chair,* for example, has *high chair* as a subordinate class and *furniture* as a superordinate class. The three categories form a hierarchy in which *furniture* contains *chair* as a member, and *chair* contains *high chair* as a member.

Psychologists have used several different experimental procedures to study how people make classifications. The first section of this chapter describes a procedure called *concept identification.* The categories in concept identification tasks typically contain geometric patterns that vary along several obvious dimensions—for example, shape, size, and color. The experimenter selects a rule to define the concept, and the task requires discovering the rule through learning which patterns are examples of the concept. The rule might be relatively simple, such as "All red patterns are examples," or it might be more complex, such as "Either red patterns or small patterns are examples."

One limitation of this approach is that many categories cannot be distinguished on the basis of a simple rule. We can usually distinguish a dog from a cat, but it is questionable whether we use a simple rule to make this distinction. The second section discusses some characteristics of natural or real-world categories and emphasizes how we use these characteristics to organize knowledge. In order to recognize objects and reduce the need for constant learning, we have to be able to classify novel objects into a familiar category. The final section discusses how people do this.

Concept identification

Testing Simple Hypotheses

The most basic distinction between two categories occurs when they can be distinguished by the values of a single relevant dimension. For example, a rule for sorting objects could state that large objects belong to one category and small objects belong to another category. Psychologists typically study how people learn to identify the relevant dimension by presenting stimuli that vary along several dimensions. The stimuli in Figure 8.1 vary along four dimensions: letter (*X* or *T*), color (*black* or *white*), size (*large* or *small*), and position (*left* or *right*). Each stimulus consists of two patterns. One pattern is an instance of the concept, and the other pattern is not an instance of the concept. The task requires that subjects select the stimulus they think is a positive instance of the concept.

It is now widely believed that people solve concept identification problems by formulating and testing hypotheses (see Levine, 1969, for a brief summary of how a different view initially predominated). There are eight possible hypotheses for the stimuli shown in Figure 8.1 if the concept is defined by a single value: *black, white, X, T, left, right, large,* and *small.* Imagine that an experimenter selected one of these values as the correct hypothesis—for example, *black.* Any black pattern would then become a positive instance of the concept, and any white pattern would become a negative instance of the concept. Your task as a subject would be to select one of the two patterns presented on each trial that was a positive instance. Initially you would not have any idea whether the pattern on the left or the right was correct. Perhaps you would guess the right pattern on the first trial and select the large, black *T*. If you guessed correctly, you would know that the concept must either be *right, large, black,* or *T*. If you guessed incorrectly and selected the pattern on the left, you would still learn that the right pattern was correct. The first feedback trial therefore provides enough information for you to eliminate four of the eight hypotheses.

One of the central issues in concept identification studies is the number of hypotheses that a person can evaluate at one time. If the first feedback trial indicates that the hypothesis is *right, large, black,* or *T*, could you evaluate all four hypotheses on the next trial, or would you select

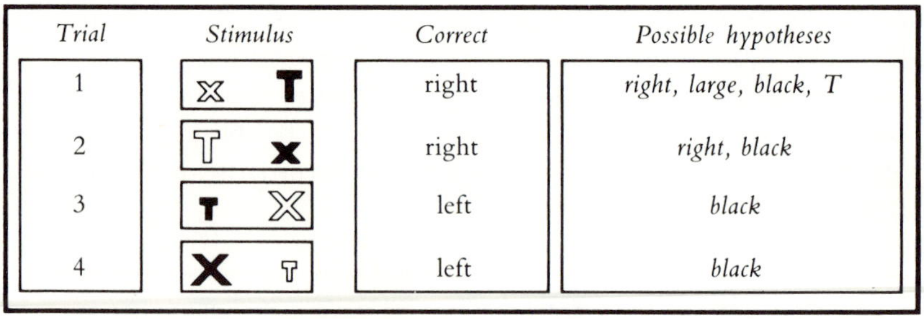

Trial	Stimulus	Correct	Possible hypotheses
1	X **T**	right	*right, large, black, T*
2	T **x**	right	*right, black*
3	**т** X	left	*black*
4	**X** т	left	*black*

Figure 8.1. Illustration of how feedback enables the subject to select the correct hypothesis after three trials. (*From "Hypothesis Behavior by Humans during Discrimination Learning," by M. Levine. In* Journal of Experimental Psychology, *1966, 71, 331–338. Copyright 1966 by the American Psychological Association. Reprinted by permission.*)

only one for evaluation? You would certainly learn more by attempting to evaluate all four. If you incorrectly picked the left pattern on the second trial, you could learn from your mistake that the correct hypothesis was either *right* or *black* because *large* and *T* are values of the incorrect pattern. However, if you decided to evaluate only one hypothesis and ignore the other three, you would learn only whether you should continue to evaluate that hypothesis (if it resulted in a correct choice) or reject it (if it resulted in an incorrect choice). Clearly, it would be advantageous to try to evaluate all hypotheses simultaneously, but, as Bruner, Goodnow, and Austin (1956) pointed out, keeping track of all possible hypotheses might exceed the limits of our capacity to process information.

The patterns shown in Figure 8.1 are actually part of a clever procedure designed by Levine (1966) to estimate how many hypotheses people can evaluate at one time. Each problem consisted of a series of three feedback trials followed by a fourth trial. The three feedback trials provided sufficient information to enable the subject always to make the correct selection on the fourth trial—if the subject could evaluate all hypotheses until they could be rejected.

Figure 8.1 illustrates the procedure for the case in which *black* is the correct hypothesis. If the right pattern is correct on trial 1, the correct hypothesis can be *right, large, black,* or *T*. If the right pattern is correct on trial 2, the correct hypothesis can be either *right* or *black*. If the left pattern is correct on trial 3, the correct hypothesis can be only *black*. Each feedback trial provides enough information to enable the subject to eliminate one-half of the potentially correct hypotheses. Subjects therefore have enough information to always select correctly on trial 4 if they are successful in evaluating all hypotheses until they can be eliminated.

Levine was able to estimate how efficiently people could eliminate hypotheses by directly testing one of their hypotheses after each feedback trial. His procedure is called the *blank trials* procedure because, after each of the feedback trials shown in Figure 8.1, the subject received four trials in which feedback was not presented. Levine assumed that the subject would respond during the nonfeedback trials by selecting one of the hypotheses that had not already been eliminated. The stimuli presented during the blank trials were selected to reveal whether the subject was consistently responding on the basis of a single hypothesis. Figure 8.2 shows a typical sequence of four blank trials. Each of the eight hypotheses results in a different sequence of choices. For example, responding on the basis of *black* would result in selecting the left pattern, followed by the right pattern, the left pattern, and the right pattern. Selecting *X* would result in choosing the left pattern on the first two trials and the right pattern on the next two trials. By analyzing the sequence of selections, Levine could determine which hypothesis served as the basis for the selections.

	Hypotheses					Hypotheses		
Black	X	Left	Large	Stimuli	Small	Right	T	White
L	L	L	L	𝗫 𝖳	R	R	R	R
R	L	L	R	🗶 **T**	L	R	R	L
L	R	L	R	**T** 🗶	L	R	L	R
R	R	L	L	🗵 **𝗫**	R	R	L	L

Figure 8.2. Blank trials showing how each hypothesis results in a different pattern of choices (*L* = left, *R* = right). *(From "Hypothesis Behavior by Humans during Discrimination Learning," by M. Levine. In* Journal of Experimental Psychology, *1966, 71, 331–338. Copyright 1966 by the American Psychological Association. Reprinted by permission.)*

Recall that, if people can effectively monitor all hypotheses, they should have only four left after the first feedback trial, two left after the second feedback trial, and one left after the third feedback trial. The hypotheses selected during the four blank trials should therefore be one of these if people can efficiently reject hypotheses. Their success in selecting an appropriate hypothesis can be used to measure how many hypotheses they are still considering after each feedback trial. Figure 8.3 shows how successful people were in rejecting inappropriate hypotheses. The bottom curve shows perfect performance, in which only a single hypoth-

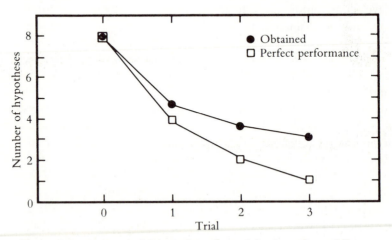

Figure 8.3. Estimate of the number of remaining hypotheses following each trial. *(From "Hypothesis Behavior by Humans during Discrimination Learning," by M. Levine. In* Journal of Experimental Psychology, *1966, 71, 331–338. Copyright 1966 by the American Psychological Association. Reprinted by permission.)*

esis remains after three feedback trials. The upper curve shows an actual performance, in which people gradually eliminated inappropriate hypotheses but still had three left after three feedback trials. The results reveal that, although people can effectively make use of feedback to eliminate hypotheses, the fact that their performance does not match the optimal performance represented by the lower curve indicates they are unsuccessful in simultaneously monitoring all hypotheses.

The ability to evaluate multiple hypotheses is a useful skill in tasks such as medical diagnosis. Experimental evidence indicates that physicians usually simultaneously evaluate from two to four hypotheses when attempting to diagnose a disease (Elstein, Shulman, & Sprafka, 1978). When they reject a hypothesis, however, they may replace it with another one, and so the number of hypotheses they consider at any one time remains relatively constant. More will be said about medical decision making in Chapter 14.

Evaluating Logical Rules

So far we have considered only a relatively simple concept, defined by a single value on a single dimension. Experimenters do not always use such simple concepts, however, and they have often studied how people learn concepts defined by logical rules typically requiring two dimensions, such as shape and color. Figure 8.4 shows how four logical rules divide stimuli into two categories. Notice that each dimension has three values—*red* (cross-hatched), *black,* and *white* for color; and *square, triangle,* and *circle* for shape. The values *red* and *square* specify the concept in the example.

The rule that is usually the easiest to learn is the *conjunctive rule*. Since the conjunctive rule uses the logical relation *and,* the concept in this case is *red and square*. A stimulus is a member of the category only if both values are present. The red square is the only stimulus that satisfies this criterion.

The *disjunctive rule* uses the logical relation *or*. A stimulus is an example of the concept if it is red or if it is a square. The three red stimuli and the three squares are now all examples of the concept.

The *conditional rule* makes use of the *if, then* relation—for example, if the stimulus is red, then it must be a square to be an example. One characteristic of the conditional rule that may seem strange is that all stimuli that are not red are positive examples. An analogy would be if you worked in a fancy restaurant and had to enforce the rule that, if a person is a male, he must wear a tie. All people that are not males would be admitted under this restriction.

The *biconditional rule* is so called because the conditional rule applies

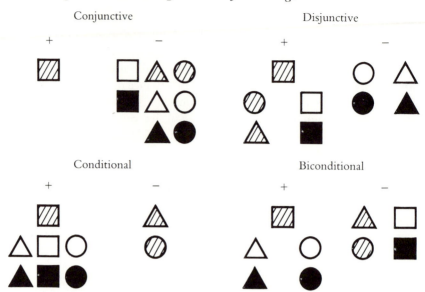

Figure 8.4. Positive and negative examples for four different logical rules. The relevant attributes are *red* and *square*. *(From "Knowing and Using Concepts," by L. E. Bourne, Jr. In* Psychological Review, *1970, 77, 546–556. Copyright 1970 by the American Psychological Association. Reprinted by permission.)*

in both directions. The biconditional rule includes the previous rule—if a stimulus is red, then it must be a square—but it also applies in the reverse direction—if a stimulus is a square, then it must be red. You should notice in Figure 8.4 that the biconditional rule excludes two squares from the positive category that were not excluded by the conditional rule. Since the biconditional rule applies in both directions, a square is not an example of the category unless it is red. The greater exclusiveness of the biconditional rule is also illustrated by the previous analogy. In addition to excluding men who were *not* wearing ties, the biconditional rule would exclude women who *were* wearing ties. The reverse of the *if male, then tie* rule is *if wearing a tie, then male.*

As you can imagine, learning the correct conceptual rule can be difficult, particularly if the stimuli consist of irrelevant dimensions. If the stimuli in Figure 8.4 varied in number and size, people not only would have to learn the correct logical rule but would have to learn that color and shape were the two relevant dimensions. One way to simplify the task would be to tell subjects that shape and color were the relevant dimensions. This task is called *rule learning* because people have to learn only the correct logical rule when they are told the relevant dimensions (Haygood & Bourne, 1965).

Bourne (1970) tested the relative difficulty of the four rules by designing an experiment in which subjects solved a series of nine successive rule-learning problems. The stimuli varied on four dimensions—color, shape, number, and size—but the experimenter always specified the two relevant dimensions before each problem. Each problem required that a person learn to classify the stimuli as either positive or negative examples of the concept. The participants were not told the correct rule, but the rule remained the same throughout the series of nine problems.

The results of the experiment are shown in Figure 8.5. There are large initial differences in the relative difficulty of the four rules. The conditional rule requires over twice as many trials to learn on the first problem as the conjunctive and disjunctive rules, and the biconditional rule requires over three times as many trials to learn. However, with practice people become very good at applying the biconditional and conditional rules and eventually perform as well on these problems as they do on the conjunctive and disjunctive problems. After solving six problems using

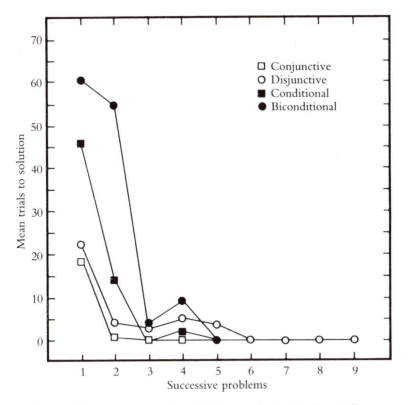

Figure 8.5. Average number of trials to solution for four different logical rules. *(From "Knowing and Using Concepts," by L. E. Bourne, Jr. In* Psychological Review, *1970, 77, 546–556. Copyright 1970 by the American Psychological Association. Reprinted by permission.)*

the same rule, all subjects solved the remaining problems without errors, no matter how difficult the rule was at the outset.

In the rule-learning problems the experimenter informed the subjects about the two relevant dimensions (attributes) but did not tell them the appropriate rule. A variation of the procedure—called *attribute learning*—is to inform people about the appropriate rule and let them discover the appropriate attributes (Haygood & Bourne, 1965). The problem is solved when people can consistently identify stimuli as either positive or negative instances of the concept.

Studies of attribute learning generally reveal that efficiency in identifying the relevant attributes depends on which rule specifies the concept. The relative difficulty of the four rules is the same as in the rule-learning tasks: attribute problems based on a conjunctive rule are the easiest, followed by the disjunctive rule, conditional rule, and biconditional rule (Bourne, Ekstrand, Lovallo, Kellogg, Hiew, & Yaroush, 1976).

Why should the four rules influence task difficulty when participants are told the relevant rule before each problem? Bourne and his colleagues proposed a frequency theory to account for these results. The frequency theory can apply to stimuli in both the positive and negative categories, but the results indicate that the positive category is more important (Bourne et al., 1976). Let's return to the partitions shown in Figure 8.4 to see how the frequency theory works when applied to the stimuli in the positive category.

When the rule is conjunctive, the only stimulus in the positive category is a red square. If size were an irrelevant dimension consisting of three values (*small, medium,* and *large*), then the red square would be small, medium, or large one-third of the time. The particular values of an irrelevant dimension will appear equally often in the positive category because the dimension is unrelated to the conceptual rule. But *red* is the only color in the positive category, and *square* is the only shape in the positive category. It is this difference in frequency between the different values along a dimension that makes it easy to identify the dimension as relevant to the concept.

It is easy to identify the relevant dimensions for a conjunctive rule because irrelevant values (*black* and *white* or *circle* and *triangle*) of these dimensions never appear in the positive category. The relevant values therefore appear 100% of the time because all positive stimuli are *red* and *square*. It is not quite so easy for the disjunctive rule. Figure 8.4 shows that three of the five positive stimuli are *red* and three of the five positive stimuli are *square*. The relevant values therefore appear 60% of the time in the positive category. Only one of the seven positive stimuli is *red* for the conditional rule, and three of the seven are *square*. The two relevant values therefore occur 29% of the time (the average of $\frac{1}{7}$ and $\frac{3}{7}$). The lowest percentage occurs for the biconditional rule. Only one of the five positive stimuli is *red,* and only one is *square.* The two relevant values occur only 20% of the time.

You should notice that the ordering of these percentages corresponds to the ordering of the difficulty of attribute identification tasks. The results suggest that people form frequency differences among the values along each dimension. When the relevant values (such as *red* and *square*) frequently occur in the positive category, it is relatively easy to identify these values as relevant. When the relevant values seldom occur in the positive category, it is much more difficult to identify them as relevant. The attribute frequency theory is consistent with several other findings in the concept identification literature. We will return to one of these findings later in the chapter when we discuss a feature frequency theory of categorization.

Critique of the Concept Identification Paradigm

Not all cognitive psychologists are satisfied with the concept identification task; some have criticized it as highly artificial and unrelated to the cognitive tasks that we usually encounter in the real world. This criticism should not imply that we are unable to draw any analogy between skills needed to do well in concept identification tasks and skills needed to do well in other tasks. As I pointed out previously, the inability of people to evaluate simultaneously a large number of hypotheses is true in real-world tasks such as medical diagnosis as well as in concept identification experiments. Yet real-world tasks are often sufficiently different from concept identification tasks that we must be very careful in making generalizations.

The predominant criticism of the concept identification paradigm is that real-world categories have characteristics that differ from the categories studied in the laboratory. This is not a new argument. Bruner, Goodnow, and Austin (1956) recognized that most real-world categories cannot be distinguished by the different values along a single dimension or by logical rules. One of the chapters in their book discussed categorizing with probabilistic cues in which the values of a dimension did not uniquely specify a category. For example, 67% of the airplanes in one category may have a straight tail, and 67% of the planes in another category may have a curved tail. The tail is a probabilistic cue because it tells us only the most likely category of a plane, not its exact category.

Although Bruner, Goodnow, and Austin reported some experiments on categorizing with probabilistic cues, their work is primarily remembered for research using the standard concept identification paradigm. A dramatic change in how psychologists viewed real-world categories had to wait until the 1970s, when Eleanor Rosch and her students at the University of California, Berkeley, began to study the characteristics of natural categories (Rosch, 1973). One of the characteristics of concept identification tasks that bothered Rosch is that all members of the concept are equally good members. Consider the five examples in Figure 8.4 that satisfy the conjunctive rule *red or square*. All of the five positive instances are equally good members because they all satisfy the rule. In contrast, natural categories are not composed of equally good members. If we gave people different variations of the color red, they would agree that some variations were more representative of the color than others (a "good" red versus an "off" red).

Another characteristic of natural categories is that they may be composed of continuous dimensions rather than discrete dimensions. Colors, for example, vary along a continuum in which red gradually becomes orange, and orange gradually becomes yellow. Natural categories are also hierarchically organized because larger categories often contain smaller categories. These characteristics of natural categories have important implications for how we make use of categories to organize knowledge. The next section discusses these implications.

Natural categories

As we saw, one characteristic of real-world, or natural, categories is that they are hierarchical—some categories contain other categories. For example, the category *furniture* contains chairs, and the category *chairs* contains living-room chairs. Each of these levels contains a variety of objects, but the variety decreases as the category becomes smaller. There are many different kinds of furniture (beds, sofas, tables, chairs), fewer kinds of chairs (living-room chairs, dining-room chairs, high chairs), and still fewer kinds of living-room chairs. The first part of this section looks at how the hierarchical organization of categories influences our behavior.

Another characteristic of natural categories is that some members seem to be better representatives of the category than others. We could all agree that chairs are furniture, but what about a piano? Shirts are certainly a good example of clothing, but what about a necklace? The second part of this section examines the implications of the fact that the members of categories are not all equally good members.

The Hierarchical Organization of Categories

Rosch and her colleagues studied the hierarchical organization of categories by using the three levels shown in Table 8.1 (Rosch, Mervis, Gray, Johnsen, & Boyes-Braem, 1976). The largest categories are the superordinate categories, such as *musical instruments*. They contain the basic-level categories (such as *drum*), which in turn contain the subordinate categories (such as *bass drum*). The most important of the three levels, according to Rosch, is the basic level because basic-level categories

TABLE 8.1.   Examples of Subordinate, Basic, and Superordinate Categories.

Superordinate	Basic level	Subordinates	
Musical instrument	Guitar Piano Drum	Folk guitar Grand piano Kettle drum	Classical guitar Upright piano Bass drum
Fruit	Apple Peach Grapes	Delicious apple Freestone peach Concord grapes	Mackintosh apple Cling peach Green seedless grapes
Tool	Hammer Saw Screwdriver	Ball-peen hammer Hack hand saw Phillips screwdriver	Claw hammer Cross-cutting hand saw Regular screwdriver
Clothing	Pants Socks Shirt	Levi's Knee socks Dress shirt	Double-knit pants Ankle socks Knit shirt
Furniture	Table Lamp Chair	Kitchen table Floor lamp Kitchen chair	Dining-room table Desk lamp Living-room chair
Vehicle	Car Bus Truck	Sports car City bus Pick-up truck	Four-door sedan car Cross-country bus Tractor-trailer truck

From "Basic Objects in Natural Categories," by E. Rosch, C. B. Mervis, W. D. Gray, D. M. Johnsen, and P. Boyes-Braem. In *Cognitive Psychology,* 1976, *8,* 382–440. Copyright 1976 by Academic Press, Inc. Reprinted by permission.

are the most differentiated from one another, and they are therefore the first categories we learn and the most important in language.

The differentiation of categories can be measured by determining how much the members of a category share attributes with other members but have attributes that are different from the members of other categories. At the superordinate level the difficulty is that members share few attributes. Examples of furniture—such as table, lamp, and chair—have few attributes in common. At the subordinate level the difficulty is that the members share many attributes with members of similar subordinate categories. For example, a kitchen table has many of the same attributes as a dining-room table. The intermediate level of categorization—the basic level—avoids the two extremes. Members of a basic-level category, such as chair, not only share many attributes but have attributes that differ from other basic-level categories, such as lamp and table.

Evidence for the differentiation of categories comes from a study in which people were asked to list the attributes of objects at different levels in the hierarchy (Rosch et al., 1976). Some people listed the attributes of superordinate objects (such as musical instruments, fruit, tools, clothing); others listed the attributes of basic-level objects (guitar, apple, hammer, pants); and still others listed the attributes of subordinate objects (classical guitar, Mackintosh apple, claw hammer, Levi's).

The experimenters analyzed the data by identifying attributes people seemed to agree were associated with the specified category. Table 8.2 shows the average number of shared attributes at each level in the hierarchy. The number of shared attributes increases from the superordinate to the subordinate level. The members of a superordinate category share very few attributes compared to the basic level. However, the increase in shared attributes from the basic level to the subordinate level was very small. The differences between levels can be illustrated by the three

TABLE 8.2 Number of Attributes in Common at Each Hierarchical Level.

| | Number of attributes in common | | | | | |
| | Raw tallies | | | Judge-amended tallies | | |
Category	Super-ordinate	Basic level	Sub-ordinate	Super-ordinate	Basic level	Sub-ordinate
Musical instrument	1	6.0	8.5	1	8.3	8.7
Fruit	7	12.3	14.7	3	8.3	9.5
Tool	3	8.3	9.7	3	8.7	9.2
Clothing	3	10.0	12.0	2	8.3	9.7
Furniture	3	9.0	10.3	0	7.0	7.8
Vehicle	4	8.7	11.2	1	11.7	16.8

From "Basic Objects in Natural Categories," by E. Rosch, C. B. Mervis, W. D. Gray, D. M. Johnsen, and P. Boyes-Braem. In *Cognitive Psychology,* 1976, *8,* 382–440. Copyright 1976 by Academic Press, Inc. Reprinted by permission.

TABLE 8.3. Examples of Shared Attributes at Different Hierarchical Levels.

Tool
make things
fix things
metal

Saw
handle
teeth
blade
sharp
cuts
edge
wooden handle

Cross-cutting hand saw
used in construction

Hack hand saw
no additional

Clothing
you wear it
keeps you warm

Pants
legs
buttons
belt loops
pockets
cloth
two legs

Levi's
blue

Double-knit pants
comfortable
stretchy

Furniture
no attributes

Chair
legs
seat
back
arms
comfortable
four legs
wood
holds people—
   you sit on it

Kitchen chair
no additional

Living-room chair
large
soft
cushion

From "Basic Objects in Natural Categories," by E. Rosch, C. B. Mervis, W. D. Gray, D. M. Johnsen, and P. Boyes-Braem. In *Cognitive Psychology,* 1976, *8,* 382–440. Copyright 1976 by Academic Press, Inc. Reprinted by permission.

examples shown in Table 8.3. There were only two attributes listed for the superordinate category *clothing*—you wear it and it keeps you warm. These same two attributes plus an additional six were listed for the basic-level category *pants*. Pants have legs, buttons, belt loops, pockets, and two legs and are made of cloth. One additional attribute was listed for the subordinate category *Levi's*—blue—and two additional attributes were listed for double-knit pants—comfortable and stretchy. Notice that, although the items in subordinate categories share slightly more attributes than those in basic-level categories, there is a considerable overlap of attributes for subordinate categories. Although Levi's and double-knit pants differ on a few attributes, they also share many of the same attributes, making it easier to distinguish between pants and shirts than to distinguish between Levi's and double-knit pants.

The same argument can be extended to motor movements. There are very few movements in common at the superordinate level. The movements that accompany working with a tool or getting dressed depend on which tool or which article of clothing is involved. Motor movements at the basic level are more standard. We put on pants the same way, regardless of whether they are Levi's or double-knit pants. The result is a large increase in common motor movements going from the superordinate to the basic level but a very small increase going from the basic to the subordinate level. We therefore say "He puts on his pants one leg at a time," rather than "He puts on his clothing one leg at a time" or "He puts on his double-knit pants one leg at a time." The reference to clothing is too general because motor movements differ for different kinds of clothes, and the reference to double-knit pants is too specific because the same motor movements apply to pants in general.

Another characteristic of categories is particularly important for prototype theories—the shape of objects within the category. The prototype of a category is usually defined as the "average" of the patterns in the category. It represents the central tendency of the category. But is it meaningful to talk about the average shape of real-world categories? The answer depends on which hierarchical level we are talking about.

The objects in Figure 8.6 represent basic-level categories, and the four objects in each row belong to the same superordinate category. Rosch and her colleagues found that people were not very good at identifying the average shape of two different basic-level objects belonging to the same superordinate category. For example, the average shape of a table and a chair together would look like neither a table nor a chair but something in between that would be difficult to identify. These results are not surprising if we try to think of what an "average" object would look like for superordinate categories such as furniture, clothing, vehicles, and animals. We can think of good examples of each category, but this is not the same as forming an average of all the examples.

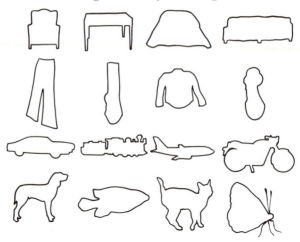

Figure 8.6. Examples of outlines of pictures representing basic-level categories. The pictures in each row belong to the same superordinate category. *(From "Basic Objects in Natural Categories," by E. Rosch, C. B. Mervis, W. D. Gray, D. M. Johnsen, and P. Boyes-Braem. In* Cognitive Psychology, *1976, 8, 382–440. Copyright 1976 by Academic Press, Inc. Reprinted by permission.)*

The concept of an average example becomes meaningful if we think of objects from the same basic level. Although the average shape of furniture is unreasonable, the average shape of a chair is a more reasonable concept. In fact, people were quite accurate in identifying the average shape of two objects from the same basic-level category—for example, the average of two chairs still looks reasonably like a chair, and the average of two shirts still looks reasonably like a shirt. Basic-level objects are sufficiently similar to each other that the average shape is identifiable. The creation of an average pattern to represent a category is therefore possible at the basic level (and at the subordinate level, where the shapes of objects in the same category are even more similar) but is not possible at the superordinate level.

Family Resemblances

So far we have emphasized comparing categories at different levels of generality. Rosch and her colleagues argued that the intermediate level of generality—the basic level—is the most important. It is the most general level at which a prototype or concrete image can be formed to represent the category as a whole. It is also the level at which categories are the most differentiated from one another because the members of basic-level categories share many attributes with each other but do not share many attributes with members of other categories.

We will now shift our emphasis to comparing the members within a category. Rosch and Mervis (1975) have used the term *family resemblance* to refer to differences in how well members of a category represent that category. For instance, people agree that chairs, sofas, and tables are good examples of furniture; cars, trucks, and buses are good examples of vehicles; and oranges, apples, and bananas are good examples of fruit. Table 8.4 lists 20 members for each of six superordinate categories, ranked from the most typical to the least typical, based on people's ratings.

Although the rank order may seem fairly obvious to us, it isn't obvious *why* the order exists. Why is a car a good example and an elevator a poor example of a vehicle? Both can transport people and materials. Rosch and Mervis hypothesized that good members will share many attributes with other members of the category and few attributes with members of other categories. Notice that Rosch is applying the same hypothesis she used to compare superordinate, basic, and subordinate categories to compare the typicality of members within a category.

Rosch and Mervis tested their hypothesis by asking people to list the attributes of each of the category members shown in Table 8.4. For example, for a bicycle people might list that it has two wheels, pedals, and handlebars; you ride on it; and it doesn't use fuel. To test the hypothesis that the good examples of categories should share many attributes with other members of the category, it is necessary to calculate a measure of family resemblance for each item by considering how many other members share each attribute of the item. Let's take a specific example. Since a car has wheels as one of its attributes, we would count the number of vehicles that also have wheels. Since a car has a windshield, we would count the number of members that have a windshield. The numerical score for each attribute can vary from 1 to 20 depending on how many of the 20 members in Table 8.4 possess that attribute. The family resemblance score for each member is obtained by adding together all of the numerical scores of each attribute possessed by that member. If 14 members of the category have wheels and 11 have windshields, the family resemblance score would be 25 for a car if it had only those two attributes. The actual score, of course, is much higher since we also have to add the numerical scores for all the other attributes listed for a car. The results revealed that good representatives of a category had high family resemblance scores. The correlations between the two variables was between .84 (for vegetable) and .94 (for weapon) for the six superordinate categories listed in Table 8.4.

Another way of viewing these results is to compare how many attributes are shared by the five most typical and five least typical examples in each category. The five most typical vehicles are car, truck, bus, motorcycle, and train. The five share many attributes since they possess many common parts—the subjects in the experiment were able to iden-

TABLE 8.4. Typicality of Members in Six Superordinate Categories.

		Category			
Item	Furniture	Vehicle	Fruit	Weapon	Vegetable	Clothing
1	Chair	Car	Orange	Gun	Peas	Pants
2	Sofa	Truck	Apple	Knife	Carrots	Shirt
3	Table	Bus	Banana	Sword	String beans	Dress
4	Dresser	Motorcycle	Peach	Bomb	Spinach	Skirt
5	Desk	Train	Pear	Hand grenade	Broccoli	Jacket
6	Bed	Trolley car	Apricot	Spear	Asparagus	Coat
7	Bookcase	Bicycle	Plum	Cannon	Corn	Sweater
8	Footstool	Airplane	Grapes	Bow and arrow	Cauliflower	Underpants
9	Lamp	Boat	Strawberry	Club	Brussels sprouts	Socks
10	Piano	Tractor	Grapefruit	Tank	Lettuce	Pajamas
11	Cushion	Cart	Pineapple	Teargas	Beets	Bathing suit
12	Mirror	Wheelchair	Blueberry	Whip	Tomato	Shoes
13	Rug	Tank	Lemon	Icepick	Lima beans	Vest
14	Radio	Raft	Watermelon	Fists	Eggplant	Tie
15	Stove	Sled	Honeydew	Rocket	Onion	Mittens
16	Clock	Horse	Pomegranate	Poison	Potato	Hat
17	Picture	Blimp	Date	Scissors	Yam	Apron
18	Closet	Skates	Coconut	Words	Mushroom	Purse
19	Vase	Wheelbarrow	Tomato	Foot	Pumpkin	Wristwatch
20	Telephone	Elevator	Olive	Screwdriver	Rice	Necklace

From "Family Resemblances: Studies in the Internal Structure of Categories," by E. Rosch and C. B. Mervis. In *Cognitive Psychology*, 1975, 7, 573–605. Copyright 1975 by Academic Press, Inc. Reprinted by permission.

tify 36 attributes that belonged to all five members. The five least typical examples are horse, blimp, skates, wheelbarrow, and elevator—the subjects identified only two attributes that belonged to all five of the least typical members (perhaps that they carry people and move). The results were similar for the other five superordinate categories.

The fact that typical members of categories tend to share attributes with other members is also true for basic-level categories. You may have noticed that the examples of the superordinate categories shown in Table 8.4 are basic-level categories. Rosch and Mervis (1975) selected six of these examples (car, truck, airplane, chair, table, lamp) to test the same hypothesis—that the most typical members of basic-level categories should share more attributes with other members than the least typical members. For each of the six categories the experimenters selected 15 pictures, varying from good to poor examples. Rosch and Mervis then asked groups of undergraduates to rate how well each picture represented their idea of the category. As was found for the members of superordinate categories, there was a high correlation between the typicality of a member and the number of shared attributes.

The other half of the hypothesis—that the attributes of good members are not shared by the members of other categories—also was supported. Rosch and Mervis asked the subjects to list possible categories for the examples shown in Table 8.4. The possibility that an item would be classified into an alternative category increased as the examples became less typical. For example, a sled and skates could be classified as toys rather than as vehicles. A horse could be classified as an animal and an elevator as part of a building. The possibility of classifying a more typical vehicle into an alternative category was less likely, suggesting that more typical members are less likely to possess attributes that are also possessed by members of other categories.

Categorizing novel patterns

At the beginning of this chapter we learned that one advantage of categories is that they enable us to recognize novel objects. A young child who encounters a new dog for the first time can use previous knowledge of dogs to recognize the new dog. Lacking this ability to classify novel objects, the child would have to be told the identity of every new object.

People are quite good at making perceptual classifications, and psychologists are naturally interested in how they do it. The characteristics of natural categories may provide a clue. One characteristic is that some category members are more prototypical or better representatives of the category than other members. People might therefore create a pattern or prototype that they feel is a very good representative of the category and use it to classify other patterns. A model based on this strategy is called a *prototype model.* Another characteristic of category members is that they share features or attributes. People might therefore classify a novel pattern by determining how frequently its feature values match the feature values of category patterns. A model based on this strategy is called a *feature frequency model.*

The two models can be illustrated by referring to the examples in Figure 8.7, taken from one of my experiments (Reed, 1972). If you were a subject in this experiment, I would first tell you that the upper row of faces represents one category, and the bottom row of faces represents another category. I would then ask you to study the two categories because you would have to classify novel faces as a member of one of the two categories. Students in my experiments classified from 20 to 25 novel faces (faces that didn't match any of the faces shown in Figure 8.7). Figure 8.8 shows three novel faces.

The feature frequency model proposes that people match the feature values of the novel pattern to the feature values of the patterns in the two categories. For example, the four features of each novel face (forehead, eyes, nose, and mouth) would be compared to the five faces in each category to determine how many features in each category matched the features of the novel face. The pattern is then classified into the category that results in the most feature matches.

The prototype model proposes that people create a pattern that best represents each category. This prototype is usually a pattern that is the average of all the other patterns in the category. The prototype for

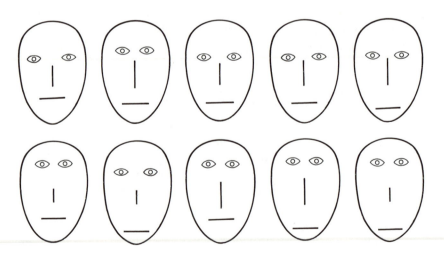

Figure 8.7. Example of a perceptual categorization task. The upper five faces represent Category 1, and the lower five faces represent Category 2. *(From "Perceptual vs. Conceptual Categorization," by S. K. Reed and M. P. Friedman. In* Memory & Cognition, *1973, 1, 157–163. Copyright 1973 by the Psychonomic Society, Inc. Reprinted by permission.)*

the top row of faces in Figure 8.7 is the pattern that is created by finding the average feature values of the five patterns in the category. It has the average forehead height, average eye separation, average nose length, and average mouth height. The middle pattern in Figure 8.8 is the prototype for the top row of faces, and the right pattern is the prototype for the bottom row of faces. We will now review evidence that supports each of these two models, beginning with the prototype model.

The Prototype Model

The prototype model proposes that the perceiver creates a prototype to represent each category and classifies a novel pattern by comparing it to the category prototypes, finding which prototype it most closely resembles, and selecting that category. If the novel pattern were more similar to the Category 1 prototype, it would be classified into Category 1. If it were more similar to the Category 2 prototype, it would be classified into Category 2.

The prototype rule has the advantage that it doesn't require many comparisons in order to classify a pattern. Instead of comparing a novel pattern to every pattern in the category, a person has to compare a novel pattern to only a single pattern in each category—the pattern that is the best representative of that category. As we encounter more patterns in a category, it would become more difficult to compare a novel pattern to all of them. The prototype strategy is therefore an economical strategy because only a single comparison is required for each category regardless of how many patterns are in it.

Initial support for the use of a prototype strategy in classifying patterns came from a study by Posner and Keele (1968). The investigators created four prototype patterns—a triangle, the letters *M* and *F*, and a random pattern. Each prototype was made up of nine dots and could be distorted by varying the dots. Figure 8.9 shows different amounts of

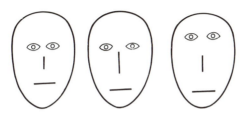

Figure 8.8. Examples of novel test faces for Figure 8.7. The middle face is the Category 1 prototype and the right face is the Category 2 prototype. *(From "Pattern Recognition and Categorization," by S. K. Reed. In* Cognitive Psychology, *1972, 3, 382–407. Copyright 1972 by Academic Press, Inc. Reprinted by permission.)*

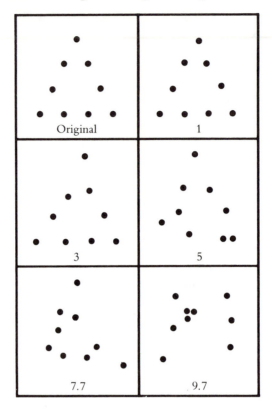

Figure 8.9. Distortions of a prototype (original) pattern at different levels of variability. *(From "Perceived Distance and the Classification of Distorted Patterns," by M. I. Posner, R. Goldsmith, and K. E. Welton. In* Journal of Experimental Psychology, *1967, 73, 28–38. Copyright 1967 by the American Psychological Association. Reprinted by permission.)*

distortion for one of the prototypes. The numbers show how much the dots were allowed to vary, the larger numbers implying greater distortions. Posner and Keele constructed distortions of each prototype at each of the three levels of variability: low variability (level 1), moderate variability (level 5), and high variability (level 7.7). Undergraduates at the University of Oregon learned a list of 12 patterns, 3 from each prototype (triangle, *M, F,* and random). Group 1 subjects learned to classify three low-variability distortions of each prototype, and Group 5 subjects learned to classify three moderate-variability distortions of each prototype. You will notice in Figure 8.9 that the prototype is fairly obvious for level 1 distortions but is not so obvious for level 5 distortions. Group 1 subjects should therefore have a much better idea than Group 5 subjects of what the prototype looks like.

After the undergraduates could correctly classify all 12 patterns into the four categories, they were asked to classify high-variability patterns they had never seen before. The crucial comparison in this experiment is whether Group 1 subjects or Group 5 subjects would be better in classifying the novel patterns. Group 1 subjects should have a better idea of what the prototype looked like, but Group 5 subjects should have a better idea of how patterns could vary within a category since they had trained on more variable patterns. The results indicated that Group 5 subjects were significantly better than Group 1 subjects in classifying the highly distorted, novel patterns. In other words, subjects were more able to recognize highly distorted patterns when they had trained on moderately distorted patterns than when they had trained on slightly distorted patterns. The implication is that making the prototype very obvious by using low-distortion patterns is not sufficient when people have to classify highly distorted patterns. It is also necessary to learn how patterns can vary within a category.

Although the superiority of the Group 5 subjects suggested that learning about category variability may be more important than learning the category prototypes, Posner and Keele also obtained results that supported the use of a prototype strategy. First, they found that ability to correctly classify a novel pattern depended on the degree of similarity between the novel pattern and the category prototype. The more similar a novel pattern was to one of the category prototypes, the easier it was to correctly classify the pattern. This result would be expected if people had created a prototype to represent each category. Second, undergraduates who had trained on the moderately distorted patterns could later classify the category prototypes as well as they could classify the patterns they studied during the training session. Remember that they had not seen the prototypes previously because all the training patterns were distortions of the prototype. This finding suggests that even Group 5 subjects could create a prototype from the training patterns.

The results of this study suggested that people could create prototypes to represent categories and use them to classify novel patterns. However, there was also evidence that people learned more than simply the category prototypes since the variability of the patterns within a category also influenced their performance on classifying novel patterns. Posner and Keele's findings were an important contribution to the study of how people classify patterns. Subsequent research by other investigators has focused largely on directly comparing the prototype model with other categorization models.

Comparing Alternative Models

The results obtained by Posner and Keele (1968) were certainly consistent with a prototype model, but how would a prototype model compare with alternative models? I became interested in this question as a graduate student and decided to devote my dissertation to it. It seemed to me that people classify a pattern into a category because that pattern is similar to other patterns in the category. If we accept this assumption, the first step in formulating a categorization model is to define a measure of similarity.

One method of measuring similarity is simply to show people pairs of patterns and ask them to rate the similarity of the two patterns in each pair. A better method, however, is to convert the similarity ratings into distances by using a multidimensional scaling program, which specifies the locations of the patterns in a multidimensional space. The *distance* between two patterns is determined by how close they are to each other. There are two advantages of using the program, which is run on a computer. First, distances are better measures of similarity than the original similarity ratings. Second, if we can interpret the dimensions of the scaled distances, we will have a better idea about which characteristics of the patterns most influenced the similarity judgments. Interested readers may want to look at articles by Shepard (1962) and Kruskal (1964) to learn more about these programs.

Let me use a specific example to clarify the second assertion. I initially showed people pairs of schematic faces and asked them to judge the similarity of the two faces. I then used a multidimensional scaling program to convert the similarity ratings into distances and found that the faces could be represented in four dimensions, one for each of the four features that varied (eye height, eye width, nose length, and mouth height). Since it is difficult to draw a four-dimensional diagram, my example in Figure 8.10 shows only two dimensions. The example is fictitious, but it corresponds fairly closely to the two categories shown in Figure 8.7 if we let the horizontal dimension (X_1) represent the height of the eyes and the vertical dimension (X_2) represent the height of the mouth. One dimension is a good distinguisher between the two categories (the horizontal dimension, or eye height), whereas the other dimension is a poor distinguisher between the two categories (the vertical dimension, or mouth height).

The fact that some dimensions are much more important than others in distinguishing between categories is true for most categories. For example, if we selected a random sample of males and females, we would find that height is a good dimension and intelligence is a poor dimension for distinguishing between the two categories. Since multidimensional scaling programs represent patterns in terms of the dimensions that influence similarity judgments, we can see how pairs of patterns and groups of patterns differ along each dimension.

After we have converted similarities into distances, we can use the distance between two patterns as a measure of similarity. The similarity between two patterns in the multidimensional space is inversely related

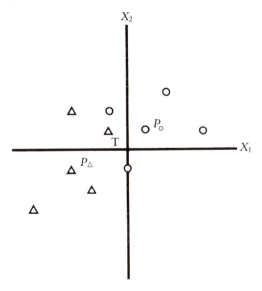

Figure 8.10. Categories of patterns represented in a multidimensional space: Category 1 patterns (△), Category 2 patterns (o), Category 1 prototype ($P_\triangle$), Category 2 prototype (P_o), and a test pattern (*T*). *(From* Psychological Processes in Pattern Recognition, *by S. K. Reed. Copyright 1973 by Academic Press, Inc. Reprinted by permission.)*

to distance—similarity increases as distance decreases. The most similar patterns are those that are close together.

The distance between two patterns is most commonly defined as the length of the straight line drawn between them. The distance measure can be illustrated by considering a simple classification rule called the *nearest neighbor rule*. The nearest neighbor rule states that a person should classify a novel pattern by comparing it to all the patterns in each category in order to find the single category pattern that is most similar to the novel pattern. The novel pattern is then classified into the category that produces the best match. To return to the example in Figure 8.10, the novel or test pattern (represented by a *T*) is closest to a pattern in Category 1, so it should be classified into Category 1 according to the nearest neighbor rule.

The problem with the nearest neighbor rule is that it requires that a person compare the test pattern to all the category patterns but uses only a single pattern (the one most similar to the test pattern) as the basis for decision. If the most similar pattern is not very representative of its category, the decision could easily be wrong. For example, a young child who had a Pekingese dog as a pet might classify a long-haired cat as a dog because the cat looks more like the Pekingese than like other cats. The error would occur because, although a Pekingese is a dog, it is not a very good representative of the category. A better rule, called the *average dis-*

tance rule, states that a person should compare the novel pattern to all the patterns in each category in order to determine the average distance between the novel pattern and the patterns in each category. If the average distance is less for Category 1 patterns, Category 1 should be selected; otherwise Category 2 should be selected. The average distance rule has the advantage over the nearest neighbor rule that it uses all category patterns as the basis for the decision instead of only a single pattern. It has the disadvantage that a person must compute the average similarity in addition to comparing the novel pattern to all category patterns.

Both of these disadvantages are eliminated by the *prototype rule.* If a person can create a prototype to represent each category, a novel pattern has to be compared only to this single pattern. The symbols $P_\triangle$ and P_o represent the two prototypes in Figure 8.10. According to the prototype rule, a person should select Category 1 whenever a novel pattern is closer to the Category 1 prototype and Category 2 whenever a novel pattern is closer to the Category 2 prototype.

The final model that we will consider is different from the first three in that it doesn't use distance in making predictions. The *feature frequency rule* is concerned with matching features rather than measuring the similarity between patterns. It looks at the features on the novel pattern and compares how many times they exactly match features of the category patterns. Consider the left pattern shown in Figure 8.8. It has a large forehead, narrow eyes, a short nose, and a high mouth. An inspection of the two categories in Figure 8.7 reveals that four faces in Category 1 have a large forehead, one has narrow eyes, and one has a high mouth. Therefore, the total number of feature matches with the novel face is six. By contrast, four faces in Category 2 have narrow eyes, three have short noses, and two have high mouths. Since the number of matches is higher for Category 2, the pattern should be classified into Category 2, according to the feature frequency rule.

You may have noticed that each of the four models—nearest neighbor, average distance, prototype, and feature frequency—states how a pattern should be classified. Since the models use different information, they sometimes differ in their selection of categories. Therefore, the models could be used to make predictions about how people would classify the patterns. If the prototype model, for example, was more successful than the other models in predicting how people classified novel patterns, this would imply that they used a prototype strategy. In fact, the results of my studies did support the prototype model.

The results do not prove that everyone used the prototype strategy, but they suggest that it was the predominant strategy used. This suggestion was confirmed by asking people which strategy of the four listed in Table 8.5 they used. The majority selected the prototype strategy, and very few selected the two strategies that required comparing the novel patterns (projected faces) with all the category patterns. These particular results are from an experiment in which UCLA undergraduates had to classify novel patterns after learning the two categories shown in Figure 8.7. Comparing a novel pattern to all the category patterns should be particularly difficult when the category patterns are stored in memory rather than physically present. However, the data supported the prototype model even when all the patterns were simultaneously present, as they are in Figure 8.7 (Reed, 1972).

One qualification of these results is necessary before we consider other research. The best predicting model was a prototype model in which the dimensions were differentially weighted or emphasized to account for the fact that some dimensions are more useful than others in distinguishing between categories. For the two categories shown in Figure 8.7 the weights calculated to reflect the usefulness of the dimensions were .46 for forehead (eye height), .24 for eye separation, .24 for nose length, and .06 for mouth height. The weights indicate that the forehead is a good dimension for distinguishing between the two categories and the mouth is a poor dimension. The results suggest that the most popular strategy was to compare the similarity of the novel pattern to the two category prototypes but to emphasize some dimensions more than others

TABLE 8.5. Subjects' Reports on Using Different Classification Strategies after Learning the Category Patterns.

Strategy	*Percentage*
1. Prototype	
I formed an abstract image of what a face in Category 1 should look like and an abstract image of what a face in Category 2 should look like. I then compared the projected face with the two abstract images and chose the category which gave the closest match.	58%
2. Nearest neighbor	
I compared the projected face with all the faces in the two categories looking for a single face which best matched the projected face. I then chose the category in which that face appeared.	10%
3. Feature frequency	
I looked at each feature on the projected face and compared how many times it exactly matched a feature in each of the two categories. I then chose the category which gave the highest number of matches.	28%
4. Average distance	
I compared the projected face with each of the five faces in Category 1 and with each of the five faces in Category 2. I then chose the category in which the faces were more like the projected face, basing my decision on all faces in the two categories.	4%

From "Pattern Recognition and Categorization," by S. K. Reed. In *Cognitive Psychology*, 1972, *3*, 382–407. Copyright 1972 by Academic Press, Inc. Reprinted by permission.

when making the comparison. The finding that people emphasized some dimensions more than others is consistent with our discussion of pattern recognition (Chapter 2), where we saw that difficulty in discriminating pairs of letters could be analyzed in terms of the relative importance of feature dimensions.

The Feature Frequency Model

Although the prototype model was much more successful than the feature frequency model in predicting how people would classify schematic faces (Reed, 1972), there are situations in which a feature frequency model is more appropriate. Schematic faces consist of features that vary along continuous dimensions such as eye separation or mouth height, so it is possible to create an average pattern or prototype to represent the category. Not all items consist of features that vary along a continuous dimension, however. Consider the following task, designed by Hayes-Roth and Hayes-Roth (1977).

The task was to classify people as belonging to Club 1, Club 2, or neither club. The variation of three features affected the classification: age, education, and marital status. Each feature had one of four values. The age of a person was 30, 40, 50, or 60; the education level was junior high, high school, trade school, or college; and the marital status was single, married, divorced, or widowed. People would have considerable difficulty creating an average person to represent each of the two clubs. It would be easy to compute the average age level, but computing an average for education or marital status is more problematical. We might translate educational level into years of education, but this would blur the distinction between trade school and college. Forming an average marital status is even more difficult.

The point of this example is simply that the kind of stimuli being classified places constraints on which strategies are the easiest to use. Hayes-Roth and Hayes-Roth found that a version of the feature frequency model was a good predictor of how students would classify people into clubs. The most successful model compared combinations of features in addition to individual features. For example, if a person were 30 years old and divorced, the model would examine how many people in each club were *both* 30 and divorced in addition to matching the two individual features. Neumann (1974) also tested a feature frequency model that matched both individual features and combinations of features. Once again, the model was successful in predicting how people would classify patterns that did not consist of continuous dimensions. The only problem with feature frequency models is that they can require a great number of comparisons if they match combinations of features in addition to the individual features (see Reitman & Bower, 1973).

Our current knowledge about categorization models suggests that either the prototype model or the feature frequency model can predict classifications, depending on the features of the classified items. When the stimuli consisted of dot patterns or schematic faces that had continuous dimensions, the data indicated that people used a prototype strategy (Posner & Keele, 1968; Reed, 1972). The possibility that the prototype could have been retained as a visual image might also have encouraged the construction of a prototype. When the items did not consist of continuous dimensions, a version of the feature frequency model was successful in predicting classifications (Neumann, 1974; Hayes-Roth & Hayes-Roth, 1977). Since items in the real world possess many different kinds of features, it is fortunate that we have some flexibility in our classification strategies.

Box 8.1 shows how both feature frequencies and category averages were used to predict the "average" Miss America. The average values of

---

Box 8.1. How the Ideal Miss America Measures Up

When Miss Mississippi was crowned Miss America 1980, Dr. George L. Miller rubbed his hands together like a crapshooter staring a "7" in the face and said, "The honey, she came through for me."

Miller, however, wasn't speaking about Cheryl Prewitt, the blue-eyed beauty from the Magnolia State. . . . He was talking about a computer.

Miller and Dr. Chipel P. Tseng, statistical analysts at Northern Illinois University, used the campus computer to determine the composite profile of Miss America winners and then to figure the odds-on favorite for the 1980 crown. Months before the crowning, the computer spit out the name "Cheryl Prewitt."

Last August, the analysts fed the computer mounds of data (but no photographs) on the last 20 Miss America pageants. Then, after processing personal information on the coming year's contestants, the computer decided that Miss Prewitt stood over a 25-percent chance of victory. After she won a swimsuit preliminary, the computer increased the odds to over 60 percent.

Miller's computer decided the "average" Miss America is a woman who is about 20½ years old, 5 feet 6 inches tall, 119 pounds, with measurements of 35.6–23.4–35.6. She tends to score high in the swimsuit contest, comes from a small town, has brown hair, green eyes, a plain name and either sings or plays the piano. She usually is a college graduate.

Miss Prewitt came very close to that description. She is 22, 5 feet 6 inches, 112 pounds and measures 35–23–36. She is from rural Ackerman, Miss., has brown hair, blue eyes, sings and plays the piano and is a graduate of Mississippi State University.

—M.L.

previous winners were used to determine height, weight, and measurements. Other data—such as the fact that winners typically come from a small town and have brown hair, green eyes, and a plain name—were determined by how frequently previous winners possessed these particular characteristics. By using a combination of category averages and feature frequencies, the statistical analysts successfully predicted the winner of the pageant.

Summary

One way we organize knowledge is through categories and hierarchies made up of categories. Categories reduce the complexity of the environment and the need for constant learning and enable us to recognize objects, respond appropriately, and order and relate classes of events.

The concept identification paradigm is one approach to the study of categorization. People attempt to learn a conceptual rule by receiving feedback on positive and negative instances of the concept. Research involving blank trials reveals that, although people can evaluate more than a single hypothesis at one time, they do not perform at the optimum level when they do this.

Concepts that are defined by logical rules are easiest to learn for a conjunctive rule, followed by the disjunctive, conditional, and biconditional rules. The same relative difficulty occurs when people are told the rule and have to identify the relevant attributes. Real-world or natural categories generally cannot be distinguished by a simple rule. Frequently they are hierarchically organized—for example, double-knit pants are included in the category *pants,* and pants are included in the category *clothes.* Rosch has argued that most classifications are made at the intermediate or basic level—the most general level at which a prototype can be constructed and the level at which categories are most differentiated. The members of natural categories vary in how well they represent the category. Oranges and apples are considered good examples of fruit, whereas coconuts and olives are considered poor examples. The attributes or features of good members are shared with other members of the category and are not shared by members of alternative categories.

The two most popular theories of classifying novel patterns are the prototype model and the feature frequency model. The prototype model proposes that people create a pattern that best represents the category and then classify novel patterns by comparing them to the category prototypes. The prototype is usually the central tendency of the category, formed by calculating the average of all the patterns in the category. Prototype theories have been most successful in predicting how people will classify perceptual patterns consisting of feature values that vary continuously along a dimension. By contrast, the feature frequency model proposes that people classify patterns by comparing how frequently their feature values match the feature values of the category patterns and then select the category that results in the greatest number of feature matches. The feature frequency theory has been most successful in predicting how people classify patterns consisting of feature values that do not vary continuously along a dimension.

Recommended reading

Two chapters in the book by Bourne, Domonowski, and Loftus (1979) provide a good introduction to concept identification. The blank trials procedure developed by Levine has been extended by Berger (1974) to provide a direct measure of a subject's hypotheses. A recent review article by Mervis and Rosch (1981) summarizes research on the categorization of natural objects. Homa (Homa, Cross, Cornell, Goldman, & Schwartz, 1975; Homa & Chambliss, 1975) investigated variables that influence prototype abstraction, such as the number of categories and the number of exemplars within a category. Strauss (1979) investigated prototype abstraction in infants and adults to determine whether the prototype or feature frequency theory could best account for his findings. Although both theories attempt to explain how people abstract categorical information, some investigators (Brooks, 1978; Medin & Schaffer, 1978) have argued that people compare a novel pattern to the category patterns rather than to abstract information. A recent paper by Martin and Caramazza (1980) builds a bridge between the concept identification and prototype abstraction literatures. The authors investigated whether people would learn logical rules in order to classify schematic faces.

9

Semantic
Organization

A scientist must organize. One makes a science with facts in the same way that one makes a house with stones; but an accumulation of facts is no more a science than a pile of stones is a house.

HENRI POINCARÉ

The need to organize knowledge is universal—it applies as much to the arts and humanities as to the sciences. Imagine that you wrote every fact you knew on a separate card and someone mixed all the cards and put them in a gigantic pile. Now imagine that someone asked you in which city the Declaration of Independence was signed and you had to retrieve the appropriate card in order to answer the question. How would you find the correct card? Even worse, what if you had to write an essay on the Declaration of Independence? Since all the cards are mixed up, finding one card would provide no clues about the location of other cards on the same topic.

In order to retrieve related information from LTM, we must be able to organize our memory. Much of this organization is semantic—based on the meaning of the information. A particularly effective way to organize semantic information is to form hierarchies. The first section of this chapter illustrates how hierarchical organization facilitates recall.

A popular procedure for studying the organization of semantic memory is to ask people to respond *true* or *false* to statements such as *A robin is a bird* or *A canary is a building*. In order to answer the question *Is a robin a bird?* we have to consider the meaning of both *robin* and *bird*. The time needed to respond provides psychologists with a clue about the organization of semantic information in LTM. The second section of this chapter describes how psychologists have followed this approach to construct models of semantic memory. Two major classes of models are used. One model assumes that people compare the features of two categories to determine their relationship. For example, we could decide whether a robin is a bird by determining whether a robin possesses the features of a bird. This model is somewhat similar to the categorization models discussed in the previous chapter. The other model assumes that the relation between two categories is stored directly in memory in a semantic network, which consists of concepts joined to other concepts by links that specify the relation between them.

The third section illustrates how semantic networks can be applied to a variety of tasks. A key assumption here is the idea of *spreading activation*. Spreading activation implies that the activation of a concept can lead to the activation of other, related concepts as the activation spreads along the paths of the network. This is a very general assumption that allows us to apply semantic network models to many different tasks. Since semantic network models might possibly provide a general theory, we will consider their strengths and limitations carefully.

Hierarchical organization

We have seen examples in the previous chapter of how some information is hierarchically organized and how a hierarchical organization can influence our performance on cognitive tasks such as classifying visual patterns. Hierarchical organization can also influence performance by facilitating the recall of semantic information.

Recall of Hierarchical Information

One advantage of a well-organized memory is that it helps us to retrieve information in a systematic way. I began this chapter by asking you to imagine that you had to retrieve information by searching a gigantic pile of cards. If the information on the cards were organized in some systematic way, this would be a manageable task. If the information were not systematically organized, the task would be very difficult and your level of achievement would not be very impressive.

An experimental analog of this task was created to study the effects of hierarchical organization on recall (Bower, Clark, Winzenz, & Lesgold, 1969). The material consisted of conceptual hierarchies of words like the one shown in Figure 9.1. Participants in the experiment saw four different hierarchies, each containing 28 words. One group of subjects, in the "organized" condition, studied the four hierarchies for approximately 1 minute each. They then attempted to recall all 112 words in

Level

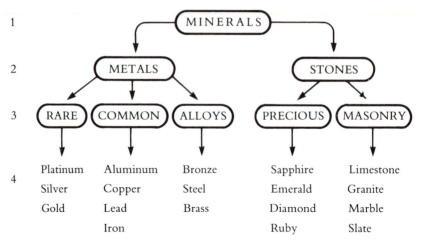

Figure 9.1. Hierarchical organization of minerals. *(From "Organizational Factors in Memory," by G. H. Bower. In* Cognitive Psychology, *1970, 1, 18–46. Copyright 1970 by Academic Press, Inc. Reprinted by permission.)*

whatever order they wished. The study and recall trial was repeated four times. The upper curve in Figure 9.2 shows how well this group performed: they recalled 73 words after the first study trial and all 112 words after three study trials.

Another group of subjects, in the "random" condition, saw the same 112 words inserted randomly in the four hierarchies. For example, if the four hierarchies consisted of plants, instruments, body parts, and minerals, each set of 28 words would contain words from all four hierarchies inserted randomly into a spatial tree like the one shown in Figure 9.1. The high level of performance of subjects in the organized condition is particularly impressive when compared to the subjects in the random condition. After four study trials the random group was still recalling fewer words than the organized group recalled on the very first trial (see Figure 9.2).

We should note at this point that the effects of organization are not limited to hierarchical organization. In another experiment Bower presented people with associated words linked together. For example, the words *bread, mouse,* and *yellow* were linked to *cheese*; the words *cat* and *trap* were linked to *mouse*; and *sun* and *butterfly* were linked to *yellow*. When the associated words were linked together, people recalled many more words than when the same words were randomly linked together (as when *cat* and *bread* were linked to *yellow*). The semantic organization of the material improved recall, even though the organization did not consist of a hierarchy. The difference between the organized and random

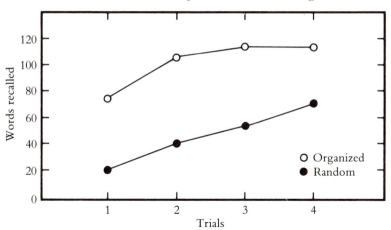

Figure 9.2. Average number of words recalled by subjects in the "organized" and "random" conditions. *(From "Organizational Factors in Memory," by G. H. Bower. In* Cognitive Psychology, *1970, 1, 18–46. Copyright 1970 by Academic Press, Inc. Reprinted by permission.)*

conditions was more striking for hierarchical organization, however, suggesting that hierarchical organization is particularly effective.

Category Size

Figure 9.1 shows that each category in the hierarchy is divided into several smaller categories. The division of a category into subcategories raises the question of how big the groups should be. The advantage of grouping items might be reduced if the groups were too small. On the other hand, information might be difficult to remember or retrieve if the groups were too large.

In Chapter 4 we learned that the capacity of STM can be increased by forming chunks consisting of several items stored as a group in LTM. The grouping of chess pieces (Chase & Simon, 1973) is an example of how chunking improves recall in an STM task—the average size of a chunk for an expert chess player was 2.5 pieces. We know from both research (Charness, 1976) and demonstrations (Box 9.1) that chess experts also have a very good LTM for chess positions. In order for such a good LTM to exist, it is likely that the smaller chunks are part of a very large hierarchy of board positions.

Psychologists have used several different techniques to study how people group information. The estimated size of the groups depends on the experimental procedure, but it generally ranges from two to five items. Chase and Ericsson (1979) demonstrated how grouping can improve recall by testing a single subject over a one-year period. The subject began with a typical digit span of seven digits. After one year of prac-

---

Box 9.1. At Age 75, Chess Master Is Still a Blindfolded Whiz

Chess master George Koltanowski set a world's record Saturday in San Francisco—at age 75—by playing and beating four opponents at once without looking at the boards.

Koltanowski, the chess editor of The Chronicle, thus became the oldest player to hold what chess players call a blindfold simultaneous exhibition.

His four opponents had full use of chessmen and boards as they called their moves out in turn to the master, who sat in a corner of his apartment with his eyes shut and his arm propped on a television.

The first player was checkmated in 13 moves and the other three resigned shortly thereafter. Mike Duncan of San Mateo lasted 26 moves before moving his rook to the wrong square and falling into a trap.

"I knew I'd lose," said Duncan, "but it's fascinating to find out just when the blow is going to come."

Koltanowski said he was nervous before the exhibition began, but, as his opponents began to slip up, he sat back, cracked an occasional joke and nibbled cookies.

"It was like the good old days," said the master, who, in 1937, took on 34 opponents in a simultaneous blindfold exhibition in Scotland, winning 24 games and drawing ten.

"I'm back on the warpath," he added. "Next month I'm going to play six at once."

His wife, Leah, who witnessed the exhibition but who does not know how to play chess, smiled when asked if Koltanowski remembers such things as bringing home items from the market.

"George remembers what he wants to remember," she said.

From the *San Francisco Chronicle*, February 26, 1979. © *San Francisco Chronicle*, 1979. Reprinted by permission.

---

tice he could recall a string of 70 digits. Pauses in his recall indicated that he organized the digits into groups of three or four and never formed groups larger than five digits. Since the subject was a long-distance runner, he initially attempted to encode many of the groups as running times. For instance, he encoded 3 4 9 2 as 3.492, a near world-record time for running a mile. He also showed evidence of using hierarchical organization because he combined digits into larger groups that usually consisted of three smaller groups. After recalling the first three groups of four digits each, he would pause longer before recalling the next three groups of four digits each. One interesting finding is that the subject's ability to recall groups of digits didn't generalize to letters. When he was tested on recalling letters, his memory span immediately fell back to about six consonants.

Broadbent (1975) also studied pauses in recall to determine how people store categorized information in LTM. He asked people to name television programs, the countries of Europe, the seven dwarfs, and the colors of the rainbow. Based on pauses in their recall and other experimental findings, he argued that people usually form groups consisting of about three items. One of the experiments he cited was a study by Wickelgren (1964) that investigated the size of rehearsal groups. Wickelgren asked people to rehearse a string of digits and instructed them on how to group the digits in the string. The instructions varied both the number and the size of the groups. Recall was best when the digits were divided into groups consisting of either three or four digits. Telephone numbers, of course, are grouped in this way, which presumably makes them easier to rehearse. And we use commas to divide long strings of digits into three-digit groups.

A good example of how small groups can form a very large hierarchy is the organization of information contained in a book or newspaper. Detterman and Ramig (1978) collected paragraphs from a wide variety of newspapers, novels, and upper-division textbooks. They found that the average number of sentences in a paragraph was about two for newspapers, three for novels, and five for textbooks. They then gave people examples of the sentences and asked them to divide each sentence into its major parts. The instructions did not specify the meaning of "major parts," nor did they suggest how many major parts should be in a sentence. People identified an average of 2.4 parts per sentence. They were then instructed to break the major parts into smaller parts if they could. They divided the major parts into an average of 3.6 smaller parts, each containing an average of 2.2 words. Each of the words contained an average of 2.3 syllables, and each syllable contained an average of 2.6 phonemes. The data illustrate how a paragraph can be partitioned into smaller and smaller categories, each consisting of two to four items.

The paragraph hierarchy contained a mixture of subjective and objective units. The objective units—sentences, words, syllables, and phonemes—are well defined and can be measured simply by counting how frequently they occur. The other two levels—the parts and subparts of sentences—were measured by asking people to break up a sentence into its parts. Of course, it is likely that objective grammatical units—noun phrases, verb phrases, and prepositional phrases—influenced the way people partitioned a sentence into its parts. We will encounter some of these units in the next chapter, on language, when we learn how the rules of a grammar can provide a hierarchical description of sentences.

Hierarchical organization could be extended even further if we had started with an entire book rather than a single paragraph. For example, I wrote this book on a hierarchical plan. The book is divided into three major parts on (1) information-processing stages, (2) the representation and organization of knowledge, and (3) cognitive skills. Each part contains four or five chapters, and each chapter contains three or four sections, which are divided into two to four subsections. I'm not certain whether this kind of organization is beneficial to readers, but it is consistent with experimental findings on hierarchical organization and category size. It also makes a very large hierarchy if we connect it to the paragraph hierarchy investigated by Detterman and Ramig.

Verification of semantic statements

In addition to influencing the amount of recall, hierarchical organization influences the time required to retrieve information from LTM. A popular procedure for studying the organization of semantic knowledge is to ask people to verify semantic statements. The experimenter might present a statement such as *A bird is an animal* and ask the subject to respond *true* or *false* as quickly as possible. The time it takes to respond to different kinds of statements provides some clues about the organization of semantic memory. As you might expect, hierarchical organization influences the time required to verify semantic statements.

Figure 9.3 shows a three-level hierarchy in which the most general category, *animal,* is divided into two subcategories—*bird* and *fish.* At the bottom of the hierarchy are specific instances of birds and fish, such as

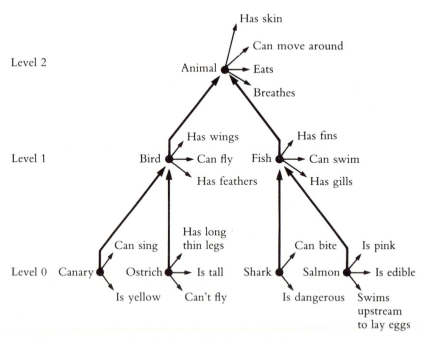

Figure 9.3. Example of a hierarchically organized memory structure. *(From "Retrieval Time from Semantic Memory," by A. M. Collins and M. R. Quillian. In* Journal of Verbal Learning and Verbal Behavior, *1969, 8, 240–248. Copyright 1969 by Academic Press, Inc. Reprinted by permission.)*

canary and shark. Hierarchical organization influences classification time in that people can generally verify that an instance is a member of a basic-level category faster than they can verify that it is a member of a super-ordinate category. For instance, they can more quickly determine that a canary is a bird than that a canary is an animal. People can also classify more typical instances faster than they can classify less typical instances. It is easier to verify that a canary is a bird than that an ostrich is a bird.

A number of theories have been proposed to account for these findings. The two most popular are the hierarchical network model of Collins and Quillian (1969, 1970) and the feature comparison model of Smith, Shoben, and Rips (1974). The distinction between the two models can be summarized briefly with the aid of the diagram in Figure 9.4. The *feature comparison model* assumes that instances are classified by comparing the features or attributes of the two nouns representing the member and the category. To verify that a robin is a bird, a person would compare the features of robin with the features of bird. In contrast, the *hierarchical network model* assumes that category information is stored directly in memory by means of associations. The right half of Figure 9.4 shows that *robin* is associated with *bird* and *bird* is associated with *animal*. In order to make predictions, both theories require more specific assumptions. We will now examine the strengths and weaknesses of these assumptions.

The Hierarchical Network Model

Figure 9.3 shows how information is stored in the hierarchical network model. Each word in the network is stored with pointers (arrows) showing how it is related to other words in the network. By following the pointers, we know that ostrich and canary are examples of birds, and

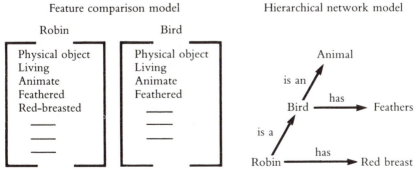

Figure 9.4. Distinction between the feature comparison model and the hierarchical network model. *(From "Theories of Semantic Memory," by E. E. Smith. In W. K. Estes (Ed.),* Handbook of Learning and Cognitive Processes *(Vol. 6). Copyright 1978 by Lawrence Erlbaum Associates, Inc., Publishers. Reprinted by permission.)*

birds and fish are examples of animals. We also know that a canary, an ostrich, a shark, and a salmon are animals since the pointers connect these instances with the superordinate category *animal*.

The pointers also show how features are stored at different levels in the hierarchy. Features that are true of all animals—such as eating and breathing—are stored at the highest level. Features that apply to basic-level categories—such as that birds have wings, can fly, and have feathers—are stored at an intermediate level. Properties stored at the lowest level are true for that particular member but not for all members of the category. It is at this level that we know that a canary is yellow and can sing.

One advantage of this kind of network is that it provides an economical way to store information because the information does not have to be repeated at each of the three levels. It isn't necessary to specify that eating and breathing are features of birds, fish, canaries, ostriches, sharks, and salmon because the network tells us that all are examples of animals, which eat and breathe. This economy of storage comes at a cost, however: retrieval of the fact that a canary eats requires two inferences—first, that a canary is a bird, and second, that a bird is an animal. In other words, it is necessary to go to the appropriate level in the hierarchy before retrieving the features stored at that level.

Although the network model was originally developed as an efficient means of storing information in a computer, it provides a number of interesting predictions if we use it as a model of human memory. Collins and Quillian (1969), in fact, used the model for that purpose by making two primary assumptions: first, that it takes time to move from one level in the hierarchy to another, and second, that additional time is required if it is necessary to retrieve the features stored at one of the levels.

Collins and Quillian tested the model by asking people to respond *true* or *false* as quickly as they could to sentences like *An elm is a plant* or *A spruce has branches*. The first sentence is an example of a question about set relations—it asks whether one category is a member of another. The second question is a question about properties—it asks about the features of a category member.

The average reaction times to six different kinds of true sentences are shown in Figure 9.5. A specific example illustrates the different points on the graph. The three lower points—the response times to questions about set relations—support the prediction that it takes time to move between levels in the network. To verify that *A canary is a canary* requires no change in level; *A canary is a bird* requires a one-level change; and *A canary is an animal* requires a two-level change. The graph indicates that response times depend on the number of changes.

The upper three points indicate that it takes longer to respond to property questions. This finding is consistent with the assumption that response time should increase if it is necessary to retrieve the features

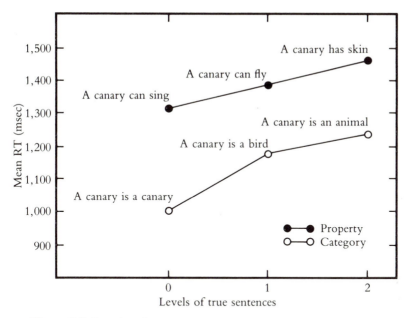

Figure 9.5. Reaction time (RT) to verify statements about feature attributes and category membership. *(From "Retrieval Time from Semantic Memory," by A. M. Collins and M. R. Quillian. In Journal of Verbal Learning and Verbal Behavior, 1969, 8, 240–248. Copyright 1969 by Academic Press, Inc. Reprinted by permission.)*

stored at one of the levels in the hierarchy. Furthermore, the level in the network where the properties are stored influences response times. The network model proposes that information about singing is stored at the lowest level, information about flying is stored at the intermediate level, and information about skin is stored at the highest level. The data support this assumption and suggest that this is how property information is stored in human memory.

Another interesting prediction based on the network model concerns facilitating retrieval from memory (Collins & Quillian, 1970). Facilitation in this case occurs when the retrieval of information is made easier because the previous question required retrieval of similar information. For example, it should be easier to verify a property of a canary if the previous question was also about a canary. The network model, however, allows us to make a more specific prediction. Collins and Quillian proposed that the degree of facilitation should depend on whether one follows the same path in the network to answer both questions. This concept can be illustrated by considering whether it would be easier to verify that *A canary is a bird* following *A canary can fly* or *A canary can sing*. The answer isn't intuitively obvious, but the network model predicts that *A canary can fly* should cause greater facilitation because the property *fly* is stored at the bird-level and *sing* is stored at the canary-level. The same path is followed only when both questions require retrieving information from the bird-level. The data were quite supportive of the prediction that the extent of semantic facilitation should depend on using the same path as the previous question (Collins & Quillian, 1970).

The successful predictions of the reaction time data in Figure 9.5 and the predictions regarding semantic facilitation are impressive accomplishments of the network model. There are two findings, however, that the model does not account for without additional assumptions. The first is that it is possible to find instances in which verification time is not a function of levels in the hierarchy. For example, it takes longer to verify that a chimpanzee is a primate than that a chimpanzee is an animal. The network model should predict the opposite because *primate,* like *bird* and *fish,* is at a lower level in the hierarchy than *animal.* The second finding is that the network model does not account for the typicality effect—the fact that more typical members of categories are easier to classify than less typical. It should be easier to verify that a canary is a bird than that an ostrich is a bird. However, since both are one level from bird, as is illustrated in Figure 9.3, the model does not predict differences in response time. The feature comparison model attempted to correct these deficiencies by offering an alternative formulation.

The Feature Comparison Model

The feature comparison model proposed by Smith, Shoben, and Rips (1974) attempts to account for classification times in somewhat the same way as the prototype model accounts for classifications. Their model assumes that the meaning of words can be represented in memory by a list of features. The features can be used to define categories, but they vary in the extent to which they are associated with a category. Smith, Shoben, and Rips considered the most essential features to be *defining* features and the remainder to be *characteristic* features. Defining features are features that are necessary in order to be a member of a category, whereas characteristic features are usually possessed by category members but are not necessary. The defining features for birds might include the fact that they are alive and have feathers and wings; the characteristic features might include that birds can fly and are of a certain size. Since the defining features are more essential, they should play a more important role in how people make classifications.

The feature comparison model has two stages. The first stage compares all the features of two concepts to determine how similar one concept is to another. For example, to determine whether a robin is a bird, we would compare the features of robin with the features of bird. If the comparison reveals that the two concepts are either very similar or dissimilar, we can respond *true* or *false* immediately. The second stage is necessary when the degree of similarity is between the two extremes. The answer isn't obvious in this case, so the model proposes that we examine only the defining features to determine whether the example possesses the necessary features of the category. The distinction between the two stages corresponds to our experience that sometimes we make classifications very quickly on the basis of the close similarity between two concepts, and sometimes we make classifications more slowly after we evaluate the criteria for category membership.

In the previous chapter we saw that psychologists often define the similarity of two items in terms of the distance between them in a multi-dimensional space. A two-dimensional representation of the similarity among birds is shown in Figure 9.6. The distances were derived by asking people to rate the similarity of all possible pairs of items, such as the similarity of two birds or the similarity of a particular bird and their concept of a bird (Rips, Shoben, & Smith, 1973). The similarity ratings were analyzed in a multidimensional scaling program and plotted in two dimensions. The horizontal dimension in this case seems to correspond to size, with the larger birds on the left and the smaller birds on the right. The experimenters interpreted the vertical dimension as "predacity"—the birds at the upper end being victims and the birds at the lower end being predators.

The first stage of the feature comparison model requires comparing

Figure 9.6. Multidimensional scaling solution for birds, showing their similarity to one another and to the category prototype. *(From "Semantic Distance and the Verification of Semantic Relations," by L.J. Rips, E.J. Shoben, and E.E. Smith. In* Journal of Verbal Learning and Verbal Behavior, *1973, 12, 1–20. Copyright 1973 by Academic Press, Inc. Reprinted by permission.)*

the distance of an example to the concept of the category, represented by the point labeled *bird*. All the features are used in the comparison in order to determine the similarity between the example and the concept. The comparison is analogous to the prototype model, particularly since the concept of the category is close to the central tendency of the category (see the point labeled *bird* in Figure 9.6). Examples that are close to the concept should usually be classified immediately without consideration of their defining features during the second stage. The probability that the second stage is necessary increases as the distance between the category concept and the example increases. The model therefore predicts that the more typical members of a category (such as robin, sparrow, blue-jay) should be classified more rapidly than the less typical members (chicken, goose, duck) because evaluating the defining features during the second stage slows down the classification. Smith, Shoben, and Rips (1974) found that people could, in fact, classify instances that are typical of the category faster than they could classify instances that are not typical of the category. The ability to account for the typicality effect is one advantage of the feature comparison model over the network model.

The other advantage of the feature comparison model is that, unlike the network model, it can account for the reversal of the category size effect. The *category size effect* refers to the fact that people are usually able to classify a member into a smaller category faster than into a larger category—for example, verifying that a collie is a dog more quickly than that a collie is an animal. The network model is consistent with the category size effect because the smaller category *(dog)* requires fewer inferences than the larger category *(animal)*. Since the smaller category is a part of the larger category, it appears lower in the hierarchy and will therefore be reached sooner. There are cases, however, that violate the category size effect because the classification times are faster for the larger category. For example, people were able to verify more quickly that Scotch is a drink than that Scotch is a liquor, even though *drink* is a larger category than *liquor*.

The feature comparison model can account for violations of the category size effect because its predictions are based on similarity rather than category size. The reason it is usually easier to verify that an example belongs to a smaller category is that the similarity between the example and one's concept of the smaller category is greater than the similarity between the example and the larger category. However, there are exceptions to this rule. Sometimes—as Smith, Shoben, and Rips showed—there is a greater similarity between the example and a larger category. The feature comparison model predicts that in this case people should be able to classify into the larger category more quickly than into the smaller category. Experimental results support this prediction (Smith, Shoben, & Rips, 1974).

Although the feature comparison model accounts for both typicality and category size effects, the model has some weaknesses. Let's now listen to what the critics have to say about its limitations.

Limitations of the Feature Comparison Model

One of the problems with the feature comparison model, as was pointed out by one of its developers (Smith, 1978), is that it relies on ratings to make most of its predictions. It's not very surprising that, if people rate an example as highly similar to their concept of a category, they will be fast to verify that it belongs to that category. The predictions regarding both typicality and category size reflect the degree of similarity between a member and its category. The predictions made by the feature comparison model are therefore rather weak predictions. Its principle asset is that the major alternative—the network model—does not make even these predictions unless it uses so many additional assumptions that it can predict almost anything.

A second criticism of the feature comparison model is its proposal that all our classifications require computations—we use the features of concepts to compute their degree of similarity. Computation is an essential part of the categorization models discussed in the previous chapter, where the emphasis was on classifying novel patterns. But once we have learned to associate examples with categories, is it still necessary to use features to compare the similarity of two concepts? Couldn't we use the associations among concepts, as suggested by the proponents of the network model (Collins & Loftus, 1975)? If we have learned that a robin is a bird, it would seem easier to use this information directly rather than to compute the similarity between robin and bird. What information is stored directly in memory and what is computed is a very important issue that is discussed by Smith (1978).

A third criticism of the feature comparison model is the argument against necessary or defining features (Collins & Loftus, 1975; Rosch & Mervis, 1975; McCloskey & Glucksberg, 1979). The feature comparison model avoids this criticism to some extent by proposing that features are more or less defining, and only the more defining features are evaluated during the second stage. This implies, however, that people can identify the more defining features of categories, and we have little direct support for this assumption. Rosch and Mervis's (1975) results, in fact, suggest the opposite—that the structure of categories is based not on defining features possessed by all members of the category but on a large number of features that are true of only some category members.

In order to avoid entirely the problem of defining features, McCloskey and Glucksberg (1979) modified the feature comparison model to consist of only a single stage. Their model proposes that decision time is determined by the number of features that have to be compared before the evidence is strong enough to make a classification. Each category is represented by features that include the values of typical members of that category. For example, the color of fruit might include the values *red, yellow, orange,* and *green,* and the height of a man might include the values *between 5 feet and 6½ feet.* The assumption that only the most typical values of a category are stored implies that some members of the category may have feature values that are not specified. Some men are taller than 6½ feet, and some fruit might have a color different from those mentioned. The stored values represent the values of only the typical members.

Category membership is verified by comparing the feature values of an example with the feature values that represent the category. The comparison of each feature yields either positive or negative evidence that the example belongs in that category. The color of a banana, an orange, or an apple would yield positive evidence that these examples are fruit because their color matches one of the four representative colors of that category. McCloskey and Glucksberg propose that a person continues to compare the different features of an example until the proportion of positive evidence or negative evidence exceeds some criterion. Their model predicts that people will verify the more typical members of a category relatively quickly since positive evidence accumulates at a faster rate for these members. The precise formulation of how their model evaluates evidence is based on Bayes's theorem, about which we will learn more in Chapter 14.

Semantic network models

The preceding discussion reflected both the strengths and the weaknesses of the hierarchical network model and the feature comparison model. Each provided an explanation for some aspects of the data but could not explain other aspects. We should remember that thus far we have emphasized only hierarchical relations, and there are other kinds of semantic relations. Even if we limit our study to only hierarchical relations, we would have to allow for the fact that a word is actually stored in many hierarchies. The word *salmon,* for example, is part of a *food* hierarchy and a *fishing* hierarchy in addition to being part of an *animal* hierarchy.

In order to represent a greater variety of semantic relations, psychologists have proposed more general semantic network models. We will look at two models that share some of the assumptions of the hierarchical network model but are not limited to specifying only hierarchical relations. The first is the spreading activation theory proposed by Collins and Loftus (1975). The model is particularly interesting because it is an attempt to correct some of the limitations of the hierarchical network model proposed by Collins and Quillian (1969). The second model, called ACT, was proposed by John Anderson (1976) in his book *Language, Memory, and Thought*. ACT attempts to formulate a very general model that is capable of integrating many of the topics studied by cognitive psychologists.

A Spreading Activation Theory

The *spreading activation model* (Collins & Loftus, 1975) is representative of semantic network models in its emphasis on concepts joined together by links that show relationship. Figure 9.7 shows how a part of human memory can be represented in the network. The length of each link represents the degree of semantic relatedness between two concepts. Thus the concept *red* is closely related to other colors and less closely related to red objects. Notice that the model can also account for the typicality effect if the links represent different degrees of semantic relatedness.

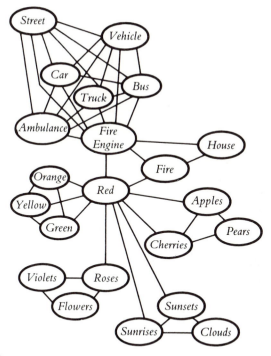

Figure 9.7. Example of a spreading activation model in which the length of each line (link) represents the degree of association between two concepts. *(From "A Spreading Activation Theory of Semantic Processing," by A. M. Collins and E. F. Loftus. In* Psychological Review, *1975, 82, 407–428. Copyright 1975 by the American Psychological Association. Reprinted by permission.)*

The shorter links reveal that *car* and *bus* are more closely related to *vehicle* than is *ambulance* or *fire engine*.

The spreading activation model assumes that, when a concept is processed, activation spreads out along the paths of a network, but its effectiveness is decreased as it travels outward. For example, presentation of the word *red* should strongly activate closely related concepts like *orange* and *fire* and should cause less activation of concepts like *sunsets* and *roses*. The model therefore predicts the typicality effect because more typical members will activate the superordinate category sooner than less typical members—for instance, *car* and *bus* will activate *vehicle* sooner than *fire engine* or *ambulance* will.

The idea of activation spreading throughout a semantic network of interconnected concepts provides a clear picture of the semantic relations among concepts. It is easy to imagine activation decreasing in strength as it travels outward. The model also assumes that activation decreases over time or intervening activity. This assumption places a constraint on the amount of activation that can occur because the activation of a second concept will decrease the activation of the first concept.

Although the model provides a convenient metaphor, its success will depend on how well it can account for experimental results. One such result is the effect of *semantic priming*. Priming occurs when a decision about one concept makes it easier to decide about another concept. An example of priming can be found in the lexical decision task studied by Meyer and Schvaneveldt (1976), which required that people judge whether a string of letters formed a word. Some of the letters did *(BUTTER),* and some did not *(NART).* Each trial consisted of a pair of strings in which the second string was presented immediately after subjects made their decision about the first string. The most interesting results occurred when both strings were words. If the two words were semantically related, people were faster in verifying that the second string was a word than if the two words were unrelated. For example, people verified faster that the string *BUTTER* was a word when it was preceded by *BREAD* than when it was preceded by *NURSE.*

The spreading activation model can account for these results since it proposes that the presentation of a word activates related words. *BUTTER* will be activated by *BREAD* but will not be activated by *NURSE.* The activation of the word makes it easier to identify, resulting in faster response times.

In addition to the direct representation of semantic relations in a network, the spreading activation model allows for the use of feature matching in verification of semantic statements. It therefore includes the assumptions of both the hierarchical network model and the feature comparison model. One way we can decide that a mallard is a bird is to find superordinate links between *mallard* and *duck* and between *duck* and *bird*. Another way is to find that there are common properties in our concept of *mallard* and our concept of *bird*. Collins and Loftus suggest that we consider the evidence obtained from both feature comparisons and superordinate links when we make a decision.

Thus the model has considerable flexibility, but it makes predictions with difficulty. Critics of the model (for instance, Smith, 1978; McCloskey & Glucksberg, 1979) have argued that, with so many assumptions, it is not surprising that the model accounts for many empirical findings. They find its main weaknesses to be both the number of assumptions it makes and its failure to make many clear-cut predictions. In fact, the model was developed primarily to show how its assumptions are consistent with existing data rather than to make interesting predictions. It remains to be seen whether psychologists can design experiments to seriously test the model.

Another possible limitation of the spreading activation model is that it does not account for the spontaneous recall of a word after an initial failure to recall it. We have all experienced the situation where we fail to recall a word and then later recall it spontaneously. Perhaps the spontaneous recall was actually triggered by the spreading activation from another word, but my own experience is that I am usually unaware of any associations between the word and current stimuli. Box 9.2 describes several examples of recall failure and a suggested remedy. Although the suggestion may save us time by curtailing search, it does not solve the problem of why momentary failures of recall occur.

ACT

In spite of their limitations, semantic network models appeal to many people because they are sufficiently general to provide a common framework for many of the issues studied by cognitive psychologists. The generality of the network models is nicely illustrated by ACT. Anderson (1976) designed ACT to apply to a wide variety of cognitive tasks ranging from scanning STM to making complex inferences. The basic assumptions of ACT are similar to those of the spreading activation model: knowledge is stored in a semantic network consisting of interconnected nodes, and activation can spread down network paths from active nodes to activate new nodes and paths. Although the basic assumptions of the two models are the same, Anderson applies ACT to many tasks that were not considered by Collins and Loftus (1975).

Many aspects of ACT are too technical to discuss in an introductory book, but we will consider how Anderson applied the model to predict how quickly people can retrieve stored knowledge. The stored knowledge in this case was information that people learned in a fact retrieval experiment. The purpose of asking them to learn information was to

Box 9.2. Total Recall? Forget It!

GOODMAN ACE

Listen. I'm going to share with you my discovery of the secret for a long and joyous life as you reach the later years. Briefly, all you have to do is what I have done: give up trying futilely to recall totally something that's on the tip of your brain—an elusive date or a happening or a quotation—when your memory is out to lunch.

After years of gradual self-destruction at this typewriter, desperately attempting to bring into focus a recollection without scurrying to lift a heavy dictionary or an encyclopedia, I've come to the medical conclusion that hours can be added to the life span by accepting my principle that total recall is for the birds.

In my case I accidentally happened upon a cartoon in *The New Yorker* some months ago. It showed a handsome, bemused young caveman, nattily attired in the latest bearskin, obviously on his way to woo his cavewoman, his fingers at his lips as if he were trying to recall some line he could hand her. The caption was "Roses are red, violets are blue, something, something, and so are you."

Now, quickly. If you are unable to supply that missing "something, something" without a peek at the end of this piece,* welcome aboard the Happy World of Non-recall. I say "happy" because after spending ten anguished minutes trying to verbalize that line, I decided to forget ever having stared at that cartoon.

As I settled back in my chair I was overcome by a warm, overwhelming, euphoric calm. In that lovely stupor, I began to realize that I had discovered the secret scientific formula for a carefree, tolerable life: ICR equals FI. Translated into lay language for your convenience, "If You Can't Recall It, Forget It." So, as have many of my fellow discoverers before me, I whispered, "Eureka."

However, before announcing this new panacea to the world or, more important, to the Food and Drug Administration, I decided, in the interest of saving myself a malpractice suit, to self-test it. Now, in the August years of my life, I can do no less than to give unstintingly to mankind what remains of myself.

It was that same afternoon of my discovery—or was it the following week?—that I sat at my typewriter composing a column for *SR* in which I was describing a man as being "as handsome as Cary Grant." But I couldn't recall Mr. Grant's first name. Ulysses S. first came to mind, then Lou Grant, the name of Mary Tyler Moore's TV boss. Also Lee Grant, one of my favorite actresses, and Grant Withers who sneaked in somehow or other.

But when the name of the governor of New York, Hugh Carey, flashed across my screen, and I found myself thinking, *Hugh Grant,* I realized that I was on my way to being caught up in another total-recall trap. I stopped cold turkey. The withdrawal pains, I admit, were severe. But I got hold of myself and settled for non-recall. And, very simply, I changed the line to read, "The man was as handsome as Paul Newman." Eureka again. And *voilà!*

*(Sugar is sweet.)

control experimentally the number of relations among the concepts. The experimental material consisted of 26 sentences of the form *A person is in the location* (see Table 9.1 for some examples). A particular individual and a particular location occurred in one, two, or three sentences; for example, *a hippie* occurred in three sentences, and *a debutante* occurred in one sentence. After the subjects had learned all the information in the sentences, they were given test sentences and instructed to respond *true* to test sentences that they had previously learned and *false* to any other sentences. Anderson was interested in how quickly people could respond *true* or *false* to each test sentence.

Table 9.1 shows examples of the test sentences, each preceded by a two-digit number. The first digit indicates the number of times the person appeared in the study material, and the second digit indicates the number of times the location appeared in the study material. Thus the sentence *A hippie is in the park* is marked 3-3 because both *hippie* and *park* appeared three times in the study material. The results of Anderson's experiment indicated that reaction time increased as a function of the number of times a person or a location occurred in the study sentences. Subjects were relatively slow in verifying a sentence like *A hippie is in the park* because *hippie* and *park* both occurred three times. In contrast, they were relatively fast in verifying a sentence like *A lawyer is in the cave* because both *lawyer* and *cave* occurred only once in the study material.

Figure 9.8 shows how information about the sentences is represented by ACT. In order to verify *A hippie is in the park,* it is necessary to find a path in the network that joins *hippie* and *park.* Since the experiment measured response times, the theoretical question is how quickly the path

TABLE 9.1. Sample Sentences Used in Anderson's (1976) Fact Retrieval Study.

Subject studies	True test probes
1. A hippie is in the park.	3–3 A hippie is in the park.
2. A hippie is in the church.	1–1 A lawyer is in the cave.
3. A hippie is in the bank.	1–2 A debutante is in the bank.
4. A captain is in the park.	.
5. A captain is in the church.	.
6. A debutante is in the bank.	.
7. A fireman is in the park.	
	False test probes
.	3–1 A hippie is in the cave.
.	1–2 A lawyer is in the park.
26. A lawyer is in the cave.	1–1 A debutante is in the cave.
	2–2 A captain is in the bank.
	.
	.

From *Language, Memory, and Thought,* by J. R. Anderson. Copyright 1976 by Lawrence Erlbaum Associates, Inc., Publishers. Reprinted by permission.

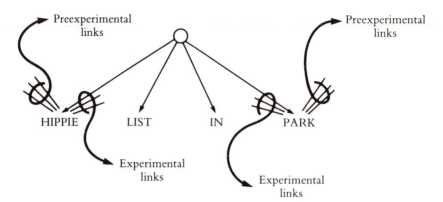

Figure 9.8. Representation of semantic information in ACT. *(From Language, Memory, and Thought, by J. R. Anderson. Copyright 1976 by Lawrence Erlbaum Associates, Inc., Publishers. Reprinted by permission).*

can be found. The presentation of the test sentence *A hippie is in the park* causes the activation of both *hippie* and *park*. The time it takes to find the path that links *hippie* and *park* depends on (1) the rate at which activation spreads from the two concepts, (2) the length of the path joining the two concepts, and (3) the possible alternative paths the activation can take.

When a concept is activated, the rate of spread down the appropriate path (the links joining *hippie* and *park*) is determined by the strength of the appropriate link relative to the strength of the other links that join the concepts. The other links include both preexperimental links that were a part of the subject's semantic network before the experiment and experimental links learned in the experiment. The preexperimental links include various associations that a person has to concepts like *hippie* and *park*. In Anderson's predictions the preexperimental links do not vary. The parameter that does vary is the number of experimental links. Since the word *hippie* occurred three times in the study material, it is linked to three different locations *(park, church,* and *bank)*. The word *park* is linked to three different persons *(hippie, captain,* and *debutante)*. Increasing the number of experimental links increases the time to find an intersecting path joining two concepts because it slows the spread of activation along the appropriate path. The activation of *hippie* and *park* is divided among three experimental links, whereas the words *lawyer* and *cave* have only a single experimental link. ACT therefore predicts that verification time should increase with an increase in the number of experimental links to either the person or the location.

There are two other parameters in ACT that determine how quickly an intersecting path can be found between two concepts. Neither of the two parameters was varied in this experiment, but they are useful in predicting the results of other experiments. One parameter is the number of links that must be activated along the intersecting path. Figure 9.8 shows that in this example only two links are involved. You may recall that the number of links is a very important parameter in the hierarchical network model since it is used to predict verification times at different hierarchical levels. The other parameter is the number of irrelevant paths that exist along the relevant path. Figure 9.8 shows two irrelevant paths. One indicates that *A hippie is in the park* was contained in the list of study sentences. The other indicates that the relation between *hippie* and *park* is that the hippie is "in" the park. The irrelevant paths have the same effect as the irrelevant links joined directly to the concept: they tend to reduce the spread of activation along the relevant path by dividing the activation among the paths.

In conclusion, ACT is an example of a spreading activation model in which the activation spreads throughout a semantic network. At each point in the network, the activation is divided among alternative links according to their relative strengths. Although only the number of experimental links varied in the experiment that we considered, the other parameters give the model considerable generality and facilitate its application to other experiments.

Evaluation of Semantic Networks

Psychologists' reactions to semantic network models have ranged from the belief that they are totally useless to the belief that they are the only hope of achieving a general theory in cognitive psychology. The two views are represented in the following two reviews of Anderson's *Language, Memory, and Thought* (1976). First, an enthusiastic argument in support of models like ACT:

> In general we must conclude that despite the high productivity in the memory industry the actual growth has not yet been sufficient to provide a framework that can cohere and direct research in cognitive psychology. Furthermore the lack of progress is not a result of not enough effort, but of the narrowness of terms of reference that researchers have implicitly accepted and which have effectively hobbled the enterprise from the beginning. One possible exception exists, however—John Anderson, who in the breadth, depth, quality and sheer volume of his work is something of a Superman in memory research. If anything can give us what we need, ACT, his latest model, can [Claxton, 1978, p. 515].

Not everyone is this enthusiastic. A critic of this approach argues that it has little to offer:

> It is also my impression that many (of course not all) information processing psychologists consider Anderson's work to be at the cutting edge of the field, to embody what they are most proud of. "Language, Memory, and

Thought" (henceforth, LMT) may perhaps be looked on as the state-of-the-art book. In addition, LMT discusses a number of methodological and analytical tools from a variety of areas which might be useful in the background and technical arsenal of a cognitive psychologist or linguist. Given this assumption of the status of the book "within" the field, it is perhaps surprising that the conclusion that one reaches after reading the book is:

1. Remarkably little is known about the range of processing issues discussed in LMT.
2. There is not much prospect of adding to scientific knowledge by pursuing the methods represented in LMT.
3. At least one of the ablest practitioners in the field (Anderson himself) has considerable (principled) doubts about the possibility of doing what he and others are trying to do.
4. There is remarkably little that a linguist (or even a psychologist) could learn by reading LMT [Wexler, 1978, p. 327].*

The reason for such divided opinion is that, like most other theories, semantic network models have both advantages and disadvantages. The advantage is that semantic network models are extremely flexible. It is very easy to introduce many assumptions into the model to make it consistent with many kinds of data. However, the price for this advantage is that it becomes very difficult to test the model. If a model becomes so flexible that it is consistent with almost any experimental finding, it loses its predictive power. A model has predictive power only if it predicts that certain events should occur and other events should not occur. One can then evaluate the model by determining which events do, in fact, occur.

The challenge for the developers of semantic network models is not only to take advantage of their flexibility, but to place some constraints on the models in order to make some interesting predictions. Now when a network model fails to make a correct prediction, the developers usually create additional assumptions to give the model greater flexibility. Consequently, the revised model usually succeeds where the original failed, but many psychologists find the revision less satisfactory. Collins and Loftus's (1975) revision of the hierarchical network model corrected the limitations of the former but sacrificed the precise predictions that made the hierarchical network model one of the more interesting semantic network theories.

Other network models, such as ACT, also require revision to accommodate new experimental findings. Consider ACT's prediction that increasing the number of links to a concept will slow down retrieval time because the spreading activation will be divided among the alternative paths. Smith, Adams, and Schorr (1978) argued that the model implies

*From "A Review of John R. Anderson's *Language, Memory, and Thought*," by K. Wexler. In *Cognition*, 1978, *6*, 327–351. Copyright 1978 by Elsevier Sequoia S. A. Reprinted by permission.

that increasing knowledge about a topic should lead to increasing difficulty in answering questions about it. In order to resolve this counterintuitive prediction, they investigated whether the integration of new knowledge could reduce the interference caused by additional links.

Their procedure was similar to the procedure used by Anderson. Subjects learned either two or three facts about a person—for example, that *Marty broke a bottle* and *Marty did not delay the trip*. The third fact either provided a common theme for the first two facts or was unrelated. *Marty was chosen to christen the ship* provides a theme for *Marty broke the bottle* and *did not delay the trip*, whereas *Marty was asked to address the crowd* is not obviously related to the first two facts. The test required that people then make rapid judgments about whether test sentences appeared in the study set. When the facts were unrelated, people required more time to recognize a statement if they had learned three facts than if they had learned two. This finding replicated Anderson's results and is consistent with the predictions of ACT. When the third fact integrated the first two, people could recognize any one of the three facts as quickly as they could when there were only two facts. In other words, integration allows one to overcome the potential interference of learning new information.

The results of this experiment indicate that increasing the number of links at a concept node does not necessarily slow down recognition time. Does this result seriously challenge ACT? In the final chapter of *Language, Memory, and Thought* Anderson provides the following answer:

> Another remark that needs to be made about the empirical accountability of ACT is that one cannot seriously expect to perform a single experiment and slay ACT. If ACT makes a prediction that proves wrong, that exact version of ACT will have to be abandoned but I am obviously going to propose a slight variant of the theory with slightly changed assumptions that is compatible with those data. It would be nice if the theory could be reduced to a few critical assumptions that could be subject to simple experimental tests. However, things just do not work that way. ACT is only going to be rejected by repeated attacks that keep forcing reformulations until the point comes when the theory becomes unmanageable with its patches and bandages [Anderson, 1976, p. 532].

Anderson has kept his promise by formulating a slight variation of the theory to meet the challenge raised by Smith, Adams, and Schorr. His modified version of ACT uses subnodes to integrate related material (Reder & Anderson, 1980). In Figure 9.9a, the original ACT representation, all four facts are linked directly to Marty. In Figure 9.9b, the modified ACT representation using subnodes, only two facts are linked directly to Marty—that he cooked spaghetti and that he participated in a ship christening. The three facts about the ship christening are all linked to the same subnode.

(a)

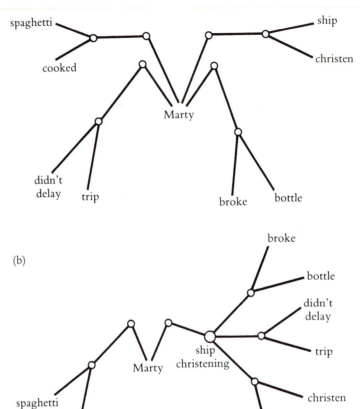

Figure 9.9. Two possible memory representations for related facts about Marty. (a) ACT representation; (b) modified ACT representation using subnodes. *(From "Partial Resolution of the Paradox of Inter-ference: The Role of Integrating Knowledge," by L. Reder and J. R. Anderson. In* Cognitive Psychology, *1980, 12, 447–472. Copyright 1980 by Academic Press, Inc. Reprinted by permission.)*

Reder and Anderson propose that, under certain conditions, people can evaluate a fact by making a consistency judgment rather than by attempting to retrieve the fact. When given the test statement *Marty broke the bottle,* people respond positively because this information is consistent with the theme that Marty christened the ship. In this case, they would respond as soon as activation reached the *ship christening* subnode and then would not attempt to retrieve the facts connected to the subnode. Response times would therefore not be influenced by the number of facts connected to the subnode, as Smith, Adams, and Schorr (1978) found.

However, the integration of facts at a common subnode does not always eliminate interference. The number of facts influences response time when a person must examine the specific facts at that subnode. Imagine that you read statements about a ship christening, but some of the statements described Marty's activities and other statements described James's activities. If you now had to evaluate the statement *Marty broke the bottle,* you might have difficulty since both were involved in the christening. Evaluating the statement therefore requires retrieving the specific facts associated with Marty. The data collected by Reder and Anderson revealed that even integrated facts can interfere with each other when the subject is forced to examine the specific facts and cannot make a general consistency judgment.

Their findings suggest that integration results in faster decisions when examining only the subnode is sufficient for making the decision. This conclusion is also supported by the influence of irrelevant information on response times. The fact *Marty cooked spaghetti* is irrelevant to his activities associated with ship christening. The inclusion of this statement delays the evaluation of statements about ship christening because activation also spreads down irrelevant paths. However, additional statements about cooking spaghetti do not further delay decisions about ship christening because these statements could be integrated at a *cooking spaghetti* subnode, and activation would stop once this irrelevant subnode was reached.

The subnode model is an example of a successful revision of ACT to incorporate new findings. The basic assumption of ACT remains the same: activation spreads along the paths of a semantic network. The revision is simply that activation can stop at a subnode rather than spread to the integrated facts linked to that subnode. If Anderson can continue to modify ACT without introducing too many patches and bandages, it should provide a general framework for integrating our expanding knowledge of semantic memory.

Summary

Psychologists have studied semantic memory to learn how people use meaning to organize information in LTM. One effective way to organize material is to use hierarchical organization by partitioning a large category into smaller and smaller categories. Experimental results have demonstrated that people can learn hierarchical information quickly, but they have considerable difficulty learning the same information when it is presented randomly. The study of how people retrieve information reveals that they typically group from two to five items together. Groups of this size can form the basis for a large hierarchy—for instance, a paragraph: the paragraph can be divided into sentences, sentences into major ideas, major ideas into smaller word groups, word groups into words, words into syllables, and syllables into phonemes.

The hierarchical organization of categories influences the amount of time it takes to verify sentences about the members of categories. It usually takes less time to verify category membership at the basic level than at the superordinate level. For example, it is easier to verify that a canary is a bird than that a canary is an animal. The hierarchical network model predicts this result by assuming that semantic information is organized in a hierarchy and that it takes time to change levels in the hierarchy. The network model also predicts that the time it takes to verify a property of an object will depend on the level in the hierarchy where the property is stored. This assumption implies that it should take longer to verify that a canary eats than that a canary can fly since eating is stored at the animal level and flying is stored at the bird level. In contrast, the feature comparison model assumes that statements are verified by using features to compute the similarity of two concepts. When there is an intermediate amount of similarity, people must evaluate only the most necessary, or defining, features of the category. The feature comparison model correctly predicts that classification time depends more on similarity than on category size and also depends on whether the example is a typical member of its category. Critics of the feature comparison model question its reliance on ratings to make predictions, its failure to make direct use of learned associations in memory, and its somewhat artificial distinction between characteristic and defining features.

The hierarchical network model is a specific example of a semantic network model in which concepts are represented by nodes in a network and relations are represented by links joining the concepts. The spreading activation model was proposed to correct some limitations of the hierarchical network model. Its principle assumption is that the activation of a concept results in the activation of related concepts spreading along the paths of the network. Another network model, ACT, uses the same assumption to provide a theoretical account of many experimental findings, including the retrieval of stored information. The advantage of semantic network models is that they are general enough to provide a broad theoretical framework for incorporating a large variety of findings. Their major disadvantage is that they often make so many assumptions that they lose their ability to make predictions.

Recommended reading

Bower (1970) reviewed research on organizational factors in memory in the first issue of the journal *Cognitive Psychology*. Rosch (1975) used the priming technique to investigate the organization of semantic categories. Mandler (1967), one of the first psychologists to investigate the hierarchical organization of memory, proposed that each level in the hierarchy contained about five categories. Nelson and Smith (1972) studied the acquisition and forgetting of hierarchically organized information. Stevens and Coupe (1978) argue that spatial knowledge is also hierarchically organized—for example, most people wrongly infer that San Diego, California, is west of Reno, Nevada, because most of California is west of Nevada. A possible criticism of semantic memory research is that it does not adequately control for stimulus familiarity (McCloskey, 1980).

PART **III**

Complex Cognitive Skills

10

Language

Words differently arranged have a different meaning, and meanings differently arranged have different effects.

PASCAL

The discussion of semantic memory in the previous chapter emphasized associations among words. We are now ready to consider how words can be combined to form sentences. One possible theory is that this combination occurs by associations. We could argue that just as *robin* is associated with *bird,* the words in a sentence can be associated with each other. The problem with this view of language is that there are so many different ways words can be combined we would have to learn an infinite number of associations in order to form sentences. An alternative theory is that we learn a *grammar*—a system of rules that is capable of producing sentences. Ideally, the rules of a grammar should generate all the sentences of a language without generating any strings of words that are not sentences. The first section of this chapter provides a brief description of two kinds of grammatical rules—phrase structure rules and transformation rules.

The second section deals with the comprehension of sentences. The comprehension of ambiguous sentences is a particularly interesting study because we must resolve the ambiguity in order to understand the sentence. The third section discusses memory for sentences and examines the extent to which people remember the exact words of a sentence, as opposed to only its general meaning. The final section considers the distinction between asserted and implied statements. Findings on how well people can make this distinction offer some applications of research on the understanding of language, particularly in relation to the evaluation of courtroom testimony and advertising claims.

Psychology and grammar

One of the important influences on the development of cognitive psychology during the 1960s was the work of the linguist Noam Chomsky. Prior to Chomsky's influence on psycholinguistics (the psychological study of language) psychologists had explored the possibility that people could learn language by learning the associations between adjacent words in a sentence. According to this view, we learn to speak correctly through paired-associate learning: each word in a sentence serves as a stimulus for the word that follows it. In the sentence *The boy hit the ball,* the word *the* is a stimulus for the response *boy,* and the word *boy* is a stimulus for the word *hit.* The speaker of a language would therefore have to learn which words could follow any other word in a sentence.

Chomsky (1957) argued that there are several problems with the association view of language. First of all, there are an infinite number of sentences in a language. It is therefore unreasonable to expect that people could learn a language by learning associations between all adjacent words. Consider simply a word like *the*. There are many, many words that could follow *the*, and a person might never learn all of them. When you consider all the possible words that can occur in a sentence and all the words that could possibly follow each word, you can see that this would be a very inefficient way to learn a language. Another problem with the association view is that it does not account for the relations among nonadjacent words. For example, in the sentence *Anyone who says that is lying,* the pronoun *anyone* is grammatically related to the verb *is lying,* but this relation is not revealed if we consider only the relation between adjacent words. The association view, in fact, ignores the hierarchical structure of sentences in proposing how people learn to speak grammatically correct sentences.

The hierarchical structure of sentences is revealed in the diagrams that you may have constructed in school. Many of us were taught how to break down a sentence into parts. We might begin by dividing a sentence into a noun phrase and a verb phrase and then divide the noun phrase into an adjective and a noun and the verb phrase into an adverb and a verb. Division into smaller units produces a hierarchical organization that reveals the grammar of the sentence. The diagram, which is based on a set of rules, provides a picture of the grammatical organization. The rules are part of what we call a *phrase structure grammar* because they reveal how we can form phrases consisting of groups of words.

Phrase Structure Grammar

An alternative to representing language as a string of words is representing it as a rule system. This approach can be illustrated by considering a very simple set of rules taken from a phrase structure grammar (Table

10.1). The rules are expressed by using an arrow that means *can be rewritten as*. The symbols refer to sentences (S), noun phrases (NP), verb phrases (VP), and determiners (Det). The first rule states that a sentence can be rewritten as a noun phrase followed by a verb phrase. The second rule states that a noun phrase can be rewritten as a determiner followed by a noun. The third rule states that a verb phrase can be rewritten as a verb followed by a noun phrase. The last three rules give examples of words that can be substituted for a determiner, a noun, and a verb.

The rules may seem more familiar to you if they are expressed visually. Figure 10.1 shows how they can be used to reveal the grammatical structure of a sentence. The sentence is first rewritten as a noun phrase followed by a verb phrase (Rule 1). Rule 2 then allows us to rewrite the noun phrase, and Rule 3 allows us to rewrite the verb phrase. Since the application of Rule 3 produces another noun phrase, it is necessary to apply Rule 2 again to rewrite the second noun phrase. Using the vocabulary rules to substitute words for the determiners, nouns, and verbs, we can now produce a small number of sentences—for instance:

The boy hit a ball.

The stick hit a boy.

A ball hit a ball.

Although the number of sentences we can produce using this particular grammar is quite limited, the grammar illustrates how sentences can be produced through the application of rules. The creation of additional rules, such as including adjectives in a noun phrase, would allow us to generate a greater variety of sentences.

Transformational Grammar

Chomsky (1957) argued that one limitation of a phrase structure grammar is that it does not reveal how a sentence can be modified to form a similar sentence. For example, how can we change (1) an active statement into a passive statement, (2) a positive statement into a negative statement, or (3) an assertion into a question? Given the sentence *The boy hit the ball*, the first change produces *The ball was hit by the boy*; the second change produces *The boy did not hit the ball*; and the third change produces

---

TABLE 10.1. Example of Phrase Structure Rules.

1. S→NP + VP	4. Det→a, the
2. NP→Det + Noun	5. Noun→boy, ball, stick
3. VP→Verb + NP	6. Verb→hit

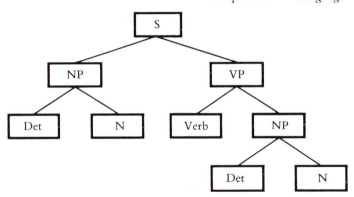

Figure 10.1. A sentence diagram based on the phrase structure rules in Table 10.1.

Did the boy hit the ball? The modification in each case transforms an entire sentence into a closely related sentence. Transformation rules therefore serve a different function than phrase structure rules, which reveal the grammatical structure of a sentence. Chomsky, however, made use of the phrase structure rules in developing his transformational grammar because the transformations are based on the grammatical structure of a sentence.

Consider the transformation of *The boy hit the ball* into *The ball was hit by the boy*. The transformation rule in this case is

$$NP1 + V + NP2 \rightarrow NP2 \ + \ was \ + V + by + NP1$$

The transformation changes the position of the two noun phrases and inserts additional words into the passive sentence. The passive sentence begins with the second noun phrase (*the ball*) and ends with the first noun phrase (*the boy*). It is also necessary to add the words *was* and *by*. Notice that the transformation uses the syntactic description of a closely related sentence. The phrase structure rules specify both of the descriptions.

The transformational grammar proposed by Chomsky in 1957 was an advance over a phrase structure grammar because, in addition to revealing grammatical structure, it showed how sentences could be transformed. Chomsky was not entirely satisfied with the transformational grammar, however, and in 1965 he wrote a second book to correct some of its limitations. The changes that he made were primarily concerned with allowing meaning to play a more important role in the grammar.

One problem with the 1957 grammar was that it could generate sentences that seemed grammatical but expressed meaningless ideas. This point can be illustrated by adding another verb—*took*—to the rules shown in Figure 10.1. The addition allows us to produce new sentences like *The boy took the ball* and *The ball took the boy*. Although both sentences appear to be grammatical, the second sentence doesn't make much sense. The reason is that the verb *took* usually requires an animate subject—someone who is alive and therefore capable of taking something. Chomsky attempted to correct this deficiency by placing constraints on which words could be substituted into a sentence. Instead of treating all verbs the same, he argued that some verbs require animate subjects. This restriction is based on the meaning of words.

Another problem with the earlier version of the transformational grammar was that it could not always distinguish between different meanings of an ambiguous sentence, although it was sometimes successful because some ambiguous sentences can be distinguished by the use of phrase structure rules. Consider the sentence *They are flying planes*. One interpretation considers *flying* to be part of the verb phrase *are flying*, whereas the other interpretation considers *flying* to be an adjective in the noun phrase *flying planes*. In the first interpretation *they* refers to someone who is flying planes; in the second interpretation *they* refers to the planes. A phrase structure grammar can make this distinction because each interpretation has a different derivation (see Figure 10.2).

There are other ambiguous sentences, however, that cannot be distinguished by phrase structure rules because both interpretations of the sentence produce the same derivation. Consider the sentence *Flying planes can be dangerous*. The sentence has the same ambiguity as the previous sentence. The two interpretations can be revealed by rephrasing the sentence as either *Flying planes is dangerous* or *Flying planes are dangerous*. The first interpretation indicates that flying is dangerous to the pilot; the second interpretation indicates that the planes themselves are dangerous.

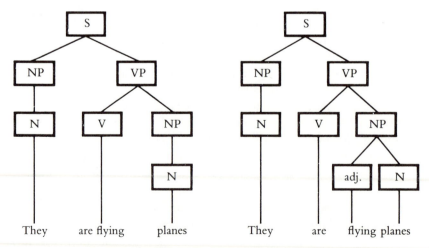

Figure 10.2. Two alternative derivations of an ambiguous sentence.

In both interpretations, however, *flying planes* is the subject of the sentence, so the ambiguity cannot be resolved by appealing to different phrase structure rules.

Chomsky (1965) proposed that, in order to resolve the ambiguity, it is necessary to postulate a level of analysis that directly represents the meaning of a sentence. He therefore modified the transformational grammar to consist of two levels: the surface level—directly related to the sentence as it is heard—and the deep level—directly related to the meaning of the sentence. The only way to resolve the ambiguity of a sentence like *Flying planes can be dangerous* is to know which of the two deep levels is intended—flying is dangerous to the pilot or the planes themselves are dangerous.

The concepts introduced by Chomsky had a major impact on the emerging field of psycholinguistics. Psychologists who were interested in language investigated the implications of a transformational grammar for theories of how people comprehend and remember sentences. A book by Lachman, Lachman, and Butterfield (1979) reviews much of the early research in psycholinguistics and illustrates how emphasis in the field has gradually shifted over time. The next two sections of this chapter focus primarily on current issues that are related to syntactic and semantic aspects of comprehending and remembering sentences. Though Chomsky's ideas had a direct influence on some of the earlier studies (MacKay, 1966; Sachs, 1967), his influence is less obvious on some of the more recent research.

Comprehension of sentences

Ambiguous Sentences

The comprehension of sentences, like the recognition of patterns, is a complex skill that we perform very well. Ambiguous sentences afford us some insight into how difficulties in comprehension might arise. One technique for studying comprehension is to measure how quickly people can complete the beginning of a sentence. Try to finish the following three sentences as quickly as you can.

1. Although he was continually bothered by the cold . . .
2. Although Hannibal sent troops over a week ago . . .
3. Knowing that visiting relatives could be bothersome . . .

Each of the three sentences represents a different kind of ambiguity studied by MacKay (1966). The first example represents *lexical* (word) *ambiguity* because the word *cold* can refer either to the temperature of the environment or to a person's health. The second example represents *surface ambiguity* because it concerns the grouping of words. The word *over* can be either part of the verb phrase (*sent troops over*) or part of the prepositional phrase (*over a week ago*). Linguistically, this distinction can be represented by the phrase structure rules since each interpretation would have a different derivation. The third example represents an *underlying ambiguity* because the ambiguity can be resolved only if we know the underlying meaning (deep structure) of the sentence. Notice that the phrase *visiting relatives* is ambiguous in the same sense that *flying planes* was ambiguous in the example given earlier. It is unclear who are the visitors—and this ambiguity cannot be resolved at the phrase structure level.

It is possible, of course, that people may never notice these ambiguities and therefore find it as easy to complete these sentences as to complete closely related unambiguous sentences. The following three sentences show unambiguous variations of each of the three examples. The italicized word is the only change.

> 4. Although he was continually bothered by the *headache* . . .
> 5. Although Hannibal sent troops *almost* a week ago . . .
> 6. Knowing that visiting *some* relatives could be bothersome . . .

MacKay investigated the effect of ambiguity on sentence completion times by giving people either ambiguous sentences or unambiguous variations of the same sentences. Their task was to finish each sentence as quickly as they could. The completions had to be short, grammatical, and related to the beginning of the sentence.

Figure 10.3 shows the average amount of time required to complete each class of sentences. There was no difference among the unambiguous control sentences but there were differences among the three kinds of ambiguous sentences—all of which took more time to complete than the control sentences. The participants had the least difficulty with lexical ambiguities, more difficulty with surface ambiguities, and still more difficulty with underlying ambiguities. Sentences that contained more than one ambiguity (multiple ambiguities) were the most difficult to complete. It is interesting that very few of the participants reported that they noticed the ambiguities, although they took significantly more time to complete the ambiguous sentences.

The reason many potentially ambiguous sentences do not seem ambiguous in our everyday use of language is that the intended meaning is usually clear from the context. If I say that I am bothered by the cold, the preceding sentences should reveal the intended meaning. We might therefore expect that context should make it as easy to comprehend ambiguous sentences as unambiguous sentences. The results of an experiment by Swinney and Hakes (1976) support this hypothesis.

The subjects in their experiments performed two tasks simultaneously while they listened to pairs of sentences. One task asked them to

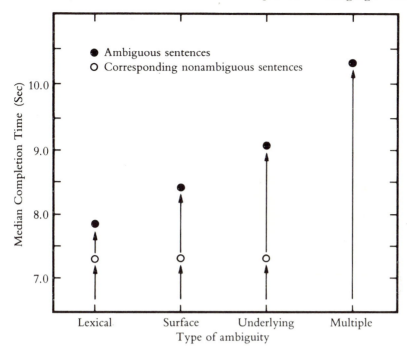

Figure 10.3. Completion times for ambiguous and nonambiguous sentences. *(From "To End Ambiguous Sentences," by D. G. MacKay. In Perception & Psychophysics, 1966, 1, 426–435. Copyright 1966 by the Psychonomic Society, Inc. Reprinted by permission.)*

judge how closely they felt the two sentences of each pair were related. This task requires comprehension of the sentences. The second task required that they press a button as soon as they heard a word beginning with a specified sound (phoneme). The rationale of this experiment is that people should be slower in responding to the phoneme whenever they are having difficulty in comprehending the sentence. The following pair of sentences is a typical example:

> Rumor had it that, for years, the government building had been plagued with problems. The man was not surprised when he found several "bugs" in the corner of his room [Swinney & Hakes, 1976, p. 686].

The target phoneme in this example occurs at the beginning of the word *corner*, shortly after the ambiguous word *bugs*. In order to determine whether the ambiguous word would delay comprehension and therefore detection of the phoneme, Swinney and Hakes compared performance on the ambiguous sentences with performance on unambiguous control sentences. The unambiguous version of the example contained the word *insects* in place of the word *bugs*. Swinney and Hakes found that subjects took significantly more time to detect the phoneme when it followed an ambiguous word than when it followed an unambiguous word. The findings were consistent with MacKay's (1966) results in suggesting that an ambiguity can delay comprehension.

However, sometimes the ambiguous word occurred in a context that made it clear which meaning of the word was intended. For example:

> Rumor had it that, for years, the government building had been plagued with problems. The man was not surprised when he found several spiders, roaches, and other "bugs" in the corner of his room [Swinney & Hakes, 1976, p. 686].

When the context clarified the meaning of the ambiguous word, people could comprehend the ambiguous word *bug* as quickly as they could comprehend the unambiguous word *insect*. There was no longer any difference in response times to the target phoneme.

We could interpret these results by arguing that only a single meaning of the ambiguous word is activated when the context indicates the intended meaning. This argument has considerable intuitive appeal, but recent findings suggest that it is wrong. In the previous chapter we saw that, when people are asked to decide whether a string of letters is a word, their decision is faster when a word is preceded by a semantically related word, such as *bread* preceded by *butter*. If people consider only a single meaning of an ambiguous word, a word like *bug* should facilitate the recognition of either *ant* or *spy,* depending on which meaning is activated.

Swinney (1979) tested this prediction by replacing the phoneme-monitoring task with a lexical-decision task. He explained to the subjects that a string of letters would appear on a screen as they listened to some of the sentences, and they were to decide as quickly as possible whether or not each letter string formed a word. He did not mention that some of the sentences and words were related. The words appeared on the screen immediately after subjects heard the ambiguous word and were contextually appropriate, contextually inappropriate, or unrelated to the meaning of the ambiguous word. A contextually appropriate word, such as *ant,* was consistent with the meaning of the ambiguous word that was suggested by the context. A contextually inappropriate word, such as *spy*, was consistent with the meaning that was not suggested by the context. An unrelated word, such as *sew*, was consistent with neither of the two meanings.

If the context causes the activation of only a single meaning, it should be easier to recognize only the contextually related word (*ant*). But if both meanings of the ambiguous word are activated, the contextually inappropriate word (*spy*) should also be easier to recognize than the unrelated word (*sew*). The results indicated that, when the visual test word immediately followed the ambiguous word, both contextually appropriate and contextually inappropriate words were easier to recognize than the un-related words. But when the test word occurred four syllables (approx-imately 750–1000 msec) after the ambiguous word, recognition of only the contextually related word was facilitated.

Swinney's findings suggest that more than one meaning of an am-biguous word is activated even when a prior context indicates which meaning is appropriate. If only one meaning of *bugs* were activated by the phrase *He found several spiders, roaches, and other bugs*, it is not clear why it would be as easy to respond to *spy* as to *ant*. However, when the test word occurred four syllables after the ambiguous word, recognition of only the word *ant* was facilitated. It therefore appears that, although both meanings of an ambiguous word are momentarily activated, the context allows the listener to select the appropriate meaning quickly. The selec-tion of the appropriate meaning occurred quickly enough to prevent interference in the phoneme-detection task. As you may recall, there was a slight delay between the ambiguous word and the target phoneme. This was sufficient time to resolve the ambiguity when there was an appropri-ate context. An appropriate context therefore seems to allow the listener to select the appropriate meaning of a word quickly rather than to prevent more than one meaning from being activated.

Understanding Noun Phrases

The preceding discussion emphasized the understanding of a single ambiguous word. Let us now consider a noun phrase consisting of an adjective and a noun. Noun phrases may also be sources of ambiguity if it is not clear which word is the adjective and which word is the noun. An extreme case is the title of the article in Box 10.1: "Adjective Substi-tution Demonstration: Noun String Findings Analysis." The title is par-ticularly awkward because each adjective looks like a potential noun. The reader therefore has to decide whether each word in the title is an adjec-tive or a noun, and this decision delays comprehension.

An important issue in studying how people understand groups of words such as noun phrases is whether the meaning of one word is influenced by the meaning of another word. When we hear a noun phrase such as *the burning house,* do we retrieve the meaning of *burning* and the meaning of *house* independently and then combine the two meanings? Or is the meaning of *house* directly influenced by the adjective that precedes it? Since it is not obvious which words are adjectives in a noun string, it is unlikely that the adjectives would immediately influence the meaning of the noun. Upon encountering a noun string like the examples in Box 10.1, a reader probably retrieves the meaning of each word and then attempts to combine the individual meanings. Comprehension would be

---

Box 10.1. Adjective Substitution Demonstration: Noun String Findings Analysis

What's this article about? A careful look at the words in the title shows that they are all nouns that are commonly used in government, business, and academe. Moreover, they are often used in "strings" like this, especially in the titles of projects, programs, agencies, and processes. These "noun strings" are one of the hallmarks of stilted, incomprehensible bureaucratic prose.

Short noun strings are everywhere in our written and spoken language. Doublets are especially common and well accepted: *day care, form letter, pressure cooker, case study, career choice, grant application, life style.* Strings of three or more nouns are not common in everyday speech or writing, but are very common in professional jargon: *health service provider, management information requirement, system level specification, Document Design Center, human factors engineering support, video training system application, U.S. Army weapons systems.* These all may seem reasonable and familiar to you, even if you don't know exactly what they mean. But excesses are also quite common, particularly in the Federal government: just what exactly is a *host area crisis shelter production planning workbook?*

Why are noun strings so difficult to understand? Why do we usually spend some time poring over a new one we encounter, trying to decipher it? It cannot be because of the words themselves; they are usually fairly common and nontechnical. It must be because of the way that they are used together and the complex process we must go through to decode them.

Let's look at the structure of a noun string first. A noun string is a sequence of nouns that function as a unit: the final noun of the string is the "head noun"; all the other nouns preceding it (and any adjacent or intervening adjectives) function as adjectives that modify this head noun. If we understand only one thing about a phrase like *ozone probability target,* we know that it is about some kind of target. The head noun in a noun string is easy to identify: it's always at the end of the string.

But how does a reader find the end of a noun string? Nouns still look like nouns, even though they may be functioning as adjectives. As a reader progresses through a noun string, each noun is a potential candidate for the head noun of that string or phrase—unless another noun follows. Everything in a noun string is therefore ambiguous until all the nouns have been identified. Consider *management information system plan.* The reader does not know whether it refers to information, a system, or a plan until the end of the string, but in the meantime the reader has been forming and abandoning false hypotheses about the meaning of the phrase. . . .

From the May 1980 issue of *Fine Print* (now called *Simply Stated*). Reproduced with permission from the Document Design Center, American Institutes for Research.

---

facilitated, however, if the meaning of an adjective directly influenced the meaning of the noun. The evidence suggests that there is a direct influence for noun phrases such as *the burning house*.

Potter and Faulconer (1979) used a picture probe task to investigate how people understand noun phrases. (Figure 10.4 shows examples of sentences and pictures used in the experiment.) Subjects listened to sentences such as *It was already getting late when the man first saw the burning house ahead of him.* Immediately after the noun *house,* a picture appeared illustrating either the noun alone (*house*) or the noun phrase (*burning house*). The subject's task was to decide whether the pictured object had been named in the sentence. When the adjective was not included in the

It was already $\begin{Bmatrix} \text{burning} \\ \text{getting late} \end{Bmatrix}$ when the man first saw the {burning} house ahead of him.

"It's {dripping} on the table," Sally said, gesturing at the {dripping} candle that she had made.

Seeing it {drooping} in the yard, the boyscout wondered how many years the {drooping} flag had been used.

Although it was $\begin{Bmatrix} \text{low} \\ \text{borrowed} \end{Bmatrix}$, Jill thought that the {low} table would be adequate.

Figure 10.4. Examples of sentences and typical versus modified picture probes. *(From "Understanding Noun Phrases," by M. C. Potter and B. A. Faulconer. In* Journal of Verbal Learning and Verbal Behavior, *1979, 18, 509–521. Copyright 1979 by Academic Press, Inc. Reprinted by permission.)*

noun phrase, subjects were faster in verifying the more typical pictures shown on the left in Figure 10.4. For example, when the subjects heard the sentence *It was already getting late when the man first saw the house,* they could verify the picture of a typical house faster than a picture of a burning house. This finding is analogous to the typicality effects discussed in the chapter on categorization (Chapter 8). Since the typical pictures are more representative of their category than the modified pictures, they can be verified more quickly.

A more interesting question is what happens when the noun is preceded by the adjective. If the meaning of the noun is retrieved independently of the meaning of the adjective, then we would expect that the more typical picture should still be verified more rapidly. However, if the meaning of the noun is influenced by the adjective, the modified picture should be verified more quickly. The results supported the second of the two alternatives: the subjects verified the modified picture more quickly than the typical picture when the noun was preceded by the adjective. These results occurred even though the task required only verification of the noun so participants could have ignored the meaning of the adjective when they made their decisions. The magnitude of the effect was related to the familiarity of the noun phrase, since the modified picture was verified faster for familiar noun phrases (for example, *roasted turkey*) than for unfamiliar noun phrases (for example, *broken screwdriver*).

In another version of this experiment the information conveyed by the adjective came at the beginning of the sentence rather than immediately before the noun. For example, people heard the sentence *It was already burning when the man first saw the house ahead of him.* People's verification times for this condition were similar to their verification times when the adjective was not presented: they were faster at verifying the typical picture than the modified picture. The results imply that retrieving the meaning of a noun can be influenced by an immediately preceding adjective but is not likely to be influenced when the same information occurs earlier in a sentence.

You may be wondering how these results relate to Swinney's (1979) findings on the interpretation of ambiguous words. Both studies are concerned with how context influences the semantic interpretation of a word, but their conclusions are somewhat different. Swinney argues that the meaning of an ambiguous word is not influenced by its context but is selected shortly after both meanings are activated. Potter and Faulconer argue that context can influence the meaning of a word because the interpretation of a noun is influenced by the adjective that precedes it. In order to compare these two findings, we have to consider how the experiments differ. Swinney investigated the alternative meanings of an ambiguous word, whereas Potter and Faulconer investigated how quickly an adjective can modify our concept of a noun. Swinney used a semantic priming task, whereas Potter and Faulconer used a picture probe task. Direct comparisons are therefore difficult, and we will have to wait for more research before we attempt to integrate their results.

One direction in which research might go is to use a picture probe task to study the effect of context on ambiguous words. For example, one could show a picture of a beetle following the word *bug* to determine whether verification times would be faster when the context clearly indicated that *bug* referred to an insect rather than a monitoring device. My intuition is that a clarifying context would result in faster verification times. Although Swinney found that both meanings of an ambiguous word were activated—even after a clarifying context—it is possible that people may be more conscious of the meaning that fits the context of the sentence.

It is interesting to note that only 3 of 40 subjects in MacKay's (1966) experiment reported that they noticed an ambiguity when they read a sentence even though the ambiguous sentences were more difficult to complete. Swinney and Hakes (1976) also reported that many of their subjects reported they were unaware of the ambiguities. Perhaps the alternative meanings of a word are represented at different levels of consciousness, and a level that is sufficient for causing semantic priming may not be sufficient to reduce response times on a picture probe task. These views are only speculations, but the kinds of experimental paradigms designed by Swinney (1979) and Potter and Faulconer (1979) should help us find the answers.

Memory for sentences

Memory for Meaning

The study of language has not been limited to the study of comprehension. Psychologists have also been interested in what people remember about sentences following comprehension. People usually attempt to remember the meaning of what is said but do not try to remember the exact words. We might therefore expect that it would be difficult to detect syntactic changes that preserve the meaning of a sentence but easy to detect syntactic changes that alter the meaning. The sentence *Tom called John* has the same meaning as *John was called by Tom* but a different meaning from *John called Tom*. A listener should find it easier to distinguish the third sentence from the first two than to distinguish the first two sentences from each other.

These speculations were supported by an experiment by Sachs (1967). Her experiment was motivated by Chomsky's (1965) distinction between deep structure and surface structure. If comprehension is primarily concerned with the meaning of a sentence, as expressed in the deep

structure, characteristics of surface structure that do not influence meaning may not be remembered after comprehension. Therefore, in many
instances we may recall a sentence not in its exact wording but in another
wording that expresses the same meaning or deep structure.

Sachs tested this hypothesis by using a recognition memory procedure in which people attempted to identify a sentence they had previously heard in a passage either immediately following the sentence or
after a delay of either 80 syllables (approximately 27 seconds) or 160
syllables (approximately 46 seconds). They were instructed that they
would hear a series of short passages, each of which would be inter-
rupted. They would then hear a sentence repeated from somewhere in the
passage—sometimes in the exact same words and sometimes changed in
some small way. The changed sentence differed from the original sentence in either meaning or syntactic form. The instructions indicated that
they should mark *identical* if the words were exactly the same and *changed*
if there was any change at all. The following example, in which the
sentence to be tested is shown in italics, illustrates the procedure:

> There is an interesting story about the telescope. In Holland a man named
> Lippershey was an eyeglass maker. One day his children were playing with
> some lenses. They discovered that things seemed very close if two lenses
> were held about a foot apart. Lippershey began experimenting, and his
> "spyglass" attracted much attention. *He sent a letter about it to Galileo, the great
> Italian scientist.* (0 syllables) Galileo at once realized the importance of the
> discovery and set about to build an instrument of his own. He used an old
> organ pipe with one lens curved out and the other in. On the first clear night
> he pointed the glass toward the sky. He was amazed to find the empty dark
> spaces filled with brightly gleaming stars! (80 syllables) Night after night
> Galileo climbed to a high tower, sweeping the sky with his telescope. One
> night he saw Jupiter, and to his great surprise discovered near it three bright
> stars, two to the east and one to the west. On the next night, however, all
> were to the west. A few nights later there were four little stars (160 syllables)
> [Sachs, 1967, p. 438].*

The subjects heard the test sentence at the points marked 0, 80, or
160 syllables, depending on the delay being tested. They then indicated
whether the test sentence was identical in wording to the original sentence. The test sentence was either the original sentence or a modification
that produced a semantic change, an active/passive change, or a formal
change. The test for the above example was one of the following four
sentences:

*From "Recognition Memory for Syntactic and Semantic Aspects of Con-
nected Discourse," by J. S. Sachs. In *Perception & Psychophysics*, 1967, *2*, 437–
442. Copyright 1967 by the Psychonomic Society, Inc. This and all other quotations from this source are reprinted by permission.

Original: He sent a letter about it to Galileo, the great Italian scientist.
Semantic: Galileo, the great Italian scientist, sent him a letter about it.
Passive/Active: A letter about it was sent to Galileo, the great Italian scientist.
Formal: He sent Galileo, the great Italian scientist, a letter about it [Sachs, 1967, p. 439].

Notice that the semantic sentence differs from the original in meaning. Galileo received the letter, rather than sent it, in the original sentence. The passive/active sentence has the same meaning as the original sentence but a different grammatical structure: the original sentence is changed from active to passive. The formal sentence also preserves the meaning of the original sentence and differs only slightly from the original in wording.

The percentage of correct judgments for each test sentence is shown in Figure 10.5. The results show that people have a good memory for the exact wording of a sentence when tested immediately after hearing it. However, memory for the exact wording rapidly deteriorates; the lack of ability to distinguish identical and formally changed sentences reveals that

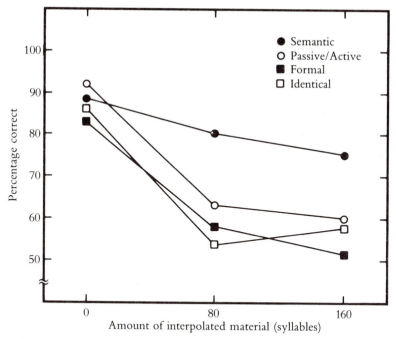

Figure 10.5. Percentage of correct classifications of sentences that either were identical to the original sentences or differed on semantic, syntactic, or formal characteristics. *(From "Recognition Memory for Syntactic and Semantic Aspects of Connected Discourse," by J. S. Sachs. In* Perception & Psychophysics, *1967, 2, 437–442. Copyright 1967 by the Psychonomic Society, Inc. Reprinted by permission.)*

80 syllables later it is already close to the level of 50% correct that would result from guessing. It is even difficult to remember major syntactic changes, such as whether the original sentence was active or passive. However, memory for the meaning of the sentence remains fairly good. Small changes in the original sentence were often detected if they altered its meaning but were often missed if they changed only its syntactic form.

The results indicate that people's ability to recognize the syntactic form of a sentence was quite low, in contrast to their memory for semantic content. The loss of syntactic information occurred quite rapidly, suggesting that memory of the original sentence was rapidly replaced by memory for the semantic information contained in the sentence. Although Sachs's findings are very representative of what usually happens during comprehension, there are a few exceptions.

Memory for Surface Structure

The exception to the rule that people usually remember only the meaning of a sentence, and not its exact surface form, was demonstrated by Keenan, MacWhinney, and Mayhew (1977). Their study is particularly interesting because the subjects—19 members of the Psychology Department at the University of Denver who attended a research luncheon—didn't know they were in an experiment. The procedure for these luncheons is that one of the participants presents research ideas while the others ask questions, expand on ideas, give criticisms, or make humorous remarks. The particular discussion that served as the basis for the experiment was carried out in the usual manner except that it was tape recorded.

The experimenters used the tape recording to select two kinds of statements. Statements that had high interactional content expressed wit, sarcasm, humor, or personal criticism—for example, "I think you made a fundamental error in this study." These statements were paired with statements that had low interactional content, such as "I think there are two fundamental tasks in this study." The experimenters hypothesized that people would be more likely to remember the surface form of the high interactional statements than of the low interactional statements because the exact choice of words helps to reveal the attitude of the speaker.

Keenan and her colleagues tested their hypothesis by giving participants a recognition memory test between one and two days following the research discussion. Some of the items on the test exactly matched the original statements, others were paraphrases of the original statements that preserved their meaning, and the remainder were completely unrelated in semantic content. Statement 1 is an example of a sentence that has low interactional content. Statement 2 is its paraphrase:

1. You put a little morpheme that says you're going to choose the Object as Subject.
2. When you get an Object topic, you add on another little morpheme [p. 552].

When the participants were given sentences that had low interactional content, they were unable to distinguish between the original statements and the paraphrases. They recognized 19% of the original statements and falsely recognized 18% of the paraphrases.

Now let's consider statements that have high interactional content. Statement 3 was actually spoken; Statement 4 is its paraphrase.

3. Italians, you know what Italians are like, they had a strike, they had a heat wave.
4. Everyone knows what happens in Italy, first they had a strike, then they had a heat wave [p. 552].

The level of performance was much better on statements that had high interactional content. The participants indicated that they recognized 56% of the original statements and 18% of the paraphrases.

The results indicate that people are capable of distinguishing a sentence from its paraphrase if the sentence is particularly noteworthy. It is seldom necessary to remember the exact words of a sentence. However, one case where it is worth remembering the exact statement involves the distinction between a direct assertion that something is true and the implication that the information is true. This distinction is the topic of the next section.

Implications of sentences

Studies have shown that language can have an impact on behavior without making direct assertions. It is often sufficient for a message simply to imply an action to convince a listener that the action actually occurred. Thus the sentence *The hungry python caught the mouse* may convince the listener that the python ate the mouse, even though that action is not explicitly stated. The fact that people may not distinguish implications and direct statements can have important consequences. For example, a consumer could be misled by the implications of an advertisement, or a jury could be misled by the implications of a testimony. We will first consider the effect of implications on courtroom testimony.

Courtroom Testimony

The asking of leading questions is one way implications can influence a person's responses. Elizabeth Loftus designed a procedure to simulate what might occur during eyewitness testimony (for example, Loftus,

1975). The procedure consists of showing people a short film depicting a car accident and, immediately after the film, asking them questions about what occurred in the film. One experimental variation involved phrasing the questions as either *Did you see a broken headlight?* or *Did you see the broken headlight?* The word *the* implies that there was a broken headlight, whereas the word *a* does not imply the existence of such an object. The results showed that people who were asked questions containing the word *the* were more likely to report having seen something, whether or not it had actually appeared in the film, than those who were asked questions containing the word *a*.

Another experiment revealed that the wording of a question can affect a numerical estimate. The question *About how fast were the two cars going when they smashed into each other?* consistently yielded a higher estimate of speed than when *smashed* was replaced by *collided, bumped, contacted,* or *hit*. These results, when combined with similar findings from other experiments conducted by Loftus and her associates, demonstrate that leading questions can influence eyewitness testimony.

Implications can influence not only how a witness responds to questions but what a jury remembers about the testimony of a witness. In another experiment (Harris, 1978) subjects listened to a simulated courtroom testimony and then rated statements about information in the testimony as true, false, or of indeterminate truth value. Half of the test statements were directly asserted (for instance, *The intruder walked away without taking any money*) and half the statements were only implied (*The intruder was able to walk away without taking any money*). The test item that the intruder did not take any money would be true for the asserted statement but of indeterminate truth value for the implied statement.

Harris found that people were more likely to indicate that asserted statements were true than that implied statements were true. There was, however, a disturbing tendency to accept implied statements—subjects responded *true* to 64% of the statements that were only implied. Furthermore, instructions warning people to be careful to distinguish between asserted and implied statements did not significantly reduce the acceptance of implied statements.

The work of Loftus and Harris should be of interest to people in the legal professions. A judge can immediately rule leading questions out of order, but not before the members of the jury have heard the question. Instructions from the judge to disregard certain evidence may not prevent the jury from considering that evidence when making their decision. More subtle uses of language, such as use of the word *crash* rather than the word *hit,* may not even be identified as potentially misleading.

Harris has speculated that the distinction between asserted and implied statements may be even more difficult to make in a real courtroom than in an experimental situation. People in his experiment made their judgments immediately after hearing a 5-minute segment of a simulated trial testimony. Members of a jury make their final decision after a much longer delay and after they have heard much more information. It is therefore important to clarify immediately any courtroom statements that are ambiguous regarding whether information was asserted or implied. If the witness is unwilling to directly assert the information—and thus become liable for perjury—the jury should be made aware of the questionable value of the information.

Advertising Claims

The acceptance of implied statements is as important an issue in advertising as it is in courtroom testimony. The Federal Trade Commission makes decisions regarding deceptive advertising, but deciding what constitutes deceptive is a complex question. The decision may be particularly difficult if a claim is only implied. Consider the following commercial:

> Aren't you tired of sniffles and runny noses all winter? Tired of always feeling less than your best? Get through the whole winter without colds. Take Eradicold Pills as directed.

Notice that the commercial does not directly assert that Eradicold Pills will get you through the whole winter without colds—it is only implied. In order to test whether people can distinguish between asserted and implied claims, Harris (1977) gave people a series of 20 fictitious commercials, half of which asserted claims and half of which implied claims. The subjects were instructed to rate the claims as true, false, or of indeterminate truth value on the basis of the presented information. Some of the people made their judgments immediately after hearing each commercial, and others made their judgments after hearing all 20 commercials. In addition, half the people were given instructions that warned them not to interpret implied claims as asserted and were shown an example of a commercial that made an implied claim.

The results of the experiment indicated that the subjects responded *true* significantly more often to assertions than to implications. Furthermore, instructions were helpful in reducing the number of implications accepted as true. Although these results are encouraging, however, they are not unqualifiedly positive. First, even in the condition that was most favorable to rejecting implications—the group that had been warned and that gave an immediate judgment after hearing each commercial—people accepted about half the implied statements as true. When the judgments were delayed until all 20 commercials were presented, people accepted as true about as many implied statements as direct statements—even when they had been specifically warned about implied statements.

The acceptance of implied statements is a problem that exists outside the psychology laboratory. In fact, one of the most frequently accepted implied statements in Harris's (1977) study was a verbatim statement from a real commercial. Another real commercial, created after Harris's study, was changed because competitors complained that it made unfair implications about their product (see Box 10.2). Their complaints resulted in a modification of the commercial.

Box 10.2. American Express Ads Challenged

NEW YORK—Those "Don't-leave-home-without-them" television commercials for American Express Travelers Cheques are under attack, and American Express reportedly plans to re-do them.

Competitors say the ads unfairly imply that people who lose travelers checks may not be able to get a refund unless the checks were issued by American Express.

NBC News reported that American Express has agreed to change its commercials. Actor Karl Malden will reshoot the endings, NBC said, and make it clear that all travelers checks are refundable, not just American Express checks.

Collot Guerard of the division of advertising practices in the Federal Trade Commission's Bureau of Consumer Protection said the agency "probably will take a look at the American Express ad."

Deciding whether it is deceptive, she said, will depend on the answers to a number of questions, including: "How easy is it to get refunds for the other companies' travelers checks?"

The American Express TV campaign introduced in June shows people in a variety of situations. They lose their travelers checks. Panic. A plea for help. But the checks were not American Express. What is to be done? The question is unanswered. At the end, comes the voice of Malden: "American Express Travelers Cheques. Don't leave home without them."

From the *San Francisco Chronicle*, August 17, 1979. © Associated Press Newsfeatures. Reprinted by permission.

Logical Implications

In the examples we have been looking at so far people often were unable to distinguish between assertions and statements with fairly obvious implications. Attempts to comprehend many logical statements, however, often reveal the opposite problem—the logical implications are not very obvious. Imagine that you are shown four cards, each containing a *D,* a *K,* a 3, or a 7 (see Figure 10.6). The experimenter informs you that each card has a letter on one side and a number on the other side and then asks which cards would you have to turn over to determine the truth of the sentence *Every card that has a D on one side has a 3 on the other side.* Try to answer this question before reading further.

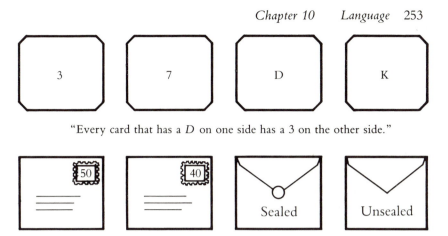

"Every card that has a *D* on one side has a 3 on the other side."

"If a letter is sealed, then it has a 50-lira stamp on it."

Figure 10.6. The four-card selection problem.

The experiment, known as the four-card selection problem, has been analyzed by Wason and Johnson-Laird (1972). It is an example of a conditional reasoning task. The correct answer is that you would have to turn over the cards containing a *D* and a 7. The selection of a *D* is fairly obvious—the rule would be false if the other side of the card did not contain a 3. The rule would also be false if you turned over the card containing the 7 and found a *D* on the other side. It is not necessary to turn over the card containing the 3, although this is a common mistake. The rule does not specify what should be on the opposite side of a 3; it only specifies what should be on the opposite side of a *D*. For example, finding a *K* on one side of the card and a 3 on the other side would not make the rule false.

The results of experiments using this task reveal that the implications of a conditional rule are not very clear to most people. The combined results of four experiments indicated that only 5 of 128 subjects correctly turned over only the two correct cards (Wason & Shapiro, 1971). The most popular choice was to turn over the two cards mentioned in the rule—the letter *D* and the number 3 for the above example.

Wason and Johnson-Laird (1972) argued that people make mistakes because they seek information that would verify the rule rather than information that would falsify it. Only the latter information is necessary. Turning over the card containing the 3 would verify the rule if a *D* were found on the other side, but it's not logically necessary to turn over this card since the rule does not specify what should be on the other side. It is necessary to turn over the 7, but people usually overlook this card because they are not seeking ways to disprove the rule.

Wason and Shapiro (1971) hypothesized that the poor performance in this task was due in part to the abstract material. They predicted that using more realistic materials related to everyday knowledge would make the task significantly easier. The realistic rules were of the general form *Every time I go to Manchester I travel by car*. The four cards contained two destinations (Manchester and Leeds) and two modes of transport (car and train). One side of the card specified the destination and the other side the transportation. Of 16 British subjects 10 selected the two correct cards (Manchester and train) when realistic material was used, compared to only 2 of 16 subjects when abstract material was used.

A problem with even greater appeal as a realistic task is the letter-sorting task used by Johnson-Laird, Legrenzi, and Legrenzi (1972). Italian subjects in the realistic condition were asked to imagine that they worked at a post office, and their job was to make sure that the letters conformed to each of the following rules: (1) if a letter is sealed, then it has a 50-lira stamp on it, and (2) a letter is sealed only if it has a 50-lira stamp on it. Two letters were face down, revealing either a sealed or an unsealed envelope, and two letters were face up, revealing either a 40-lira or a 50-lira stamp (see Figure 10.6). Subjects in the symbolic condition were asked to test two abstract rules involving letters with an *A* or a *D* on one side and a 3 or a 5 on the other side. Seventeen of the 24 subjects in the realistic condition were correct on both rules, compared to none of the 24 subjects in the symbolic condition.

The results clearly demonstrate that people improve when the conditional statement contains familiar information. The semantic content of the statement is thus an important determinant of performance. Investigations of how semantic content influences performance currently make up the majority of psychological studies of comprehension (Lachman et al., 1979). This emphasis on semantic variables rather than syntactic variables represents a shift from the early studies in psycholinguistics—today psychologists are less interested in the syntactic issues discussed by Chomsky (1957). This may be due partially to the greater emphasis Chomsky himself placed on semantics in the revision of his theory (Chomsky, 1965). But it is also due to the realization that the semantic knowledge of the listener or reader plays a major role in comprehension. The interaction between the knowledge of the comprehender and the semantic nature of the material is particularly evident in studies of text comprehension. The next chapter, on text comprehension, expands the unit of analysis from the sentence to the paragraph. Just as the comprehension of a word usually depends on its context in a sentence, the comprehension of a sentence often depends on the context of the paragraph.

Summary

One of the major questions that has fascinated psychologists interested in language is how people learn to speak in grammatically correct sentences.

An early view suggested that children learn to associate the adjacent words in a sentence. According to this view, each word serves as a stimulus for the word that follows it. There are several problems with this theory, the major one being that a person would have to learn an infinite number of associations. The alternative view is that a child learns a grammar consisting of rules for generating sentences. The transformational grammar proposed by Chomsky stimulated much research as psychologists investigated how well it could account for the results of language experiments. The grammar consisted of both phrase structure rules for describing the parts of a sentence (such as noun phrase and verb phrase) and transformation rules for changing a sentence into a closely related sentence (such as an active sentence into a passive sentence).

Psychologists have occasionally used ambiguous sentences to study comprehension and have found that it takes more time to complete an ambiguous sentence than an unambiguous one. A clarifying context apparently allows the listener to quickly select the appropriate meaning of an ambiguous word, although both meanings have been activated. The study of how people comprehend noun phrases indicates that the meaning of a noun is immediately influenced by the adjective that precedes it. The research on comprehension attempts to identify how context influences the meaning of words and raises the question of whether alternative meanings can exist at different levels of conscious awareness.

After people comprehend a sentence, they usually quickly forget the exact wording and retain only the meaning. The results of one experiment indicated that when people listened to a passage and were tested on a sentence that occurred about a minute earlier, they could easily identify the sentence from among alternatives that differed in meaning. However, they were not very good at identifying syntactic changes that preserved the meaning of the sentence. In the one exception, from a different study, participants had a fairly good verbatim memory for sentences that expressed wit, sarcasm, or personal criticism.

An aspect of language that has direct practical applications is the distinction between assertions and implications. The impact of a sentence that only implies certain events may be as great as a sentence that directly asserts these events. Making people aware of the distinction between an asserted and an implied statement is particularly important in courtroom testimony. Research using simulated testimony has found that people often do not distinguish or do not remember what information was only implied rather than asserted. Similar results have been found for advertising claims. In contrast to these studies—in which people easily accepted the implications—studies on logical reasoning show that the implications of logical statements are not very apparent. People are seldom correct when abstract material is used but improve when they can relate the statement to everyday knowledge.

Recommended reading

An easy introduction to the theoretical contributions of Chomsky is a book by Lyons (1970). Jenkins (1969) discusses the influence of grammatical theories on the way psychologists think about language acquisition. Lachman, Lachman, and Butterfield (1979) review the shift in psycholinguistics from a preoccupation with syntax to a preoccupation with semantics. Schvaneveldt, Meyer, and Becker (1976) used their lexical-decision task to study the effect of semantic context on visual word recognition. Blank and Foss (1978) studied how an appropriate semantic context facilitates the comprehension of sentences.

There have been many studies on memory for sentences. Jarvella (1979) reviews studies on immediate memory for the exact words of a sentence. Bransford and Franks (1971) performed a classic study on the integration of ideas in sentences, in which they demonstrated that people have difficulty recognizing the exact words in a sentence because they combine the ideas in related sentences. Kintsch and Bates (1977) studied recognition memory outside the laboratory by testing students' memory for statements made during a classroom lecture. Danks and Glucksberg (1980) summarized recent work in psycholinguistics in their chapter for the *Annual Review of Psychology*.

11

Comprehension and Memory for Text

Reading a book should be a conversation between you and the author.
MORTIMER ADLER AND CHARLES VAN DOREN

It may be difficult to single out any one cognitive skill as more important than the others, but if we had to make a choice, comprehension would be a prime contender for the honor. Much of what we learn depends on our ability to comprehend or understand written material. The comprehension of written material has attracted considerable interest.

This interest in comprehension has resulted in attempts to rewrite regulations and instructions to make them easier to understand. For instance, President Jimmy Carter issued an order requiring each federal regulation to be written in plain English and be understandable to those who had to comply with it. One example of the attempt to improve instructions is the study conducted by Charrow and Charrow (1979). The goal of the study was to make it easier to understand jury instructions by identifying difficulties in comprehension. Box 11.1 shows two versions of instructions to a jury. The first version is the original; the second version is a modification designed to be easier to understand.

Charrow and Charrow tested the success of their modifications by asking prospective jury members to paraphrase the instructions. After the members heard the instructions, they attempted to recall them in their own words. The jury members who listened to the modified instructions were more successful than the members who listened to the original instructions. For the example shown in Box 11.1 there was about a 50% improvement in ability to recall the instructions.

Box 11.1.

Original

You must not consider as evidence any statement of counsel made during the trial; however, if counsel for the parties have stipulated to any fact, or any fact has been admitted by counsel, you will regard that fact as being conclusively proved as to the party or parties making the stipulation or admission.

As to any question to which an objection was sustained, you must not speculate as to what the answer might have been or as to the reason for the objection.

You must not consider for any purpose any offer of evidence that was rejected, or any evidence that was stricken out by the court; such matter is to be treated as though you had never known of it.

You must never speculate to be true any insinuation suggested by a question asked a witness. A question is not evidence and may be considered only as it supplies meaning to the answer.

Modified

As I mentioned earlier, it is your job to decide from the evidence what the facts are. Here are five rules that will help you decide what is, and what is not, evidence.

1. Lawyers' Statements.   Ordinarily, any statement made by the lawyers in this case is not evidence. However, if all the lawyers agree that some particular thing is true, you must accept it as the truth.

2. Rejected Evidence.   At times during this trial, items or testimony were offered as evidence, but I did not allow them to become evidence. Since they never became evidence, you must not consider them.

3. Stricken Evidence.   At times, I ordered some piece of evidence to be stricken, or thrown out. Since that is no longer evidence, you must ignore it, also.

4. Questions to a Witness.   By itself, a question is not evidence. A question can only be used to give meaning to a witness's answer. Furthermore, if a lawyer's question to a witness contained any insinuations, you must ignore those insinuations. And

5. Objections to Questions.   If a lawyer objected to a question, and I did not allow the witness to answer the question, you must not try to guess what the answer might have been. You must also not try to guess the reason why the lawyer objected to the question.

From "Making Legal Language Understandable: A Psycholinguistic Study of Jury Instructions," by R. P. Charrow and V. R. Charrow. In *Columbia Law Review*, 1979, 79, 1306–1374. Reprinted by permission of the authors.

Psychologists have used primarily two measures of comprehension, and we will encounter examples of each in this chapter. One is a subjective measure of understanding. They ask people to rate on a scale how easy various texts were to understand, or they might ask people to press a button as soon as they think that they understand a sentence. The second measure is the number of ideas that people can recall from a text. This measure assumes that, if someone has really understood the ideas, he should be able to recall more ideas than someone who didn't understand the ideas.

Two important components influence comprehension—the reader and the text. The reader comes equipped with prior knowledge that can help her understand the text by relating what she reads to what she already knows. The quotation at the beginning of this chapter—"Reading a book should be a conversation between you and the author"—reflects this interaction between the reader and the author. But unlike a real conversation, the conversation proceeds in only one direction. This places an added burden on the author to anticipate how the reader might respond—to attempt to foresee difficulties and answer questions that the reader might have.

The three sections of this chapter emphasize the reader, the text, and the interaction between the reader and the text. The first section looks at how the reader's knowledge influences the comprehension and recall of ideas in a text. The second section is about the organization of ideas in a text. The final section discusses a specific model of how comprehension occurs. Although the model is not completed, it is already successful in predicting how easy it is to read different paragraphs.

Prior knowledge of the reader

Effect on Comprehension

A central issue for psychologists interested in studying comprehension is specifying how people use their knowledge to understand new or abstract ideas. The influence of prior knowledge on the comprehension and recall of ideas was dramatically illustrated in a study by Bransford and Johnson (1973). They asked people to listen to a paragraph and try to comprehend and remember it. At the end of the paragraph the subjects rated how easy it was to comprehend and then attempted to recall as many ideas as they could. You can get some feeling for the task by reading the following passage once and, after you have finished, attempting to recall as much as you can.

> If the balloons popped, the sound wouldn't be able to carry, since everything would be too far away from the correct floor. A closed window would also prevent the sound from carrying, since most buildings tend to be well insulated. Since the whole operation depends on a steady flow of electricity, a break in the middle of the wire would also cause problems. Of course, the fellow could shout, but the human voice is not loud enough to carry that far. An additional problem is that a string could break on the instrument. Then

there could be no accompaniment to the message. It is clear that the best situation would involve less distance. Then there would be fewer potential problems. With face to face contact, the least number of things could go wrong [p. 392].*

Bransford and Johnson intentionally designed the passage to consist of abstract, unfamiliar statements. If you found it difficult to recall the ideas, your experience was similar to the experience of the people who participated in the experiment. They recalled only 3.6 ideas from a maximum of 14. The ideas can be made less abstract by showing people an appropriate context, as is illustrated in Figure 11.1. Does the picture help you recall any more ideas?

Bransford and Johnson (1973) tested the effect of context by comparing a "no-context" group with two other groups. The "context-before" group saw the picture before they read the passage. They recalled an average of 8.0 ideas, a substantial improvement over the no-context group. The "context-after" group saw the picture immediately after reading the passage. They recalled only 3.6 ideas—the same number as the no-context group. The effect of context was useful, but only if people were aware of the context before reading the passage.

The results suggest that context does much more than simply provide hints about what might have occurred in the passage. If the picture provided useful retrieval cues, the people who saw the picture after reading the passage should have recalled more ideas than the group who didn't see the picture. Since recall was improved only when people saw the picture before reading the passage, the experiment suggests that the context improved comprehension, which in turn improved recall. People in the context-before group rated the passage as easy to comprehend, in contrast to the context-after group. When the abstract ideas were difficult to comprehend, they were quickly forgotten, and providing the context after the passage had no effect on recall.

The balloon passage is an example of a novel context since most of us have never encountered this particular situation. But even a familiar context is useful only if we know when it is appropriate. Consider the following passage:

The procedure is actually quite simple. First you arrange things into different groups. Of course, one pile may be sufficient depending on how much there is to do. If you have to go somewhere else due to lack of facilities, that is the next step; otherwise you are pretty well set. It is important not to overdo things. That is, it is better to do too few things at once than too many. In the short run this may not seem important, but complications can

*From "Consideration of Some Problems of Comprehension," by J. D. Bransford and M. K. Johnson. In W. G. Chase (Ed.), *Visual Information Processing.* Copyright 1973 by Academic Press, Inc. This and all other quotations from this source are reprinted by permission.

easily arise. A mistake can be expensive as well. At first the whole procedure will seem complicated. Soon, however, it will become just another facet of life. It is difficult to foresee any end to the necessity for this task in the immediate future, but then one never can tell. After the procedure is completed, one arranges the materials into different groups again. Then they can be put into their appropriate places. Eventually they will be used once more, and the whole cycle will then have to be repeated. However, that is part of life [Bransford & Johnson, 1973, p. 400].

The paragraph actually describes a very familiar procedure, but the ideas are presented so abstractly that the procedure is difficult to recognize. People who read the passage had as much trouble recalling ideas as the people who read the balloon passage—they recalled only 2.8 ideas from a maximum of 18. A different group of subjects, who were informed after reading the passage that it referred to washing clothes, didn't

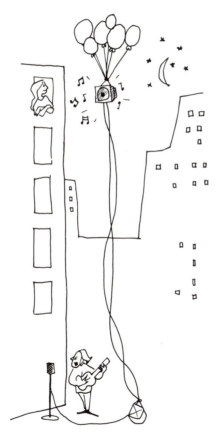

Figure 11.1. Appropriate context for the balloon passage. *(From "Considerations of Some Problems of Comprehension," by J. D. Bransford and M. K. Johnson. In W. G. Chase (Ed.),* Visual Information Processing. *Copyright 1973 by Academic Press, Inc. Reprinted by permission.)*

do any better; they recalled only 2.7 ideas. But those subjects who were told before they read the passage that it described washing clothes recalled 5.8 ideas. The results are consistent with the results on the balloon passage and indicate that background knowledge isn't sufficient if people don't recognize the appropriate context. Although everyone is familiar with the procedure used to wash clothes, people didn't recognize the procedure because the passage was so abstract. Providing the appropriate context before the passage therefore increased both comprehension and recall, as it did for the balloon passage.

Effect on Retrieval

The failure of the context-after group to recall more ideas than the no-context group was caused by the difficulty in comprehending material when there was not an obvious context. The results might have been different, however, if the material had been easier to understand as presented. Bransford and Johnson, in fact, suggest that if people initially understand a text and are then encouraged to think of the ideas in a new perspective, they might recall additional ideas that they failed to recall under the old perspective.

A study by Anderson and Pichert (1978) supports the hypothesis that a shift in perspective may result in the recall of additional ideas. The participants in their study read about two boys who played hooky from school. The story told that they went to one of the boys' homes because no one was there on Thursdays. It was a very nice home on attractive grounds, set back from the road. But because it was an older home, it had some defects—a leaky roof and a damp basement. The family was quite wealthy and owned a lot of valuable possessions, such as ten-speed bikes, a color television, and a rare coin collection. The entire story contained 72 ideas, which had previously been rated in terms of their importance to a prospective burglar or to a prospective homebuyer. For example, a leaky roof and damp basement would be important to a homebuyer, but valuable possessions and the fact that no one was usually home on Thursday would be important to a burglar.

The subjects read the story from one of the two perspectives and, after a short delay, were asked to write down as much of the exact story as they could remember. Following another short delay they again attempted to recall ideas from the story. Half did so from the same perspective and half from a new perspective. The experimenters told the students in the "same perspective" condition that the purpose of the study was to determine whether people could remember things they thought they had forgotten if they were given a second chance. Students in the "new perspective" condition were told that the purpose of the study was to determine whether people could remember things they thought they had forgotten if they were given a new perspective.

As might be expected, the perspective influenced the kind of information people recalled during the first recall period. The group that had the burglar perspective recalled more burglar information, and the group that had the homebuyer perspective recalled more homebuyer information. The results during the second recall attempt supported the hypothesis that a change in perspective can result in recall of additional information. The group that shifted perspectives recalled additional ideas that were important to the new perspective—7% more ideas in one experiment and 10% more in another. In contrast, the group that did not shift perspective recalled slightly less information on their second attempt than on their first attempt.

Notice that these findings differ from the findings of Bransford and Johnson (1973) in that the shift to a new perspective aided the retrieval, rather than the comprehension, of ideas. Since the story was easy to comprehend, comprehension wasn't a problem; the problem was being able to recall all the ideas. Anderson and Pichert proposed three possible explanations for why changing perspectives aided recall. One possibility is that people simply guessed ideas that they didn't really remember but that were consistent with the new perspective. The chance of guessing correctly, however, is rather low. A second alternative is that people did not recall all they could remember because they thought it was not important to the original perspective. The instructions, however, were to recall all the information. The third possibility was the one favored by Anderson and Pichert because it was the most consistent with what the participants reported during interviews that followed their recall. Many subjects reported that the new perspective provided them with a plan for searching memory. They used their knowledge about what would interest a homebuyer or a burglar to retrieve new information that was not suggested by the original perspective.

Scripts: Representing Prior Knowledge

The previous studies support the idea that prior knowledge influences either the comprehension or the retrieval of information in a text. People who could interpret abstract ideas as related to a serenade or washing clothes had an advantage in comprehending and recalling the ideas. In addition, adopting a particular perspective enabled people to retrieve more concrete ideas that they were initially able to comprehend. The argument that prior knowledge is important has much intuitive appeal. Can we be more specific about the organization of prior knowledge, particularly the knowledge of everyday activities that most people share?

Schank and Abelson (1977) proposed that our knowledge is organized around many kinds of routine activities—for example, going to a restaurant, visiting a dentist, or riding a bus. They used the term *script* to refer to what we know about each of these situations. For example, a restaurant script would specify what we know about going to a restaurant. At a very general level a restaurant script consists of standard roles, props or objects, conditions, and results. The conditions for going to a restaurant are that a customer is hungry and is able to pay for the meal. The props are tables and chairs, a menu, food, a bill, and money or a credit card. The results are that the customer has less money but is no longer hungry, while the owner has more money. Between the time that a customer enters and leaves, there is a fairly standard sequence of events that include selecting a table, looking at the menu, ordering the food, eating, and paying the bill.

Since the sequence of events is quite standard, if someone asks us about a particular restaurant, there is no need to mention all the actions that took place. Instead we would mention events that are not standard— such as the quality of the food, the service, the decor, and perhaps the cost. The advantage of all the standard information stored in a script is that it enables the listener to fill in the missing details without having to recapitulate everything.

A study by Bower, Black, and Turner (1979) used the concept of scripts to investigate how people's knowledge of routine activities helps them understand and remember information. The first question they asked is to what extent people agree about the events that occur in standard activities such as going to a restaurant, attending a lecture, getting up in the morning, grocery shopping, or visiting a doctor. They asked people to list about 20 actions or events that occur during each of these activities. Table 11.1 presents the lists in the order the events were usually mentioned. All the events listed in Table 11.1 were mentioned by at least 25% of the subjects. The lists indicate that there is considerable agreement regarding the actions that occur during routine activities.

What effect does knowledge of script-related activities have on memory for text? One effect is that scripts determine what is emphasized as we read a text. The typical events in a script provide a framework for comprehension but are themselves uninteresting because we already know about them. What is usually interesting is the occurrence of an event that is related to the script but unexpected. For example, a customer may need help translating a menu because it is in French, or the waiter may spill soup on the customer. Schank and Abelson (1977) refer to such events as *obstacles* or *distractions* because they interrupt the major goals of the script, such as ordering and eating.

Bower and his colleagues (1979) hypothesized that such interruptions should be remembered better than the routine events in the scripts listed in Table 11.1. From the viewpoint of the reader they are the only "point" of the story. Bower also hypothesized that events that are irrelevant to the goals of the script should be remembered less well than the routine events in the script. For example, the type of print on the

TABLE 11.1. Activities Associated with Different Events.

Going to a restaurant	Attending a lecture	Getting up	Grocery shopping	Visiting a doctor
Open door	ENTER ROOM	*Wake up*	ENTER STORE	*Enter office*
Enter	*Look for friends*	Turn off alarm	GET CART	CHECK IN WITH RECEPTIONIST
Give reservation name	FIND SEAT	Lie in bed	Take out list	SIT DOWN
Wait to be seated	SIT DOWN	Stretch	Look at list	Wait
Go to table	Settle belongings	GET UP	Go to first aisle	Look at other people
BE SEATED	TAKE OUT NOTEBOOK	Make bed	*Go up and down aisles*	READ MAGAZINE
Order drinks	*Look at other students*	*Go to bathroom*	PICK OUT ITEMS	*Name called*
Put napkins on lap	*Talk*	Use toilet	Compare prices	Follow nurse
LOOK AT MENU	Look at professor	*Take shower*	Put items in cart	*Enter exam room*
Discuss menu	LISTEN TO PROFESSOR	*Wash face*	Get meat	Undress
ORDER MEAL	TAKE NOTES	Shave	Look for items forgotten	*Sit on table*
Talk	CHECK TIME	DRESS	Talk to other shoppers	Talk to nurse
Drink water	Ask questions	Go to kitchen	Go to checkout counters	NURSE TESTS
Eat salad or soup	Change position in seat	Fix breakfast	*Find fastest line*	Wait
Meal arrives	Daydream	EAT BREAKFAST	WAIT IN LINE	Doctor enters
EAT FOOD	Look at other students	BRUSH TEETH	*Put food on belt*	Doctor greets
Finish meal	Take more notes	Read paper	Read magazines	Talk to doctor about problem
Order dessert	*Close notebook*	*Comb hair*	WATCH CASHIER RING UP	Doctor asks questions
Eat dessert	*Gather belongings*	*Get books*	PAY CASHIER	DOCTOR EXAMINES
Ask for bill	Stand up	Look in mirror	*Watch bag boy*	Get dressed
Bill arrives	Talk	Get coat	Cart bags out	Get medicine
PAY BILL	LEAVE	LEAVE HOUSE	Load bags into car	Make another appointment
Leave tip			LEAVE STORE	LEAVE OFFICE
Get coats				
LEAVE				

Items in all capital letters were mentioned by the most subjects, items in italics by fewer subjects, and items in lowercase letters by the fewest subjects.

From "Scripts in Memory for Text," by G. H. Bower, J. B. Black, and T. J. Turner. In *Cognitive Psychology*, 1979, 11, 177–220. Copyright 1979 by Academic Press, Inc. Reprinted by permission.

menu or the color of the waitress's hair is irrelevant to the goals of the script. The results supported the predictions. People who read stories about the script activities shown in Table 11.1 recalled 53% of the interruptions, 38% of the script actions, and 32% of the irrelevant information.

Although background knowledge usually makes comprehension and recall easier, it can also be the source of errors. When we already know something about the given topic and then read more about it, we may have difficulty distinguishing between what we read and what we already know. This can create a problem if we are asked to recall the source of the information. Consider the following biographical passage:

> Gerald Martin strove to undermine the existing government to satisfy his political ambitions. Many of the people of his country supported his efforts. Current political problems made it relatively easy for Martin to take over. Certain groups remained loyal to the old government and caused Martin trouble. He confronted these groups directly and so silenced them. He became a ruthless, uncontrollable dictator. The ultimate effect of his rule was the downfall of his country [Sulin & Dooling, 1974, p. 256].

People who read this passage should not associate it with their knowledge of famous people since Gerald Martin is a fictitious person. It would be easy, however, to modify the passage by changing the name of the dictator. In an experiment designed by Sulin and Dooling (1974) half of the subjects read the Gerald Martin passage, and half of the subjects read the same passage with the name changed to Adolf Hitler. Either 5 minutes or one week after reading the passage, the subjects were given a recognition memory test consisting of seven sentences from the passage randomly mixed with seven sentences that were not in the passage. Subjects were asked to identify the sentences that occurred in the passage.

Four of the sentences not in the passage were completely unrelated (neutral), and the other three varied in their relatedness to the Hitler theme. The low-related sentence was *He was an intelligent man but had no sense of human kindness*. The medium-related sentence was *He was obsessed by the desire to conquer the world*. The high-related sentence was *He hated the Jews particularly and so persecuted them*. Figure 11.2 shows the recognition of sentences for the two retention intervals. At the short retention interval there were few false recognitions, and the results were uninfluenced by whether the passage was about a famous person (Hitler) or a fictitious person (Martin). After one week, however, it was more difficult for people who read the Hitler passage to distinguish between what was in the passage and what they knew about Hitler. People were likely to recognize a sentence incorrectly as having occurred in the passage if it described Hitler. False recognitions also increased with the retention interval for people who read the Gerald Martin (fictitious) passage, but to a lesser degree.

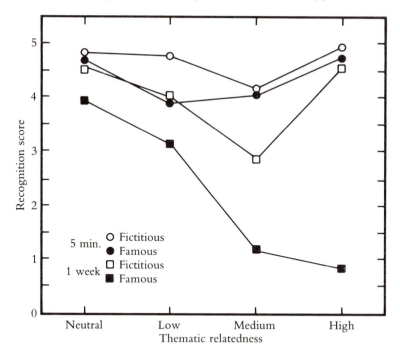

Figure 11.2. Recognition performance (high score = high performance) on new information as a function of main character, retention interval, and thematic relatedness. *(From "Intrusion of a Thematic Idea in Retention of Prose," by R. A. Sulin and D. J. Dooling. In* Journal of Experimental Psychology, *1974, 103, 255–262. Copyright 1974 by the American Psychological Association. Reprinted by permission.)*

In conclusion, there is a variety of ways prior knowledge can influence the comprehension and recall of text. Prior knowledge can make abstract ideas seem less abstract and easier to comprehend. It can also determine what we emphasize in a text and provide a framework for recalling ideas. The price we pay for these benefits is that it may be more difficult to locate the source of our knowledge if what we read is integrated with what we know. In most cases the price is fairly small relative to the benefits.

Organization of text

In this section we will look at how the organization of ideas in a text can influence recall.

Story Structure

One characteristic of simple narrative stories is that the structure determines how the events in the story are organized. We can study this structure at a very general level by representing a story as consisting of a setting, a theme, a plot, and a resolution (Thorndyke, 1977). The *setting* describes time, location, and major characters. The *theme* provides the general focus of the story, often a goal that the main character attempts to achieve. The *plot* consists of a series of actions attempting to achieve the goal. There may be several subgoals or intermediate goals that have to be accomplished before the main goal is reached. The *resolution*—the final outcome of the story—often describes whether the main character was successful in achieving the goal. Each of the components is evident in the following story. (Statements are numbered for the purpose of the discussion below.)

> (1) Circle Island is located in the middle of the Atlantic Ocean (2) north of Ronald Island. (3) The main occupations on the island are farming and ranching. (4) Circle Island has good soil but (5) few rivers and (6) hence a shortage of water. (7) The island is run democratically. (8) All issues are decided by a majority vote of the islanders. (9) The governing body is a senate (10) whose job is to carry out the will of the majority. (11) Recently, an island scientist discovered a cheap method (12) of converting salt water into fresh water. (13) As a result, the island farmers wanted (14) to build a canal across the island, (15) so that they could use water from the canal (16) to cultivate the island's central region. (17) Therefore, the farmers formed a procanal association (18) and persuaded a few senators (19) to join. (20) The procanal association brought the construction idea to a vote. (21) All the islanders voted. (22) The majority voted in favor of construction. (23) The senate, however, decided that (24) the farmers' proposed canal was ecologically unsound. (25) The senators agreed (26) to build a smaller canal (27) that was 2 feet wide and 1 foot deep. (28) After starting construction on the smaller canal, (29) the islanders discovered that (30) no water would flow into it. (31) Thus the project was abandoned. (32) The farmers were angry (33) because of the failure of the canal project. (34) Civil war appeared inevitable [Thorndyke, 1977, p. 80].*

The setting is described in the first ten statements, which inform us about the location and central characters. The next six statements establish the theme and introduce the goal of building a canal across the island. Statements 17–31 contain the plot, which describes how the islanders attempted to accomplish the goal but were overruled by the senate. The last three statements describe the final resolution or outcome.

The structure of this simple narrative is very apparent. It proceeds from the setting to the theme, plot, and resolution. In order to evaluate how useful the overall structure of a story is in facilitating comprehen-

---

sion, Thorndyke modified the story to make the structure less apparent. One modification placed the theme at the end of the story, so it would not be encountered until after people had read the plot and resolution. People read or heard the story only once, so when they finally reached the information about the goal, they had to use it to interpret what they had previously read about the plot. A more extreme modification was to delete the goal statement entirely. The most extreme modification was to present the sentences in a random order so readers would have to completely reconstruct the organization, if they used it at all.

The subjects in Thorndyke's experiment either read or listened to two stories. One story was the Circle Island story; the other was about an old farmer who wanted to put his donkey into a shed. A subject read or heard each story once—in either its original or the modified form— and then attempted to recall all the ideas in the story. Figure 11.3 shows how the organization of the story influenced the recall of ideas. Providing the theme at the end of the story was more effective than providing no theme at all, but it was less effective than providing it before the plot. These findings suggest that the theme helped people understand the plot, particularly when it preceded the plot. The recall of sentences presented in a random order was very difficult, again demonstrating the importance of story structure. The same pattern of results occurred when people rated how easy it was to understand the stories.

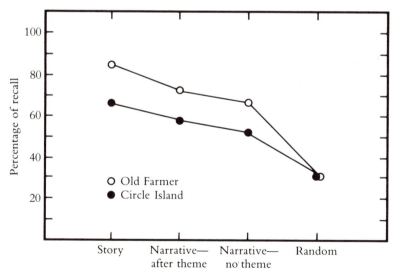

Figure 11.3. Recall of the Old Farmer and Circle Island passages for the different experimental conditions.   *(From "Cognitive Structures in Comprehension and Memory of Narrative Discourse," by P. W. Thorndyke. In* Cognitive Psychology, *1977, 9, 77–110. Copyright 1977 by Academic Press, Inc. Reprinted by permission.)*

Psychologists usually study rather simple stories, but the same ideas can be applied to more complex stories. At least one major publisher has been very successful in producing novels that always follow a very standard setting, theme, plot, and resolution. The global structure of the story changes very little from novel to novel, and yet each new book is very successful (see Box 11.2). A good story structure is apparently worth keeping.

Sentence Structure

In addition to the global structure of a text—represented by its setting, theme, plot, and resolution—the structure of individual sentences can influence the recall of details. For example, a student might be asked to learn the following facts:

> *Text 1:* George Washington was the first president of the United States. He lived in Mount Vernon.
>
> *Text 2:* Thomas Jefferson was the third president of the United States. He lived in Monticello.
>
> *Text 3:* Abraham Lincoln was the 16th president of the United States. He lived in a log cabin.
>
> *Text 4:* Theodore Roosevelt was the 26th president of the United States. He lived in Sagamore Hill.

The sentence structure of each example is: _____ was the _____ president of the United States. He lived in _____. The examples differ only in the details that fill the blanks. In order to investigate the effect of sentence structure on learning, Thorndyke and Hayes-Roth (1979) conducted the following experiment.

They varied the number of training passages that preceded a test passage. Each sentence in the test passage had a corresponding, related sentence in all of the training passages. For example, suppose the training passage was about constellations and the test passage contained the sentence *This constellation was originally charted at Palomar Observatory.* In the "repeated" condition the sentence would be repeated exactly in all the training passages. Although each training passage would describe a different constellation (for example, the Apus Constellation, the Eridanus Constellation, and the Lepus Constellation) all would be charted at Palomar Observatory. This should make it easy to remember that the constellation in the test passage (the Pavo Constellation) was also charted at Palomar Observatory. In the "changed" condition the training and test passages all shared the same sentence structure (*This constellation was charted at*), but the location differed for each passage—it could be Palomar Observatory for one constellation and Mount Wilson for another. Notice

Box 11.2. The Harlequin Series

LLOYD WATSON

He held her body between his roving hands and she made no effort to stop him, shuddering with pleasure under the kiss which seemed to last endlessly, as though in itself it were an act of possession.

—From *Duel of Desire* by Charlotte Lamb

She had the terrifying thought that she had provoked him too far, that he had so lost control that he would take her by force. "You have every reason to be afraid," he said softly, half under his breath. "What the hell do you want, you cheap little flirt?"

—From *Shadow of the Past* by Robyn Donald

"Oh, Simon," she whispered, her mind whirling in the sea of her emotions. Suddenly he pulled away from her, lying beside her with his hand covering his face. "Dear God, what's happening to me? What am I doing to you?" he groaned with undisguised desperation.

—From *Early Summer* by Jan MacLean

Great literature? Hardly. Big bucks? You betcha.

Authors Lamb, Donald and MacLean are part of a stable of 100 women writers who collectively turn out 12 "romances" a month, 12 months a year.

Together, they have written one of the most sensational success stories in publishing history—and they have done so without once getting down to the sexual nitty-gritty.

As the publicity release puts it: "No matter how passionate the protagonists, the heroine's virtue remains intact until marriage.... While problems and misunderstandings delay the happy ending, there are no shocks to disturb the 'beautiful dream.'"

The women are under exclusive contract to Harlequin Enterprises Ltd. of Toronto, the world's largest fiction factory.

Last year, Harlequin sold 125 million books. That's something like four every second.

The novels were printed in 18 languages and marketed in 80 countries....

Unlike other publishers, who promote their titles and authors, Harlequin promotes only "Harlequins."

To a Harlequin reader, the title and author are irrelevant.

The formula seldom varies: Girl, usually poor, always attractive, but rarely beautiful, meets boy—more often than not in some far-off, exotic land—and ultimately, after the standard 190 pages, girl gets boy.

Along the way, not only is there no overt sex, there's no tragedy, no serious illness nor the slightest hint of violence.

Love conquers all.

that this condition is analogous to the example of the four presidents, in which the sentence structure was the same for all four presidents, but the details differed.

Figure 11.4 shows the results of the experiment. Increasing the number of training passages improved recall of information in the test passage when that information was identical (repeated) to the information in the training passages. In other words, repetition improves recall. This isn't very surprising. The interesting question is whether repetition of the same sentence structure improves recall when the information changes. The results show that repetition of only the sentence structure initially improves recall, but then recall declines and finally reaches a level about equivalent to that with no training passages. Although one or two training passages improved recall, it became increasingly difficult to remember which details went with the test passage when subjects read many passages and the details changed from passage to passage. If each passage mentioned a different observatory, the observatories mentioned in the training passages could make it difficult to remember which observatory was mentioned in the test passage. The curve marked *intrusions* in Figure 11.4 shows the number of times subjects incorrectly recalled a detail from a training passage rather than from the test passage.

The number of intrusions can be reduced by making it easier to distinguish between the information presented in the training passages

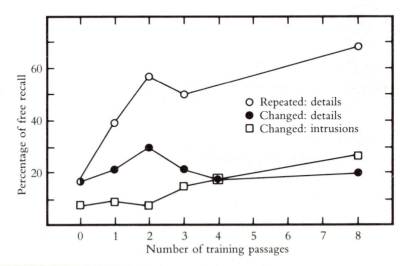

Figure 11.4. Recall of repeated and changed details as a function of the number of training passages.   *(From "The Use of Schemata in the Acquisition and Transfer of Knowledge," by P. W. Thorndyke and B. Hayes-Roth. In* Cognitive Psychology, *1979, 11, 82–106. Copyright 1979 by Academic Press, Inc. Reprinted by permission.)*

and the information presented in the test passage. Thorndyke and Hayes-Roth investigated the effect of delaying the test passage in a second experiment. They varied the number of training passages, as in the previous experiment, but didn't present the test passage until a day after the training passages. This change in procedure made it easy to distinguish between details in a training and a test passage. The number of intrusions was very low and did not increase with the number of training passages. Furthermore, recall of changed information increased as a function of the number of training passages—unlike the results shown in Figure 11.4, which increased only for the initial two training passages. The reason for the improvement in recall is that repeating the same sentence structure across passages teaches people what kind of information they should recall. If every passage mentioned an observatory, students should learn that they have to recall the name of an observatory. Increasing the delay between the training passages and the test passage makes it easier to remember which observatory was mentioned in the test passage.

Implications for the Design of Instructional Materials

Does the effect of temporal separation on recall have any implications for instruction? Perhaps. A writer might present material in different parts of a book or a lecturer in separate lectures if integration of the material would be confusing. A more direct approach, however, is to alter the wording of the material to either promote or discourage integration, depending on whether integration is likely to be beneficial. The similar sentence structure in the previous study promoted integration because the wording was kept identical across passages except for the changes in details.

Hayes-Roth (1978) demonstrated that paraphrasing statements so the sentence structure is not identical reduces integration. Consider the following two texts, which describe similar political events in two different countries.

> *Text 1:* The Spring Episode was the first revolution in Morinthia. The outbreak occurred shortly before dawn on April 17, 1843. The revolution was undoubtedly caused by the tyranny imposed upon the Morinthian people by King Egbert, the dictator. For months, Egbert had extracted half of all the earnings of the people. However, the immediate cause of the outbreak appeared to be a minor crime committed several days earlier. A peasant had poached several chickens from the royal henhouse to serve at his daughter's wedding. It seemed a minor offense to the people, but in Morinthia, everyone who disobeyed the law was punished severely. . . [p. 87].

> *Text 2:* The November Episode was the first revolution in Caledia. The outbreak occurred shortly after midnight on November 1, 1737. The revo-

lution was undoubtedly caused by the tyranny imposed upon the Caledian people by King Ferdinand, the dictator. For months, Ferdinand had refused to allow the representatives of the people to participate in the government. However, the immediate cause of the outbreak appeared to be a minor crime committed several days earlier. A stable boy had drunk a bit too freely at the local tavern and disturbed the town with his singing while making his way home. It seemed a minor offense to the people, but in Caledia, everyone who disobeyed the law was punished severely. . . [p. 87].*

In both texts a first revolution is named, dated, and attributed to the tyranny of a dictatorial king. The cause of each revolution is a minor crime committed by an ordinary person, who is severely punished. However, the details differ in the two texts: the name and time of occurrence of the revolution, the name of the king, and the particular crime. Since both texts are worded nearly identically, it should be difficult to remember which details occurred in which text. The integration of details can be reduced, however, if one text is paraphrased so the wording is not identical. Hayes-Roth found, over a variety of topics, that students remembered about 20% more details when one text was a paraphrase of the other. Thus a simple procedure for improving recall of material that is similar in outline, but different in detail, is to word the material as differently as possible to encourage separate memory structures.

There are, of course, many situations in which the integration of ideas is desired, and the use of similar wording should promote integration. If the first Morinthian revolution were followed by a second Morinthian revolution, there would likely be some details that would be relevant to both revolutions. A reader would therefore want to integrate some of the details to determine how the two revolutions were related. The integration should be facilitated by using the same words. Hayes-Roth (1978) showed that, when integration was useful, the identical wording across texts resulted in a 50% improvement in making accurate inferences. We will now take a closer look at variables that influence the integration of ideas in a text and determine how easy it is to read.

Readability

The first two sections of this chapter reviewed research on two very important components of comprehension—the prior knowledge of the reader and the organization of the text. The development of a detailed

---

*From "Structurally Integrated versus Structurally Segregated Memory Representations: Implications for the Design of Instructional Materials," by B. Hayes-Roth. In A. M. Lesgold, J. W. Pellegrino, S. D. Fokkema, and R. Glaser (Eds.), *Cognitive Psychology and Instruction.* Copyright 1978 by Plenum Publishing Corporation. Reprinted by permission.

model of comprehension is obviously a challenging task, but Walter Kintsch and his students at the University of Colorado have already been quite successful. One attractive aspect of Kintsch's model is that it is now complete enough to allow predictions about the ease of reading different kinds of text.

Predicting readability is an important applied problem. The developers of educational materials want to be assured that their materials can be understood by the students who read them. A former professor of mine once wrote a chapter for *The Mind,* a book in one of the Time-Life series. His chapter required nine revisions before it satisfied the editors of Time-Life. Although he was a good writer and familiar with the topic, he was inexperienced at writing for students in junior high school—the reading level selected for the series.

There have been many attempts to predict readability. According to Kintsch and Vipond (1979), the earliest formulas appeared in the 1920s. There are now about 50 readability formulas, most containing word and sentence variables—unfamiliar words and long sentences generally make a text more difficult to read. What the formulas lack, however, is a good measurement of text organization. If someone placed all the words in a sentence in a scrambled order, the sentence would be very difficult to comprehend, but the predictions of most formulas would be unchanged because they don't consider the order of words in sentences or the order of sentences in a paragraph. The formulas are limited because they are not based on a theory of text comprehension.

The theory that is currently being developed by Kintsch has already contributed to overcoming many of these limitations by providing an account of how the information-processing capabilities of the reader interact with the organization of the text. This section provides a summary of the major assumptions of Kintsch's theory. We begin by looking at how readers attempt to relate new ideas in the text with ideas they have already encountered. The results of this research will tell us what assumptions should be included in a theory of comprehension. The second part of this section describes Kintsch's theory (Kintsch & Vipond, 1979; Kintsch, 1979), and the final part shows how it attempts to predict readability.

Integration of Ideas

Haviland and Clark (1974) have effectively argued that a sentence is usually understood within the context of the sentences that precede it. For example, the statement *George thinks vanilla* is rather bizarre by itself but becomes understandable when preceded by the question *What kind of ice cream does Vivian like?* The understanding of a sentence should therefore depend on how easy it is to relate the ideas in the sentence to the ideas that came before it. This prediction can be illustrated by the following pairs of sentences:

1. Ed was given an alligator for his birthday. The alligator was his favorite present.
2. Ed was given lots of things for his birthday. The alligator was his favorite present.

The first sentence provides an appropriate context for the second sentence in both cases, but the first case makes it clear that Ed received an alligator on his birthday. The second case requires an inference that one of the things Ed received was an alligator.

Participants in Haviland and Clark's experiment saw pairs of sentences in a tachistoscope. After reading the first sentence, they pressed a button to see the second sentence. When they thought they understood the second sentence, they pushed another button, which stopped a clock that measured how long the second sentence was displayed. As predicted by Haviland and Clark, it took significantly less time to comprehend the second sentence when the same ideas (such as alligator) were mentioned in both sentences than when the relation between the two sentences had to be inferred.

The ease with which new ideas can be related to old ideas also depends on the order of the sentences in a paragraph (Kieras, 1978). Consider the sequence of sentences in Table 11.2. The letter preceding each sentence indicates whether the information in the sentence is given (*g*) or new (*n*). The sentence is classified as given if it contains at least one noun that appeared in the preceding sentences. The first example contains only one new sentence; all sentences but the first refer to information that preceded them. The second example contains four new sentences that do

TABLE 11.2. Examples of Presentation Orders Showing the Given (g) or New (n) Status of Each Sentence.

Example 1	*Example 2*
n – The ants ate the jelly.	n – The kitchen was spotless.
g – The ants were hungry.	n – The table was wooden.
g – The ants were in the kitchen.	n – The ants were hungry.
g – The kitchen was spotless.	g – The ants were in the kitchen.
g – The jelly was grape.	n – The jelly was grape.
g – The jelly was on the table.	g – The jelly was on the table.
g – The table was wooden.	g – The ants ate the jelly.

From "Good and Bad Structure in Simple Paragraphs: Effects on Apparent Theme, Reading Time, and Recall," by D. E. Kieras. In *Journal of Verbal Learning and Verbal Behavior*, 1978, *17*, 13–28. Copyright 1978 by Academic Press, Inc. Reprinted by permission.

not refer to preceding information. Kieras predicted that the ideas in the first example should be easier to integrate and recall than the ideas in the second example, and the results supported his prediction.

You may have noticed that all but one of the given sentences in Example 1 repeats a noun from the immediately preceding sentence. The one exception—*The jelly was grape*—repeats a noun (*jelly*) from a sentence that occurred four steps earlier. This sentence may be more difficult to integrate with the preceding sentences because the given information may no longer be in STM, requiring a search of LTM to retrieve the first sentence. Evidence in fact suggests that comprehension is influenced by whether the preceding relevant information is still active in STM or whether it must be retrieved from LTM (Lesgold, Roth, & Curtis, 1979).

The following sentences should be easy to integrate because the first sentence contains relevant information that should still be available in STM when the reader encounters the second sentence.

3. A thick cloud of smoke hung over the forest. The forest was on fire [Lesgold, Roth, & Curtis, p. 294].

Now let's insert two sentences that change the topic and make it less likely that the information about the smoke over the forest is still in STM when the reader learns about the fire.

4. A thick cloud of black smoke hung over the forest. Glancing to one side, Carol could see a bee flying around the back seat. Both of the kids were jumping around but made no attempt to free the insect. The forest was on fire [p. 295].

The inserted information is irrelevant to the fire in the forest and should make it more difficult to comprehend the final sentence than in Case 3. Now consider the insertion of two sentences that are consistent with the initial topic.

5. A thick cloud of smoke hung over the forest. The smoke was thick and black, and began to fill the clear sky. Up ahead Carol could see a ranger directing traffic to slow down. The forest was on fire [p. 295].

The two inserted sentences continue the initial topic, making it easier for the reader to keep active in STM information about the cloud of black smoke. Lesgold, Roth, and Curtis predicted that less time should be required to comprehend the final sentence in Case 5 than in Case 4. Their results supported their predictions.

A number of variables influence comprehension, according to these studies. All the variables reflect how easy it is to integrate what a person is reading with what that person has already read. One variable is whether the reader can relate newly acquired information to ideas that were already expressed in the text. Kieras's (1978) research indicated that it was easier to recall ideas in the text if the sentences referred to previous information rather than contained only new information. A second variable is whether previously expressed ideas are still active in STM or whether they must be retrieved from LTM. Comprehension is easier when related ideas are still active in STM (Lesgold, Roth, & Curtis, 1979). A third variable is whether newly acquired information can be related directly to previous information or whether the reader must infer the relation. Inferences slow down comprehension (Haviland & Clark, 1974). Each of these three variables should be incorporated into a theory of comprehension.

Kintsch's Model of Comprehension

The model of comprehension proposed by Kintsch is still incomplete, although it is already fairly complex. I will therefore give only a brief summary of its major assumptions, emphasizing those that are related to the previous three studies. Figure 11.5 illustrates a theoretical framework for discussing how the information-processing capabilities of the reader interact with the organization of the text. There are two inputs in the model—the text and the goals of the reader. The knowledge and goals of the reader are represented at the top of the figure by the *goal schema*. The goal schema indicates what is relevant; it establishes expectations, calls for certain facts, and may infer facts if they are not directly stated in the text. The text itself is represented in the model by *propositions*. The propositions divide the text into meaningful units; the *coherence rules* arrange them in a network called a *coherence graph* to show how they are related. The network is similar to the semantic networks discussed in Chapter 9. The propositions are also grouped together whenever they belong to the same fact. The *macrostructure* of the text consists of a set of summarization rules called *macro-operators*—they indicate which facts are most relevant and are therefore determined by the goals of the reader. For example, if we asked people to summarize the story about the two boys who stayed home from school (Anderson & Pichert, 1978), which we discussed earlier in this chapter, we would expect that the summaries would differ depending on whether people adopted the burglar or the homebuyer perspective.

The general characteristics of the model can be illustrated with a simple example (Kintsch, 1979). Consider the following text:

> The Swazi tribe was at war with a neighboring tribe because of a dispute over cattle. Among the warriors were two unmarried men, Kakra and his younger brother Gum. Kakra was killed in a battle [p. 6].

The model specifies rules for dividing the text into propositions, but we will not be concerned with the details of these rules. We will consider

Goal Schema

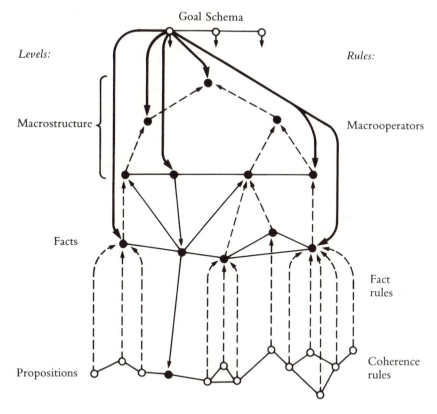

Levels:

Macrostructure

Facts

Propositions

Rules:

Macrooperators

Fact
rules

Coherence
rules

Figure 11.5. The global structure of Kintsch's model of comprehension. *(From "On Modeling Comprehension," by W. Kintsch. In* Educational Psychology, *1979, 14, 3–14. Copyright 1979 by Division 15 of the American Psychological Association. Reprinted by permission.)*

word groups that correspond approximately to the underlying propositions. Figure 11.6 shows how the first sentence is divided into five groups and how the groups are related in a coherence graph. The proposition *was at war with* is the most important proposition, and the others are joined to it. An important parameter in the model is the number of propositions that can be kept active in STM. Since STM is limited in capacity, only a few propositions can be kept active; our example assumes that the capacity limit is three propositions. Both the most important and the most recent propositions are retained in STM (indicated in the figure by the broken circle).

Figure 11.7 shows the propositions of the second sentence and the propositions from the first sentence that are still active in STM. The reader first attempts to connect the new propositions with the old one in STM, but the words in the second sentence don't match any of the words in STM. The reader next determines whether the new propositions can be related to any propositions in LTM. Kintsch proposes that the search

Coherence analysis: Cycle I

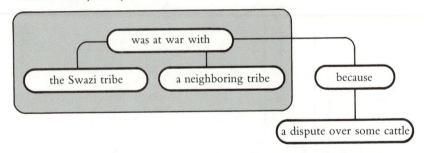

Figure 11.6. Analysis of the first sentence. *(From "On Modeling Comprehension," by W. Kintsch. In* Educational Psychologist, *1979, 14, 3–14. Copyright 1979 by Division 15 of the American Psychological Association. Reprinted by permission.)*

of LTM, which he refers to as a *reinstatement search,* is one of the factors that makes a text difficult to read. If information in the text can be related to ideas that are still active in STM, comprehension is easier than if the reader must search LTM in order to integrate new information with the old. This assumption is consistent with the findings of Lesgold, Roth, and Curtis (1979).

The reinstatement search also fails for the example because there are no concepts that are common to the first two sentences. The model must

Coherence analysis: Cycle II

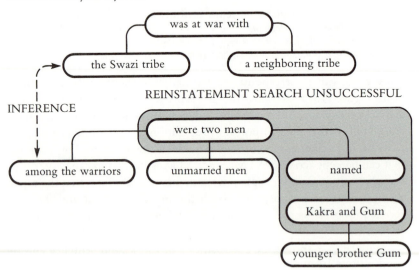

Figure 11.7. Analysis of the second sentence. *(From "On Modeling Comprehension," by W. Kintsch. In* Educational Psychologist, *1979, 14, 3–14. Copyright 1979 by Division 15 of the American Psychological Association. Reprinted by permission.)*

therefore construct a new coherence graph rather than add on to the old graph. It may also make an inference at this point to interrelate the two graphs. The inference is that the warriors mentioned in the second sentence were members of the Swazi tribe. This seems like a reasonable inference, but it is not stated directly. Kintsch's model assumes that inferences, like reinstatement searches, slow down the reader and make comprehension more difficult. The evidence supports this assumption, as was demonstrated by Haviland and Clark (1974).

The model once again selects three propositions from the second sentence to keep active in STM. Figure 11.7 shows that the three selected specify the names of the two men. The third sentence—*Kakra was killed in battle*—is easy to relate to previous information because information about Kakra is still available in STM. Therefore, the new information can be added directly to the coherence graph without having to search LTM or make an inference.

This example should give you an approximate idea of how the model works. The major theme of the model is that incoming information can be understood more easily when it can be integrated with information that the reader has already encountered. The easiest case is when the new information can be related to information that is still active in STM. If it cannot be related, a reinstatement search attempts to relate the new information to propositions stored in LTM. If the reinstatement search fails, a new coherence graph must be started, resulting in a memory for ideas that are not very well integrated. The result should be poorer recall, as was found by Kieras (1978) when the new sentences could not be related to previous sentences. The integration of ideas can sometimes be achieved by an inference, but the need for inferences also contributes to the difficulty of the text.

Predicting Readability

Kintsch's (1979) model is not yet complete, but it has already been quite successful in predicting the relative readability of 20 paragraphs, selected to represent a wide range of readability. Kintsch defined *readability* as the number of propositions recalled divided by the reading time. The measure takes into account both recall and reading time because it is easy to improve either measure at the expense of the other. Three parameters were estimated to make predictions. One parameter was the capacity of STM, which was usually about four propositions. Another parameter was the number of new propositions that were considered at one time. This number usually depended on the number of propositions in each sentence since the model worked on one sentence at a time (as in the example) unless the sentence was too long. The maximum number ranged from 5 to 8 propositions, with a mean of 6.2. The final parameter was the probability that a proposition would be stored in LTM and subsequently recalled. The mean learning probability was rather high for the short texts and was equal to .64. The parameter estimates suggest that a reader processes all the propositions in a sentence unless the sentence contains more than six propositions. The probability of storing each proposition in LTM is rather high for short paragraphs. About four propositions can be kept active in STM.

Kintsch used his model, along with more traditional measures, to predict the readability of paragraphs. The two best predictors of readability were word frequency and the number of reinstatement searches. The first measure is contained in most readability formulas. As we might expect, the use of common, frequently occurring words improves comprehension. The second measure—the number of reinstatement searches—is calculated from Kintsch's model. Application of the model determines how often a person must search LTM to relate new information to previous information. A reinstatement search is required only when the new information cannot be related to the propositions in STM. Another theoretical measure that helps to improve the readability predictions is the number of inferences that are required. An inference is required whenever a concept is not directly repeated—for example, when *war* was mentioned in the first sentence and *warriors* in the second sentence. The number of inferences influenced readability, although not as much as word frequency and the number of reinstatement searches. The required inferences were fairly easy, however; their influence might increase if they were more difficult.

The results indicate that a theory of comprehension can contribute to predicting readability. The theoretical measures—the number of reinstatement searches and the number of inferences—are determined by how well the ideas in the text relate to other ideas in the text. These measures were not included in the traditional measures of readability. Kintsch's model also provides a framework for considering the interaction between the reader and the text. The model implies that readability is not only determined by the text; it is also the result of the interaction between a particular reader and a particular text (Kintsch and Vipond, 1979). For example, a reinstatement search is required only when new information cannot be related to information in STM. A person who can retain many propositions in STM therefore has an advantage in having to make fewer reinstatement searches than a person with a more limited STM. There are several different ways the facilitating effect of background knowledge could be incorporated into the model. Background knowledge might increase the number of propositions held in STM because of their greater familiarity. In addition, it might be easier to make inferences in order to relate different concepts in the text.

Kintsch and Vipond (1979) began their article by reviewing the interaction between the fields of psychology and education. The interaction was very apparent in the early part of this century but diminished during the following decades as psychologists began to study simple and somewhat artificial materials. The amount of current research activity on complex skills like comprehension suggests that the interaction between the two fields should increase. Good theoretical models, like the one developed by Kintsch and Vipond, should certainly stimulate this interaction.

Summary

Psychologists study comprehension by investigating how people's prior knowledge and information-processing characteristics interact with the organization of ideas in a text. The importance of prior knowledge is evident when people have to comprehend very abstract ideas. A meaningful context improves recall when the context is given before, but not after, people read abstract material. It is necessary to improve comprehension in order to improve recall. The recall of more concrete ideas may be improved by providing a context after people have read the text if the context causes a change in perspective. People's knowledge about everyday activities can be represented by scripts that describe the most common events associated with the activities. Scripts influence what a person emphasizes when reading a text. One disadvantage of prior knowledge is that it sometimes makes difficult distinguishing between recently read material and prior knowledge about the topic.

Comprehension is determined not only by what a person already knows but by the organization of ideas in a text. The global structure of narrative stories includes setting, theme, plot, and resolution. The theme provides the general focus of the story and often consists of a goal that the main character tries to achieve. Comprehension is best when the theme precedes the plot, deteriorates when the theme follows the plot, and deteriorates even more when the theme is left out. The recall of ideas is also influenced by sentence structure. The results of an experiment that repeated the same sentence form but changed the details indicated that repetition initially improved recall, but further repetitions made it difficult to distinguish which details occurred in which passage. Increasing the amount of delay between related details or paraphrasing the sentences to make them more distinguishable makes it easier to keep the details separate.

It is usually the case, however, that comprehension is improved by integration of the material. The reader attempts to relate the ideas in the text to ideas already read. Comprehension is easiest when the ideas can be related to ideas that are still available in STM. If no relations are found, the reader can search LTM to look for a relation. If no relations are found in LTM, the new material must be stored separately rather than integrated with the old material. Relations can sometimes be found by making inferences, but inferences slow down comprehension compared to the direct repetition of the same concepts.

A model of comprehension proposed by Kintsch has been quite successful in predicting relative readability. The model can account for the organization of text by considering how many LTM searches and inferences are required. Its parameters include the number of propositions that are processed at one time, the probability of storing a proposition in LTM, and the number of propositions that can be kept active in STM. In addition to improving previous readability formulas, the model provides a theoretical framework for investigating how the information-processing characteristics of a person interact with the organization of the text to influence comprehension.

Recommended reading

Reder (1980) provides an excellent summary of research on the comprehension and retention of prose. Just and Carpenter (1980) have proposed a theory of reading based on the eye fixations of the reader. Kieras (1981) developed a simulation model to predict the reading time of individual sentences. Britton, Westbrook, and Holdredge (1978) related the effect of text difficulty to the capacity demands of attention. Other studies have investigated the effect of the reader's prior knowledge on learning information in a text (Chiesi, Spilich, & Voss, 1979; Spilich, Vesonder, Chiesi, & Voss, 1979). Bushke and Schaier (1979) and McKoon and Ratcliff (1980) studied the organization of text propositions in memory, and Walker and Meyer (1980a, 1980b) discuss the integration of text information. The model developed by Kintsch and his associates provides the best formal account of text comprehension. The model is described in a paper by Kintsch and Van Dijk (1978). Papers by Graesser, Hoffman, and Clark (1980), Miller and Kintsch (1980), and Vipond (1980) discuss how the variables specified in the model influence the comprehension of prose. Daneman and Carpenter (1980) show how individual differences in STM influence performance on a reading comprehension task.

12

Problem Solving

Solving a problem means finding a way out of a difficulty, a way around an obstacle, attaining an aim that was not immediately understandable. Solving problems is the specific achievement of intelligence, and intelligence is the specific gift of mankind: Solving problems can be regarded as the most characteristically human activity.

GEORGE POLYA (1962)

Humans are not the only creatures who can solve problems, yet identifying problem solving as the most characteristically human activity, as Polya has done, emphasizes its importance in the development of civilization. The next two chapters discuss problem solving and emphasize recent progress in our attempt to understand how people solve problems. This chapter attempts to establish the basic components of a theory of problem solving. The first section contains examples of different kinds of problems. A question that has interested psychologists is how general problem-solving skills are. At one extreme the answer is that the skills are very general, and a person who is good at solving one type of problem will also be very good at solving other types of problems. At the other extreme is the claim that skills are very specific, and a person who is good at solving one type of problem may be poor at solving other types. The claim made in the first section falls between these two extremes. The proposed classification identifies three general kinds of problems based on the skills required to solve them.

The second section describes the general characteristics of a theory of problem solving proposed by Newell and Simon (1972). The theory attempts to describe how problem solving is influenced by (1) the information-processing capabilities of people as determined by STM and LTM, (2) the structure of the problem and its effect on the search for a solution, and (3) the effectiveness of different strategies and sources of information. The third section discusses strategies such as means/end analysis and the use of subgoals. We will be interested in identifying both the limitations of the strategies and the reasons they work well when they are successful. The fourth section examines the role of memory in problem solving. It discusses how we use STM and LTM and what we remember after solving a problem. Memory for problem solutions is necessary whenever we attempt to use our previous experience to solve the same problem or an analogous problem.

The problems discussed in this chapter are mainly puzzles. You may wonder why psychologists are interested in puzzles—wouldn't it be more appropriate to study the kinds of problems people encounter in school or work? One reason for studying problems like the anagram and series completion problems shown in Table 12.1 is that they often appear on intelligence tests. If we want to understand what intelligence tests really measure, we must take a closer look at the specific skills required to answer the questions. Another reason is that, when studying puzzles, psychologists can be less concerned about differences in people's education. Everyone should have more of an "equal chance" on puzzles than on problems taken from a textbook. However, psychologists have become more interested in classroom problems, as we will see in the next chapter. Fortunately, most of the issues discussed in this chapter will still be relevant when we discuss classroom problem solving.

Classifying problems

Any attempt to improve problem-solving skills raises the question of what skills are needed for different kinds of problems. Students are taught how to solve statistics problems in a statistics class and chemistry problems in a chemistry class. Have they learned any general skills in a statistics class that can make them better problem solvers in a chemistry class, or do the problems in each class require a different set of skills? The question would be easier to answer if we could classify problems according to the skills needed to solve them.

Table 12.1 shows examples of problems that have been studied by psychologists. You will better understand this chapter if you attempt to solve these problems before reading further. When you are finished working on the problems, try to classify them according to the skills needed to solve them. We will examine one method of classification that proposes the six problems can be divided into three categories.

The proposed classification is based on the general kinds of psychological skills and knowledge needed to solve different problems (Greeno, 1978). Greeno suggested that there are three types of prob-

TABLE 12.1.   Examples of Problems.

A. Analogy

What word completes the analogy?

Merchant : Sell :: Customer : _____

Lawyer : Client :: Doctor : _____

B. String problem

Two strings hang from a ceiling but are too far apart to allow a person to hold one and walk to the other. On the floor are a book of matches, a screwdriver, and a few pieces of cotton. How could the strings be tied together?

C. Missionaries and cannibals

Five missionaries and five cannibals who have to cross a river find a boat, but the boat is so small that it can hold no more than three people. If the missionaries on either bank of the river are outnumbered at any time by cannibals, they will be eaten. Find the simplest schedule of crossings that will allow everyone to cross safely. At least one person must be in the boat at each crossing.

D. Water jar

You have an 8-gallon pail and a 5-gallon pail. How could you obtain 2 gallons of water?

E. Anagram

Rearrange the letters in each row to make an English word.

RWAET

KEROJ

F. Series completion

What number or letter completes each series?

1 2 8 3 4 6 5 6 ____

A B M C D M ____

lems: arrangement, inducing structure, and transformation. The classification does not imply that we will be able to classify every problem into one of the three categories. Rather, it provides three ideal types in order to determine whether a given problem requires primarily rearrangement, inducing structure, transformation, or some combination of the three skills. We will now consider examples of each type in order to see how they differ from one another.

Arrangement

Arrangement problems present some objects and require the problem solver to arrange them in a way that satisfies some criterion. The objects usually can be arranged in many different ways, but only one or a few of the arrangements forms a solution. An excellent example is the rearrangement of the letters of an anagram to form a word—such as rearranging the letters *KEROJ* to spell *JOKER* and *RWAET* to spell *WATER*. Solving an arrangement problem often involves much trial and error, during which partial solutions are formed and evaluated. Greeno argued that the skills needed to solve arrangement problems include the following:

1. Fluency in generating possibilities. Flexibility is needed to generate many partial solutions and discard those that appear unpromising.
2. Retrieval of solution patterns. The ability to retrieve words from memory should be related to ability in solving anagrams.
3. Knowledge of principles that constrain search. Knowing the relative frequency with which various letters occur together should help guide the search. Since the pair *J R* is an unlikely combination, for instance, it should be avoided when forming partial solutions.

Gestalt psychologists were particularly interested in how people solve arrangement problems. Gestalt psychology, which began as the study of perception, emphasized the structure of patterns, and consequently it analyzed problem solving from this perspective. Many Gestalt tasks required the rearrangement of objects in order to find the correct relation among the parts.

A well-known example is the problem described by Köhler (1925) in his book *The Mentality of Apes*. Köhler hung some fruit from the top of a cage to investigate whether a chimpanzee or ape could discover how to reach it. The cage contained several sticks and crates. The solution depended on finding a correct way to rearrange the objects—for example, standing on a crate and using a stick to knock down the fruit. According to the Gestalt analysis, solving the problem required the reorganization of the objects into a new structure.

One factor that makes it difficult to find a correct arrangement is *functional fixedness*—the tendency to perceive an object only in terms of its most common use. The candle problem, studied by Duncker (1945), illustrates how functional fixedness can influence performance. The goal is to place three small candles at eye level on a door. Among other objects on a nearby table are a few tacks and three small boxes about the size of match boxes. In one condition the boxes were filled with candles, tacks, and matches. In another condition the boxes were empty. The solution requires tacking the boxes to the door so they can serve as platforms for the candles (see Figure 12.1). A greater number of subjects solved the problem when the boxes were empty (Duncker, 1945; Adamson, 1952). The use of boxes as containers, rather than as platforms, was emphasized when they contained objects, and so it was more difficult to recognize their novel function.

The string problem in Table 12.1 requires finding a novel use for a tool. The screwdriver is tied to one string to create a pendulum that can be swung to the other string. One of the best examples of overcoming functional fixedness outside the laboratory is the attempt of prisoners to

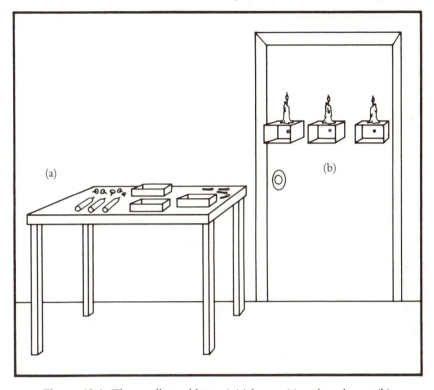

(a)

(b)

Figure 12.1. The candle problem—initial state (a) and goal state (b).

break out of jail. Since tools are not readily available in prison, prisoners have to use items that are available. Box 12.1 describes the ingenuity of two prisoners in finding novel uses for common objects.

Box 12.1. Pair of Crafty Inmates Melt Way Out of Jail

SALINAS (AP)—Two crafty inmates used a length of shower pipe, a sheet and a wall socket to melt an unbreakable plastic window and escape from Monterey County's new jail, officials said Wednesday.

A sheriff's deputy said the pair escaped Tuesday night after using a make-shift cutting torch to reduce part of the cell window to mushy goo.

Lt. Ted Brown said the inmates wrapped a sheet around a piece of flattened shower pipe, wired the contraption and plugged it into a wall socket.

The gizmo heated up and the inmates pressed it against the window until its edge had melted away, Brown said.

Then they snapped a leg off the cell bed, placed it into the newly burned hole, pried out the entire window and skipped to freedom, Brown said.

From the *Los Angeles Times,* January 6, 1978. © Associated Press Newsfeatures. Reprinted by permission.

Inducing Structure

Rearrangement problems require the rearrangement of objects to form a new relation among them. In problems of inducing structure, by contrast, the relation is fixed and the problem is to discover it. Some objects are given and the task is to discover how they are related. For example, series extrapolation problems consist of a series such as 1 2 8 3 4 6 5 6 ____. The task is to find the next element of the series. Notice that there are two series in the example. One is the ascending series 1 2, 3 4, 5 6; the other is the descending series 8, 6, ____. So the correct answer is 4. Similarly, the answer to the letter series in Table 12.1 is *E*.

Another example of inducing structure is analogy problems like Merchant : Sell : : Customer : Buy. The instructions might indicate that the analogy should be labeled *true* or *false,* or the last word could be replaced by a blank, with instructions to fill in the word that best completes the analogy. Analogical reasoning is of particular interest because of its use in intelligence tests. The Miller Analogies Test, which is widely used for admission to graduate school, is composed exclusively of verbal analogies. Other ability tests, such as the GRE and SAT, include analogies among the test items.

The psychological processes used in solving an analogy or series extrapolation problem involve identifying relations among the components and fitting the relations together in a pattern (Greeno, 1978). The importance of discovering relations among the terms of an analogy is illustrated in a model proposed by Sternberg (1977). There are four processes in Sternberg's model: encoding, inference, mapping, and application. Consider the problem *Washington is to 1 as Lincoln is to 10 or 5.* The task requires choosing either 10 or 5 to complete the analogy. The *encoding* process identifies attributes of the words that could be important in establishing relations. The first term, *Washington,* might be identified as a president, a portrait on a $1 bill, and a war hero. The *inference* process establishes valid relations between the first two terms. Washington was the first president of the United States, and his portrait appears on a $1 bill. The *mapping* process establishes relations between the first and third terms. Both Washington and Lincoln were presidents, and both portraits appear on bills, so both possibilities remain as the basis for the analogy. The *application* process attempts to establish a relation between Lincoln and 10 or 5 that is analogous to the one between Washington and 1. Since Lincoln was the 16th president of the United States, neither answer fits the presidential relation. However, Lincoln's portrait appears on a $5 bill, so the choice of 5 is consistent with the currency relation.

The importance of discovering relations is revealed by this example. Suppose we had considered only the presidential relation. If we did not know that Lincoln was the 16th president, we would be more likely to guess that he was the tenth president than the fifth, and so we would have chosen the wrong answer. Sternberg measured how quickly students were able to answer different kinds of problems in order to estimate how much time was needed to complete each of the four processes—encoding, inference, mapping, and application. One goal of his research is to study how these times vary across individuals and correlate the times with other measures of intellectual performance.

Transformation Problems

Transformation problems consist of an initial state, a goal state, and a sequence of operations for changing the initial state into the goal state. Transformation problems differ from problems of inducing structure and arrangement by providing the goal state rather than requiring solvers to produce it. An anagram problem requires finding the word that solves the anagram, and Duncker's candle problem requires finding the correct arrangement of parts that supports the candle. In contrast, a transformation problem like the missionaries and cannibals problem provides the goal state.

The missionaries and cannibals problem requires transporting missionaries and cannibals across a river under the constraint that cannibals can never outnumber missionaries, in the boat or on either side of the river. In one version of this problem, the initial state consists of five missionaries, five cannibals, and a boat that can hold three people, all on the left bank of the river. The goal state consists of the ten people and the boat, all on the right bank of the river. The operations consist of moving from one to three people in the boat back and forth across the river. The problem can be solved in 11 moves, but people usually require about 20 to 30 moves to reach a solution.

According to Greeno (1978), solving transformation problems primarily requires skills in planning based on a method called *means/end analysis*. Since a definite goal state is given in transformation problems, the problem solver can compare the current problem state with the goal state. Means/end analysis requires identifying differences that exist between the current state and the goal state and selecting operators that will reduce these differences.

The problems that we will consider in the rest of this chapter are mostly transformation problems. This will provide us the opportunity to study means/end analysis and alternative planning strategies. Much of what psychologists know about how people solve these problems is the result of the pioneering work of Simon and Newell at Carnegie Mellon University. We will review the major aspects of their theory of human problem solving before looking at the applications of their ideas to particular problems.

Newell and Simon's theory

Objectives and Method

The initial development of the theory was described in a paper titled "Elements of a Theory of Human Problem Solving" (Newell, Shaw, & Simon, 1958b), which, as we saw earlier, had an important influence on the development of information-processing theory. The paper described the first two years of a project that involved programming a digital computer to solve problems. One objective of the project, in fact, was to consider how programming a computer could contribute to a theory of human problem solving. The initial step was to use all available evidence about human problem solving to program processes resembling those used by humans. The second step was to collect detailed data on how humans solve the same problems as those solved by the computer. The program could then be modified to provide a closer approximation of human behavior. Once success was achieved in simulating performance on a particular task, the investigators could examine a broader range of tasks, attempting to use the same set of elementary information processes and program organization in all of the simulation programs. A long-term goal would be to draw implications from the theories for improving human performance.

Why does the computer play a central role in theory construction? Simon and Newell's (1971) answer is that much of our thinking is not directly observable. The covert nature of thought can make it seem magical or mysterious, leading to vague theories that obscure more than they clarify. The advantage of computer programs is that terms like *memory* and *strategy* can be defined in precisely stated instructions for a computer. Furthermore, the requirement that the programs must work—that is, must be able to solve the problem—provides a guarantee that no steps have been left unspecified. A successful program provides a measure of sufficiency—a test that the steps in the program are sufficient for solving the problem. A successful program does not guarantee that a person would solve the problem the same way; it is still necessary to make detailed observations on how people solve problems and modify the program to simulate their behavior.

In order to obtain details about how people solve problems, Newell and Simon (1972) usually collected verbal protocols from their subjects. They instructed the subjects to report verbally everything they thought about as they worked on the problem. The verbal statements often provided enough details to build a computer simulation program that would solve the problem in the same way that people solved it.

The method of collecting verbal protocols and constructing a simulation program has not been widely adopted by other investigators, although the approach is slowly gaining more appeal. One deterrent is simply that this method requires a lot of work for the investigator. The investigator therefore usually studies only a few subjects and assumes that they are fairly typical in the way they solve problems. Another limitation is that the method yields many details, and it is not always clear how to summarize the results in order to emphasize what is most important. The failure to collect verbal protocols, however, can result in the loss of valuable information because a subject's behavior may reveal little about what he is thinking.

Although the particular method used by Newell and Simon has not been widely adopted, their theory of problem solving has been very influential in determining how psychologists think about human information processing in general, and problem solving in particular. The theory provides a general framework for specifying how information-processing characteristics, the structure of the problem, and different sources of knowledge interact to influence behavior.

Theoretical Assumptions

An important component of Newell and Simon's theory is the identification of the basic characteristics of human information processing that influence problem solving. These characteristics are the same ones that we discussed in earlier chapters: performance on a problem-solving task is influenced by the capacity, storage time, and retrieval time of short-term and long-term memory. The limited capacity of short-term memory (STM) places a constraint on the number of sequential operations that can be carried out mentally. Although most people can multiply 17×8 without using paper and pencil, multiplying 17×58 is much more difficult because the number of required operations (multiplying 17×8 and 17×5, storing the products, aligning, and adding) can exceed the limit of STM. Long-term memory (LTM) does not have these capacity limitations, but it takes time to enter new information into LTM. This can make it difficult to remember the steps that were used to solve a problem, causing us to repeat incorrect steps. Thus both the limited capacity of STM and the time required to store new information in LTM can greatly influence the efficiency of a human problem solver. The simulation model proposed by Atwood and Polson (1976) nicely demonstrates this point; we will return to this model later.

Simon and Newell's (1971) theory is concerned not only with the person but with the task. The sequential nature of many problems raises the question of what options are available at each point in solving the problem. If there are many choices available, only a few of which lead to a solution, the problem can be very difficult. However, if one has a good plan for solving the problem and can therefore ignore unpromising paths, the number of unpromising paths will have little effect on performance. Simon and Newell illustrate this point by referring to the problem DONALD + GERALD = ROBERT.

$$D \ O \ N \ A \ L \ D$$
$$+ \ G \ E \ R \ A \ L \ D$$
$$\overline{R \ O \ B \ E \ R \ T}$$

The problem is to substitute a digit—0 to 9—for each of the ten letters in order to satisfy the constraint that the substitution obeys the rules of addition. The hint is $D = 5$. Therefore, $T = 0$, and a 1 has to be carried into the next column to the left. Although the number of possible choices is very large (there are 362,880 ways of assigning nine digits to nine letters), by following the rules of arithmetic and using accumulated information (such as that R must be odd), it is possible to explore relatively few promising choices. You can observe this for yourself by attempting to solve the problem. What is important, therefore, is not the number of incorrect paths but how effectively one can discover a plan that avoids the incorrect paths. To use Newell and Simon's analogy, we need not be concerned how large the haystack is if we can identify a small part of it in which we are quite sure to find the needle.

Newell and Simon use the term *problem space* to refer to the choices that the problem solver evaluates while solving a problem. The problem itself determines the number of possible choices and paths that could be followed in searching for a solution, but the problem solver determines which of these he will actually explore. Among the sources of information that influence how a person constructs a problem space are the following:

1. The task instructions that give a description of the problem and may contain helpful information
2. Previous experience with the same task or a nearly identical one
3. Previous experience with analogous tasks
4. Plans stored in LTM that generalize over a range of tasks
5. Information accumulated while solving a problem

Let us now take a closer look at how these different sources of information influence problem solving. We will first consider plans or strategies that generalize over a range of tasks. General strategies are important because they may be useful when we encounter novel problems that are completely different from problems we have solved before. After considering general strategies, we will examine how sources of more specific information depend on memory. For example, information accumulated while solving a problem can be useful, but we have to remember the information in order to use it. Memory is also necessary for us to use our previous experience in solving analogous problems. As we examine these different sources of information, we will also have the opportunity to learn how other aspects of the Newell and Simon (1972) theory—such as the limited capacity of STM and the structure of the problem space—influence the search for a solution.

General strategies

A knowledge of general problem-solving strategies can be particularly useful because general strategies apply to many different kinds of problems. For this reason books like Wickelgren's (1974) on how to solve problems emphasize general strategies such as forming subgoals or working backward. The ability to use another general strategy—means/end analysis—was suggested by Greeno (1978) as the major determinant of success in solving transformation problems.

Strategies like means/end analysis, forming subgoals, and working backward are called *heuristics* because they are often successful but do not guarantee success. In contrast, an *algorithm* is a procedure of steps that does guarantee a solution if one follows the steps correctly. The rules for multiplication constitute an algorithm because a correct answer is guaranteed if a person correctly follows the rules. We will first consider two general heuristics—means/end analysis and forming subgoals—to evaluate both their potential usefulness and their limitations as general strategies. After we have the opportunity to examine the role of memory in the next section, we will consider a third heuristic that depends on memory—the use of analogy.

Means/End Analysis

The use of means/end analysis is illustrated by a computer program called the General Problem Solver (Ernst & Newell, 1969). The program consists of general procedures that should apply across a variety of problems. A general procedure for solving transformation problems is to select operators that result in a problem state that is closer to the goal state. This is accomplished by attempting to reduce the differences between the current problem state and the goal state. In order to follow this procedure, the General Problem Solver (GPS) must be given the differences that exist between problem states and the operators that are capable of eliminating these differences. A *table of connections* combines these two sets of information by showing which differences can be eliminated by each of the operators. The specific operators and differences will, of course, vary across problems, but the general strategy of consulting a table of connections in order to determine which operators are useful for reducing differences should remain the same across problems.

In most cases the principles used to construct GPS form a reasonable model of how people attempt to solve transformation problems. In fact, GPS was specifically used as a model of human performance on a symbol transformation task studied by Newell and Simon (1972). The problems were similar to the kind of derivations students encounter in an introductory logic course. Students were given some initial statements, a set of 12 transformation rules, and a goal statement. The task was to use the rules to transform the initial statements in order to produce the goal statement. Newell and Simon identified six differences that distinguish logic statements. The table of connections specified which of these differences could be changed by each of the 12 transformation rules.

Figure 12.2 shows a simple problem involving only three transformation rules and three differences. Stated verbally, the problem is to prove that, if A implies B ($A \supset B$), then the absence of B implies the absence of A ($-B \supset -A$). The solution requires showing that $-B \supset -A$ can be derived from $A \supset B$ by the transformation rules. The two-headed arrow in Rules 2 and 3 means that these rules can be applied in either direction. The three differences in the table of connections are sign (positive or negative), connective, and position. The connectives represent *implies* ($\supset$), *and* ($\cdot$), and *or* ($\vee$). The students were not informed of their meaning, however, and treated the problems strictly as symbol transformation problems rather than as logic problems. The table of connections indicates that Rule 1 changes only the position of the symbols, but Rules 2 and 3 change both the signs of the symbols and their connectives.

A comparison of the initial state and the goal state reveals that they differ in both sign and position. Rule 1 changes position, but it can be used only when the connective is $\cdot$ or $\vee$. Rule 3 can be applied to the initial statement to change the connective to $\vee$. The result is shown in

a. *Problem*

Given:	$A \supset B$
Derive:	$-B \supset -A$

b. *Rules*

1.	$A \vee B \;\rightarrow\; B \vee A$
	$A \cdot B \;\rightarrow\; B \cdot A$
2.	$A \vee B \longleftrightarrow -(-A \cdot -B)$
3.	$A \supset B \longleftrightarrow -A \vee B$

c. *Table of connections*

Difference:		Rules	
	1	2	3
Sign		X	X
Connective		X	X
Position	X		

d. *Solution*

1.	$A \supset B$	Premise
2.	$-A \vee B$	Rule 3/Line 1
3.	$B \vee -A$	Rule 1/Line 2
4.	$-B \supset -A$	Rule 3/Line 3

Figure 12.2. Solution of a logic problem.

Line 2. Now Rule 1 can be applied to Line 2 to change the position of the symbols. The result, shown in Line 3, still differs from the goal in the sign of *B* and the connective. The application of Rule 3 to Line 3 changes both of these differences and produces the goal statement. Newell and Simon asked their subjects to verbalize their strategies as they solved the symbol transformation problems. Many aspects of their thinking could be represented by the kind of means/end analysis used in the General Problem Solver.

Limitations of Means/End Analysis

The prescription of trying to gradually reduce the differences between the current problem state and the goal state sounds like good common sense. Why can't we always use this strategy to solve problems? The answer is that sometimes it is necessary to apply an operation that does not seem to take us closer to the goal. Let us return to the water jar problem given in Table 12.1. You have an 8-gallon pail and a 5-gallon pail and have to obtain 2 gallons of water. Figure 12.3 illustrates one way of solving the problem.

The squares in the matrix are possible problem states, distinguished by the amount of water in each of the two pails. The initial state shows there is no water in either pail. The goal state is reached whenever there are two gallons of water in either pail; hence the shaded squares all represent potential goal states. The operators are: fill the 5-gallon pail (F5); empty the 5-gallon pail into the 8-gallon pail (E5); fill the 8-gallon pail (F8); and empty the 8-gallon pail into the 5-gallon pail (E8).

The most straightforward way of measuring whether we are getting closer to the goal state is to determine the difference between the current content of each pail and the desired content, or 2 gallons. This difference is 2 gallons for each pail at the beginning of the problem. The solution is illustrated in Figure 12.3. By filling the 5-gallon pail, we reach state 2, but we are still 2 gallons away from the closest solution state. Now we pour the 5 gallons into the 8-gallon pail. This brings us to state 3, but we are still 2 gallons away from a solution state. Now we fill the 5-gallon pail again and arrive at state 4, placing us 3 gallons away from a solution state. By pouring as much as we can into the 8-gallon pail, we are left with 2 gallons in the 5-gallon pail.

Our solution of the problem may have been aided by planning a few steps ahead, by the fact that there were not many choices at each decision point, or simply by luck—but it was not aided by means/end analysis because we were unable to gradually reduce the difference between the initial state and the goal state. If means/end analysis always guaranteed a solution, it would be an algorithm rather than a heuristic. Fortunately, means/end analysis is a fairly good heuristic, and it works for many

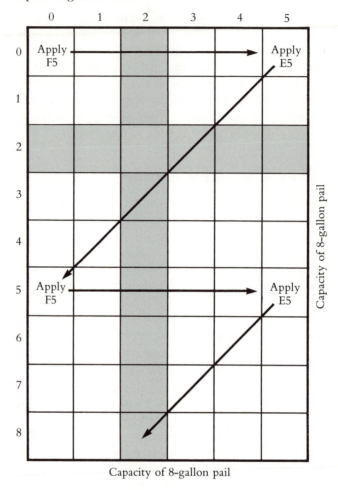

Figure 12.3. Solution of the water jar problem.

transformation problems. But this does not mean that everyone will spontaneously use it, as we will see in the next section.

Subgoals

A commonly suggested heuristic for solving problems is to divide the problem into parts—that is, to formulate subgoals. Subgoals are problem states intermediate between the initial state and the goal state; hopefully they are on the solution path. Some problems have fairly obvious subgoals, and research has shown that people take advantage of them. Consider the puzzle called the Tower of Hanoi (see Figure 12.4). The puzzle consists of three pegs and a set of rings that vary in size. The

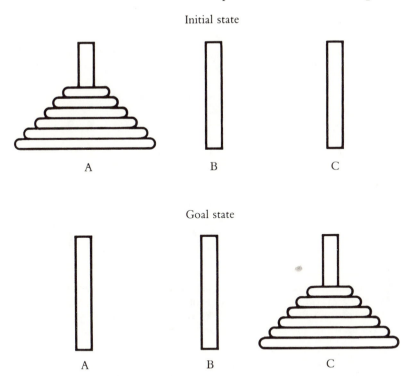

Figure 12.4. The Tower of Hanoi puzzle.

initial state has all the rings stacked on peg A in order of decreasing size. The goal is to move the stack, one ring at a time, to peg C, under the constraint that a larger ring can never be placed on a smaller ring. A reasonable subgoal is to move the largest ring to peg C. But how does one begin in order to achieve this subgoal? The answer is not obvious, and people often make the wrong choice. But as they make other moves and come closer to achieving the subgoal, the correct moves become more obvious and errors decline (Egan & Greeno, 1974).

Using subgoals can make solving a problem easier because knowing that an intermediate problem state is on the solution path makes it possible to avoid searching many unpromising paths. Figure 12.5 shows a search space that contains 16 paths, each four steps in length. Only one path ends in the goal state. If we are given a subgoal state that we know can be reached in two steps, then we can reach the subgoal by searching only four paths, each two steps in length. From the subgoal state there are another four paths, each two steps in length. The search space has been reduced from 16 four-step paths to the eight two-step paths represented by the shaded area in Figure 12.5.

Forming subgoals is often helpful, but it does not guarantee an easier

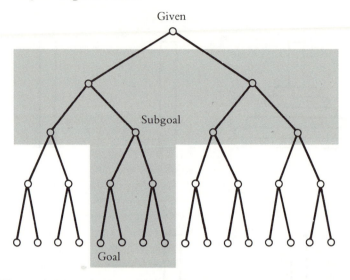

Figure 12.5. Search space. Knowledge of a subgoal limits search to the shaded area. *(From* How to Solve Problems: Elements of a Theory of Problems and Problem Solving, *by W. W. Wickelgren. Copyright © 1974 by W. H. Freeman and Company. Reprinted by permission.)*

solution. There are several limitations to keep in mind when using this method. First, it is not always obvious what are helpful intermediate problem states as some problems do not have obvious subgoals. Second, reaching a subgoal may create confusion about what to do next. Hayes (1966) found that giving people a subgoal helped them solve the part of the problem that came before the subgoal. However, some problems actually took longer to solve with a subgoal because it took a long time to figure out what to do after reaching the subgoal.

An example of a problem in which a subgoal improved performance is the missionaries and cannibals problem (described in Table 12.1) requiring the transportation of five missionaries and five cannibals across a river using a boat that can hold three people. Figure 12.6 shows the search space of legal moves for this problem (Simon & Reed, 1976). The ovals represent legal problem states—states in which the cannibals do not outnumber missionaries (unless no missionaries are present). The first number is the number of missionaries on the left bank, the second number is the number of cannibals on the left bank, the third number is the number of missionaries on the right bank, and the fourth number is the number of cannibals on the right bank. The asterisk shows the location of the boat. State A is the initial state, and state Z is the goal state; *a* indicates a backward move—the problem solver then must return to A. The numbers connecting the problem states show the number of mis-

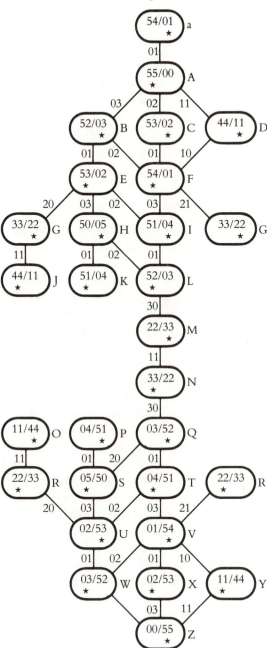

Figure 12.6. Search space for the five missionaries and cannibals problem. *(From "Modeling Strategy Shifts in a Problem-Solving Task," by H. A. Simon and S. K. Reed. In* Cognitive Psychology, *1976, 8, 86–97. Copyright 1976 by Academic Press, Inc. Reprinted by permission.)*

sionaries (first number) and the number of cannibals (second number) being transported in the boat.

One group of students, the control group, was simply asked to solve the problem. Another group, the "subgoal" group, was told that, in order to solve the problem, they would have to reach a state in which there were three cannibals across the river by themselves and without the boat. This corresponds to state L in the search space. Students in the control group required an average of 30 moves to solve the problem, compared to an average of only 20 moves for students in the subgoal group.

Strategies and Subgoals

In order to try to understand why the subgoal was so effective, Simon and I developed a simulation model of the way students in the two groups explored the search space. The goal of the model was to predict, for each of the possible legal moves, the average number of times students in each group would make that particular move. We thought that students would follow a means/end strategy in which they would move as many people across the river as possible and bring as few back as possible. A model based on the means/end strategy was fairly successful in predicting their choices, but some of their moves did not follow this strategy. For example, when at state A, students in the control group made an average of 0.5 moves to state B, 0.2 moves to state C, and 1.1 moves to state D. The means/end strategy would predict that subjects would move three people across (to state B) rather than two people (to state D), so why was moving one missionary and one cannibal such a popular choice? Violations of the means/end strategy could be accounted for by proposing that people follow a *balance strategy,* which attempts to create an equal number of missionaries and cannibals on each side of the river. The balance strategy makes it easy to avoid illegal moves since cannibals will never outnumber missionaries as long as the numbers of missionaries and cannibals are equal on both sides. The trouble with the balance strategy is that it tends to lead people away from the solution path and toward the blind alley represented by states G and J, both balanced states.

The model that we developed is called a *strategy shift model* because it proposes that students initially use a balance strategy but have to shift to a means/end strategy in order to avoid the blind alley and solve the problem. By shifting strategies sooner, they will make fewer bad moves and therefore require fewer moves to reach the solution. By assuming that students in the subgoal group would shift strategies after making only 4 moves (on the average) and students in the control group would shift strategies after making 15 moves (on the average), we were able to predict not only the total number of moves required by each group to solve the problem, but exactly how each group would explore the search space. The fact that the subgoal—three missionaries and no cannibals—is an unbalanced state makes it intuitively likely that students in the subgoal group would not persist in following a balance strategy.

The research on the effectiveness of strategies reveals that the structure of the search space is one of the factors that influence the success of a particular strategy. It is not obvious, for example, that the balance strategy is a bad strategy. It is only after we examine the search space in Figure 12.6 that we realize the consequences of following the balance strategy. A similar argument can be made for the means/end strategy. The means/end strategy is often effective because reducing differences between the current problem state and the goal state usually implies that the problem solver is moving closer to the goal. However, sometimes it is necessary to increase the difference temporarily in order to solve the problem. Think of a cat looking at its food through a piece of glass. Since the cat cannot take the shortest route—through the plate—it must walk around it and thereby momentarily increase the distance to the goal.

In addition to the characteristics of the search space, the characteristics of STM and LTM influence the effectiveness of strategies. One difficulty in using means/end analysis to solve logic problems is that there are many options available when there are many transformation rules. The limited capacity of STM makes it difficult to remember the potential consequences of different rule applications. LTM is also needed to remember the consequences of previous moves. In order to avoid reentering the blind alley in the missionaries and cannibals problem, it would be helpful to recall the sequences of moves that lead to the blind alley. Memory for subgoals would also be useful in this problem because they are difficult to generate.

Memory and problem solving

There are several ways memory can influence success in solving a problem. First, short-term memory is needed to store information about alternative choices in order to evaluate them and select one. Second, memory is needed to store information about previously visited problem states, previously evaluated hypotheses, and previously selected operators. By remembering what she previously attempted, the problem solver can avoid repeating earlier mistakes. Third, long-term memory is needed to remember how the solution was obtained after the problem is solved. Memory for problem solutions can help a person solve the same problem again or a similar problem.

We will next examine how memory influences performance during the search for a solution. We will then consider what a person remembers about the search after obtaining a solution. Finally, we will examine the role of memory in solving analogous problems.

Using Memory while Solving Problems

The use of memory while solving problems is nicely illustrated in a model of an attempt to solve the water jar problem (Atwood & Polson, 1976). The water jar problem, like the missionaries and cannibals problem, has a relatively small and well-defined search space, making it feasible to predict in detail how people will search for a solution. Atwood and Polson chose a problem that was a slightly more complex version of the one discussed in the previous section. There are now three pails, and the goal is to distribute the water equally between the two largest pails. Initially, the largest pail is full, and the other two pails are empty. For example, in the (8, 5, 3) problem the pails can hold 8, 5, or 3 gallons of water. The goal is to divide the 8 gallons of water in the largest pail equally between the 8 and 5 gallon pails.

The Atwood and Polson model assumes that people will attempt to solve the problem by using a means/end heuristic. The means/end heuristic attempts to reduce the difference between the current content and the desired content of the two largest pails. If $C(A)$ and $C(B)$ are the current contents of the two largest pails, and $G(A)$ and $G(B)$ are the contents specified in the goal, the overall difference is given by $|C(A) - G(A)| + |C(B) - G(B)|$. In the initial state of the (8, 5, 3) problem, there are 8 gallons in A and 0 gallons in B. Since the goal state requires 4 gallons in each, the initial discrepancy is $|8 - 4| + |0 - 4|$, or 8 gallons. This discrepancy should be gradually reduced if the problem can be solved using a means/end analysis.

We saw in the previous section that means/end analysis doesn't always work very well for the water jar problem; in fact, the solution of the (8, 5, 3) problem requires several violations of the means/end strategy. The (24, 21, 3) problem has a similar search space but can be solved without violating the means/end strategy. If people use a means/end strategy, they should find the latter problem easier than the former. Atwood and Polson's results supported this prediction. People required over twice as many moves to solve the (8, 5, 3) problem even though it is possible to solve both problems in the same number of moves.

The optimal way of using the means/end strategy would be to evaluate all possible moves and select the one that minimizes the discrepancy between the resulting state and the goal state. However, the limited capacity of short-term memory places a constraint on the number of possible moves that can be evaluated and compared simultaneously. The model therefore assumes that people will simply look for a good move rather than always attempt to find the best move. If the discrepancy between the resulting state and the goal state is not too large, the probability of making the evaluated move depends upon whether the problem solver recognizes the resulting problem state. The problem solver will recognize the problem state if she remembers being at that state. It is generally helpful to remember previously visited states in order not to return to them. Returning to old states generally implies that one is backing up and moving away from the goal state. Backing up is particularly detrimental in the problems studied by Atwood and Polson because it is possible to return all the way to the beginning states by making the wrong move.

To account for how people progress through the search space, Atwood and Polson estimated the probability of making a move to an old state as .20, the probability of making a move to a new state as .60, the probability of remembering previously visited states as .90, and the number of moves that can be evaluated in STM as three. These parameter estimates reveal that people do in fact prefer to move to new states rather than return to old states. They also reveal that people are able to recognize old states with a fairly high probability. The estimate that only three moves can be compared in STM is consistent with previous estimates of STM capacity since, for each move, the problem solver has to remember not only the move but how much the resulting state differs from the goal state.

If the problem solver does not select a move during the first stage described above, the model specifies other criteria for move selection. The essential characteristics of the model are evident in this brief summary, however. First, there is the use of a means/end strategy to evaluate progress toward the goal. If the problem can be solved by gradually reducing the difference between the current state and the goal state, people solve it in fewer moves than if they are forced to make moves that violate the means/end strategy. Second, the limited capacity of STM places a constraint on the number of moves that can be evaluated. Even if you had a perfect strategy that enabled you always to select the best move at each point, you would not necessarily find the shortest solution if you could not evaluate all the moves at each decision point. For example, if there were four possible moves but you could only evaluate three because of the limitations of STM, the best move might be the one you did not evaluate.

Atwood and Polson's finding that people are much more likely to make a move if it leads to a new problem state is consistent with the idea that it is generally better to move to new states than to return to old states. However, an old state will appear to be a new state if the problem solver does not remember being there. It is therefore useful to remember what states you visited when solving a problem by attempting to store this information in LTM. Atwood and Polson estimate that people were quite successful at storing such information as they solved the water jar problem. LTM is also needed to remember solutions after they have been discovered if we are to improve on our second attempt to solve the same problem.

Memory for Problem Solutions

It is likely that our problem-solving ability depends to a great extent on our memory for how we have solved previous problems. After emphasizing that plans are important for guiding complex behavior, Miller, Galanter, and Pribram (1960) argued that the major source of new plans is old plans. According to their argument, plans are usually remembered and not created. What do we remember after solving a problem for the first time?

If people do remember something about how they solved a problem, they should perform better on their second attempt than on their first attempt. Johnsen and I (Reed & Johnsen, 1977) measured how much people improved in solving the missionaries and cannibals problem as a function of whether they knew in advance that they would have to solve the problem twice. An "intentional learning" group was told that they would have to solve the problem twice and should try to remember their solution. An "incidental learning" group was simply asked to solve the problem; they were not told that they would have to solve it twice. The distinction between intentional and incidental learning is appropriate for problem solving because sometimes we try to remember solutions (for instance, to pass a math exam) and sometimes we care only about finding the solution (for example, to finish a crossword puzzle). Another variable in this experiment was whether students were given an intervening task between their two solutions. Half the students in each group were given a recognition memory task before solving the problem for the second time, and the other half simply rested for 1 minute before solving the problem again. The recognition memory task consisted of all the problem states shown in Figure 12.6, presented in a random order. The students were asked if they had encountered that particular problem state while searching for a solution.

Figure 12.7 shows the extent to which performances improved on the second trial as a function of intentional versus incidental learning and the presence of the intervening task. Students who knew they would have to solve the problem twice and did not have an intervening task showed the greatest improvement. They were 450 seconds faster on their second attempt than on their first and made 5 fewer legal moves and 2.6 fewer illegal moves (moves that would result in the missionaries being outnum-

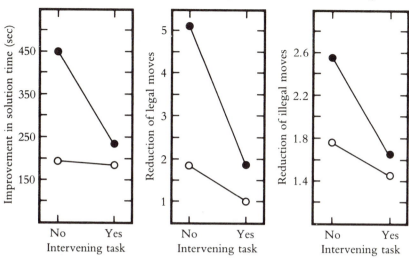

Figure 12.7. Degree of improvement for the intentional (solid line) and incidental (broken line) learning groups. *(From "Memory for Problem Solutions," by S. K. Reed and J. A. Johnsen. In G. H. Bower (Ed.), The Psychology of Learning and Motivation (Vol. 11). Copyright 1977 by Academic Press, Inc. Reprinted by permission.)*

bered). But much of the advantage of the intentional group over the incidental group disappeared when there was an intervening task. What did the intentional group learn that enabled them to improve more than the incidental group when there was no intervening task?

One possibility is that their memory for details was better. Students who were asked to remember their solution might be better at recognizing problem states, at remembering what move they made at a particular problem state, or at identifying the best move at a problem state. But the results from the intervening task revealed that there was no difference between the two groups in their ability to identify which problem states they had encountered while solving the problem. Two subsequent experiments confirmed this finding and revealed that there was no difference between the two groups in their ability to recall what move they made at a particular problem state or in their ability to identify what would be the best move at each problem state.

After students had solved the problem once, they were asked whether they would use a subgoal if they had to solve the problem again and, if so, to identify their subgoal. Two-thirds of the students in the intentional group and one-half of the students in the incidental group responded positively—a significant difference. Furthermore, the students in the intentional group were more likely to select states L, M, N, or Q as their subgoal. These problem states are particularly good subgoals, not only because they are in the middle of the search space but because it is necessary to reach them in order to solve the problem (see Figure 12.6). Students in the intentional group were also better at selecting a plan for solving the problem. You will notice in Figure 12.6 that a good plan is first to move cannibals across, then missionaries, and finally the remaining cannibals. Students in the intentional group were more likely than students in the incidental group to select this plan as a means for solving the problem on their second attempt.

These results indicate that the degree of improvement on the second trial was influenced more by differences in general planning than by differences in memory for detail. Memory for detail, in fact, was not very good for either group. We should keep in mind, however, that the problem states for the missionaries and cannibals problem all consist of different numbers of missionaries and cannibals on each side of the river. The states are therefore very similar, which makes it difficult to identify them uniquely. When the problem states are more discriminable, the problem consists of fewer steps, or there are more learning trials, memory for details should play a more important role in determining performance differences. Experimental studies, in fact, support the hypothesis that it is easier to use an analogous solution for problems with fewer steps because the solution is easier to remember.

Analogy

Analogy is another of the major heuristics for solving problems. Analogy requires that the problem solver use the solution of a similar problem to solve a current problem. Success in using analogy depends on both recognizing the similarity between two problems and recalling the solution of the analogous problem. Since the recall of a solution is required, analogy depends more on LTM than do means/end analysis and subgoals.

Let us look now at another version of the missionaries and cannibals problem, called the *jealous-husbands problem*:

> Three jealous husbands and their wives, having to cross a river at a ferry, find a boat. However, the boat is so small that it can hold no more than two people. Find the simplest schedule of crossings that will permit all six people to cross the river so that no woman is left in company with any of the men unless her husband is present. It is assumed that all passengers on the boat unboard before the next trip and that at least one person has to be in the boat for each crossing.

The jealous-husbands and the missionaries and cannibals problems are similar because the solution of one problem can be used to solve the other. Someone who knows the solution to the missionaries and cannibals problem can solve the jealous-husbands problem by (1) substituting husbands for missionaries, (2) substituting wives for cannibals, and (3) pairing the couples when men and women are on the same bank of the river. If people can make use of analogy to solve the problems, then it should be easier to solve either problem if a person first solved the analogous problem. However, experimental results indicated that people were in fact not better at solving one problem if they first solved the other problem (Reed, Ernst, & Banerji, 1974).

One explanation of why people could not improve their performance by using the similarity of the two problems is that they did not know the relation between the two problems. In a second experiment the experimenter encouraged subjects to use their solution of the first problem to solve the second problem, informing them that husbands corresponded to missionaries and wives corresponded to cannibals. The information about how the problems were related helped subjects solve the missionaries and cannibals problem but did not help them solve the jealous-husbands problem.

The results indicate that the successful use of analogy does not occur as readily as we might expect. Even when the instructions reveal the exact relation between two problems, the solution of one does not guarantee that it will be easier to solve the other. One explanation of this finding is that it is difficult to remember the correct solution when it consists of a long sequence of moves. This hypothesis suggests that the use of analogy should be more effective when the solution is easier to remember.

The problems studied by the Gestalt psychologists typically consisted of problems that could be solved in a few steps. Examples include the crate and stick (Köhler, 1925) and candle (Duncker, 1945) problems that we looked at earlier. Another problem studied by Duncker (1945) was the tumor, or radiation, problem. Table 12.2 describes this problem and a solution. The dispersion solution involves dividing the rays so they will have a high intensity only when they converge on the tumor. Although this is a clever solution, Duncker found that very few people solved the problem in this way.

Gick and Holyoak (1980) investigated whether more people would discover the dispersion solution if they were first exposed to an analogous solution. Their subjects read the attack-dispersion story before attempting to solve the radiation problem. The attack-dispersion story described a solution to a military problem in which the army had to be divided in order to converge on a fortress. The instructions indicated that the first story might give them some hints for solving the radiation problem. The results showed that most people made use of the analogy. Over half of those who read the story included the dispersion solution among their proposed solutions, compared to only 8% of the people who did not read the story before solving the radiation problem. But when Gick and Holyoak omitted the hint to use the story, the number of

TABLE 12.2.   A Summary of the Attack-Dispersion Story and of a Corresponding Solution to the Radiation Problem.

Proposition number	
	Attack-dispersion story
1–2	A fortress was located in the center of the country.
2a	Many roads radiated out from the fortress.
3–4	A general wanted to capture the fortress with his army.
5–7	The general wanted to prevent mines on the roads from destroying his army and neighboring villages.
8	As a result the entire army could not attack the fortress along one road.
9–10	However, the entire army was needed to capture the fortress.
11	So an attack by one small group would not succeed.
12	The general therefore divided his army into several small groups.
13	He positioned the small groups at the heads of different roads.
14–15	The small groups simultaneously converged on the fortress.
16	In this way the army captured the fortress.
	Radiation problem and dispersion solution[a]
1'–2'	A tumor was located in the interior of a patient's body.
3'–4'	A doctor wanted to destroy the tumor with rays.
5'–7'	The doctor wanted to prevent the rays from destroying healthy tissue.
8'	As a result the high-intensity rays could not be applied to the tumor along one path.
9'–10'	However, high-intensity rays were needed to destroy the tumor.
11'·	So applying one low-intensity ray would not succeed.
12'	*The doctor therefore divided the rays into several low-intensity rays.*
13'	*He positioned the low-intensity rays at multiple locations around the patient's body.*
14'–15'	*The low-intensity rays simultaneously converged on the tumor.*
16'	*In this way the rays destroyed the tumor.*

[a]Italicized propositions summarize the target dispersion solution.

From "Analogical Problem Solving," by M. L. Gick and K. Holyoak. In *Cognitive Psychology*, 1980, *12*, 306–355. Copyright 1980 by Academic Press, Inc. Reprinted by permission.

dispersion solutions greatly decreased. Their findings therefore demonstrated that people could generate an analogous solution when prompted, but they did not spontaneously recognize the similarity between the two problems.

Although there has been relatively little research on the use of analogy in problem solving, the current evidence shows that people often fail to notice the relation between two problems unless the instructions describe the relation (Reed et al., 1974) or at least suggest that it exists (Gick & Holyoak, 1980). Even when the relation is made explicit, analogy can be an ineffective heuristic if the analogous solution requires many steps and is difficult to remember. However, we should not dismiss analogy as useless. The relation between the problems studied thus far may not have been as obvious as the problems we usually encounter. For example, the problems that students encounter on their exams are usually similar, but not identical, to the problems they solved as homework, so they must perceive the analogy between test problems and homework problems in order to pass the test. The better students, of course, may find it easier than the poorer students to recognize the analogies. Indeed, we will see in the next chapter that more successful problem solvers are better than poorer problem solvers at recognizing the similarity of algebra word problems. Although the emphasis in the next chapter will shift to problems encountered in the classroom, many of the theoretical issues will remain the same as those we have been considering.

Summary

As there are many different kinds of problems, constructing a theory of problem solving would be easier if we were able to classify problems according to the skills needed to solve them. One method of classification distinguishes among problems of arrangement, inducing structure, and transformation. Arrangement problems require the problem solver to arrange the elements of a problem in a way that satisfies some criterion. Anagrams are a good example because the letters have to be arranged to spell a word. In problems of inducing structure, some elements are given, and the task is to discover how the elements are related. Analogy or series completion problems are examples. Transformation problems consist of an initial state, a goal state, and operations for changing the initial state into the goal state. Many puzzles are of this type, including the missionaries and cannibals, Tower of Hanoi, and water jar problems.

Much of what psychologists know about how people solve problems is the result of the pioneering work of Newell and Simon. Their theory specifies how the basic characteristics of the human information processor, the search space, and different strategies affect problem solving. Performance on a task is influenced by the capacity, storage time, and retrieval time of short-term and long-term memory. It is also influenced by the search space, which determines the number of legal moves available at each point in solving the problem. Newell and Simon have depended on computer simulation models and verbal protocols as a means for testing and developing the many details of their theory.

Two general strategies for solving problems are means/end analysis and forming subgoals. Both strategies are called heuristics because, although they are often useful, neither guarantees a successful solution. The means/end strategy states that the problem solver should select operators that reduce the difference between the current problem state and the goal state. A table of connections shows which differences can be eliminated by each of the operators. Although the means/end strategy can be used across a wide range of problems, it is sometimes necessary to select operators that do not reduce the difference between a current state and the goal state. A knowledge of subgoals is valuable because it reduces the size of the search space. A detailed simulation of how people solved the missionaries and cannibals problem revealed that a subgoal enabled them to avoid blind alleys by selecting a better strategy than the one that is frequently used.

There are several ways that memory can influence success in solving a problem. Short-term memory is needed to evaluate the alternative choices at each point when searching for a solution. Memory is also needed to store information about previously visited problem states, previously evaluated hypotheses, and previously selected operators. The important role of memory in solving problems is revealed in a simulation model of how people solve the water jar problem. Memory for problem solutions is also necessary to use analogy successfully. In order to use the solution of a similar problem, it is necessary both to recognize the similarity of the two problems and to remember the analogous solution.

Recommended reading

The chapter on thinking by Erickson and Jones (1978) provides an extensive summary of recent work on reasoning, concept identification, and problem solving. The classic work on the effect of set on problem solving was conducted by Luchins (1942) in a study using the water jar problem. The Atwood-Polson model, originally developed for the water jar problem, was extended by Jeffries, Polson, Razran, and Atwood (1977) to describe performance on the missionaries and cannibals problem.

Information-processing models have also been developed to account for performance on Duncker's candle problem (Weisberg & Suls, 1973) and on geometric analogies (Mulholland, Pellegrino, & Glaser, 1980). Ericsson and Simon (1980) critically analyzed the role of verbal reports in constructing theories and argued that verbal reports can be very useful if they are treated like other kinds of data.

The past decade has witnessed a growing interest in developing information-processing models of how people answer questions on intelligence tests. This interest has been accompanied by the study of individual differences in problem solving. Articles by Hunt and Lansman (1975), Pellegrino and Glaser (1979), and Sternberg (1979) provide an overview of work in this area. A book edited by Sternberg and Detterman (1979) contains a number of interesting chapters on the growing interaction between intelligence testing and cognitive psychology.

13

Classroom Problem Solving

It is strange that we expect students to learn, yet seldom teach them anything about learning. We expect students to solve problems, yet seldom teach them about problem solving. And, similarly, we sometimes require students to remember a considerable body of material, yet seldom teach them the art of memory. It is time we made up for this lack, time that we developed the applied disciplines of learning and problem solving and memory. We need to develop the general principles of how to learn, how to remember, how to solve problems, then to develop applied courses, and then to establish the place of these methods in an academic curriculum.

DON NORMAN (1980)

How can we put cognitive psychology to use in improving instruction? Norman (1980) recommended four steps:

1. To understand enough about the psychology of learning or problem solving that applied techniques can be developed.
2. To develop applied methods and formal courses in these methods that can aid in the general problem-solving and learning abilities of our students.
3. To use this knowledge in two ways:
   a. To develop courses in methods of learning, memory, and problem solving to provide students with important cognitive tools.
   b. To develop better instructional systems for conventional teaching and make use of new technological developments and new techniques of cognitive science to make interactive, intelligent tutoring systems a reality.

4. To demonstrate the effectiveness of these techniques and to gain sufficient academic and public acceptance that not only will they be taught, they will be sought after.*

Although they are not yet widespread, courses on problem solving already exist. One of the best known was first offered on the UCLA campus in 1969 to a class of 32 students (Rubinstein & Pfeiffer, 1979). The course was intended, first, to develop abilities to classify problems and, secondly, to identify and even restructure the skills needed to solve the problems. The organizers hoped that explicit instruction in a wide variety of practical applications of heuristic and algorithmic problem-solving methods would facilitate use of the methods and their generalization to new situations. They also felt that bringing together students with diverse majors would provide exposure to different problem-solving strategies. The course is based primarily on Rubinstein's (1975) book *Patterns of Problem Solving,* but it is taught by faculty and teaching assistants from many different disciplines. The popularity of the course is revealed by the fact that enrollment since 1976 has been about 1200 students a year, with 12 sections of the course taught each quarter.

Problem-solving courses are also popular at Carnegie-Mellon University, where they are currently taught in four of the colleges—science, engineering, humanities, and fine arts (Hayes, 1979). Some of the courses currently taught in different subject areas attempt to teach mainly specialized skills in the content area of the course. The history course, for example, makes explicit the search and evaluation procedures that should be used to find and evaluate historical information. The course taught in the psychology department assumes no prior knowledge and is not aimed at a particular field. It emphasizes general skills such as mnemonic techniques, decision making, representation and search, and creativity. The common theme of all the courses is their concern with *procedural knowledge*—knowledge of how to do something—rather than *declarative knowledge*—that is, knowledge of facts and principles.

The attempt to teach good problem-solving techniques raises the question of how research on problem solving can improve instruction. Larkin (1980) has argued that attempts to teach problem solving in the classroom face three limitations. First, it is hard to teach people to solve problems, and even the best teachers often have limited success. Second, the methodologies most often used in educational research do not provide information about effective problem solving. Statistical comparisons of

*From "Cognitive Engineering and Education," by D. A. Norman. In D. T. Tuma and F. Reif (Eds.), *Problem Solving and Education: Issues in Teaching and Research.* Copyright 1980 by Lawrence Erlbaum Associates, Inc., Publishers. This and all other quotations from this source are reprinted by permission.

test scores, for instance, do not provide good insights into the processes of effective problem solving, the manner in which these processes are acquired, and the kinds of defects unskilled problem solvers experience. Third, although instructional programs in problem solving can achieve benefits, it is not clear how. If we could understand in detail how the instructional programs achieve their effects, then the knowledge could be applied to other programs and educational materials.

Larkin believes that there has been impressive progress in understanding the detailed mechanisms of problem solving. However, since much of this progress has been achieved by studying puzzles and games, its direct application to the classroom is not immediately apparent. Nevertheless, the knowledge gained from this research is currently being used to study classroom problems, and a fruitful interaction between laboratory problem solving and classroom instruction is emerging.

This chapter discusses promising approaches to the study of how people solve classroom problems. The representation and initial analysis of problems is discussed in the first section. One way to represent a problem—drawing a picture—is often helpful, but it is not always clear when this approach should be used. The initial analysis of a problem may also require categorization in order to identify the problem as belonging to a larger class of problems. The ability to categorize a problem correctly is one source of individual differences in performance. Another source is planning, discussed in the second section. People who solve classroom problems also differ widely in their specific knowledge about a particular subject. For example, a physics professor certainly knows much more about how to solve physics problems than an undergraduate who is taking an introductory physics course. Cognitive psychologists and educators have recently begun to study the differences between how a beginner and an expert approach a problem. Much of this work focuses on differences in formulating a plan for solution.

The third section examines how problem solving might be improved through appropriate instruction. There is some evidence that teaching heuristics can improve performance on mathematics problems. The search for problem-solving methods is becoming increasingly important as computers begin to assume a more central role in education.

Representation and initial analysis

Representation and Design Problems

The previous chapter indicated that an important determinant of performance on a problem-solving task is the structure of the search space. Representation—for example, drawing a diagram to illustrate the problem—is concerned with how the problem solver translates instructions into a procedure for searching for a solution. The importance of representation is illustrated by the fact that two problems with identical search spaces (*problem isomorphs*) may differ greatly in how easy they are to solve. One set of instructions may cause the solver to represent the problem in a way that leads to an easy solution and another set of instructions may cause a representation that impedes the solution. Furthermore, a person who solves both of the problems may not recognize any similarity between them (Hayes & Simon, 1977).

Carroll, Thomas, and Malhotra (1980) investigated the role of representation in design by creating two problem isomorphs. The *temporal isomorph* required that subjects arrange seven stages of a manufacturing process in order to satisfy as many constraints as possible. They were given 19 constraints, such as stage F is of higher priority than stage B, stage A should follow stage C, and stage G uses different resources than stage F. The *spatial isomorph* involved designing a business office for seven employees. Each employee was to be assigned to a corridor a certain number of offices down from a central hallway containing a reception area at one end and accounting records at the other end. Employees with higher prestige preferred to have their offices near this central hallway. The 19 constraints for the spatial isomorph included employee F has more prestige than employee B, employee A is compatible with employee C, employee G uses the accounting records more than employee F, and so on.

Performance was measured by how many constraints were satisfied in the design. The importance of representation is illustrated by the finding that subjects did significantly better on the spatial isomorph even though both problems had equivalent constraints. Subjects given the spatial isomorph not only satisfied more of the constraints but took less time to complete their design. All 17 subjects in the spatial task used a sketch of the business office to formulate their design, but only 2 of the 18 subjects in the temporal task used a graphic representation to assist their design.

In order to determine whether graphic representation made the problem easier for the spatial group, the experimenters conducted a second experiment, in which both groups were instructed to use a matrix (see Figure 13.1). In the spatial isomorph the horizontal dimension represents the position of the offices with respect to the reception and accounting areas, the vertical dimension represents prestige, and each column is a possible corridor. In the temporal isomorph the horizontal dimension represents time, and the vertical dimension represents priority. Each column represents a possible work shift. One of the 19 constraints was to try to minimize the number of corridors or work shifts, so both groups tried to use as few columns as possible.

The results of the second experiment indicated that there were no significant differences between the two groups, either in performance scores or in solution times. The differences in experiment 1 therefore appear to be caused by the facilitating effects of a graphic representation of the problem. The usefulness of the graphic representation was obvious in the spatial task, and students spontaneously adopted it. It was not obvious in the temporal task. Performance on the two tasks became equivalent only when both tasks were represented in the same way by requiring both groups to use a graphic representation.

An interesting question raised by these findings is whether students could use analogy to improve their performance on the temporal task if they had first worked on the spatial task. The spontaneous use of a graphic procedure to solve the spatial task might then transfer to the temporal task. If students recognized the analogy between the two tasks, the experimenter would not have to instruct them explicitly to use the graphic procedure on the temporal task. Another example of how analogy can be useful in solving classroom problems is in the recognition of similarity among algebra word problems, which we will look at in the next section.

Categorization of Algebra Word Problems

After we have learned how to solve different kinds of problems, it is useful to be able to categorize a new problem as belonging to a certain

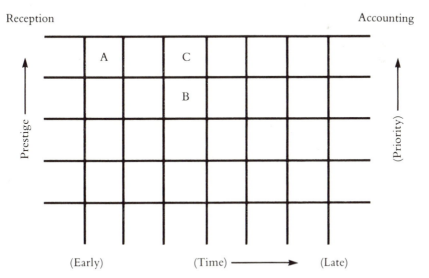

Figure 13.1. Graphic representation of a design problem. *(From "Presentation and Representation in Design Problem Solving," by J. M. Carroll, J. C. Thomas, and A. Malhotra. In* British Journal of Psychology, *1980, 71, 143–153. Copyright 1980 by the British Psychological Society. Reprinted by permission.)*

class of problems. We can then apply procedures for solving problems in that class. For example, a student in an algebra course might be given the following problem:

> One vegetable oil contains 6% saturated fats, and a second contains 26% saturated fats. In making a salad dressing, how many ounces of the second may be added to 10 ounces of the first if the percentage of saturated fats is not to exceed 16%?

The initial analysis of this problem should identify it as an example of a *mixture* problem. The student should then attempt to recall the procedure for solving mixture problems rather than the procedure for solving age, area, or interest problems. In order to determine whether students are able to classify algebra word problems systematically, Hinsley, Hayes, and Simon (1977) selected 76 problems from a high school algebra text. They then asked high school and college students to classify the problems by problem types, where the meaning of *problem types* was unspecified. When the students finished classifying the problems, they were asked to describe the properties of the categories they had identified. On the average, students identified 13.5 categories containing more than one problem, and there was considerable agreement among students about the identity of the categories. Examples included distance-rate-time, interest, ratio, triangle, area, mixture, and river-current problems.

Although the results showed that students are capable of categorizing algebra word problems, they did not demonstrate that the categories are used to formulate solutions. In fact, students may have had to formulate a solution before they could make a classification. This possibility would be very unlikely if it could be shown that students can categorize a problem very early in the course of reading it. In a second experiment, problems were read to subjects one part at a time, and after each part subjects were asked to attempt to classify the problem. Half of the subjects were able to classify the problems correctly after hearing less than one-fifth of the problem. The results verified the assumption that students can categorize problems before they have enough information to formulate a solution.

The use of categories to guide the search for a solution was nicely demonstrated in a third experiment, which used a single, complex problem:

> Because of their quiet ways, the inhabitants of Smalltown were especially upset by the terrible New Year's Eve auto accident that claimed the life of one Smalltown resident. The facts were these. Both Smith and Jones were New Year's Eve babies, and each had planned a surprise visit to the other on their mutual birthday. Jones had started out for Smith's house traveling due east on Route 210 just 2 minutes after Smith had left for Jones's house. Smith was traveling directly south on Route 140. Jones was traveling 30

miles per hour faster than Smith even though their houses were only 5 miles apart as the crow flies. Their cars crashed at the right-angle intersection of the two highways. Officer Franklin, who observed the crash, determined that Jones was traveling half again as fast as Smith at the time of the crash. Smith had been driving for just 4 minutes at the time of the crash. The crash occurred nearer to the house of the dead man than to the house of the survivor. What was the name of the dead man? [Hinsley, Hayes, & Simon, 1977, p. 102]*

The problem is an example of a distance-rate-time problem, but it contains some irrelevant information (their houses were 5 miles apart as the crow flies) that suggests that it might be a triangle problem. Verbal protocols collected from six subjects who solved the problem revealed that three of the six attended to the irrelevant triangle information. All three drew triangles and identified the 5-mile distance as the hypotenuse of the triangle. The other three subjects classified the problem as a distance-rate-time problem—in fact, initially formulating the problem as one driver going east and the other going west, a typical way of presenting problems belonging to this class. The knowledge associated with each of the two categories determined what the subject attended to in the problem, what information he expected, what information he regarded as relevant, and even what errors he made in reading the text.

From their findings the authors concluded:

1. Students can recognize problem categories and agree considerably on the categories.
2. They can usually recognize the categories early in reading the text. Sometimes reading as little as the initial noun phrase is sufficient.
3. Students have information about the problem categories that is useful for formulating solutions. This information includes knowledge about useful equations and diagrams and procedures for identifying relevant information.
4. They often use this information to solve algebra word problems when the instructions are simply to solve the problems and do not require classification.

Individual Differences in Categorization

The Smalltown problem illustrated individual differences in categorization: three of the students initially classified the problem as a

*From "Words to Equations: Meaning and Representation in Algebra Word Problems," by D. A. Hinsley, J. R. Hayes, and H. A. Simon. In P. A. Carpenter and M. A. Just (Eds.), *Cognitive Processes in Comprehension.* Copyright 1977 by Lawrence Erlbaum Associates, Inc., Publishers. Reprinted by permission.

distance-rate-time problem and three classified it as a triangle problem. The Smalltown problem was intentionally constructed to be complex and ambiguous in order to maximize the opportunity to study individual differences. Individual differences in categorization were not very apparent when standard problems were used.

Another approach to studying individual differences is to use standard problems but less sophisticated subjects. Silver (1981) asked seventh-grade students to form groups of problems that were "mathematically related" and to explain the basis for categorizing them. He used 16 problems that could be represented by a 4 × 4 matrix. The four problems in each horizontal row were mathematically related, and the same mathematical procedure could be used to solve each. The four problems in each vertical column described a similar story context but required different procedures to solve them. The first two problems in Table 13.1 are mathematically related since the same procedure is used to solve each. The third problem has the same story context as the first but requires a different mathematical procedure.

Although Silver asked his students to classify mathematically related problems, students who had difficulty perceiving the mathematical structure of the problems might use story context as a basis of classification. Students were asked to solve 12 of the problems after they made their classification in order to determine whether there was any relation between the ability to classify and to solve problems. Silver classified the students as good, average, or poor problem solvers on the basis of the number of problems they solved.

The relation between the ability to classify and to solve problems is illustrated in Table 13.2. The *association* score was obtained by counting the number of related pairs that a student put into the same category. The *pure* category score was obtained by counting the number of categories

TABLE 13.1.   A Word Problem and Related Problems.

Word problem	A farmer is counting the hens and rabbits in his barnyard. He counts a total of 50 heads and 140 feet. How many hens and how many rabbits does the farmer have?
Related structure	Bill has a collection of 20 coins that consists entirely of dimes and quarters. If the collection is worth $4.10, how many of each kind of coin are in the collection?
Related context	A farmer is counting the hens and rabbits in his barnyard. He counts six coops with four hens in each, two coops with three hens in each, five cages with six rabbits in each, and three cages with four rabbits in each. How many hens and how many rabbits does the farmer have?

From "Recall of Mathematical Problem Information: Solving Related Problems," by E. A. Silver. In *Journal for Research in Mathematics Education*, 1981, *12*, 54–64. Copyright 1981 by the National Council of Teachers of Mathematics. Reprinted by permission.

TABLE 13.2.   Effect of Ability on Categorizing Problems by Structure and Context.

Ability	Structure		Context	
	Association	*Pure*	*Association*	*Pure*
Good	17.0	3.1	0.6	0.1
Average	12.0	1.8	3.4	0.6
Poor	6.3	0.4	8.9	2.3

From "Recall of Mathematical Problem Information: Solving Related Problems," by E. A. Silver. In *Journal for Research in Mathematics Education,* 1981, *12,* 54–64. Copyright 1981 by the National Council of Teachers of Mathematics. Reprinted by permission.

that contained at least three related problems and no unrelated problems. The maximum association score was 24, and the maximum pure category score was 4. The results indicate that the better problem solvers formed categories on the basis of mathematical structure, and the poor problem solvers formed categories on the basis of story context.

Similar results were obtained when students were asked to recall information about story problems. Good problem solvers were able to recall information about mathematical structure. Poor problem solvers rarely recalled this information, even when the solutions were discussed prior to their recall. However, they could often remember details about the story context and were sometimes better than the good problem solvers at recalling these details. The results suggest that an important source of individual differences in mathematical problem solving is the ability to categorize problems initially according to the mathematical procedure needed to solve them.

Planning and solution strategies

Most of the difficulty in solving a problem lies in the initial analysis if the solution requires standard procedures that are identified during this analysis. Little planning is necessary to solve a problem if its categorization reduces the number of relevant equations to one or two. The problem solver simply recalls the equations and substitutes the relevant values for the variables.

More complex problems, however, often require the construction of a plan for producing the solution. Miller, Galanter, and Pribram (1960) defined a *plan* as a hierarchical process that controls the order in which a sequence of operations is to be performed. Planning implies that the problem solver is looking ahead and is not simply taking one step at a time. This, of course, is usually not possible the first time that a person encounters a problem. Planning has not been emphasized in much of the research on puzzles because people usually do not have detailed knowledge about how to solve a particular puzzle. Successful models of puzzle solving have therefore been based on general strategies such as means/end analysis (Atwood & Polson, 1976; Simon & Reed, 1976). Once a person has solved a particular puzzle, however, subsequent solutions can use planning techniques such as forming subgoals or identifying sequences of moves (Reed & Johnsen, 1977).

The solution of problems in courses like physics or engineering depends on a considerable degree of organized knowledge about a particular topic and how well this knowledge can be translated into efficient plans. Before examining how people make use of plans to solve problems, we will attempt to make the concept of planning more precise by looking at how it has been used in the field of artificial intelligence. As we saw in the previous chapter, the computer implementation of problem solving requires a detailed specification of the operations used to define a concept.

An Example from Artificial Intelligence

Many key ideas about planning have been formalized by Sacerdoti's work in artificial intelligence. His initial contribution was to modify a general-purpose problem-solving program called STRIPS to allow for planning. The modification was called ABSTRIPS (Abstraction Based Strips) because the planning took place in an abstraction of the search space that ignored many details (Sacerdoti, 1974). ABSTRIPS solved a problem in a hierarchy of abstraction spaces in which successively finer levels of details were introduced.

Figure 13.2 shows an example of a problem that was solved by ABSTRIPS. The problem is to use the robot to push box 1 next to box 2 and then put the robot in room A. Figure 13.2 shows the initial problem state. The robot is capable of performing operations such as pushing boxes, opening doors, and entering rooms. However, each operation has preconditions that must be satisfied before it can be used. For instance, in order to push box 1 to box 2, (1) box 1 must be a pushable object, (2) the two boxes and the robot must be in the same room, and (3) the robot must be next to box 1. Associated with each operation is a level of criticality. For this operation, precondition 1 is the most critical (the problem couldn't be solved if box 1 couldn't be pushed), precondition 2 is moderately critical, and precondition 3 is the least critical. ABSTRIPS plans solutions by first ignoring all but the most critical preconditions. It then uses its solution of the simpler problems to solve more complex problems as more details (preconditions) are introduced. The solution of the simpler problems provides subgoals for solving the more complex problems.

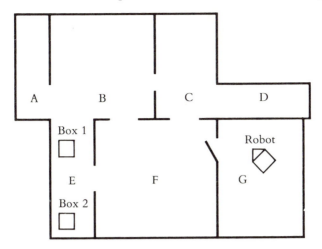

Figure 13.2. Initial state of robot problem. *(From "Planning in a Hierarchy of Abstraction Spaces," by E. D. Sacerdoti. In* Artificial Intelligence, *1974, 5, 115–135. Copyright 1974 by North-Holland Publishing Company, Amsterdam. Reprinted by permission.)*

ABSTRIPS began solving the robot problem by first establishing two subgoals: (1) push box 1 to box 2 and (2) enter room A. In establishing these two subgoals, it checked only the most critical preconditions, such as box 1 could be pushed and there was a room A that could be entered. Since these preconditions were satisfied, it then attempted to reach the two subgoals by satisfying preconditions that had an intermediate level of criticality. A precondition for pushing box 1 is that the robot is in the same room as box 1; a new subgoal was therefore needed to move the robot to room E. A precondition for moving the robot to a room is that the robot is in an adjoining room. An attempt to move the robot to room B (an adjoining room) failed because the robot was not in a room next to room B. The attempt to move the robot to room F succeeded, thereby satisfying the precondition for moving the robot to room E. The intermediate preconditions for pushing box 1 to box 2 were now satisfied, and so this subgoal could be reached at an intermediate level of planning.

But two lesser preconditions had to be satisfied in order to reach the subgoal in the actual search space. A precondition for moving from one room to an adjacent room is that the door between the two rooms is open. It was therefore necessary to open the door between rooms F and G. It was also necessary to move the robot next to box 1 after it entered room E since this is a lower level precondition for moving objects.

Although many of these preconditions may seem rather trivial to us human problem solvers, they are important determinants of the effectiveness of a problem-solving program. Figure 13.3 illustrates the success

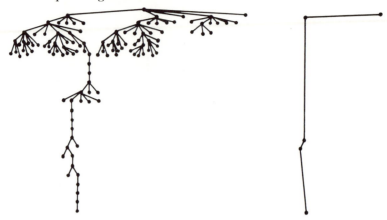

a. STRIPS search tree for the sample problem   b. ABSTRIPS search tree in the
space of criticality 6

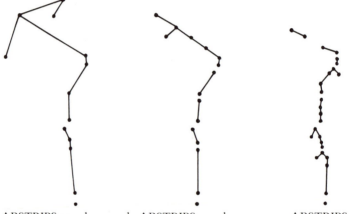

c. ABSTRIPS search
tree in the space
of criticality 5

d. ABSTRIPS search
tree in the space
of criticality 4

e. ABSTRIPS search
tree in the problem
space

Figure 13.3. Searches for a solution: STRIPS versus ABSTRIPS.
*(From "Planning in a Hierarchy of Abstraction Spaces," by E. D. Sacerdoti.
In* Artificial Intelligence, *1974, 5, 115–135. Copyright 1974 by North-
Holland Publishing Company, Amsterdam. Reprinted by permission.)*

of a hierarchical planning system. The original program, STRIPS, initially explored many unpromising paths in the search space before finding a
path that resulted in the solution. It explored 119 problem states in the
search space, only 23 of which were on the successful path. The dots in
Figure 13.3a represent problem states explored by STRIPS. You can see
that many of the paths did not lead to a solution (represented by the dot
at the bottom of the search tree).

ABSTRIPS first attempted to solve a simpler version of the problem
by considering only the most important preconditions. It required only

a few steps to solve the simpler problem (Figure 13.3b). By considering preconditions of lower criticality in subsequent searches (Figures 13.3c–13.3e), ABSTRIPS solved the problem without exploring unpromising paths. The procedure was successful because the solution of the simpler problems provided subgoals that constrained the search as more details were added (Figures 13.3b–13.3e). ABSTRIPS required less than 6 minutes of computer time to solve this problem, compared to over 30 minutes for STRIPS.

This brief description of ABSTRIPS oversimplifies the nature of planning. One potential difficulty is that achieving one subgoal may make it impossible to achieve another. For example, if ABSTRIPS first attempted to achieve the subgoal of moving the robot to room A, it would have to abandon this subgoal in order to use the robot to move the box in room E.

Furthermore, ABSTRIPS cannot make use of the relationships among the various levels of plans; therefore it runs into trouble if its higher level solutions are wrong. A more sophisticated program called NOAH (Network of Action Hierarchies) was designed to eliminate some of these deficiencies (Sacerdoti, 1977). NOAH performs its planning in a hierarchical fashion as ABSTRIPS does but tries not to overconstrain its search for a solution. NOAH is more flexible in the order in which subgoals are achieved, so it is less likely to have to abandon one subgoal because it must achieve another first. The ordering of subgoals is delayed until enough details have been obtained to specify the order. NOAH also saves the plans made at different levels in the hierarchy so that this information can be reused if it is necessary to modify a plan because some subgoals cannot be reached or are not part of the required solution.

Does Sacerdoti's work add to our knowledge of planning? As he points out in the concluding section of his book (1977), Miller, Galanter, and Pribram discussed the concept of planning in 1960. Their book discussed plan generation, execution monitoring, planning in spaces where details are ignored, the integration of subplans into larger plans, and learning as the development of hierarchical structures.

Sacerdoti's contribution is that his computer program avoids the lack of specificity common to verbal formulations. There are so many ways even a small number of moves or problem states can interrelate that it is very easy for inconsistencies to go unnoticed or interrelationships to go unspecified. Although Miller, Galanter, and Pribram provided insights into the importance of planning, many of their concepts were insufficiently defined. Artificial intelligence provides a methodology for avoiding inconsistencies, for discovering new insights that were not apparent in a verbal description, and for testing variations in the initial formulation of a concept. To use Sacerdoti's words, "the discipline imposed by computer implementation helps to debug our own insights" (1977, p. 107).

Hierarchical Planning as a Model of Human Problem Solving

Sacerdoti's theory provides a precise description of how planning can be efficiently organized, but are his ideas relevant to human behavior? Perhaps you can think of situations in which you wished you had planned more carefully before attempting a task. I can.

One example occurred on the morning that I left on my trip westward to spend a year at the University of California, Berkeley. Shortly before we left, the toilet broke and I had to repair a metal bar that connected the handle to a plunger. If we ignore the details, the task can be represented by two high-level subgoals: connect the bar to the handle and connect the plunger to the bar. One virtue of NOAH is that it can delay specifying the order of subgoals until it obtains information about lower level details. I wasn't as smart.

After attaching the bar to the handle, I noticed that the bar was curved slightly upward, but it would have to curve downward in order to reach the plunger. I unscrewed the bar and once again attached it to the handle so it would curve downward. I then noticed that it still wouldn't reach the plunger unless I attached it before connecting the bar to the handle. Fortunately, the search space was small enough that having to start over twice did not delay my trip. Still, I wished I had planned before beginning.

Planning becomes more and more important as the search space grows larger. A good example of a task that depends on hierarchical planning is the writing of computer programs. This task has been studied by Atwood, Polson, Jeffries, and Ramsey (1978). The theoretical assumptions that guided their research were greatly influenced by the ideas expressed in NOAH. They assumed:

1. A plan is a series of abstractions of the final solution, ranging from schematic high-level plans to detailed plans that produce the solution.
2. A plan is constructed by a process of stepwise refinement; that is, construction starts at the higher, more abstract levels and the details are added later.
3. Planning involves the utilization of previously learned knowledge structures.
4. Various components of the plan or even the entire plan can be retrieved from long-term memory and incorporated into a solution.
5. Planning involves the synthesis of many types of knowledge structures.

The subjects in this experiment were three highly experienced computer programmers. The task was to write a program that would accept as input the text of a book and would produce as output a list of specified index terms and page numbers on which each term appeared. The results demonstrated that subjects differed in the extent to which they followed a hierarchical, top-down planning procedure. The protocols of the three subjects showed fairly clear differences in the overall quality, completeness, and organization of their knowledge. The knowledge of one subject was sufficiently developed to allow for the construction of plans in a top-down expansion. This subject's procedure was most similar to the procedure used by NOAH. The knowledge of a second subject was less well developed, and, as a result, backtracking was necessary in order to correct deficiencies in the design. The knowledge of the third subject was developed to such an extent that this subject was able to retrieve most of the design directly from memory and therefore required less planning than the other two subjects. These findings suggest that hierarchical planning is most likely to be carried out by someone who has enough knowledge to approach the task systematically but is unable to retrieve the solution directly from memory.

Individual Differences in Planning

The view that hierarchical planning is more characteristic of an expert than of a novice is supported by Larkin and Reif's (1979) research on how a novice and an expert solve physics (mechanics) problems. The expert was a physics professor who had recently taught a mechanics course. The "novice" was an excellent student who had recently completed his first university-level course in mechanics. Both subjects solved five problems, which were taken from a widely used textbook. Figure 13.4 shows one of the problems. The subjects were asked to work normally but to think aloud as much as possible. Both solved all five problems, but neither subject recognized any problem as having an immediately obvious solution.

Although both subjects solved all five problems, they did not proceed in the same way. The novice began immediately to identify relevant principles and apply them individually to generate equations. When relevant equations were identified, he combined them to eliminate undesirable quantities. The expert did not immediately construct a mathematical description of the problem. Instead, he used a more general planning procedure in which details were added by successive refinements. The expert did not try to write equations and eliminate undesirable quantities but used a more coherent approach to guide the subsequent construction of relevant equations. The expert applied principles not individually but as part of a well-defined plan.

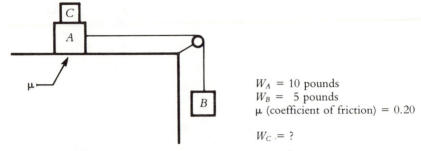

$W_A = 10$ pounds
$W_B = 5$ pounds
μ (coefficient of friction) $= 0.20$

$W_C = ?$

Figure 13.4. A physics problem requiring calculation of how much block *C* must weigh to keep block *A* from sliding off the table. *(From "Understanding and Teaching Problem Solving in Physics," by J. H. Larkin and F. Reif. In European Journal of Science Education, 1979, 1, 191–203. Copyright 1979 by the Institute for Science Education. Reprinted by permission.)*

The result was that the equations generated by the expert were clustered together in time, corresponding to a rapid application of pre-planned methods. In contrast, the novice generated equations more randomly in time. Figure 13.5 shows how much time separated successive pairs of equations generated by the expert and novice. The broken lines are the graphs that would occur if the equations had been generated

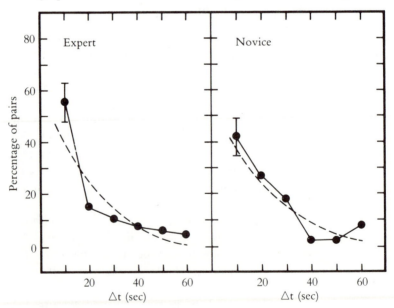

Figure 13.5. Percentage of equation pairs, as a function of intervening time (Δt), generated in problem solutions. *(From "Understanding and Teaching Problem Solving in Physics," by J. H. Larkin and F. Reif. In European Journal of Science Education, 1979, 1, 191–203. Copyright 1979 by the Institute for Science Education. Reprinted by permission.)*

TABLE 13.3. Hypothesized Differences between a Novice and an Expert.

	Novice	*Expert*
Problem representation	Rely on verbal problem statement; no use of semantic and auxiliary information	Construct diagram when useful; rely on strong spontaneous mediating representation
Knowledge structure	No problem category information used; principles stored separately	Strong problem category information available, with associated solution procedures
Initial analysis	No informal qualitative analysis; identify unknown and given values; go directly to equations	Qualitative elaboration of problem features to determine most promising procedure if solution is not immediately clear
Solution strategy	Nearly random search for equations containing desired quantities; substitute values until answer is isolated	Implement plan for solution; rarely need to rework by alternative procedure

From "Information Processing Analysis of Mathematical Problem Solving," by J. I. Heller and J. G. Greeno. Paper presented at the Applied Problem Solving Conference, Evanston, Illinois, 1979. Reprinted by permission of Joan I. Heller.

randomly in time. The novice's graph closely corresponds to the prediction of random generation, whereas the expert's graph shows a large number of equation pairs with small intervening times, reflecting a significant amount of clustering.

The studies on individual differences in planning and problem solving have typically used a very limited number of subjects. These studies are continuing, and future theoretical models should be less tentative than current models. But some consistency is already emerging in interpretations of how the expert problem solver differs from the beginning problem solver. Heller and Greeno (1979) reviewed the evidence on individual differences in solving word problems in arithmetic, algebra, physics, and thermodynamics. They suggested that several characteristics of the solution procedures change as the problem solvers become more competent. Table 13.3 summarizes the differences for two ends of a continuum. Heller and Greeno's analysis provides a good first approximation of the differences between the novice and the expert and a useful summary of current knowledge.

Problem solving and instruction

The distinction between the operations used by the novice and the expert leads us to consider whether problem-solving strategies can be explicitly taught. If we can identify what the expert is doing, can we use this information to teach the novice to become a better problem solver? The expert has acquired considerable knowledge over a long period of time, and it would be unreasonable to expect that the novice could acquire the same amount of knowledge over a short period of time. However, the expert may have learned some problem-solving strategies that, if explicitly taught, would make the novice a better problem solver.

Teaching Heuristics

A recent paper by Schoenfeld (1979) illustrates how we might teach heuristic strategies. Although Schoenfeld compared the performances of only seven students, his paper reflects both the potential benefits and the limitations of teaching heuristics.

The students were science and mathematics majors who were recruited as volunteers from upper-division courses in mathematics. Four of the seven students were randomly assigned to a "heuristics" group and the remaining three were assigned to a "nonheuristics" group. All students took a pretest consisting of five challenging mathematics problems. They then participated in five instruction sessions spread over a two-week period, during which time they worked on and saw the solutions to 20 problems. Students in both groups spent the same amount of time working on the problems and saw the same solutions. After the instruction sessions students took a posttest of five problems. All problems in the pretest, instruction sessions, and posttest were chosen from five classes of similar problems—similar in that they could be solved by a particular strategy.

At the first instruction session the four heuristics students were given a list of the five strategies (see Table 13.4). They were then given the problems grouped according to strategy, with each session devoted to a particular strategy. Students in the nonheuristics group did not see the list of strategies and were given the 20 practice problems in random order. Although all students saw the same solutions, students in the heuristics group also saw an overlay to each solution that indicated where a particular strategy had been used.

The three students in the nonheuristics group successfully solved a total of five problems on the pretest and five problems on the posttest. The four students in the heuristics group correctly solved a total of four problems on the pretest and thirteen problems on the posttest. All four heuristics students improved their performance and had at least two more correct solutions on the posttest.

Schoenfeld is careful in interpreting his results and presents a balanced discussion of the implications of the study. The results are encouraging because they demonstrated that a training procedure can improve

TABLE 13.4.   The Five Problem-Solving Strategies.

1. Draw a diagram if at all possible.
   Even if you finally solve the problem by algebraic or other means, a diagram can help give you a "feel" for the problem. It may suggest ideas or plausible answers. You may even solve a problem graphically.

2. If there is an integer parameter, look for an inductive argument.
   Is there an "*n*" or other parameter in the problem which takes on integer values? If you need to find a formula for $f(n)$, you might try one of these:
   A. Calculate $f(1)$, $f(2)$, $f(3)$, $f(4)$, $f(5)$; list them in order, and see if there's a pattern. If there is, you might verify it by induction.
   B. See what happens as you pass from *n* objects to $n + 1$. If you can tell how to pass from $f(n)$ to $f(n + 1)$, you may build up $f(n)$ inductively.

3. Consider arguing by contradiction or contrapositive.
   Contrapositive: Instead of proving the statement "If X is true then Y is true," you can prove the equivalent statement "If Y is false then X must be false."
   Contradiction: Assume, for the sake of argument, that the statement you would like to prove is false. Using this assumption, go on to prove either that one of the given conditions in the problem is false, that something you know to be true is false, or that what you wish to prove is true. If you can do any of these, you have proved what you want.
   Both of these techniques are especially useful when you find it difficult to begin a direct argument because you have little to work with. If negating a statement gives you something solid to manipulate, this may be the technique to use.

4. Consider a similar problem with fewer variables.
   If the problem has a large number of variables and is too confusing to deal with comfortably, construct and solve a similar problem with fewer variables. You may then be able to
   A. Adapt the method of solution to the more complex problem.
   B. Take the result of the simpler problem and build up from there.

5. Try to establish subgoals.
   Can you obtain part of the answer, and perhaps go on from there? Can you decompose the problem so that a number of easier results can be combined to give the total result you want?

From "Explicit Heuristic Training as a Variable in Problem-Solving Performances," by A. H. Schoenfeld. In *Journal for Research in Mathematics Education,* 1979, *10,* 173–187. Copyright 1979 by the National Council of Teachers of Mathematics. Reprinted by permission.

students' abilities to solve problems. Thus if we expect students to learn such strategies, we should label them explicitly and illustrate their use. But Schoenfeld also argues that we should not expect a dramatic improvement in performance on the basis of a limited number of practice sessions. There is no guarantee that students will use or know when to apply a particular technique even though they could use it successfully during a practice session. In part, this is the fault of the vagueness of some of the strategies. The instruction to use subgoals, for example, did not transfer very well to other problems because the strategy itself usually requires considerable specific knowledge to use effectively.

Schoenfeld's conclusion is therefore both cautious and optimistic:

> We are still a long way from success. If we can succeed in identifying truly useful problem-solving strategies (and here we have done well); if we can

understand and exploit the mechanisms by which experts call these strategies into play; and if we can create efficient means by which this knowledge can be passed on to our students, the potential rewards are great indeed. The obstacles are many, the field vast. This experiment shows that, under appropriate circumstances, explicit instruction in general problem-solving strategies (heuristics) does have an impact on students' problem-solving performance. The rest will, with luck and work, come with time [1979, p. 186].

The Computer as Tutor

Contributions to a better understanding of problem solving have come from many disciplines. Rubinstein's problem-solving course at UCLA originated in the Department of Engineering, Hayes's course in the Department of Psychology. Carroll, Thomas, and Malhotra are psychologists who worked on design problems at the IBM Watson Research Center. The research on categorization of word problems was done by psychologists at Carnegie-Mellon University. Silver and Schoenfeld are both members of mathematics departments, and Sacerdoti is a member of the artificial intelligence group at the Stanford Research Institute. Larkin and Reif have backgrounds in physics and did their study as members of the Group in Science and Mathematics Education at the University of California, Berkeley.

The multidisciplinary nature of research on complex skills has resulted in a multidisciplinary journal called *Cognitive Science*, first published in January 1977, with an emphasis on research in artificial intelligence, psychology, and language. The progress being made in these areas, combined with the rapid decline in costs of computers, should result in increasing use of the computer as an intelligent tutor that can help people solve problems. This goal is now attainable because the computer itself has become a good problem solver (see Box 13.1).

Box 13.1. How Smart Can Computers Get?

On a Monday morning at Yale University, Margot Flowers sits down with her friend Abdul for another debate on Mideast politics:

MARGOT: Who started the 1967 war?

ABDUL: The Arabs did, by blockading the Strait of Tiran.

MARGOT: But Israel attacked first.

ABDUL: According to international law, blockades are acts of war.

MARGOT: Were we supposed to let you import American arms through the strait?

(Box 13.1 continues)

Box 13.1 (*continued*)

ABDUL: Israel was not importing arms through the strait. The reason for the blockade was to keep Israel from importing oil from Iran.

They don't have the finesse of U.N. diplomats, but then Margot Flowers is one of three scientists who created Abdul, a computer program that dips into its memory of data to reason out answers to questions. The dialogue is an exercise in a 25-year-old field called artificial intelligence (AI), and with the remarkable advances in computer technology at their command, hundreds of AI researchers are testing the potential of the new electronic brains. Their goal is as remarkable as their technology: to determine how close a computer can come to simulating the human mind and, perhaps, transcending it.

The results thus far are both tantalizing and reassuring. In scores of AI experiments, well-programed computers can play chess and backgammon, draw analogies among Shakespearean plays and understand tales involving friendship and adultery. Computers can use facts to make inferences and draw on experience to reach unprogramed conclusions. But only up to a point: what AI researchers are learning is that the human brain is even more astonishing than they thought—and that true intelligence involves elements of will, consciousness and creativity of which today's computers are incapable. "So far, artificial intelligence falls under the definition of problem solving," says AI scientist Terry Winograd of Stanford. "That's the first step."

The first "thinking" problem solver was probably a 1956 computer program called the Logic Theorist, which could choose from a set of facts and use logical operations to prove mathematical statements. Its first triumph was finding a proof of a theorem in mathematical logic that both Bertrand Russell and Alfred North Whitehead had missed.

Today's problem solvers are even more sophisticated. One of the most impressive is the backgammon champ programed by Hans J. Berliner of Carnegie-Mellon University in Pittsburgh. The program chooses among all possible legal moves by reducing each to a mathematical equation that measures threats and opportunities and then picks the move whose equation has the highest value. BACON, another program developed by Nobel laureate Herbert A. Simon and his colleagues at Carnegie-Mellon, looks for patterns in scientific data. On its own, BACON "discovered" a rule of planetary mechanics first established by Johannes Kepler in 1609. And when it was fed all the facts that were known about chemistry in the year 1800, BACON deduced the principle of atomic weight—a feat that took human scientists another 50 years.

From *Newsweek* (June 30, 1980). Reprinted by permission.

The initial development of computer-assisted instruction (CAI) in the 1960s was based on multiple-choice questions. A student's responses determined how she would progress through the program, but there was no attempt to understand the student's misconceptions. Howe (1978) has characterized the most recent approaches to CAI as based on a "learning by doing" rather than a "learning by being told" philosophy. The newer view represents learning as an active construction of knowledge in which creativity and problem-solving skills play an important role. According to Howe, the major reason for the limitations of the traditional CAI program is that it neither knows nor understands the topic being taught. This means that it is unable to interpret alternative or interesting answers, to understand why a student made a mistake, or to supply her with useful information. The goal of the most recent learner-based programs is to model the knowledge and skill acquired by an individual in order to best assist her in learning these skills.

An example of this newer approach is Brown and Burton's (1978) diagnostic analysis of a student's misconceptions in basic mathematical skills. Using techniques developed in the field of artificial intelligence, they constructed a computer model for diagnosing why a student is making a mistake. Their model is based on the assumption that mistakes usually occur not because students do not follow procedures very well, but because they often follow the wrong procedure. If students follow the wrong procedure, there should be a systematic pattern in their errors. A good diagnostic model should be able to identify the misconception ("bug") that causes the systematic pattern.

Brown and Burton's analysis revealed that there is a remarkable number of possible bugs even for relatively simple procedures like addition and subtraction. Furthermore, it's a challenging task for a teacher or a computer program to identify these bugs. Figure 13.6 shows three addition problems and three subtraction problems. Each set of three problems has a bug that produces the erroneous answers. See if you can identify the two bugs before reading further.

Addition problems

17	18	43
+ 5	+ 6	+79
13	15	23

Subtraction problems

662	831	563
−357	−158	−241
215	583	322

Figure 13.6. Example of an addition bug and a subtraction bug.

If you tried diagnosing the errors, you will realize that error diagnosis can be difficult. The addition bug is that the student is treating each digit as a single digit. Thus 17 + 5 is treated as 1 + 7 + 5. The subtraction bug is that the student subtracts all borrows from the left-most digit in the top number. Diagnosing bugs becomes even more difficult when (1) any one of several different bugs can account for the errors, (2) there is more than one bug producing the errors, or (3) a student occasionally makes random errors when applying a buggy procedure.

Brown and Burton discuss three applications of their diagnostic model. The first is an instructional game for training student teachers. The prospective teachers were first shown a single problem with an incorrect answer. They then gave the computer new problems, and the computer gave buggy answers. When the students felt that they had diagnosed the bug, the computer gave them problems and they had to produce buggy answers. The problems were selected so it would be difficult to give the correct buggy answers unless one had correctly diagnosed the bug. A second use of a diagnostic model was to analyze errors on subtraction problems given by elementary school students in an attempt to identify bugs in their answers. A third application of the model was to judge the diagnostic quality of a test. If a test is used to diagnose specific misconceptions rather than simply to assign a numerical score, it is necessary to select problems that will reveal the misconceptions. A good diagnostic model can do this. The three applications illustrate the potential benefit of diagnostic models, computer tutors, and applications of theories in cognitive science to educational problems.

Summary

Courses on improving problem-solving skills are currently being taught at a few universities, and many educational courses require problem solving. Many of the ideas we have discussed previously are being applied in the study of how people solve problems.

The importance of representation in solving design problems is illustrated by differences in formulating a spatial (office layout) and a temporal (production schedule) design. The spontaneous use of a graphic representation resulted in better performance on the spatial design, but there was no difference when a graphic representation was used to solve both design problems. College students' initial analysis of algebra word problems resulted in a categorization of the problem into one of about 14 categories. Students then used the information about the categories—including knowledge about useful equations, diagrams, and procedures for identifying relevant information—to formulate solutions. The development of categorization skills is illustrated by individual differences among seventh graders. When asked to classify problems according to their mathematical structure, good problem solvers were able to form categories on the basis of the mathematical procedures used to solve the problems, whereas poor problem solvers formed categories on the basis of story context. Good problem solvers were also better at recalling the mathematical structure of problems.

As problems become more complex, the skilled use of planning becomes important in determining how efficiently they can be solved. Planning involves establishing subgoals that guide the search for a solution. Many of the key ideas used in planning have been formalized by work in artificial intelligence. Programs like NOAH use a hierarchical technique in which details are considered only after the initial solutions are formulated in an abstraction of the search space. A study of how computer programmers design software revealed three levels of performance—one characterized by considerable backtracking to correct incorrect procedures, one characterized by the efficient use of hierarchical planning, and one characterized by the retrieval of a detailed solution. Planning was also the main distinguishing characteristic between how a novice and an expert solved physics problems.

The distinction between the operations used by the novice and by the expert suggests that it might be beneficial to teach problem-solving strategies. As one example of this approach, upper-division science and mathematics majors were taught strategies about drawing a diagram, looking for an inductive argument, arguing by contradiction, formulating a simpler problem, and establishing subgoals. The group taught the strategies improved their performance on a posttest, whereas a control group did not. Another application of knowledge about problem solving is the design of intelligent computer tutors. Recent progress in the areas of artificial intelligence, education, and cognitive psychology has resulted in CAI programs that treat learning as an active construction of knowledge, involving skills in problem solving. An example of this new approach is a program that attempts to diagnose misconceptions about addition and subtraction. Applications of this work include using the computer to diagnose errors or to train teachers to diagnose errors, and using the conceptual ideas to improve the diagnostic quality of tests.

Recommended reading

Paige and Simon (1966) discuss cognitive processes in solving algebra word problems. The effect of meaningfulness on solving algebraic equations has been studied by Mayer and Greeno (1975) and Kieras and Greeno (1975). Mayer and Greeno (1972) have also investigated how different instructional procedures influence what people learn about a statistical formula called the *binomial theorem*. Rasmussen and Jensen (1974) investigated individual differences in how electricians search for a failure in an electronic circuit. Research on individual differences in solving physics problems was summarized in an article published in *Science* (Larkin, McDermott, Simon, & Simon, 1980). A book edited by Tuma and Reif (1980) contains a collection of papers on problem solving and education. Resnick (1981) reviews recent research on instructional psychology.

14

Decision Making

I cannot, for want of sufficient premises, advise you what to determine, but if you please I will tell you how. . . . My way is to divide half a sheet of paper by a line into two columns; writing over one Pro, and over the other Con. Then, doing three or four days' consideration, I put down under the different heads short hints of the different motives, that at different times occur to me for or against the measure. When I have thus got them all together in one view, I endeavor to estimate the respective weights . . . [to] find at length where the balance lies. . . . And, though the weight of reasons cannot be taken with the precision of algebraic quantities, yet, when each is thus considered, separately and comparatively, and the whole matter lies before me, I think I can judge better, and am less liable to make a rash step; and in fact I have found great advantage for this kind of equation, in what may be called moral or prudential algebra.

BENJAMIN FRANKLIN (1772/1887)

Every day we make many decisions. Most of these are relatively unimportant—what to eat for breakfast, for example. Others—such as selecting a car, a home, or a job—are more important. Making decisions is often difficult because each alternative usually consists of many dimensions, and very seldom does the best alternative excel on all dimensions. One way to simplify the decision process is to emphasize only a single dimension. Box 14.1 illustrates this approach. The Morrisons evaluated many dimensions before buying a house, but they made their final selection on the basis of a single dimension—the quality of the local school. Although this is a very important dimension for parents with school-age children, there was such a small difference in the quality of the schools that the Morrisons really overemphasized this dimension.

Box 14.1. Dream Home Bypassed for School

KATHY O'TOOLE *Education Writer*

Mike and Patty Morrison had hopes this time of getting their dream home—a new one, with carpeting in just the colors they wanted, with a fireplace in the family room and a breakfast area in the kitchen.

The Morrisons, newcomers from Southern California with two pre-school children, found their dream home in a new San Ramon subdivision.

But they didn't buy it.

The house lacked one feature. It wasn't near the elementary school whose pupils had the highest test scores in the San Ramon School District.

Instead, the Morrisons bought a more expensive home in Walnut Creek with a floor plan they didn't like, and the carpet a color they didn't like.

They made their decision based on standardized school test score information supplied by a San Ramon Valley real estate agent, Sherry Schiff.

The Morrisons' decision illustrates the relatively small differences parents sometimes consider in deciding what home to buy.

In state reading tests given last May, third-graders at the school near the home the Morrisons bought scored higher than those in 91 percent of the state's schools. The third-graders at the school near the home the Morrisons preferred scored better than those in 84 percent of the schools.

The Morrisons and their real estate agent have played a meaningless statistical game, contend several testing experts for Eastbay school districts and the state Department of Education.

The test scores of the two schools compared were so close, say the test experts, that they can't possibly tell parents in which school their child will do better.

Reproduced with permission from the *Oakland Tribune,* Oakland, California.

The first section of this chapter describes models of how people select an alternative from a set of alternatives. Examples include selecting a home, a car, or dinner from a menu. These models do not consider probabilities because they assume that a person knows the values of relevant dimensions, such as price, gas mileage, and optional equipment in the case of buying a car. The following two sections are concerned with examples of risky decision making—those in which the decision maker must consider probabilities. We will first examine how people make probability estimates, including ways they revise their estimates when they receive new information. We will then consider how people use the estimates to make decisions. The study of decision making has been influenced by both normative and descriptive models. Normative models specify what a person should do. They often provide a standard for comparing how closely actual decisions match normative decisions. Descriptive models attempt to describe how people actually arrive at decisions. The relation between normative and descriptive models is a theme that occurs throughout the discussion of risky decision making. The final section of this chapter discusses medical decision making as an example of a complex skill. The discussion illustrates how psychological models can be used to describe medical diagnosis.

Making choices

Compensatory Models

One reason decisions can be difficult is that alternatives usually consist of many dimensions. If one of the dimensions is not very attractive, the decision maker must decide whether to eliminate that alternative or continue to consider it because its other dimensions may be very attractive. For example, a person may purchase a car with low gas mileage because of the smooth ride and spaciousness of a large car. Decision-making models that allow attractive dimensions to compensate for unattractive dimensions are called *compensatory models*. The advice given by Benjamin Franklin quoted at the beginning of this chapter is consistent with a compensatory model because Franklin attempted to combine both the pros and cons of each option.

An *additive model* is a kind of compensatory model. An additive model combines both attractive and unattractive dimensions to arrive at a total score for each alternative. Consider the case of John Smith. John has lived in a college dormitory for three consecutive years. It is now his senior year, and he feels that it is time to enjoy the greater freedom that an apartment can offer. He has found two rather attractive apartments and must select one. John decides to follow Ben Franklin's advice and systematically list the advantages and disadvantages of each. First he lists the attributes that will influence his decision, and then he rates each on a scale that ranges from -3 (a very negative impression) to $+3$ (a very positive impression). Here are his ratings:

	Apartment A	*Apartment B*
Rent	+1	+2
Noise level	-2	+3
Distance to campus	+3	-1
Cleanliness	+2	+2
	+4	+6

The sums of the ratings for the various dimensions of the two apartments reveal that John's best choice is to select apartment B, which is rated higher.

There are several ways of modifying the summation rule that could change the results. First, the four attributes were equally weighted in the example. If some attributes are more important to John than others, he would want to emphasize these attributes when making his decision. For instance, he might want to emphasize distance from campus if he lives in a cold climate and has to walk to classes. If this variable is twice as important as the others, he could multiply his ratings of distance by 2 to give this dimension greater emphasis. The sum of the ratings would then be +7 for apartment A and +5 for apartment B. Second, adding the ratings of the four attributes does not account for how the attributes might interact. Although apartment A is very noisy, it is so close to campus that it would be convenient to use the library as a place to study. The high noise level is therefore not as detrimental as it would be if the apartment were the only convenient place to study. The low rating for noise level should perhaps be modified to take into account the interaction between that dimension and distance to campus.

A model that is very similar to the additive model is called the *additive-difference model*. The latter compares two alternatives by totaling the differences between their values on each dimension. The values on each dimension are shown below. The third column shows the value obtained from subtracting the second column from the first.

	Apartment A	Apartment B	Difference
Rent	+1	+2	−1
Noise level	−2	+3	−5
Distance to campus	+3	−1	+4
Cleanliness	+2	+2	0
	+4	+6	−2

The sum of the differences is −2, which implies that apartment A is two units less attractive than apartment B. The additive model implies the same conclusion: the sum of the ratings for apartment A is 2 less than the sum of the ratings for apartment B. Although the additive and the additive-difference models usually result in the same conclusion, the search for information is different. The additive model evaluates all dimensions of one alternative before considering the next alternative. The additive-difference model compares the two alternatives attribute by attribute. If there are more than two alternatives, a given alternative is compared to the best of the preceding alternatives.

Both the additive and the additive-difference models describe a good procedure for evaluating alternatives. Both evaluate alternatives on all of their dimensions and allow for attractive values to compensate for unattractive values. The models can be used to make realistic decisions, as is illustrated in Box 14.2. The article describes an additive model in which points are assigned to six dimensions depending on how much information each provides. The decision to proceed with further investigation is based on the sum of the points.

Although Benjamin Franklin's advice was good, we may question how often we follow it. The examples demonstrate that the additive model provides a systematic procedure for making decisions, but are we really this systematic in making decisions? How often do we take the time to make the kind of calculations required by the models? Perhaps some other model might better describe how we actually make choices. The alternative to a compensatory model is a *noncompensatory* model, in which unattractive dimensions result in elimination of alternatives.

Noncompensatory Models

If we do not calculate, how *do* we make decisions? Tversky (1972) has proposed that we make choices by gradually eliminating less attractive alternatives. His theory is called *elimination by aspects* because it assumes that the elimination is based on the sequential evaluation of the attributes—aspects—of the alternatives. If the attribute of an alternative does not satisfy some minimum criterion, that alternative is eliminated from the choice set.

Consider the case of Mrs. Green, who is looking for a new car. If Mrs. Green has only $7000 to spend, she may first eliminate from her set of possible choices those cars that cost over $7000. She may also be interested in gas economy and eliminate cars that cannot travel at least 25 miles on a gallon of gas. By continuing to select attributes and rejecting those that do not satisfy some minimum criterion, she will continue to eliminate alternatives until there is only a single car remaining that satisfies all her criteria.

The final choice, based on this procedure, depends on the order in which the attributes are evaluated. If the price of the car was one of the last attributes evaluated by Mrs. Green, she could have previously eliminated all cars costing under $7000, an undesirable situation if she only has $7000 to spend. The model therefore proposes that the attributes differ in importance, and the probability of selecting an attribute for evaluation depends on its importance. If price were a very important attribute, it would have a high probability of being selected early in the sequence.

The elimination-by-aspects model has the advantage that it does not require any calculations. The decision maker simply selects an attribute according to some probability that depends on the importance of that attribute. She then determines whether an alternative satisfies a minimum criterion for that attribute and eliminates those alternatives that do not meet the criterion.

The *conjunctive model*—a variant of elimination by aspects—requires that all the attributes satisfy minimum criteria before being selected. It differs from elimination by aspects by proposing that people finish evaluating one alternative before considering another. The first alternative

---

Box 14.2. Report Says Police Can Predict Which Burglaries Can Be Solved

WASHINGTON (AP)—A new study indicates that police can reliably predict which burglaries can be solved and recommends that they stop investigating cases unlikely to lead to an arrest.

The report, released yesterday by the Police Executive Research Forum, said "the characteristics of burglary cases, not follow-up investigations, determine the overall success or failure rate of burglary investigations."

The FBI reported there were 3.1 million burglaries in 1978, but fewer than one in five led to an arrest. It is the most common felony crime in the United States.

The study recommends police departments consider six key elements of preliminary burglary reports to decide whether to investigate further.

The forum, a national organization of state and local police executives, used police personnel in 26 cities, including Toledo, to test a rating system first developed in 1972 by the Stanford Research Institute in Alameda County [sic], Calif.

The six elements and the numerical value assigned to them were:
• Police arrival at scene: Five points for police arrival less than one hour after the crime; one point for arrival between one and 12 hours after the crime; three-tenths of a point for arrival 12 to 24 hours afterwards; no points for arrival more than 24 hours later.
  • Seven points for a civilian witness report.
  • One point if a policeman discovered the crime.
  • Seven points for usable fingerprints of a stranger at the scene.
  • Nine points for the name or description of a suspect.
  • One-tenth of a point for a description of a suspicious vehicle at the scene.
  • No points for all other information.

If the preliminary report had a total value of 10 points or less, the study predicted further investigation would not lead to an arrest. It predicted an arrest if the total was more than 10 points.

Analyzing the results of 12,001 past burglary investigations, the forum found that its method of weighing the factors was 85% accurate in predicting which cases led to a suspect being arrested, charged and turned over for prosecution.

Under the screening procedure used by the forum, 86.7% of the burglary cases would not be assigned for further investigation.

From the *Plain Dealer,* Cleveland, January 28, 1980. © Associated Press Newsfeatures. Reprinted by permission.

---

that satisfies all the minimum criteria is selected. The conjunctive model is an example of what Simon (1957) has called a *satisficing search.* Simon argued that limited capability to evaluate many alternatives often prevents people from selecting the best alternative. Instead, they are willing to settle for a good alternative—that is, one that satisfies all the minimum criteria. Other constraints, such as limits in time or availability, may also influence us to choose a good alternative rather than wait for the best alternative. For example, we may simply become tired of looking at apartments, or an apartment we liked may be rented by the time we return, so we will choose that alternative rather than continue searching for a better one.

Selecting a Strategy

The four models we have looked at differ with respect to how people search for information. John Payne (1976) took advantage of this difference in designing a procedure for evaluating which strategies people use. He presented information describing the dimensions of apartments, such as rent, cleanliness, noise level, and distance to campus (see Figure 14.1). The information describing each apartment was printed on the back of a card, which had to be turned over in order to reveal its value. Subjects were allowed to turn over as many cards as they needed to make their decision. The order in which they turned over the cards should reveal how they searched for information. Payne gathered additional evidence about how they arrived at a decision by asking them to think aloud as they evaluated the information on the cards.

Payne argued that the four decision-making models could be distinguished by the ways people search for information. Figure 14.2 shows a classification of the models according to whether the search is intradimensional or interdimensional and whether the number of dimensions searched is constant or variable across alternatives. This distinction can be clarified by comparing the additive model and the elimination-by-aspects model.

The additive model proposes that a person turns over cards representing one alternative and forms an overall score to represent the attractiveness of that alternative. The procedure is then repeated for the other alternatives. The search for information is *interdimensional* (across dimensions) because all relevant dimensions are evaluated for one alternative

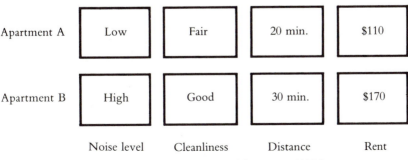

Figure 14.1. Information search task used by Payne (1976).

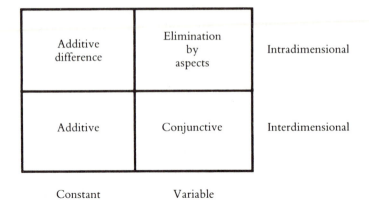

Additive difference	Elimination by aspects	Intradimensional
Additive	Conjunctive	Interdimensional
Constant	Variable	

Figure 14.2. Classification of decision models according to whether search is intra- or interdimensional across a constant or variable number of dimensions.

before the next alternative is evaluated. This method would require turning over cards in one row before going on to the next row (see Figure 14.1). Although it is not necessary to turn over all cards in each row (since some dimensions may not be important), the decision maker should turn over the same number of cards in each row so all alternatives can be compared along the same dimensions. The search therefore involves looking at a "constant" number of dimensions across alternatives.

The elimination-by-aspects procedure uses an *intradimensional* (within dimensions) search. The decision maker selects a dimension and evaluates that dimension across all the alternatives remaining in the choice set. In other words, the cards in one column would be turned over before the decision maker goes to another column. If some alternatives had already been eliminated, it would not be necessary to turn over the cards for those alternatives. This implies that the search evaluates a "variable" number of dimensions across alternatives. Some very expensive apartments could be eliminated after looking only at rent, whereas the final choice might require looking at many dimensions.

The other two models—the additive-difference model and the conjunctive model—can also be classified along the two dimensions (see Figure 14.2). The additive-difference and elimination-by-aspects models propose that people search by dimensions, selecting a dimension and evaluating alternatives on that dimension before selecting another dimension. The search is intradimensional. The additive and conjunctive models propose that people search by alternatives, selecting an alternative and evaluating the dimensions of that alternative before selecting another alternative. The search is therefore interdimensional. The models can also be differentiated by whether the same or a different number of dimensions is evaluated for each alternative. The additive and additive-difference models evaluate the same number of dimensions for each alternative, whereas the conjunctive and elimination-by-aspects models evaluate a variable number of dimensions for each alternative—as soon as a dimension fails to satisfy the criterion, the alternative is no longer considered. Some alternatives might be rejected after evaluation of the first dimension, and other alternatives might remain in the choice set after many dimensions are evaluated.

Payne did not expect that everyone would follow the same strategy in searching for information. His expectations were influenced by work on problem solving that demonstrated how individuals adapted their strategies to the demands of the task. An important characteristic of problem-solving strategies is that they attempt to keep the demands of the task within the limited capacity of the problem solver. Payne argued that the heuristics used by decision makers should also be adaptive to the information-processing demands of the task. One implication of this view is that the decision maker might change strategies as the demands of the task change.

Payne's results supported his expectations. Students were given a variety of tasks that differed in both the number of alternatives (2, 6, or 12) and the number of dimensions (4, 8, or 12). Table 14.1 shows how the search strategies varied with the number of alternatives in the choice set. The principal finding is that the students changed from searching a constant number of dimensions for two alternatives to a variable number of dimensions as the number of alternatives increased. The search strategies and verbal protocols revealed that, when asked to evaluate many alternatives, subjects reduced the complexity of the task by using the conjunctive and elimination-by-aspects procedures to eliminate some of the alternatives quickly. When only a few alternatives remained in the choice set, the subjects might then use one of the cognitively demanding

TABLE 14.1. Classification of Search Patterns as a Function of Alternatives Available.

	Search pattern			
	Interdimensional		Intradimensional	
Number of alternatives	Constant	Variable	Constant	Variable
2	12	3	18	3
4	6	11	2	17
8	3	15	0	18
12	2	12	0	22

From "Task Complexity and Contingent Processing in Decision Making: An Information Search and Protocol Analysis," by J. W. Payne. In *Organizational Behavior and Human Performance*, 1976, *16*, 366–387. Copyright 1976 by Academic Press, Inc. Reprinted by permission.

procedures—such as the additive or additive-difference strategies—to make the final evaluation and choice.

The following excerpt from a protocol illustrates the use of the elimination-by-aspects model to reduce the number of alternatives:

> I'm going to look at landlord attitude. In H it's fair. In D it's poor. In B it's fair, and in A it's good. In L the attitude is poor. In K it's poor. In J it's good, and in I it's poor. . . . So, that's important to me. . . . So, I'm not going to live any place where it's poor [Payne, 1976, p. 379].

The subject never again examined alternatives D, I, K, and L. Contrast this protocol with an excerpt illustrating the use of the additive-difference model to compare two alternatives.

> O.K., we have an A and a B. First look at the rent for both of them. The rent for A is $170 and the rent for B is $140. $170 is a little steep, but it might have a low noise level. So we'll check A's noise level. A's noise level is low. We'll go to B's noise level. It's high. Gee, I can't really very well study with a lot of noise. So I'll ask myself the question, is it worth spending that extra $30 a month for, to be able to study in my apartment [p. 378].

The two protocols reveal how a low value on a dimension results in elimination of an alternative in the elimination-by-aspects model. However, when the additive-difference model is used, an alternative scoring low on one dimension might still be selected if it scores high on other dimensions—in the example above the decision requires determining whether a lower rent will compensate for a high noise level.

Payne's (1976) analysis reveals how studying information search and verbal protocols can provide evidence on the kind of decision strategies people use to evaluate alternatives. It would be interesting to apply these techniques to "field research," where people would actually hunt for apartments. We would probably start with a list of potential apartments from a housing office or newspaper. These listings would provide us with only a few dimensions, but we would likely eliminate some alternatives on the basis of rent or location. When we actually visited the apartments, we would be receiving information by alternatives rather than by dimensions. In order to use an intradimensional search strategy, we would have to store the information and reorganize it. The most efficient strategy might be simply to retain the values of the most attractive apartment and compare the values with each new alternative, using an additive or additive-difference rule.

Estimating probabilities

We turn now to a somewhat more complex problem—making decisions under conditions of uncertainty. There was some amount of uncertainty in the previous examples. Although the distance of an apartment from campus is not likely to change, the noise level could drastically change if quiet students were replaced by members of a rock band. In the examples discussed in the rest of the chapter, however, uncertainty is a major factor.

Box 14.3 gives an example of a situation in which there is much uncertainty. Based on the best evidence available at that time, the National Aeronautics and Space Administration proposed that the odds were 152 to 1 against Skylab's injuring human beings. Odds are a ratio of two probabilities. In this particular case, the estimate of the probability that Skylab would not harm human life was 152 times as large as the estimate of the probability that it would.

Box 14.3. 152-to-1 Skylab Will Hurt No One

WASHINGTON (AP)—Skylab likely will tumble from orbit within weeks, but the odds are 152-to-1 against it harming human life anywhere in the world, space agency chief Robert A. Frosch said yesterday.

"For those who would like to know the likelihood that a particular person will be injured, it is about one chance in 600 billion," he said.

But Frosch, head of the National Aeronautics and Space Administration, conceded that the agency still has little idea exactly when or where the 79-ton space station will re-enter the earth's atmosphere.

He told a House Government Operations subcommittee that re-entry date "presently is predicted . . . between June 27 and July 21. There is a 50–50 probability that this will happen by July 9."

Scientists will have a better idea as time moves along, he said, but "at best we may be able to delay re-entry by a few hours through exercise of the spacecraft's stabilization system."

"The uncertainties are so large that nothing can be said at present as to where Skylab will re-enter, except that it will be within the limits of 50 degrees north and south latitude," he said. That includes all of the United States and Africa, much of Canada, and most of South America, Europe and Asia.

"Because 75 percent of the earth's surface in that band is water, it is quite likely reentry will occur over water," he said.

From the *Oakland Tribune,* Oakland, California, June 5, 1979.

The potential threat to human life caused by Skylab illustrates the importance of accurate estimates of probabilities in order to make wise decisions. Kahneman and Tversky have shown that probability estimates are based on heuristics that sometimes yield reasonable estimates but often do not. Two of these heuristics are availability and representativeness. Before reading further, answer the questions in Box 14.4 to determine how you might make use of these heuristics.

Box 14.4. Questions about Subjective Probabilities

1. How many cities that begin with the letter *F* do you think you can recall? Give your estimate before you start recalling examples.
2. Are there more words in the English language that start with the letter *K* or that have a *K* as their third letter?
3. Which is the more likely cause of death—breast cancer or diabetes?
4. If a family has three boys (B) and three girls (G), which sequence of births is more likely—B B B G G G or B G G G B G B?
5. Are you more likely to find 60 boys in a random sample of 100 children or 600 boys in a random sample of 1000 children?

Availability

The *availability* heuristic proposes that we evaluate the probability of an event by judging the ease with which relevant instances come to mind (Tversky & Kahneman, 1973). For example, we may assess the divorce rate in a community by recalling divorces among our acquaintances. When availability is highly correlated with actual frequency, estimates should be accurate. But there are other factors besides the actual frequency of occurrence that can influence availability and cause systematic biases.

In the first experiment conducted by Tversky and Kahneman (1973) subjects were shown nine letters, which were to be used to construct words. They were given 7 seconds to estimate the number of words they believed they could produce in 2 minutes. The average number of words actually constructed varied from 1.3 (for the letters $XUZONLCJM$) to 22.4 (for $TAPCERHOBO$). The correlation between the estimates and the number of words produced over 16 problems was .96.

In another experiment subjects were asked to estimate the number of instances they could recall from a category in 2 minutes. The average number of instances recalled varied from 4.1 (city names beginning with the letter *F*) to 23.7 (four-legged animals). The correlation between estimation and word production was .93 over 16 categories. The high correlation between estimation and production revealed that subjects were quite accurate in estimating the relative availability of instances in the different conditions.

Some instances, however, might be difficult to retrieve from memory even though they occur frequently. The availability hypothesis would predict that frequency should be underestimated in this case. Suppose you sample a word at random from an English text. Is it more likely that the word starts with a *K* or that *K* is its third letter? The availability hypothesis proposes that people attempt to answer this question by judging how easy it is to think of examples in each category. Since it is easier to think of words that begin with a certain letter, people should be biased toward responding that there are more words that start with the letter K than have a K in the third position. The median estimated ratio for each of five letters was that there were twice as many words in which that letter was the first letter, rather than the third letter, in the word. The estimates were obtained despite the fact that all five letters were actually more frequent in the third position.

Slovic, Fischhoff, and Lichtenstein (1976) have used the availability hypothesis to account for how people estimated the relative probability of 41 causes of death—including diseases, accidents, homicide, suicide, and natural hazards—which were combined into 106 pairs. A large sample of college students judged which member of the pair was the more likely cause of death; Table 14.2 shows how often they were correct as a function of the relative frequency of the two events. Examination of the events most seriously misjudged provided indirect support for the hypothesis that availability, particularly as influenced by the media, biases probability estimates. The frequencies of accidents, cancer, botulism, and tornadoes—all of which receive heavy media coverage—were greatly overestimated. Asthma and diabetes, which receive less media coverage,

TABLE 14.2. Judgments of Relative Frequency for Selected Pairs of Lethal Events.

Less likely	*More likely*	*True ratio*	*% Correct discrimination*
Asthma	Firearm accident	1.20	80
Breast cancer	Diabetes	1.25	23
Lung cancer	Stomach cancer	1.25	25
Leukemia	Emphysema	1.49	47
Stroke	All cancer	1.57	83
All accidents	Stroke	1.85	20
Pregnancy	Appendicitis	2.00	17
Tuberculosis	Fire and flames	2.00	81
Emphysema	All accidents	5.19	88
Polio	Tornado	5.30	71
Drowning	Suicide	9.60	70
All accidents	All diseases	15.50	57
Diabetes	Heart disease	18.90	97
Tornado	Asthma	20.90	42
Syphilis	Homicide	46.00	86
Botulism	Lightning	52.00	37
Flood	Homicide	92.00	91
Syphilis	Diabetes	95.00	64
Botulism	Asthma	920.00	59
Excess cold	All cancer	982.00	95
Botulism	Emphysema	10,600.00	86

From "Cognitive Processes and Societal Risk Taking," by P. Slovic, B. Fischhoff, and S. Lichtenstein. In J. S. Carroll and J. W. Payne (Eds.), *Cognition and Social Behavior*. Copyright 1976 by Lawrence Erlbaum Associates, Inc., Publishers. Reprinted by permission.

were underestimated. Similarly, the spectacular event fire—which often takes many victims and receives much media coverage—was perceived as considerably more frequent than the less spectacular event drowning, even though both are about equally frequent causes of death.

Representativeness

The *representativeness* heuristic states that the probability of an event is estimated by evaluating how similar it is to the essential properties of its population. Let us attempt to clarify this definition by considering some specific examples.

Kahneman and Tversky (1972) studied representativeness through a questionnaire given to students in college-preparatory high schools. Some of the questions were designed to measure the concept of randomness. A major characteristic of apparent randomness is the absence of any systematic patterns. The representativeness heuristic implies that people should judge orderly events as having low probability if they believe they were generated by a random process. This prediction was supported by the answers to one of the questions on the questionnaire:

> On each round of a game, 20 marbles are distributed at random among five children: Alan, Ben, Carl, Dan and Ed. Consider the following distributions:

	I			II	
Alan	4		Alan	4	
Ben	4		Ben	4	
Carl	5		Carl	4	
Dan	4		Dan	4	
Ed	3		Ed	4	

> In many rounds of the game will there be more results of type I or type II? [Kahneman & Tversky, 1972, p. 434]

The uniform distribution of marbles (II) is objectively more probable than the nonuniform distribution (I), but it appears too orderly to be generated by a random process. A significant majority of students selected distribution I as more probable than distribution II; the presence of some perturbation made the former seem more representative of a random process. Intuition regarding randomness is also illustrated by the fact that subjects estimated that the sequence of boy/girl births in the order B B B G G G was significantly less likely than the order G B B G B G, even though the two sequences are equally probable.

Furthermore, it was found that people ignore sample size when making probability estimates. A sample of events or objects is only part of the total population of those objects or events. Since the size of the sample does not reflect any particular property of its population, size should not influence representativeness. For example, finding 600 boys in a sample of 1000 babies was judged as likely as finding 60 boys in a sample of 100 babies, even though the latter event is much more likely. Although increasing sample size reduces the variance of a distribution, the students' estimates of probability distributions were uninfluenced by sample size.

This result was also obtained when students were asked to estimate posterior probabilities. Estimating posterior probabilities requires the revision of a probability on the basis of new evidence. A typical problem reads as follows:

> Consider two very large decks of cards, denoted A and B. In deck A, ⅚ of the cards are marked *X,* and ⅙ are marked *O*. In deck B, ⅙ of the cards are marked *X* and ⅚ are marked *O*. One of the decks has been selected by chance and 12 cards have been drawn from it, of which 8 are marked *X* and 4 are marked *O*. What do you think the probability is that the 12 cards were drawn from deck A, that is, from the deck in which most of the cards are marked *X*? [Kahneman & Tversky, 1972, p. 447]

The question was repeated for samples containing 4 *X*'s and 2 *O*'s, 40 *X*'s and 20 *O*'s, and 5 *X*'s and 1 *O*. The median estimate that deck A was selected was .70 when the sample ratio of *X* : *O* was 4 : 2, 8 : 4, and 40 : 20. The estimate was .83 when the ratio of *X* : *O* was 5 : 1. The results reveal that the probability estimates were influenced by the ratio of *X*'s to *O*'s, which does not consider differences in sample size. The true posterior probabilities depend on the difference between the number of *X*'s and *O*'s. Notice that, for a constant ratio, the difference between *X*'s and *O*'s increases as the sample size increases. A sample of 40 *X*'s and 20 *O*'s provides the most evidence in favor of deck A, not the sample containing 5 *X*'s and 1 *O*.

Revising Probability Estimates

A central issue in the study of risky decision making is how people revise their probability estimates when they obtain new evidence. A normative model called *Bayes's theorem* has made this an interesting area of study because it is possible to evaluate human performance by observing how closely it corresponds to the model. There are several ways of writing Bayes's theorem; the following is the easiest to remember:

New odds = Old odds × Likelihood ratio

$$\frac{pr(H1|D)}{pr(H2|D)} = \frac{pr(H1)}{pr(H2)} \times \frac{pr(D|H1)}{pr(D|H2)}$$

The *new odds* is the ratio of the probabilities of hypothesis 1 (*H1*) and hypothesis 2 (*H2*) after the probabilities have been revised on the basis of new data (D). The *old odds* is the ratio of the probabilities of the two hypotheses before the data were obtained. The *likelihood ratio* is the probability of obtaining the data if $H1$ were true divided by the probability of obtaining the data if $H2$ were true. The new odds are calculated by multiplying the old odds and the likelihood ratio.

If the old odds are 3:1 in favor of $H1$ and the likelihood ratio is 1:2, then the new odds are 3:2. Odds can be converted into probabilities by keeping the numerator the same and forming a new denominator by adding the numerator and the original denominator. If the odds are 3:2, then the probability of $H1$ is $3/(3 + 2)$ or .6.

The major finding in studies that have used Bayes's theorem as a model is that people are usually conservative in revising their probability estimates (Edwards, 1968). Conservatism implies that people do not revise their estimates enough, and therefore their subjective probabilities are less extreme than the actual probabilities. Conservatism results in an underestimation of high probabilities and an overestimation of low probabilities. An example of conservatism is the question about the deck of cards in the Kahneman and Tversky questionnaire. The probability that deck A was selected is .96 when the sample consisted of 4 X's and 2 O's and higher for the other three samples. The subjective estimates were .70 for three of the four samples and .83 for the fourth sample.

The question about whether deck A or deck B was selected is typical of the kind of questions in many of the studies that have used Bayes's theorem as a model. If $H1$ is the probability that deck A was selected and $H2$ is the probability that deck B was selected, then $pr(H1) = pr(H2) = \frac{1}{2}$, since a deck was randomly selected. The old odds—the ratio of these two probabilities—is simply equal to 1 in this case since the probabilities are equal. The likelihood ratio is calculated by dividing $pr(D|H1)$ by $pr(D|H2)$, where the data are the number of X's and O's in the sample of cards. These probabilities can be calculated by using standard statistical procedures.

When Bayes's theorem is applied to real-world decision tasks, it is sometimes necessary to estimate either the old odds or the likelihood ratio because objective probabilities are not known. Consider a hypothetical case in which the Soviet Union dramatically increases its military budget. Do the data imply that the Soviet Union is now more likely to be involved in a war? In order to calculate the new odds for this event, it is necessary to know the old odds—$pr(\text{war})/pr(\text{no war})$—and the likelihood ratio—$pr(\text{budget increase}|\text{war})/pr(\text{budget increase}|\text{no war})$. Since we do not know either of these values, we would have to estimate them. One difficulty in evaluating how well people do in realistic decision tasks is that the correct answer can be computed only when the old odds and likelihood ratio are known. If we assume, however, that people will be conservative in complex, real-world tasks, as they usually are in laboratory tasks, then the best decision makers should be those who are least conservative. The next section illustrates how this assumption has been used to evaluate performance in a complex military task (Edwards, Phillips, Hays, & Goodman, 1968).

Probabilistic Information Processing Systems (PIP)

One way to improve decision making is to use a computer to carry out calculations based on a normative model. Edwards, Phillips, Hays, and Goodman (1968) designed a Probabilistic Information Processing System (PIP) that combined human and machine to carry out a realistic Bayesian task efficiently. The experiment, which was begun in 1964, described a hypothetical state of the world as it might appear in 1975. Subjects were given a 27-page fictitious history of the world between 1964 and 1975. The history provided information that would help them evaluate five hypotheses ($H1$ through $H5$):

> $H1$: Russia and China are about to attack North America. $H2$: Russia is about to attack the United Confederation of European States. $H3$: Russia is about to attack the United Arab Republic. $H4$: China is about to attack Japan. $H5$: Some other major conflict is about to break out.

Subjects were told that, at the beginning of the experiment, the odds are $5:1$ in favor of peace for each hypothesis. During the course of the experiment they received 60 items of data from three different sources: a ballistic missile early warning system, an intelligence system, and a reconnaissance satellite system. After receiving each new piece of evidence, subjects were required to revise their estimates for each of the five hypotheses.

A typical intelligence system report might look like this:

> Judging from a careful study by our agents of the production of Soviet parachute factories and military boot shops, our military panel estimates that Soviet paratroop units have been increased by about 20 percent in the last eight months [Edwards et al., 1968, p. 257].

A typical satellite system report might look like this:

> At 0630 this morning, two squadrons of conventional submarines sailed from Vladivostok. They steamed in a southerly direction until they were clear of the harbor and then submerged. Evaluation: probably routine exercises, though this is an unusually large force [p. 257].

The purpose of the experiment was to determine whether the use of a computer would assist people in revising their probability estimates. One group (PIP) used the computer system. Subjects in this group supplied a likelihood ratio for each hypothesis ($H1$–$H5$) that specified the likelihood of receiving that piece of evidence if the hypothesis were true. The computer then multiplied the current (old) odds for that hypothesis and the likelihood ratio to compute the new odds. The PIP group was not shown the old odds or the new odds; they simply estimated a likelihood ratio for each of the five hypotheses whenever they received new evidence. The other group (POP) directly estimated the new odds for each of the five hypotheses whenever they received new evidence.

If I were a subject in the PIP group and received the report that two squadrons of submarines sailed from Vladivostok, I might reason as follows: The report increases the probability of an attack by the Soviet Union, but since submarines travel so slowly, the attack is more likely to involve Europe than North America. I will set the likelihood ratio favoring an attack as 2:1 against North America, 3:1 against the United Arab Republic, and 4:1 against the United Confederation of European States. I don't think the evidence is relevant to hypotheses 4 and 5, so I will leave these probabilities unchanged by using 1 as a likelihood ratio. The computer then multiplies the old odds by the likelihood ratio to compute new odds for each of the five hypotheses. If I were a subject in the POP group, I would estimate the new odds directly rather than estimate the likelihood ratio. If the old odds were 2:5 that Russia and China would attack North America, I might decide to change them to 3:5 after learning about the submarines.

The results of an extensive research project revealed that the odds computed from the likelihood ratios supplied by subjects in the PIP group were much less conservative than the odds estimated by subjects in the POP group. For example, when the odds of the PIP group were 99:1 in favor of war, the odds of the POP group were 4.0:1, and when the odds of the PIP group were 99:1 in favor of peace, the odds of the POP group were 11.9:1.

When a computer used a likelihood ratio supplied by a person and Bayes's theorem, its calculation of the new odds was much less conservative than the odds estimated by a person. One reason this was so is that subjects in the PIP group simply estimated likelihood ratios and never knew the value of the current odds. If they knew the current odds before estimating the likelihood ratio, subjects might change their estimates of the likelihood ratio to manipulate the odds rather than simply estimate the likelihood of the data. When subjects in the PIP group were shown the current odds before estimating the likelihood ratio, they did respond with more conservative estimates of the likelihood ratio in order to avoid extreme odds. Their degree of conservatism was intermediate between the PIP group without feedback and the POP group.

The results of this study clearly demonstrated that the use of a computer can dramatically reduce the degree of conservatism often found in Bayesian tasks. Unfortunately, it is not possible in Edwards's task to calculate the correct odds since there are no objective probabilities to use in the likelihood ratios. However, when the PIP and POP groups were compared on a more artificial task, in which the correct odds could be calculated, the PIP group performed more accurately. Even the PIP group was slightly conservative when compared with the correct odds, although the POP group was much more conservative and therefore much less accurate.

Expected value

Estimating probabilities accurately is an important decision-making skill, but it is not sufficient for making good decisions. Imagine a situation in which the United States' oil interests in the Middle East are threatened. The response to this situation will depend in part on the probability that the threat is a real one. But the response also depends on the perceived consequences of various courses of action the government might take. For example, one response might be to increase American military forces in the Middle East. This course of action, like other alternative actions, has both advantages and disadvantages. It is therefore necessary to assess both the probability of events and the consequences of various actions when making decisions.

When we considered the different choice models in the first section of this chapter, we assigned values to the different dimensions of each alternative in the choice set. It is also necessary to assign values in risky decision making, but in addition we have to combine the values of different outcomes with the probabilities that they will occur. A normative procedure for combining probabilities and values is called *expected value*. Like other normative models, expected value provides a standard of reference against which psychologists can compare how people make decisions. Psychologists have usually made this comparison by designing rather simple gambling situations in which they can inform people about probabilities (of winning and losing) and values (amount won or lost). The expected value is the average amount of money people can expect to win or lose each time they decide to gamble. Let us see how it is calculated.

Calculating Expected Value

Expected value is calculated by multiplying the value of each possible outcome by its probability and adding the products. Its use can be illustrated by a simple game. I'm going to offer you the opportunity to play the game, and you must decide whether it would be to your advantage to play. I'm going to roll a fair die. If the number 6 appears, you win $5. If one of the other five numbers appears, you win nothing. It costs $1 every time you play. Should you participate?

Expected value allows you to estimate the average amount of money you can expect to win or lose on every roll of the die. You can calculate this amount if you know the probability of a win—$pr(W)$; the amount of a win—$v(W)$; the probability of a loss—$pr(L)$; and the amount of a loss—$v(L)$. Substituting these amounts into the equation below yields

$$\text{Expected value} = pr(W) \times v(W) + pr(L) \times v(L)$$
$$\text{Expected value} = \tfrac{1}{6} \times \$4 + \tfrac{5}{6} \times -\$1 = -\$\tfrac{1}{6}$$

The probability of a win is $\tfrac{1}{6}$, and the amount of a win is $4 ($5 minus the $1 entry fee). The probability of a loss is $\tfrac{5}{6}$, and the value of a loss is $1. The expected value of this game is $-\$\tfrac{1}{6}$, implying that you would lose an average of about 17 cents every time you played the game. A decision based on a normative model should be to play the game for a positive expected value and not to play the game for a negative expected value.

A problem with using expected value as a descriptive model is that it does not always predict behavior. Gambling casinos are usually crowded with people playing games that have negative expected values. People also buy insurance in spite of its negative expected value. Since insurance companies pay out less money in claims than they collect as premiums, a purchaser of insurance can expect to lose money. And yet the purchase of insurance can be justified on the basis that it provides protection against a large financial setback.

Subjective Expected Utility

Two changes were made in the concept of expected value in order to make it more descriptive of actual behavior. The first change replaced the value of an outcome by its utility. *Utility* is the subjective value of an outcome, or what the outcome is actually worth to an individual. If people enjoy gambling, the act of gambling has utility in addition to the money that is won or lost. If you enjoy winning money and don't mind losing money, then you could formulate a positive expected utility for the game I described earlier. If the utility of a win—$u(W)$—is $6 rather than $4, and the utility of a loss—$u(L)$—remains at $1, the expected utility would be positive rather than negative.

$$\text{Expected utility} = pr(W) \times u(W) + pr(L) \times u(L)$$
$$\text{Expected utility} = \tfrac{1}{6} \times \$6 + \tfrac{5}{6} \times -\$1 = \$\tfrac{1}{6}$$

The expected utility model could also account for the reason people buy insurance if the utility of money increases faster than the actual value of money as the amount increases. A person would then be relatively more concerned about losing a substantial amount of money at one time than about paying out the much smaller premiums each year.

A second change in the expected value model was to make it more descriptive by replacing probabilities by subjective probabilities. When decision makers don't know the actual probabilities, they must use subjective probabilities, or what they think the actual probabilities are. As we learned in the previous section, subjective probabilities often differ from actual probabilities. *Subjective expected utility* is calculated the same way as expected value, but probabilities are replaced by subjective probabilities (*spr*) and values are replaced by utilities. The subjective probability of each outcome is multiplied by its utility, and the products are added.

$$\text{Subjective expected utility} = spr(W) \times u(W) + spr(L) \times u(L)$$

By replacing probabilities with subjective probabilities and values with utilities, the subjective expected utility model bases its predictions on subjective information. Therefore, it should be more accurate than the expected value model in predicting people's decisions. Like the expected value model, however, it assumes that people place an equal emphasis on the four components—$u(W)$, $spr(W)$, $u(L)$, and $spr(L)$. It also implies that people have to calculate since it is necessary to multiply the utility of events by their subjective probabilities.

Information-Processing Models

We learned earlier that decision rules like elimination by aspects or the conjunctive rule simplified decision making by allowing the decision maker to eliminate alternatives without having to calculate. When evaluating the attractiveness of a gamble, people are likely to consider the probability of winning, the amount of a win, the probability of losing, and the amount of a loss. But they may find it difficult to mentally compute expected value or even to place equal emphasis on the four risk dimensions, as implied by the model.

Slovic and Lichtenstein (1968) tested the hypothesis that people will be more influenced by some dimensions than others. They had subjects evaluate the attractiveness of gambles, using a special type of gamble illustrated in Figure 14.3. A duplex gamble requires that the subject spin two spinners. The first spinner determines whether he will win money, and the second spinner determines whether he will lose money. There are four possible outcomes for the gamble shown in Figure 14.3: win $1 and

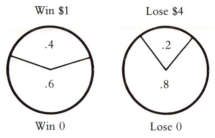

Figure 14.3. Example of a duplex gamble where $pr(W)=.4$, $v(W)=\$1$, $pr(L)=.2$, and $v(L)=\$4$. *(From "Relative Importance of Probabilities and Payoffs in Risk Taking," by P. Slovic and S. Lichtenstein. In* Journal of Experimental Psychology Monograph, *1968, 78(3, Pt. 2). Copyright 1968 by the American Psychological Association. Reprinted by permission.)*

lose \$4 (a net loss of \$3), win \$1 and lose nothing, win nothing and lose nothing, or win nothing and lose \$4. Slovic and Lichtenstein used duplex gambles in order to change the probability of winning and the probability of losing independently. This is not possible in a standard gamble (represented by only one spinner) because the probability of winning is equal to 1 minus the probability of losing. It is not possible to determine whether people are more influenced by the probability of winning or the probability of losing if the two probabilities cannot be varied independently.

Slovic and Lichtenstein used two methods to evaluate the attractiveness of gambles. One method used a simple rating scale that varied from −5 (strong preference for not playing) to +5 (strong preference for playing). The second method required that subjects indicate the largest amount of money they would be willing to pay the experimenter in order to play the gamble (for attractive gambles) or in order to not have to play the gamble (for unattractive gambles). In both cases Slovic and Lichtenstein correlated the judged attractiveness of gambles with the four risk dimensions. The correlations should be approximately equal if people were placing an equal emphasis on all four dimensions. The results indicated that there was a large difference in the correlations. A subject's highest correlation was, on the average, twice the size of the lowest correlation. The data indicated that the responses of many subjects were determined by one or two risk dimensions and were unresponsive to changes in the values of the less important dimensions.

The data also revealed that the particular dimension emphasized varied across subjects and that the most important dimension was influenced by whether the subject responded with a numerical rating or a monetary response. Table 14.3 shows that, when subjects used a rating scale, the probability of a win was the most important dimension for 50% of the subjects. When subjects responded in terms of the amount of

**TABLE 14.3.   Percentage of Subjects for Whom
a Given Risk Dimension Was Most Important.**

	Risk dimension			
	$pr(W)$	$v(W)$	$pr(L)$	$v(L)$
Rating group	50	9	15	26
Bidding group	18	19	10	53

From "Relative Importance of Probabilities and Payoffs in Risk Taking," by P. Slovic and S. Lichtenstein. In *Journal of Experimental Psychology Monograph,* 1968, *78*(3, Pt. 2). Copyright 1968 by the American Psychological Association. Reprinted by permission.

money they would be willing to pay the experimenter (bid), the amount of a loss was the most important dimension for 53% of the subjects. In other words, the response scale influences the way a gamble is evaluated. When responses were expressed in terms of money, subjects attended more to a monetary dimension—$v(L)$—than when the responses were numerical ratings.

Normative models cannot explain either the finding that people place an unequal emphasis on the risk dimensions or the finding that the emphasized dimension is influenced by the response scale. If people are not following normative models, do their ratings of relative attractiveness differ from the relative attractiveness of the gambles as determined by expected value? The average correlation between subjects' ratings and expected value was .79 for numerical ratings and .80 for monetary ratings. The correlations indicate that the expected value model is a fairly accurate predictor of ratings even though subjects attend more to some dimensions than to others. Although models based on expected value are often useful in predicting responses, results like those obtained by Slovic and Lichtenstein help reveal how people simplify the task and how their decisions depart from expected value.

To summarize, expected value models are reasonably good, though not perfect, predictors of decision-making behavior. Their predictions can often be improved when utilities are substituted for values and subjective probabilities for probabilities. It should also be possible to improve their predictions by taking into account the fact that people may emphasize some dimensions of risk more than others.

Medical decision making

Medical diagnosis is an excellent example of a complex skill that we can relate to many of the issues raised in this chapter. A recent book, *Medical Problem Solving* (Elstein, Shulman, & Sprafka, 1978), summarizes the results of an extensive investigation of how doctors arrive at a diagnosis.

The book is important not only because of the importance of medical decision making, but because the results are discussed within the context of models of human information processing and normative decision making.

Simulation of Medical Cases

Elstein, Shulman, and Sprafka report a series of experiments employing various methodologies. Some experiments used actors who played the role of patients; others simply used written descriptions of symptoms. Some experiments allowed the physicians to request whatever information they wanted; other experiments presented information in a fixed order. Some experiments studied what the physicians did; others attempted to train medical students to become better decision makers.

I will summarize the results of one experiment that used "high-fidelity simulation": the simulation attempted to create a situation that closely resembled the actual world of the physician. Actors from the Department of Theater at Michigan State University were carefully trained to simulate patients. The cases were based upon actual clinical records and presented problems that a general internist practicing in a community hospital could expect to see. Each physician could decide how much information to collect, including the results of (simulated) laboratory findings. The physicians knew the cases were simulated, but most of the 24 who participated thought the simulations were convincing.

The interactions between physicians and patients were recorded on videotape. The physicians were instructed to think aloud during the interaction and comment on what they had learned or were about to do and why. Additional information was obtained after the session, when an experimenter questioned each physician while both reviewed the videotape.

The simulation experiment presented three cases, all played by college students. The first case was a female student with three main complaints—extreme fatigue and excessive sleeping, poor appetite, and severe headache. Further history showed mild chills and fever with general aching of about five days' duration. Information that could be obtained from a physical examination included enlarged tonsils and mild jaundice.

Results of the Simulation

Table 14.4 shows the most frequent hypotheses for this case and the number of physicians who considered each during different stages of the examination. The initial hypotheses are general—infection, for example.

One of the major findings across all the simulation experiments was that physicians start to form hypotheses early in the examination, before they have much data. The number of physicians who generated at least one hypothesis during the first 5 minutes was 20 (of 24) in simulation 1, 18 in simulation 2, and 23 in simulation 3. The process of gathering data can be thought of as a search through a large search space. If the physician simply gathered data unsystematically until a solution emerged, the size of the search space would be so large that a diagnosis could never be reached in a reasonable amount of time. Forming hypotheses early in the sequence guides the acquisition of additional data, thus limiting the search by verifying or modifying current hypotheses. Table 14.4 reveals that the number of physicians who considered mononucleosis as a hypothesis increased as additional data were obtained.

The number of hypotheses that were considered at any one time was very consistent across problems, with the means ranging between 2 and 4. On all three simulations the average number of hypotheses considered at any one time remained relatively constant through various stages of the examination, implying that, when a hypothesis was rejected, it was replaced by another or by a reformulation of the rejected hypothesis. It is likely that the hypotheses serve as organizers of data in STM since the range of 2 to 4 is consistent with the number of chunks of complex material that can be retained at once in memory (Simon, 1974).

TABLE 14.4. Hypotheses Considered during Various Stages of the Diagnosis.

Hypothesis[a]	Total at any point	As first hypothesis	At quarter mark	At halfway mark	At conclusion
Infection[b]	21	14	15	19	5
Infectious mononucleosis	20	2	9	15	20
Infectious hepatitis	18	5	9	11	5
Hemolytic anemia	17				
Hereditary spherocytic anemia	10				8
Viral illness or viral respiratory infection	8		4	6	1
Meningitis	7		5	4	0
Anemia	6			3	
Influenza	4		3	1	0
Encephalitis	4		2	3	0
Leukemia	4			1	0
Lymphoma	4		0	0	1

[a]Twelve hypotheses in addition to those listed were each considered by one or two subjects at some point in the problem.

[b]Includes acute febrile illness, viral illness, bacterial infection, and viral respiratory infection.

From *Medical Problem Solving*, by A. S. Elstein, L. S. Shulman, and S. A. Sprafka. Copyright 1978 by Harvard University Press. Reprinted by permission.

A central issue in the study was how physicians combine information to form hypotheses. Elstein's search for a model that describes what physicians do, rather than what they ought to do, began with the observation that in all the protocols the physicians were consistently able to rank hypotheses but were unable to give more precise estimates of probability. Attempts to obtain estimates of the odds or probability assigned to each hypothesis, likelihood ratios, or estimates of the correlation between cues and hypotheses were all unsuccessful.

The physicians did, however, spontaneously classify the cues as positive, negative, or noncontributory for each hypothesis. A simple additive model, in which cues that were interpreted as positive evidence were rated $+1$, cues that were interpreted as negative evidence were rated -1, and noncontributory cues were rated 0, was fairly successful in predicting which hypotheses would be selected. Note that this procedure is identical to the procedure suggested by Ben Franklin. Although it is possible to represent medical diagnosis as a Bayesian task, physicians apparently use a much simpler procedure to evaluate hypotheses. The simpler procedure avoids the cognitive demands of estimating the initial probabilities of diseases, estimating likelihood ratios, and carrying out the computations to compute the new odds.

Heuristics for Medical Students

In the concluding chapter of their book Elstein and his coinvestigators offer a set of guidelines for medical students.

1. Generating a list of alternative hypotheses:
    a. *Multiple competing hypotheses.* Think of a number of diagnostic possibilities compatible with the major complaints and preliminary findings. Avoid making snap diagnoses.
    b. *Probability.* Consider the most common diagnoses first.
    c. *Utility.* Consider seriously those diagnoses for which effective therapies are available and in which failure to treat would be a serious omission.
2. Gathering data:
    d. *Planned testing.* Form a reasoned plan for testing your hypotheses, one that considers both probability and utility. Sequence laboratory tests to rule out first the most common diseases (probability) and next the disease most needing treatment (utility).
    e. *Branching and screening.* The physical examination should use branching procedures. Develop adequate screening techniques to make overly detailed examinations unnecessary.
    f. *Cost/benefit calculation.* Consider the harm tests might do and their cost. Balance these against the information to be gained.

g. *Precision.* Strive for the degree of reliability needed for the decision. More is unnecessary.

3. Combining data and selecting a course of action:

h. *Disconfirmatory evidence.* Actively seek out and evaluate evidence that tends to rule out any hypothesis as well as the evidence that tends to confirm it.

i. *Multiple diagnoses.* Don't forget the possibility that a patient with multiple complaints has more than one disease.

j. *Bayes's theorem.* Revise probabilities after collecting data. If the findings are relatively more likely in diagnosis A than in diagnosis B, revise your opinion in favor of A.

k. *Probability and utility.* When a course of action is selected, consider both the probability of the diagnoses for which the action is appropriate and the benefits and penalties that would follow. Combine these two considerations to estimate expected value and choose so as to maximize expected value.

These guidelines represent an attempt to combine the insights of normative decision models and cognitive psychology to formulate a practical tool for students. They are guidelines that should be useful for many tasks concerned with risky decision making. How well they can be followed, both with and without computer aids, remains one of the exciting questions for future investigation.

Summary

Making decisions usually requires evaluating at least two alternatives, each differing from the other along a number of dimensions. Selecting an alternative requires the decision maker to combine this information to form an overall evaluation for each alternative. The study of how people search for information provides evidence about decision strategies.

Four of the more popular decision models can be differentiated by whether people compare the alternatives dimension by dimension (intradimensional) or alternative by alternative (interdimensional), and whether they evaluate the same number or a variable number of dimensions for each alternative. In the elimination-by-aspects model alternatives are compared by dimensions, and the number of dimensions evaluated varies across alternatives. The conjunctive model is similar but considers only one alternative at a time; the first alternative that satisfies the minimum criteria for each dimension is selected. The additive and additive-difference models require that the same number of dimensions be evaluated across alternatives. The additive model assigns a numerical score to each dimension and sums the scores to determine the relative attractiveness of each alternative. The additive-difference model compares alternatives dimension by dimension and determines the difference between the scores on each dimension; the sum of the differences determines which alternative is more attractive.

Risky decision making refers to decisions that are concerned with uncertainty—for example, evaluating the potential threat of a nuclear reactor, buying insurance, and diagnosing medical problems. In order to make good decisions, it is necessary to make accurate estimates of probabilities. Probability estimates are often based on heuristics, which sometimes yield reasonable estimates but often do not. Two heuristics are availability and representativeness. The availability heuristic proposes that we evaluate the probability of an event by judging the ease with which relevant instances can be recalled. The representativeness heuristic states that the probability of an event is estimated by evaluating how similar it is to the essential properties of its population.

Bayes's theorem is a normative procedure for revising probabilities on the basis of new data. Studies of how people revise their probability estimates usually find that people are conservative, resulting in estimates that are less extreme than the probabilities calculated from Bayes's theorem. Conservatism can be greatly reduced if people estimate the likelihood ratio, and a computer multiplies the estimate and the current odds to compute the new odds.

Expected value is a normative procedure for making decisions. Expected value is calculated by multiplying the value of events by their probability of occurring and summing the products. Subjective expected utility is a modified version of this procedure in which subjective values (utilities) replace values and subjective probabilities replace probabilities. The expected value model can be further modified by allowing for the possibility that people may emphasize some components of the model more than others.

Physicians use several heuristics to simplify the task of diagnosing medical problems. They form hypotheses early in the diagnosis to guide their collection of data. They seem to use a simple additive model to combine the data, adding the number of positive cues and subtracting the number of negative cues. The authors of the book *Medical Problem Solving* use the results of their research to recommend a list of heuristics for training medical students. Future studies should focus on how well students can follow these heuristics and whether medical decision making can be improved if a computer is used to combine probabilities by using Bayes's theorem.

Recommended reading

A review article by Slovic, Fischhoff, and Lichtenstein (1977) summarizes recent research on decision making. A statistical model that has influenced many studies of decision making is multiple linear regression.

Dawes (1979) evaluated the success of this approach, and Hammond (1971) recommended using the linear model and computer-implemented feedback to improve performance on decision-making tasks. Slovic and Lichtenstein (1971) compared the multiple linear regression and Bayesian approaches, and Shanteau (1975) evaluated an information-integration approach to risky decision making. The development of expected value as a psychological model was discussed by Payne (1973). Beach (1975) reviewed studies on the application of Bayesian models to military, business, and medical decisions. Other applications include the study of jury (Penrod & Hastie, 1980) and medical (Fox, 1980) decision making.

References

Adams, M. J. Models of word recognition. *Cognitive Psychology*, 1979, *11*, 133–176.

Adamson, R. E. Functional fixedness as related to problem solving: A repetition of those experiments. *Journal of Experimental Psychology*, 1952, *44*, 288–291.

Anderson, J. R. *Language, memory and thought*. Hillsdale, N. J.: Erlbaum, 1976.

Anderson, J. R. Arguments concerning representations for mental imagery. *Psychological Review*, 1978, *85*, 249–277.

Anderson, J. R., & Reder, L. M. An elaborative processing explanation of depth of processing. In L. S. Cermak & F. I. M. Craik (Eds.), *Levels of processing in human memory*. Hillsdale, N. J.: Erlbaum, 1979.

Anderson, R. C., & Pichert, J. W. Recall of previously unrecallable information following a shift in perspective. *Journal of Verbal Learning and Verbal Behavior*, 1978, *17*, 1–12.

Aronson, E. *The social animal*. San Francisco: W. H. Freeman, 1972.

Atkinson, R. C. Ingredients for a theory of instruction. *American Psychologist*, 1972, *27*, 921–931. (a)

Atkinson, R. C. Optimizing the learning of a second-language vocabulary. *Journal of Experimental Psychology*, 1972, *96*, 124–129. (b)

Atkinson, R. C., & Raugh, M. R. An application of the mnemonic keyword method to the acquisition of a Russian vocabulary. *Journal of Experimental Psychology: Human Learning and Memory*, 1975, *104*, 126–133.

Atkinson, R. C., & Shiffrin, R. M. Human memory: A proposed system and its control processes. In K. W. Spence & J. T. Spence (Eds.), *The psychology of learning and motivation* (Vol. 2). New York: Academic Press, 1968.

Atkinson, R. C., & Shiffrin, R. M. The control of short-term memory. *Scientific American*, 1971, *225*, 82–90.

Atwood, M. E., & Polson, P. G. A process model for water jar problems. *Cognitive Psychology*, 1976, *8*, 191–216.

Atwood, M. E., Polson, P. G., Jeffries, R., & Ramsey, H. R. Planning as a process of synthesis (Technical Report SAI–78–144–DEN). Englewood, Colo.: Science Applications, December 1978.

Baddeley, A. D. *The psychology of memory*. New York: Basic Books, 1976.

Baddeley, A. D. The trouble with "levels": A re-examination of Craik and Lockhart's framework for memory research. *Psychological Review*, 1978, *85*, 139–152.

Baddeley, A., & Hitch, G. Working memory. In G. H. Bower (Ed.), *The psychology of learning and motivation* (Vol. 8). New York: Academic Press, 1974.

Bahrick, H. P. Maintenance of knowledge: Questions about memory we forgot to ask. *Journal of Experimental Psychology: General*, 1979, *108*, 296–308.

Bahrick, H. P., & Boucher, B. Retention of visual and verbal codes of the same stimuli. *Journal of Experimental Psychology*, 1968, *78*, 417–422.

Baron, J. Intelligence and general strategies. In G. Underwood (Ed.), *Strategies of information processing*. New York: Academic Press, 1978. (a)

Baron, J. The word-superiority effect: Perceptual learning from reading. In W. K. Estes (Ed.), *Handbook of learning and cognitive processes*. Hillsdale, N. J.: Erlbaum, 1978. (b)

Bartlett, F. C. *Remembering: A study in experimental and social psychology*. New York: Macmillan, 1932.

Beach, B. H. Expert judgment about uncertainty: Bayesian decision making in realistic settings. *Organizational Behavior and Human Performance*, 1975, *14*, 10–59.

Berger, D. E. Measures of information processing in concept identification. *Journal of Experimental Psychology*, 1974, *102*, 384–392.

Biederman, I. On the semantics of a glance at a scene. In M. Kubovy & J. R. Pomerantz (Eds.), *Perceptual organization*. Hillsdale, N. J.: Erlbaum, 1981.

Blank, M. S., & Foss, D. J. Semantic facilitation and lexical access during sentence processing. *Memory & Cognition*, 1978, *6*, 644–652.

Bourne, L. E., Jr. Knowing and using concepts. *Psychological Review*, 1970, *77*, 546–556.

Bourne, L. E., Jr., Domonowski, R. L., & Loftus, E. F. *Cognitive processes*. Englewood Cliffs, N. J.: Prentice-Hall, 1979.

Bourne, L. E., Jr., Ekstrand, B. R., Lovallo, W. R., Kellogg, R. T., Hiew, C. C., & Yaroush, R. A. Frequency analysis of attribute identification. *Journal of Experimental Psychology: General*, 1976, *105*, 294–312.

Bower, G. H. Organizational factors in memory. *Cognitive Psychology*, 1970, *1*, 18–46.

Bower, G. H., Black, J. B., & Turner, T. J. Scripts in memory for text. *Cognitive Psychology*, 1979, *11*, 177–220.

Bower, G. H., Clark, M., Winzenz, D., & Lesgold, A. Hierarchical retrieval schemes in recall of categorized word lists. *Journal of Verbal Learning and Verbal Behavior*, 1969, *8*, 323–343.

Bower, G. H., & Glass, A. L. Structural units and the redintegrative power of picture fragments. *Journal of Experimental Psychology*, 1976, *2*, 456–466.

Bower, G. H., & Winzenz, D. Comparison of associative learning strategies. *Psychonomic Science*, 1970, *20*, 119–120.

Bransford, J. D. *Human cognition: Learning, understanding and remembering*. Belmont, Calif.: Wadsworth, 1979.

Bransford, J. D., & Franks, J. J. The abstraction of linguistic ideas. *Cognitive Psychology*, 1971, *2*, 331–350.

Bransford, J. D., & Johnson, M. K. Considerations of some problems of comprehension. In W. G. Chase (Ed.), *Visual information processing*. New York: Academic Press, 1973.

Britton, B. K., Westbrook, R. D., & Holdredge, T. S. Reading and cognitive capacity usage: Effects of text difficulty. *Journal of Experimental Psychology: Human Learning and Memory*, 1978, *4*, 582–591.

Broadbent, D. E. The role of auditory localization in attention and memory span. *Journal of Experimental Psychology*, 1954, *47*, 191–196.

Broadbent, D. E. A mechanical model for human attention and immediate memory. *Psychological Review*, 1957, *64*, 205–215.

Broadbent, D. E. *Perception and communication*. London: Pergamon Press, 1958.

Broadbent, D. E. The magic number seven after fifteen years. In A. Kennedy & A. Wilkes (Eds.), *Studies in long term memory*. London: Wiley, 1975.

Brooks, L. R. Spatial and verbal components of the act of recall. *Canadian Journal of Psychology*, 1968, *22*, 349–368.

Brooks, L. R. Nonanalytic concept formation and memory for instances. In E. Rosch & B. Lloyd (Eds.), *Cognition and categorization*. Hillsdale, N. J.: Erlbaum, 1978.

Brown, A. L. Knowing when, where, and how to remember: A problem of metacognition. In R. Glaser (Ed.), *Advances in instructional psychology* (Vol. 1). Hillsdale, N. J.: Erlbaum, 1978.

Brown, A. L., & Campione, J. C. Training strategic study time apportionment in educable retarded children. *Intelligence*, 1977, *1*, 94–107.

Brown, E., Deffenbacher, K., & Sturgill, W. Memory for faces and the circumstances of encounter. *Journal of Applied Psychology*, 1977, *62*, 311–318.

Brown, J. S., & Burton, R. R. Diagnostic models for procedural bugs in basic mathematical skills. *Cognitive Science*, 1978, *2*, 155–192.

Bruner, J. S., Goodnow, J. J., & Austin, G. A. *A study of thinking*. New York: Wiley, 1956.

Buckhout, R. Eyewitness testimony. *Scientific American*, 1974, *231*, 23–31.

Buschke, H., & Schaier, A. H. Memory units, ideas, and propositions in semantic remembering. *Journal of Verbal Learning and Verbal Behavior*, 1979, *18*, 549–563.

Campione, J. C., & Brown, A. L. Training general metacognitive skills in retarded children. In M. M. Gruneberg, P. E. Morris, & R. N. Sykes (Eds.), *Practical aspects of memory*. New York: Academic Press, 1978.

Carroll, J. M., Thomas, J. C., & Malhotra, A. Presentation and representation in design problem solving. *British Journal of Psychology*, 1980, *71*, 143–153.

Cavanagh, J. P. Relation between the immediate memory span and the memory search rate. *Psychological Review*, 1972, *79*, 525–530.

Cermak, L. S., & Craik, F. I. M. (Eds.). *Levels of processing in human memory*. Hillsdale, N. J.: Erlbaum, 1979.

Chapanis, A. *Man-machine engineering*. Monterey, Calif.: Brooks/Cole, 1965.

Charness, N. Memory for chess positions: Resistance to interference. *Journal of Experimental Psychology: Human Learning and Memory*, 1976, *2*, 641–653.

Charrow, R. P., & Charrow, V. R. Making legal language understandable: A psycholinguistic study of jury instructions. *Columbia Law Review*, 1979, *79*, 1306–1374.

Chase, W. G., & Ericsson, K. A. A mnemonic system for digit span: One year later. Paper presented at the 20th annual meeting of the Psychonomic Society, Phoenix, Arizona, November 1979.

Chase, W. G., & Simon, H. A. Perception in chess. *Cognitive Psychology*, 1973, *4*, 55–81.

Cherry, C. Some experiments on the recognition of speech with one and with two ears. *Journal of the Acoustical Society of America*, 1953, *25*, 975–979.

Chiesi, H. L., Spilich, G. J., & Voss, J. F. Acquisition of domain-related information in relation to high and low domain knowledge. *Journal of Verbal Learning and Verbal Behavior*, 1979, *18*, 257–273.

Chomsky, N. *Syntactic structures*. The Hague: Mouton, 1957.

Chomsky, N. *Aspects of the theory of syntax*. Cambridge, Mass.: MIT Press, 1965.

Claxton, G. Special review feature: Memory research. *British Journal of Psychology*, 1978, *69*, 513–520.

Clowes, M. Transformational grammars and the organization of pictures. In A. Graselli (Ed.), *Automatic interpretation and the organization of pictures*. New York: Academic Press, 1969.

Collins, A. M., & Loftus, E. F. A spreading activation theory of semantic processing. *Psychological Review*, 1975, *82*, 407–428.

Collins, A. M., & Quillian, M. R. Retrieval time from semantic memory. *Journal of Verbal Learning and Verbal Behavior,* 1969, *8,* 240–248.

Collins, A. M., & Quillian, M. R. Facilitating retrieval from semantic memory: The effect of repeating part of an inference. *Acta Psychologica,* 1970, *33,* 304–314.

Conrad, R. Acoustic confusions in immediate memory. *British Journal of Psychology,* 1964, *55,* 75–84.

Conrad, R. Speech and reading. In J. F. Kavanagh & I. G. Mattingly (Eds.), *Language by ear and by eye: The relationships between speech and reading.* Cambridge, Mass.: MIT Press, 1972.

Cooper, L. A., & Shepard, R. N. Chronometric studies of the rotation of mental images. In W. G. Chase (Ed.), *Visual information processing.* New York: Academic Press, 1973.

Craik, F. I. M. Human memory. *Annual Review of Psychology,* 1979, *30,* 63–102. (a)

Craik, F. I. M. Levels of processing: Overview and closing comments. In L. S. Cermak & F. I. M. Craik (Eds.), *Levels of processing in human memory.* Hillsdale, N. J.: Erlbaum, 1979. (b)

Craik, F. I. M., & Lockhart, R. S. Levels of processing: A framework for memory research. *Journal of Verbal Learning and Verbal Behavior,* 1972, *11,* 671–684.

Craik, F. I. M., & Tulving, E. Depth of processing and the retention of words in episodic memory. *Journal of Experimental Psychology: General,* 1975, *104,* 268–294.

Craik, F. I. M., & Watkins, M. J. The role of rehearsal in short-term memory. *Journal of Verbal Learning and Verbal Behavior,* 1973, *12,* 599–607.

Crovitz, H. F. The capacity of memory loci in artificial memory. *Psychonomic Science,* 1971, *24,* 187–188.

Crowder, R. G. *Principles of learning and memory.* Hillsdale, N. J.: Erlbaum, 1976.

D'Agostino, P. R., O'Neill, B. J., & Paivio, A. Memory for pictures and words as a function of level of processing: Depth or dual coding? *Memory & Cognition,* 1977, *5,* 252–256.

Daneman, M., & Carpenter, P. A. Individual differences in working memory and reading. *Journal of Verbal Learning and Verbal Behavior,* 1980, *19,* 450–466.

Danks, J. H., & Glucksberg, S. Experimental psycholinguistics. *Annual Review of Psychology,* 1980, *31,* 391–417.

Dawes, R. B. The robust beauty of improper linear models in decision making. *American Psychologist,* 1979, *7,* 571–582.

de Groot, A. D. *Thought and choice in chess.* The Hague: Mouton, 1965.

de Groot, A. D. Perception and memory versus thought: Some old ideas and recent findings. In B. Kleinmuntz (Ed.), *Problem solving: Research, method and theory.* New York: Wiley, 1966.

Denes, P. B., & Pinson, E. N. *The speech chain.* Bell Telephone Laboratories, 1963.

DeRosa, D. V., & Tkacz, D. Memory scanning of organized visual material. *Journal of Experimental Psychology: Human Learning and Memory,* 1976, *2,* 688–694.

Detterman, D. K., & Ramig, P. The relationship between vocabulary size and memory. Paper presented at the 19th annual meeting of the Psychonomic Society, San Antonio, Texas, November 1978.

Deutsch, J. A., & Deutsch, D. Attention: Some theoretical considerations. *Psychological Review,* 1963, *70,* 80–90.

Dooling, D. J., & Christiansen, R. E. Levels of encoding and retention of prose. In G. H. Bower (Ed.), *Psychology of learning and motivation* (Vol. 11). New

York: Academic Press, 1977.

Duncker, K. On problem solving. *Psychological Monographs,* 1945, *58* (5, Whole No. 270).

Edwards, W. Conservatism in human information processing. In B. Kleinmuntz (Ed.), *Formal representation of human judgment.* New York: Wiley, 1968.

Edwards, W., Phillips, L. D., Hays, W. L., & Goodman, B. C. Probabilistic information processing systems: Design and evaluation. *IEEE Transactions on Systems Science and Cybernetics,* 1968, *SSC-4,* 248–265.

Egan, D. E., & Greeno, J. G. Theory of rule induction: Knowledge acquired in concept learning, serial pattern learning, and problem solving. In L. Gregg (Ed.), *Knowledge and cognition.* Potomac, Md.: Erlbaum, 1974.

Egan, D. E., & Schwartz, B. J. Chunking in recall of symbolic drawings. *Memory & Cognition,* 1979, *7,* 149–158.

Egan, J. P. Recognition memory and the operating characteristic (Technical Note AFCR–TN 58–51). Bloomington, Ind.: Indiana University Hearing and Communication Laboratory, 1958.

Egeland, B. Effects of errorless training on teaching children to discriminate letters of the alphabet. *Journal of Applied Psychology,* 1975, *60,* 533–536.

Egeth, H., & Bevan, W. Attention. In B. B. Wolman (Ed.), *Handbook of general psychology.* Englewood Cliffs, N. J.: Prentice-Hall, 1973.

Elstein, A. S., Shulman, L. S., & Sprafka, S. A. *Medical problem solving.* Cambridge, Mass.: Harvard University Press, 1978.

Ericsson, K. A., & Simon, H. A. Verbal reports as data. *Psychological Review,* 1980, *87,* 215–251.

Erickson, J. R., & Jones, M. R. Thinking. *Annual Review of Psychology,* 1978, *29,* 61–90.

Ernst, G. W., & Newell, A. *GPS: A case study in generality and problem solving.* New York: Academic Press, 1969.

Estes, W. K. The information processing approach to cognition: A confluence of metaphors and methods. In W. K. Estes (Ed.), *Handbook of learning and cognitive processes* (Vol. 5). Hillsdale, N. J.: Erlbaum, 1978. (a)

Estes, W. K. Perceptual processing in letter recognition and reading. In E. C. Carterette & M. P. Friedman (Eds.), *Handbook of perception* (Vol. 9). New York: Academic Press, 1978. (b)

Estes, W. K., & Taylor, H. A. Visual detection in relation to display size and redundancy of critical elements. *Perception & Psychophysics,* 1966, *1,* 9–16.

Eysenck, M. W. Levels of processing: A critique. *British Journal of Psychology,* 1978, *69,* 157–169.

Eysenck, M. W. Depth, elaboration, and distinctiveness. In L. S. Cermak & F. I. M. Craik (Eds.), *Levels of processing in human memory.* Hillsdale, N. J.: Erlbaum, 1979.

Finke, R. A. Levels of equivalence in imagery and perception. *Psychological Review,* 1980, *87,* 113–132.

Fischler, I., Rundus, D., & Atkinson, R. C. Effects of overt rehearsal processes on free recall. *Psychonomic Science,* 1970, *19,* 249–250.

Fisher, R. P., & Craik, F. I. M. Interaction between encoding and retrieval operations in cued recall. *Journal of Experimental Psychology: Human Learning and Memory,* 1977, *3,* 701–711.

Fox, J. Making decisions under the influence of memory. *Psychological Review,* 1980, *87,* 190–211.

Franklin, B. *Complete works* (J. Bigelow, Ed.; Vol. 4). New York: Putnam, 1887.

Garner, W. R. *The processing of information and structure.* Potomac, Md.: Erlbaum, 1974.

Garner, W. R. Letter discrimination and identification. In A. D. Pick (Ed.), *Perception and its development: A tribute to Eleanor J. Gibson.* Hillsdale, N. J.: Erlbaum, 1979.

Geyer, L. H., & De Wald, C. G. Feature lists and confusion matrices. *Perception & Psychophysics,* 1973, *14,* 479–482.

Gibson, E. *Principles of perceptual learning and development.* New York: Appleton-Century-Crofts, 1969.

Gibson, E. J., & Levin, H. *The psychology of reading.* Cambridge, Mass.: MIT Press, 1975.

Gibson, E. J., Osser, H., Schiff, W., & Smith, J. An analysis of critical features of letters, tested by a confusion matrix. In *A basic research program on reading* (Cooperative Research Project No. 639). Washington, D. C.: U. S. Office of Education, 1963.

Gibson, E., Schapiro, R., & Yonas, A. Confusion matrices for graphic patterns obtained with a latency measure. *The analysis of reading skill: A program of basic and applied research* (Final report, project No. 5–1213). Ithaca, N. Y.: Cornell University and U. S. Office of Education, 1968.

Gick, M. L., & Holyoak, K. Analogical problem solving. *Cognitive Psychology,* 1980, *12,* 306–355.

Goldman, S. R., & Pellegrino, J. W. Processing domain, encoding elaboration, and memory trace strength. *Journal of Verbal Learning and Verbal Behavior,* 1977, *16,* 29–43.

Goldstein, A. G. The fallibility of the eyewitness: Psychological evidence. In B. D. Sales (Ed.), *Psychology in the legal process.* New York: Spectrum, 1977.

Gopher, D., & Kahneman, D. Individual differences in attention and the prediction of flight criteria. *Perceptual and Motor Skills,* 1971, *33,* 1335–1342.

Graesser, A. C., Hoffman, N. L., & Clark, L. F. Structural components of reading time. *Journal of Verbal Learning and Verbal Behavior,* 1980, *19,* 135–151.

Greeno, J. G. Natures of problem solving abilities. In W. K. Estes (Ed.), *Handbook of learning and cognitive processes* (Vol. 5). Hillsdale, N. J.: Erlbaum, 1978.

Gruneberg, M. M., Morris, P. E., & Sykes, R. N. (Eds.). *Practical aspects of memory.* New York: Academic Press, 1978.

Gunter, B., Clifford, B. R., & Berry, C. Release from proactive interference with television news items: Evidence for encoding dimensions within televised news. *Journal of Experimental Psychology: Human Learning and Memory,* 1980, *6,* 216–223.

Haber, R. N. Introduction. In R. N. Haber (Ed.), *Information-processing approaches to visual perception.* New York: Holt, Rinehart and Winston, 1969.

Hammond, K. R. Computer graphics as an aid to learning. *Science,* 1971, *172,* 903–908.

Hardyck, C. D., & Petrinovich, L. F. Subvocal speech and comprehension levels as a function of the difficulty level of reading materials. *Journal of Verbal Learning and Verbal Behavior,* 1970, *9,* 647–652.

Harris, R. J. Comprehension of pragmatic implications in advertising. *Journal of Applied Psychology,* 1977, *62,* 603–608.

Harris, R. J. The effect of jury size and judge's instructions on memory for pragmatic implications from courtroom testimony. *Bulletin of the Psychonomic Society,* 1978, *11,* 129–132.

Hasher, L., & Zacks, R. T. Automatic and effortful processes in memory. *Journal of Experimental Psychology: General,* 1979, *108,* 356–388.

Haviland, S. E., & Clark, H. H. What's new? Acquiring new information as a process of comprehension. *Journal of Verbal Learning and Verbal Behavior,* 1974, *13,* 512–521.

Hayes, J. R. Memory span for several vocabularies as a function of vocabulary size. *Quarterly Progress Report,* Acoustics Laboratory, Massachusetts Institute of Technology, 1952.

Hayes, J. R. Memory, goals, and problem solving. In B. Kleinmuntz (Ed.), *Problem solving: Research, method, and theory.* New York: Wiley, 1966.

Hayes, J. R. Problem solving courses at Carnegie-Mellon University. Paper presented at the AERA annual meeting, San Francisco, April 1979.

Hayes, J. R., & Simon, H. A. Psychological differences among problem isomorphs. In N. J. Castellan, D. B. Pisoni, & G. R. Potts (Eds.), *Cognitive theory* (Vol. 2). Hillsdale, N. J.: Erlbaum, 1977.

Hayes-Roth, B. Structurally integrated versus structurally segregated memory representation: Implications for the design of instructional materials. In A. M. Lesgold, J. W. Pellegrino, S. D. Fokkema, & R. Glaser (Eds.), *Cognitive psychology and instruction.* New York: Plenum Press, 1978.

Hayes-Roth, B., & Hayes-Roth, F. Concept learning and the recognition and classification of examples. *Journal of Verbal Learning and Verbal Behavior,* 1977, *16,* 321–338.

Haygood, R. C., & Bourne, L. E., Jr. Attribute and rule learning aspects of conceptual behavior. *Psychological Review,* 1965, *72,* 175–195.

Healy, A. F. Proofreading errors on the word "The": New evidence on reading units. *Journal of Experimental Psychology: Human Perception and Performance,* 1980, *6,* 45–57.

Heidbreder, E. *Seven psychologies.* New York: Appleton-Century-Crofts, 1961.

Heller, J. I., & Greeno, J. G. Information processing analyses of mathematical problem solving. Paper presented at the Applied Problem Solving Conference, Evanston, Illinois, January 1979.

Herrmann, D. J., & Neisser, U. An inventory of everyday memory experiences. In M. M. Gruneberg, P. E. Morris, & R. N. Sykes (Eds.), *Practical aspects of memory.* New York: Academic Press, 1978.

Hinsley, D. A., Hayes, J. R., & Simon, H. A. From words to equations: Meaning and representation in algebra word problems. In P. A. Carpenter & M. A. Just (Eds.), *Cognitive processes in comprehension.* Hillsdale, N. J.: Erlbaum, 1977.

Hirst, W., Spelke, E. S., Reavés, C. C., Caharack, G., & Neisser, U. Dividing attention without alternation or automaticity. *Journal of Experimental Psychology: General,* 1980, *109,* 98–117.

Hitch, G. J., & Baddeley, A. D. Verbal reasoning and working memory. *Quarterly Journal of Experimental Psychology,* 1976, *23,* 603–621.

Hock, H. S., & Tromley, C. L. Mental rotation and perceptual uprightness. *Perception & Psychophysics,* 1978, *24,* 529–533.

Holbrook, M. B. A comparison of methods for measuring the interletter similarity between capital letters. *Perception & Psychophysics,* 1975, *17,* 532–536.

Homa, D., & Chambliss, D. The relative contributions of common and distinctive information on the abstraction of ill-defined categories. *Journal of Experimental Psychology: Human Learning and Memory,* 1975, *104,* 351–359.

Homa, D., Cross, J., Cornell, D., Goldman, D., & Schwartz, S. Prototype abstraction and classification of new instances as a function of number of instances defining the prototype. *Journal of Experimental Psychology: Human Learning and Memory,* 1975, *104,* 351–359.

Howe, J. A. M. Artificial intelligence and computer-assisted learning: Ten years on. *Programmed Learning and Educational Technology,* 1978, *15,* 114–125.

Hunt, E., & Lansman, M. Cognitive theory applied to individual differences. In W. K. Estes (Ed.), *Handbook of learning and cognitive processes* (Vol. 1). Hillsdale, N. J.: Erlbaum, 1975.

Hunt, R. R., & Elliott, J. M. The role of nonsemantic information in memory:

Orthographic distinctiveness effects on retention. *Journal of Experimental Psychology: General*, 1980, *109*, 49–74.

Hyde, T. S., & Jenkins, J. J. The differential effects of incidental tasks on the organization of recall of a list of highly associated words. *Journal of Experimental Psychology*, 1969, *82*, 472–481.

James, W. *The principles of psychology*. New York: Holt, 1890.

Jarvella, R. J. Immediate memory and discourse processing. In G. H. Bower (Ed.), *The psychology of learning and motivation* (Vol. 13). New York: Academic Press, 1979.

Jeffries, R., Polson, P. G., Razran, L., & Atwood, M. E. A process model for missionaries-cannibals and other river-crossing problems. *Cognitive Psychology*, 1977, *9*, 412–440.

Jenkins, J. J. The acquisition of language. In D. A. Goslin (Ed.), *Handbook of socialization theory and research*. Chicago: Rand McNally, 1969.

Johnson, S. Hierarchical clustering schemes. *Psychometrika*, 1967, *32*, 241–254.

Johnson-Laird, P. N., Legrenzi, P., & Legrenzi, M. S. Reasoning and a sense of reality. *British Journal of Psychology*, 1972, *63*, 395–400.

Johnston, W. A., & Heinz, S. P. Flexibility and capacity demands of attention. *Journal of Experimental Psychology: General*, 1978, *107*, 420–435.

Juola, J. F., Fischler, I., Wood, C. T., & Atkinson, R. C. Recognition time for information stored in long-term memory. *Perception & Psychophysics*, 1971, *10*, 8–14.

Just, M. A., & Carpenter, P. A. A theory of reading: From eye fixations to comprehension. *Psychological Review*, 1980, *87*, 329–354.

Kahneman, D. *Attention and effort*. Englewood Cliffs, N. J.: Prentice-Hall, 1973.

Kahneman, D., Ben-Ishai, R., & Lotan, M. Relation of a test of attention to road accidents. *Journal of Applied Psychology*, 1973, *58*, 113–115.

Kahneman, D., & Tversky, A. Subjective probability: A judgment of representativeness. *Cognitive Psychology*, 1972, *3*, 430–454.

Keele, S. W., & Neill, W. T. Mechanisms of attention. In E. C. Carterette & M. P. Friedman (Eds.), *Handbook of Perception* (Vol. 9). New York: Academic Press, 1978.

Keenan, J. M., MacWhinney, B., & Mayhew, D. Pragmatics in memory: A study of natural conversation. *Journal of Verbal Learning and Verbal Behavior*, 1977, *16*, 549–560.

Keppel, G., & Underwood, B. Proactive inhibition in short-term retention of single items. *Journal of Verbal Learning and Verbal Behavior*, 1962, *1*, 153–161.

Kieras, D. E. Good and bad structure in simple paragraphs: Effects on apparent theme, reading time, and recall. *Journal of Verbal Learning and Verbal Behavior*, 1978, *17*, 13–28.

Kieras, D. E. Component processes in the comprehension of simple prose. *Journal of Verbal Learning and Verbal Behavior*, 1981, *20*, 1–23.

Kieras, D. E., & Greeno, J. G. Effect of meaningfulness on judgments of computability. *Memory & Cognition*, 1975, *3*, 349–355.

Kintsch, W. On modeling comprehension. *Educational Psychologist*, 1979, *14*, 3–14.

Kintsch, W., & Bates, E. Recognition memory for statements from a classroom lecture. *Journal of Experimental Psychology: Human Learning and Memory*, 1977, *3*, 150–159.

Kintsch, W., & Van Dijk, T. A. Toward a model of text comprehension and production. *Psychological Review*, 1978, *85*, 363–394.

Kintsch, W., & Vipond, D. Reading comprehension and readability in educational practice and psychological theory. In L. G. Nilsson (Ed.), *Perspectives on memory research*. Hillsdale, N. J.: Erlbaum, 1979.

Klatzky, R. L. *Human memory: Structures and processes* (2nd ed.). San Francisco: W. H. Freeman, 1980.

Kleiman, G. M. Speech recoding in reading. *Journal of Verbal Learning and Verbal Behavior*, 1975, *14*, 323–339.

Klein, K., & Saltz, E. Specifying the mechanisms in a levels-of-processing approach to memory. *Journal of Experimental Psychology: Human Learning and Memory*, 1976, *2*, 671–679.

Köhler, W. *The mentality of apes.* New York: Harcourt, 1925.

Kosslyn, S. M. Information representation in visual images. *Cognitive Psychology*, 1975, *7*, 341–370.

Kosslyn, S. M. The medium and the message in mental imagery: A theory. *Psychological Review*, 1981, *88*, 46–66.

Kosslyn, S. M., Ball, T. M., & Reiser, B. J. Visual images preserve metric spatial information: Evidence from studies of image scanning. *Journal of Experimental Psychology: Human Perception and Performance*, 1978, *4*, 47–60.

Kosslyn, S. M., & Pomerantz, J. R. Imagery, propositions, and the form of internal representations. *Cognitive Psychology*, 1977, *9*, 52–76.

Kroll, N. E. A., & Parks, T. E. Interference with short-term visual memory produced by concurrent central processing. *Journal of Experimental Psychology: Human Learning and Memory*, 1978, *4*, 111–120.

Krueger, L. E., & Shapiro, R. G. Letter detection with rapid serial visual presentation: Evidence against word superiority of feature extraction. *Journal of Experimental Psychology: Human Perception and Performance*, 1979, *5*, 657–673.

Kruskal, J. B. Multidimensional scaling by optimizing goodness of fit to a nonmetric hypothesis. *Psychometrika*, 1964, *29*, 1–27.

LaBerge, D., & Samuels, S. J. Toward a theory of automatic information processing in reading. *Cognitive Psychology*, 1974, *6*, 293–323.

Lachman, R., Lachman, J. L., & Butterfield, E. C. *Cognitive psychology and information processing: An introduction.* Hillsdale, N. J.: Erlbaum, 1979.

Larkin, J. H. Teaching problem solving in physics: The psychological laboratory and the practical classroom. In D. T. Tuma & F. Reif (Eds.), *Problem solving and education: Issues in teaching and research.* Hillsdale, N. J.: Erlbaum, 1980.

Larkin, J. H., McDermott, J., Simon, D. P., & Simon, H. A. Expert and novice performance in solving physics problems. *Science*, 1980, *208*, 1335–1342.

Larkin, J. H., & Reif, F. Understanding and teaching problem solving in physics. *European Journal of Science Education*, 1979, *1*, 191–203.

Laughery, K. R. Computer simulation of short-term memory: A component decay model. In G. H. Bower & J. T. Spence (Eds.), *The psychology of learning and motivation* (Vol. 3). New York: Academic Press, 1969.

Lea, G. Chronometric analysis of the method of loci. *Journal of Experimental Psychology: Human Perception and Performance*, 1975, *104*, 95–104.

Lesgold, A. M., Roth, S. F., & Curtis, M. E. Foregrounding effects in discourse comprehension. *Journal of Verbal Learning and Verbal Behavior*, 1979, *18*, 291–308.

Levine, M. Hypothesis behavior by humans during discrimination learning. *Journal of Experimental Psychology*, 1966, *71*, 331–338.

Levine, M. Neo-noncontinuity theory. In G. H. Bower & J. T. Spence (Eds.), *The psychology of learning and motivation* (Vol. 3). New York: Academic Press, 1969.

Levy, B. A. Speech processing during reading. In A. M. Lesgold, J. W. Pellegrino, S. D. Fokkema, & R. Glaser (Eds.), *Cognitive psychology and instruction.* New York: Plenum, 1978.

Light, L. L., & Carter-Sobell, L. Effects of changed semantic context on recognition memory. *Journal of Verbal Learning and Verbal Behavior*, 1970, *9*, 1–11.

Lockhead, G. R., & Crist, W. B. Making letters distinctive. *Journal of Educational Psychology,* 1980, *72,* 483–493.

Loftus, E. F. Leading questions and the eyewitness report. *Cognitive Psychology,* 1975, *7,* 560–572.

Loftus, E. F. *Eyewitness testimony.* Cambridge, Mass.: Harvard University Press, 1979.

Long, G. M. Iconic memory: A review and critique of the study of short-term visual storage. *Psychological Bulletin,* 1980, *88,* 785–820.

Lorayne, H., & Lucas, J. *The memory book.* New York: Ballantine Books, 1974.

Luchins, A. S. Mechanization in problem solving. *Psychological Monographs,* 1942 (54, Whole No. 248).

Lutz, K. A., & Lutz, R. J. Effects of interactive imagery on learning: Applications to advertising. *Journal of Applied Psychology,* 1977, *62,* 493–498.

Lyons, J. *Chomsky.* London: Collins, 1970.

MacKay, D. G. To end ambiguous sentences. *Perception & Psychophysics,* 1966, *1,* 426–435.

MacLeod, C. M., Hunt, E. B., & Mathews, N. N. Individual differences in the verification of sentence-picture relationships. *Journal of Verbal Learning and Verbal Behavior,* 1978, *17,* 493–507.

Mandler, G. Organization and memory. In K. W. Spence & J. T. Spence (Eds.), *The psychology of learning and motivation* (Vol. 1). New York: Academic Press, 1967.

Marks, D. F. Individual differences in the vividness of visual imagery and their effect on function. In P. W. Sheehan (Ed.), *The function and nature of imagery.* New York: Academic Press, 1972.

Marslen-Wilson, M. D., & Welsh, A. Processing interactions and lexical access during word recognition in continuous speech. *Cognitive Psychology,* 1978, *10,* 29–63.

Martin, R. C., & Caramazza, A. Classification in well-defined and ill-defined categories: Evidence for common processing strategies. *Journal of Experimental Psychology: General,* 1980, *109,* 320–353.

Massaro, D. Letter information and orthographic context in word perception. *Journal of Experimental Psychology: Human Perception and Performance,* 1979, *5,* 595–609.

Masur, E. F., McIntyre, C. W., & Flavell, J. H. Developmental changes in apportionment of study time among items in a multitrial free recall task. *Journal of Experimental Child Psychology,* 1973, *15,* 237–246.

Mayer, R. E., & Greeno, J. G. Structural differences between learning outcomes produced by different instructional methods. *Journal of Experimental Psychology,* 1972, *63,* 165–173.

Mayer, R. E., & Greeno, J. G. Effects of meaningfulness and organization on problem solving and computability judgments. *Memory & Cognition,* 1975, *3,* 356–362.

McCarty, D. L. Investigation of a visual imagery mnemonic device for acquiring face–name associations. *Journal of Experimental Psychology: Human Learning and Memory,* 1980, *6,* 145–155.

McCloskey, M. The stimulus familiarity problem in semantic memory research. *Journal of Verbal Learning and Verbal Behavior,* 1980, *19,* 485–502.

McCloskey, M., & Glucksberg, S. Decision processes in verifying category membership statements: Implications for models of semantic memory. *Cognitive Psychology,* 1979, *11,* 1–37.

McKoon, G., & Ratcliff, R. Priming in item recognition: The organization of propositions in memory for text. *Journal of Verbal Learning and Verbal Behavior,* 1980, *19,* 369–386.

Medin, D. L., & Schaffer, M. M. Context theory of classification learning. *Psychological Review*, 1978, *85*, 207–238.

Mervis, C. B., & Rosch, E. Categorization of natural objects. *Annual Review of Psychology*, 1981, *32*, 89–115.

Meyer, D. E., & Schvaneveldt, R. W. Meaning, memory structure, and mental processes. *Science*, 1976, *192*, 27–33.

Mihal, W. L., & Barett, G. V. Individual differences in perceptual information processing and their relation to automobile accident involvement. *Journal of Applied Psychology*, 1976, *61*, 229–233.

Milgram, S. The experience of living in cities. *Science*, 1970, *167*, 1461–1468.

Miller, G. A. The magical number seven, plus or minus two: Some limits on our capacity for processing information. *Psychological Review*, 1956, *63*, 81–97.

Miller, G. A., Galanter, E., & Pribram, K. *Plans and the structure of behavior.* New York: Holt, Rinehart and Winston, 1960.

Miller, J. R., & Kintsch, W. Readability and recall of short prose passages: A theoretical analysis. *Journal of Experimental Psychology: Human Learning and Memory*, 1980, *6*, 335–354.

Moray, N. Attention in dichotic listening: Affective cues and the influence of instructions. *Quarterly Journal of Experimental Psychology*, 1959, *11*, 56–60.

Morris, C. D., Bransford, J. D., & Franks, J. J. Levels of processing versus transfer appropriate processing. *Journal of Verbal Learning and Verbal Behavior*, 1977, *16*, 519–533.

Morris, P. E., Jones, S., & Hampson, P. An imagery mnemonic for the learning of people's names. *British Journal of Psychology*, 1978, *69*, 335–336.

Moscovitch, M., & Craik, F. I. M. Depth of processing, retrieval cues, and uniqueness of encoding as factors in recall. *Journal of Verbal Learning and Verbal Behavior*, 1976, *15*, 447–458.

Mulholland, T. M., Pellegrino, J. W., & Glaser, R. Components of geometric analogy solution. *Cognitive Psychology*, 1980, *12*, 252–284.

Narasimhan, R., & Reddy, V. S. N. A generative model for handprinted English letters and its computer implementation. *ICC Bulletin*, 1967, *6*, 275–287.

Nash-Weber, B. The role of semantics in automatic speech understanding. In D. G. Bobrow & A. Collins, *Representation and understanding.* New York: Academic Press, 1975.

Navon, D., & Gopher, D. On the economy of the human-processing system. *Psychological Review*, 1979, *86*, 214–255.

Neisser, U. *Cognitive Psychology.* New York: Appleton-Century-Crofts, 1967.

Neisser, U., & Becklen, R. Selective looking: Attending to visually specified events. *Cognitive Psychology*, 1975, *7*, 480–494.

Nelson, T. O. Repetition and depth of processing. *Journal of Verbal Learning and Verbal Behavior*, 1977, *16*, 151–171.

Nelson, T. O., & Smith, E. E. Acquisition and forgetting of hierarchically organized information in long-term memory. *Journal of Experimental Psychology*, 1972, *95*, 388–396.

Neumann, P. G. An attribute frequency model for the abstraction of prototypes. *Memory & Cognition*, 1974, *2*, 241–248.

Newell, A., Shaw, J. C., & Simon, H. A. Chess-playing problems and the problem of complexity. *IBM Journal of Research and Development*, 1958, *2*, 320–335. (a)

Newell, A., Shaw, J. C., & Simon, H. A. Elements of a theory of human problem solving. *Psychological Review*, 1958, *65*, 151–166. (b)

Newell, A., & Simon, H. A. *Human problem solving.* Englewood Cliffs, N. J.: Prentice-Hall, 1972.

Nickerson, R. S., & Adams, M. J. Long-term memory for a common object. *Cognitive Psychology*, 1979, *11*, 287–307.

Nielsen, G. D., & Smith, E. E. Imaginal and verbal representations in short-term recognition of visual forms. *Journal of Experimental Psychology*, 1973, *101*, 375–378.

Norman, D. A. Toward a theory of memory and attention. *Psychological Review*, 1968, *75*, 522–536.

Norman, D. A. Cognitive engineering and education. In D. T. Tuma & F. Reif (Eds.), *Problem solving and education: Issues in teaching and research*. Hillsdale, N. J.: Erlbaum, 1980.

Paige, J. M., & Simon, H. A. Cognitive processes in solving algebra word problems. In B. Kleinmuntz (Ed.), *Problem solving: Research, method, and theory*. New York: Wiley, 1966.

Paivio, A. Mental imagery in associative learning and memory. *Psychological Review*, 1969, *76*, 241–263.

Paivio, A. *Imagery and verbal processes*. New York: Holt, Rinehart and Winston, 1971.

Paivio, A. Coding distinctions and repetition effects in memory. In G. H. Bower (Ed.), *Psychology of learning and motivation* (Vol. 9). New York: Academic Press, 1975.

Paivio, A., Smythe, P. E., & Yuille, J. C. Imagery versus meaningfulness of nouns in paired-associate learning. *Canadian Journal of Psychology*, 1968, *22*, 427–441.

Palmer, S. E. Hierarchical structure in perceptual representation. *Cognitive Psychology*, 1977, *9*, 441–474.

Payne, J. W. Alternative approaches to decision making under risk. *Psychological Bulletin*, 1973, *80*, 439–453.

Payne, J. W. Task complexity and contingent processing in decision making: An information search and protocol analysis. *Organizational Behavior and Human Performance*, 1976, *16*, 366–387.

Pellegrino, J. W., & Glaser, R. Cognitive correlates and components in the analysis of individual differences. *Intelligence*, 1979, *3*, 187–216.

Penrod, S., & Hastie, R. A computer simulation of jury decision making. *Psychological Review*, 1980, *87*, 133–159.

Peterson, L. R. Verbal learning and memory. *Annual Review of Psychology*, 1977, *28*, 393–415.

Peterson, L. R., & Peterson, M. J. Short-term retention of individual verbal items. *Journal of Experimental Psychology*, 1959, *58*, 193–198.

Phillips, W. A. On the distinction between sensory storage and short-term visual memory. *Perception & Psychophysics*, 1974, *16*, 283–290.

Pittenger, J. B., & Shaw, R. E. Ageing faces as viscal-elastic events: Implications for a theory of nonrigid shape perception. *Journal of Experimental Psychology: Human Perception and Performance*, 1975, *1*, 374–383.

Polya, G. *Mathematical discovery* (Vol. 1). New York: Wiley, 1962.

Posner, M. I., Goldsmith, R., & Welton, K. E. Perceived distance and the classification of distorted patterns. *Journal of Experimental Psychology*, 1967, *73*, 28–38.

Posner, M. I., Boies, S. J., Eichelman, W. H., & Taylor, R. L. Retention of visual and name codes of single letters. *Journal of Experimental Psychology Monograph*, 1969, *79*, 1–13.

Posner, M. I., & Keele, S. W. On the genesis of abstract ideas. *Journal of Experimental Psychology*, 1968, *77*, 353–363.

Posner, M. I., & Snyder, C. R. R. Attention and cognitive control. In R. L. Solso (Ed.), *Information processing and cognition: The Loyola Symposium*. Hillsdale, N. J.: Erlbaum, 1975.

Postman, L., & Phillips, L. W. Short term temporal changes in free recall. *Quarterly Journal of Experimental Psychology*, 1965, *17*, 132–138.

Potter, M. C., & Faulconer, B. A. Understanding noun phrases. *Journal of Verbal Learning and Verbal Behavior*, 1979, *18*, 509–521.

Pressley, M., Levin, J. R., Hall, J. W., Miller, G. E., & Berry, J. K. The key word method and foreign word acquisition. *Journal of Experimental Psychology: Human Learning and Memory*, 1980, *6*, 163–173.

Pylyshyn, Z. W. What the mind's eye tells the mind's brain: A critique of mental imagery. *Psychological Bulletin*, 1973, *80*, 1–24.

Pylyshyn, Z. W. The imagery debate: Analogue media versus tacit knowledge. *Psychological Review*, 1981, *88*, 16–45.

Rasmussen, J., & Jensen, A. Mental procedures in real-life tasks: A case study of electronic trouble shooting. *Ergonomics*, 1974, *17*, 293–307.

Reder, L. M. The role of elaboration in the comprehension and retention of prose. *Review of Educational Research*, 1980, *50*, 5–53.

Reder, L. M., & Anderson, J. R. Partial resolution of the paradox of interference: The role of integrating knowledge. *Cognitive Psychology*, 1980, *12*, 447–472.

Reed, S. K. Pattern recognition and categorization. *Cognitive Psychology*, 1972, *3*, 382–407.

Reed, S. K. *Psychological processes in pattern recognition.* New York: Academic Press, 1973.

Reed, S. K., Ernst, G. W., & Banerji, R. The role of analogy in transfer between similar problem states. *Cognitive Psychology*, 1974, *6*, 436–450.

Reed, S. K., & Friedman, M. P. Perceptual vs. conceptual categorization. *Memory & Cognition*, 1973, *1*, 157–163.

Reed, S. K., & Johnsen, J. A. Detection of parts in patterns and images. *Memory & Cognition*, 1975, *3*, 569–575.

Reed, S. K., & Johnsen, J. A. Memory for problem solutions. In G. H. Bower (Ed.), *The psychology of learning and motivation* (Vol. 11). New York: Academic Press, 1977.

Reicher, G. M. Perceptual recognition as a function of meaningfulness of stimulus material. *Journal of Experimental Psychology*, 1969, *81*, 275–280.

Reitman, J. Without surreptitious rehearsal, information in short-term memory decays. *Journal of Verbal Learning and Verbal Behavior*, 1974, *13*, 365–377.

Reitman, J. S., & Bower, G. H. Storage and later recognition of exemplars of concepts. *Cognitive Psychology*, 1973, *4*, 194–206.

Resnick, L. B. Instructional psychology. *Annual Review of Psychology*, 1981, *32*, 659–704.

Rips, L. J., Shoben, E. J., & Smith, E. E. Semantic distance and the verification of semantic relations. *Journal of Verbal Learning and Verbal Behavior*, 1973, *12*, 1–20.

Roediger, H. L. Memory metaphors in cognitive psychology. *Memory & Cognition*, 1980, *8*, 231–246.

Rosch, E. Natural categories. *Cognitive Psychology*, 1973, *4*, 328–350.

Rosch, E. Cognitive representations of semantic categories. *Journal of Experimental Psychology: General*, 1975, *3*, 192–233.

Rosch, E., & Mervis, C. B. Family resemblances: Studies in the internal structure of categories. *Cognitive Psychology*, 1975, *7*, 573–605.

Rosch, E., Mervis, C. B., Gray, W. D., Johnsen, D. M., & Boyes-Braem, P. Basic objects in natural categories. *Cognitive Psychology*, 1976, *8*, 382–440.

Rubinstein, M. F. *Patterns of problem solving.* Englewood Cliffs, N. J.: Prentice-Hall, 1975.

Rubinstein, M. F., & Pfeiffer, K. R. Theoretical and practical aspects of the UCLA problem solving course. Paper presented at the AERA annual meeting, San Francisco, April 1979.

Rumelhart, D. E. A multicomponent theory of perception of briefly exposed stimulus displays. *Journal of Mathematical Psychology*, 1970, *7*, 191–218.

Rumelhart, D. E. Toward an interactive model of reading. In S. Dornic (Ed.), *Attention and performance* (Vol. 6). Hillsdale, N. J.: Erlbaum, 1977.

Rumelhart, D. E., & Siple, P. Process of recognizing tachistoscopically presented words. *Psychological Review*, 1974, *81*, 99–118.

Rundus, D. Analysis of rehearsal processes in free recall. *Journal of Experimental Psychology*, 1971, *89*, 63–77.

Rushmer, R. F. *Cardiovascular dynamics*. Philadelphia: Saunders, 1970.

Sacerdoti, E. D. Planning in a hierarchy of abstraction spaces. *Artificial Intelligence*, 1974, *5*, 115–135.

Sacerdoti, E. D. *A structure for plans and behavior*. Amsterdam: Elsevier, 1977.

Sachs, J. S. Recognition memory for syntactic and semantic aspects of connected discourse. *Perception & Psychophysics*, 1967, *2*, 437–442.

Sanders, A. F., & Schroots, J. J. F. Cognitive categories and memory span: III. Effects of similarity on recall. *The Quarterly Journal of Experimental Psychology*, 1969, *21*, 21–28.

Schank, R., & Abelson, R. *Scripts, plans, goals, and understanding*. Hillsdale, N. J.: Erlbaum, 1977.

Schneider, W., & Shiffrin, R. M. Controlled and automatic human information processing: I. Detection, search, and attention. *Psychological Review*, 1977, *84*, 1–66.

Schoenfeld, A. H. Explicit heuristic training as a variable in problem-solving performances. *Journal for Research in Mathematics Education*, 1979, *10*, 173–187.

Schvaneveldt, R. W., Meyer, D. E., & Becker, C. A. Lexical ambiguity, semantic context, and visual word recognition. *Journal of Experimental Psychology: Human Perception and Performance*, 1976, *2*, 243–256.

Shanteau, J. An information-integration analysis of risky decision making. In M. F. Kaplan & S. Schwartz (Eds.), *Human judgment and decision processes*. New York: Academic Press, 1975.

Sheehan, P. W. *The function and nature of imagery*. New York: Academic Press, 1972.

Shepard, R. N. The analysis of proximities: Multidimensional scaling with an unknown distance function: I. *Psychometrika*, 1962, *27*, 125–140; II. *Psychometrika*, 1962, *27*, 219–246.

Shepard, R. N. Recognition memory for words, sentences, and pictures. *Journal of Verbal Learning and Verbal Behavior*, 1967, *6*, 156–163.

Shepard, R. N., & Metzler, J. Mental rotation of three dimensional objects. *Science*, 1971, *171*, 701–703.

Shepard, R. N., & Podgorny, P. Cognitive processes that resemble perceptual processes. In W. K. Estes (Ed.), *Handbook of learning and cognitive processes* (Vol 5). Hillsdale, N. J.: Erlbaum, 1978.

Shiffrin, R. M., & Schneider, W. Controlled and automatic human information processing: II. Perceptual learning, automatic attending, and a general theory. *Psychological Review*, 1977, *84*, 127–190.

Shulman, H. G. Similarity effects in short-term memory. *Psychological Bulletin*, 1971, *75*, 399–415.

Siegel, J. A., & Siegel, W. Absolute judgment and paired-associate learning: Kissing cousins or identical twins? *Psychological Review*, 1972, *79*, 300–316.

Silver, E. A. Recall of mathematical problem information: Solving related problems. *Journal for Research in Mathematics Education*, 1981, *12*, 54–64.

Simon, H. A. *Models of man*. New York: Wiley, 1957.

Simon, H. A. How big is a chunk? *Science*, 1974, *183*, 482–488.

Simon, H. A., & Gilmartin, K. A simulation of memory for chess positions. *Cognitive Psychology*, 1973, *5*, 29–46.

Simon, H. A., & Newell, A. Human problem solving: The state of the theory in 1970. *American Psychologist*, 1971, *26*, 145–159.

Simon, H. A., & Reed, S. K. Modeling strategy shifts in a problem-solving task. *Cognitive Psychology*, 1976, *8*, 86–97.

Slovic, P., Fischhoff, B., & Lichtenstein, S. Cognitive processes and societal risk taking. In J. S. Carroll & J. W. Payne (Eds.), *Cognition and social behavior.* Potomac, Md.: Erlbaum, 1976.

Slovic, P., Fischhoff, B., & Lichtenstein, S. Behavioral decision theory. *Annual Review of Psychology*, 1977, *28*, 1–39.

Slovic, P., & Lichtenstein, S. Relative importance of probabilities and payoffs in risk taking. *Journal of Experimental Psychology Monograph*, 1968, *78*(3, Pt. 2).

Slovic, P., & Lichtenstein, S. Comparison of Bayesian and regression approaches to the study of information processing in judgment. *Organizational Behavior and Human Performance*, 1971, *6*, 649–744.

Slowiaczek, M. L., & Clifton, C. Subvocalization and reading for meaning. *Journal of Verbal Learning and Verbal Behavior*, 1980, *19*, 573–582.

Smith, E. E. Theories of semantic memory. In W. K. Estes (Ed.), *Handbook of learning and cognitive processes* (Vol. 6). Hillsdale, N. J.: Erlbaum, 1978.

Smith, E. E., Adams, N., & Schorr, D. Fact retrieval and the paradox of interference. *Cognitive Psychology*, 1978, *10*, 438–464.

Smith, E. E., & Nielsen, G. D. Representation and retrieval processes in short-term memory: Recognition and recall of faces. *Journal of Experimental Psychology.* 1970, *85*, 397–405.

Smith, E. E., Shoben, E. J., & Rips, L. U. Structure and process in semantic memory: A featural model for semantic decision. *Psychological Review*, 1974, *81*, 214–241.

Sperling, G. The information available in brief visual presentations. *Psychological Monographs*, 1960, *74*(11, Whole No. 498).

Sperling, G. A model for visual memory tasks. *Human Factors*, 1963, *5*, 19–31.

Sperling, G. Successive approximations to a model for short-term memory. *Acta Psychologica*, 1967, *27*, 285–292.

Spilich, G. J., Vesonder, G. T., Chiesi, H. L., & Voss, J. F. Text processing of domain-related information for individuals with high and low domain knowledge. *Journal of Verbal Learning and Verbal Behavior*, 1979, *18*, 275–290.

Standing, L. Learning 10,000 pictures. *Quarterly Journal of Experimental Psychology*, 1973, *25*, 207–222.

Stein, B. S., & Bransford, J. D. Constraints on effective elaboration: Effects of precision and subject generation. *Journal of Verbal Learning and Verbal Behavior*, 1979, *18*, 769–777.

Sternberg, R. J. Component processes in analogical reasoning. *Psychological Review*, 1977, *84*, 353–378.

Sternberg, R. J. The nature of mental abilities. *American Psychologist*, 1979, *34*, 214–230.

Sternberg, R. J., & Detterman, D. K. (Eds.). *Human intelligence: Perspectives on its theory and measurement.* Norwood, N. J.: Ablex Publishing, 1979.

Sternberg, S. High-speed scanning in human memory. *Science*, 1966, *153*, 652–654.

Sternberg, S. Two operations in character recognition: Some evidence from reaction time measurements. *Perception & Psychophysics*, 1967, *2*, 45–53.

Stevens, A., & Coupe, P. Distortions in judged spatial relations. *Cognitive Psychology*, 1978, *10*, 411–437.

Strauss, M. S. Abstraction of prototypical information by adults and 10-month-old infants. *Journal of Experimental Psychology: Human Learning and Memory*, 1979, *5*, 618–632.

Sulin, R. A., & Dooling, D. J. Intrusion of a thematic idea in retention of prose. *Journal of Experimental Psychology*, 1974, *103*, 255–262.

Sutherland, N. S. Outlines of a theory of visual pattern recognition in animals and man. *Proceedings of the Royal Society,* 1968, *171,* 297–317.

Swinney, D. A. Lexical access during sentence comprehension: Reconsideration of some context effects. *Journal of Verbal Learning and Verbal Behavior,* 1979, *18,* 645–659.

Swinney, D. A., & Hakes, D. T. Effects of prior context upon lexical access during sentence comprehension. *Journal of Verbal Learning and Verbal Behavior,* 1976, *15,* 681–689.

Thomson, D. M., & Tulving, E. Associative encoding and retrieval: Weak and strong cues. *Journal of Experimental Psychology,* 1970, *86,* 255–262.

Thorndyke, P. W. Cognitive structures in comprehension and memory of narrative discourse. *Cognitive Psychology,* 1977, *9,* 77–110.

Thorndyke, P. W., & Hayes-Roth, B. The use of schemata in the acquisition and transfer of knowledge. *Cognitive Psychology,* 1979, *11,* 82–106.

Thorndyke, P. W., & Stasz, C. Individual differences in procedures for knowledge acquisition from maps. *Cognitive Psychology,* 1980, *12,* 137–175.

Townsend, J. T. Theoretical analysis of an alphabetic confusion matrix. *Perception & Psychophysics,* 1971, *9,* 40–50.

Treisman, A. M. Contextual cues in encoding listening. *Quarterly Journal of Experimental Psychology,* 1960, *12,* 242–248.

Tulving, E., & Thomson, D. M. Encoding specificity and retrieval processes in episodic memory. *Psychological Review,* 1973, *80,* 352–373.

Tuma, D. T., & Reif, R. (Eds.). *Problem-solving and education: Issues in teaching and research.* Hillsdale, N. J.: Erlbaum, 1980.

Tversky, A. Elimination by aspects: A theory of choice. *Psychological Review,* 1972, *79,* 281–299.

Tversky, A., & Kahneman, D. Availability: A heuristic for judging frequency and probability. *Cognitive Psychology,* 1973, *5,* 207–232.

Tyler, S. W., Hertel, P. T., McCallum, M. C., & Ellis, H. C. Cognitive effort and memory. *Journal of Experimental Psychology: Human Learning and Memory,* 1979, *5,* 607–617.

Uhr, L. *Pattern recognition.* New York: Wiley, 1966.

Vipond, D. Micro and macroprocesses in text comprehension. *Journal of Verbal Learning and Verbal Behavior,* 1980, *19,* 276–296.

Walker, C. H., & Meyer, B. J. F. Integrating different types of information in text. *Journal of Verbal Learning and Verbal Behavior,* 1980, *19,* 263–275. (a)

Walker, C. H., & Meyer, B. J. F. Integrating information from text: An evaluation of current theories. *Review of Educational Research,* 1980, *50,* 421–437. (b)

Wason, P. C., & Johnson-Laird, P. N. *Psychology of reasoning: Structure and content.* Cambridge, Mass.: Harvard University Press, 1972.

Wason, P. C., & Shapiro, D. Natural and contrived experience in a reasoning problem. *Quarterly Journal of Experimental Psychology,* 1971, *23,* 63–71.

Watson, J. B. *Behaviorism.* New York: Norton, 1924.

Waugh, N. C., & Norman, D. A. Primary memory. *Psychological Review,* 1965, *72,* 89–104.

Weber, R. M. First graders' use of grammatical context in reading. In H. Levin & J. T. Williams (Eds.), *Basic studies in reading.* New York: Basic Books, 1970.

Weisberg, R., & Suls, J. M. An information-processing model of Duncker's candle problem. *Cognitive Psychology,* 1973, *4,* 255–276.

Wexler, K. A review of John R. Anderson's *Language, memory and thought. Cognition,* 1978, *6,* 327–351.

Wickelgren, W. A. Size of rehearsal group and short-term memory. *Journal of Experimental Psychology,* 1964, *68,* 413–419.

Wickelgren, W. A. Acoustic similarity and intrusion errors in short-term memory. *Journal of Experimental Psychology,* 1965, *70,* 102–108.

Wickelgren, W. A. *How to solve problems*. San Francisco: W. H. Freeman, 1974.

Wickens, D. D. Characteristics of word encoding. In A. W. Melton & E. Martin (Eds.), *Coding processes in human memory*. Washington, D. C.: Winston, 1972.

Wickens, D. D., Born, D. G., & Allen, C. K. Proactive inhibition and item similarity in short-term memory. *Journal of Verbal Learning and Verbal Behavior*, 1963, *2*, 440–445.

Yarmey, A. D. *The psychology of eyewitness testimony*. New York: Free Press, 1979.

Yates, F. A. *The art of memory*. London: Routledge and Kegan Paul, 1966.

d'Ydewalle, G., & Rosselle, H. Text expectations in text learning. In M. M. Gruneberg, P. E. Morris, & R. N. Sykes (Eds.), *Practical aspects of memory*. New York: Academic Press, 1978.

Yerkes, R. M., & Dodson, J. D. The relation of strength of stimulus to rapidity of habit-formation. *Journal of Comparative Neurology of Psychology*, 1908, *18*, 459–482.

Name Index

Subject Index